DEVELOPING A PUBLIC FAITH

DEVELOPING A PUBLIC FAITH

New Directions in Practical Theology

Essays in Honor of James W. Fowler

Richard R. Osmer and
Friedrich L. Schweitzer, eds.

CHALICE
PRESS

ST. LOUIS, MISSOURI

Biblical quotations, unless otherwise noted, are from the *New Revised Standard Version Bible*, copyright 1989, Division of Christian Education of the National Council of the Churches of Christ in the United States of America. Used by permission. All rights reserved.

Cover art: Motiv X from the Misereor Hunger Cloth from Ethiopia, van
    Alemayehu Bizuneth, © 1978, Misereor Medienproduktion, Germany,
    Aachen
Cover and interior design: Elizabeth Wright

This book is printed on acid-free, recycled paper.

Visit Chalice Press on the World Wide Web at
www.chalicepress.com

10 9 8 7 6 5 4 3 2 1   03   04   05   06   07   08

Library of Congress Cataloging–in–Publication Data

Developing a public faith : new directions in practical theology /
Richard R. Osmer and Friedrich L. Schweitzer, eds.
    p. cm.
Includes bibliographical references.
 ISBN 0-8272-0631-3 (alk. paper)
 1. Faith development. 2. Theology, Practical. 3. Fowler, James W.,
1940- I. Fowler, James W., 1940- II. Osmer, Richard Robert, 1950- III.
Schweitzer, Friedrich. IV. Title.
 BT771.3.F35 2002
 261.'342—dc21

2002007784

Printed in the United States of America

Contents

Contributors   vii

Preface   ix

Introduction   1

     Richard Osmer and Friedrich Schweitzer

PART ONE: Fowler's Contribution: Characterization and Contrast

1. Faith Development Research at Twenty Years   15

     Heinz Streib

2. The Development of Public Responsibility in James William Fowler's Theology and Psychology   43

     Gabriele Klappenecker

3. To Venture and to Abide: The Tidal Rhythm of Our Becoming   61

     Sharon Daloz Parks

PART TWO: Philosophical and Theological Issues Raised by Fowler's Work

4. Moral Development, the Good life, and Faith: Continuity or Conflict?   81

     Maureen Junker-Kenny

5. H. Richard Niebuhr and Fowler's Evolution as a Theologian   101

     Gordon Mikoski

6. Theology, Truth, and Scripture   117

     Michael Welker

PART THREE: Faith Development and Public Life as Practical Theological Matters

7. Public Church and Public School Systems in Pluralistic Contexts: A European Perspective   127

     Karl Ernst Nipkow

8. Globalization, Global Reflexivity, and Faith Development Theory: 141
The Continuing Contribution of Fowler's Research
   Richard R. Osmer and Friedrich L. Schweitzer

9. Postconventional Faith for Public Life   157
   Hyun-Sook Kim

10. Speak Truth to Power: Theology and Public Policy   175
    Duncan B. Forrester

11. Religious Freedom and the Public Church   189
    Johannes A. van der Ven

12. Children and Parents: Two-way Partners in Faith Development   203
    Thomas Groome

13. Family and Moral and Spiritual Development   213
    Don Browning

PART FOUR: A Response

14. Faith Development Theory and the Challenges of Practical   229
    Theology
    James W. Fowler

Bibliography of James W. Fowler's Work   251

Contributors

Don Browning is the Alexander Campbell Professor of Religion and the Social Sciences, Emeritus, at the Divinity School, University of Chicago. He currently is the director and senior researcher of the Religion, Culture, and Family Project.

Duncan Forrester is a professor of Christian ethics and practical theology, emeritus, New College, University of Edinburgh, where he also is dean of the Faculty of Divinity and director of the Centre for Theology and Public Issues.

James W. Fowler is a professor of theology and human development, Emory University. He formerly served as the Director of the Center for Faith Development and currently is the director of Emory's Center for Ethics in Public Policy.

Thomas Groome is a professor of theology and religious education in the Department of Theology, Boston College. He is the author of numerous books, including his well-known *Christian Religious Education: Sharing Our Story and Vision.*

Maureen Junker-Kenny is an associate professor of theology/ethics and practical theology, University of Dublin, Dublin, Ireland.

Hyun-Sook Kim is an adjunct professor of Christian education, Yonsei University, Seoul, Korea, and Research Fellow of the Institute of Christianity and Korean Culture. She currently is an officer in the Korea Society for Christian Education and Information.

Gabriele Klappenecker is an assistant professor of religious education, University of Münster, Münster, Germany.

Gordon Mikoski is an ordained minister of the Presbyterian Church (USA) and a Ph.D. student in the Division of Religion, Emory University. He currently is serving as the project manager for the Graduate Education in Religious Practices Project, The Candler School of Theology.

Karl Ernst Nipkow is Emeritus Professor of Practical Theology/Religious Education and General Education, University of Tübingen, Tübingen, Germany.

Richard R. Osmer is Thomas W. Synnott Professor of Christian Education at Princeton Theological Seminary, where he also has served as the director of the Tennent School of Christian Education. He currently is the editor of the *International Journal of Practical Theology.*

Sharon Daloz Parks was formerly a member of the faculty of Harvard University Divinity School and currently is the associate director of the Whidbey

Institute. She recently participated in a major research project on the common good, published in *Common Fire: Leading Lives of Commitment in a Complex World.*

Friedrich L. Schweitzer is a professor of practical theology/religious education, University of Tübingen, Tübingen, Germany.

Heinz Streib is a professor of religious education and ecumenical theology, University of Bielefeld, Bielefeld, Germany.

Johannes A. van der Ven is a professor of pastoral and empirical theology, dean of the Faculty of Theology, University of Nijmegen, Nijmegen, Netherlands, and Extraordinary Professor of Practical Theology, University of Pretoria, Pretoria, South Africa.

Michael Welker is a professor of systematic theology/dogmatics, University of Heidelberg, Heidelberg, Germany.

Preface

Our relationship with James Fowler stretches back over several decades and has passed through different phases. Osmer studied with Fowler as a Masters of Divinity student at The Divinity School, Harvard University, taking Fowler's yearlong course on faith and human development and participating in his early research on faith development theory. Fowler later served as the director of Osmer's dissertation in the Theology and Personality Ph.D. program at Emory University. While a doctoral student at Emory, Osmer was the Director of Research and Educational Development in the Center for Faith Development, of which Fowler served as the director. When Schweitzer came to Harvard for a Th.M. degree in 1979, Fowler had just left for Emory. But Harvard was still a good place to get to know Fowler's work, through his former students such as Sharon Parks and through his research associates such as Robert Kegan. Fowler and Schweitzer finally met in person during an international conference near Tübingen in 1987, which led to a joint book first in German and then in English (Fowler, Nipkow, and Schweitzer, eds., *Stages of Faith and Religious Development,* New York: Crossroad, 1991). This became the starting point for long-standing friendship and cooperation, including the joint organization of international conferences. In the 1990s, it was the newly founded International Academy of Practical Theology that brought Fowler, Osmer, and Schweitzer together at various times and in different places: Princeton, New Jersey; Bern, Switzerland; Seoul, Korea; and Stellenbosch, South Africa.

We want to offer special thanks to Kay Vogen, former administrative assistant of the Tennent School of Christian Education, Princeton Theological Seminary, and Jane Neuwirth, former secretary of the same institution. Both of them contributed in various ways to the completion of this project. Theresa Latini, a doctoral student in Practical Theology at Princeton Theological Seminary, has served as the editorial assistant for this project. We are deeply grateful for her fine work in helping this manuscript, whose authors come from various parts of the world, reach its final form.

We wish to express gratitude to President Thomas Gillespie and Dean James Armstrong of Princeton Theological Seminary, whose generous support during Osmer's sabbaticals by way of faculty research grants allowed Osmer to travel to Tübingen on two occasions to work directly with Schweitzer on this manuscript. Parts of this book also were written while both scholars were on study leave at The Center for Theological Inquiry, Princeton, New Jersey. Special thanks are offered to Wallace Alston, director of the CTI, and Don Browning and Robert Jensen, who, successively, served as the senior scholar for research during the times when Schweitzer and Osmer were at the Center.

Introduction

The title of this volume—*Developing a Public Faith*—requires explanation in several respects. Since the primary methodological focus of most of the contributors to this volume is practical theology, we will begin by pointing out how we see James Fowler's faith development theory in its relationship to the tasks of practical theology. In a second step we will focus on the issue of its contribution to the maintenance and restoration of public life.

When teaching or lecturing on the work of James Fowler, it is not uncommon to encounter questions like the following: In what field does Fowler work? Is he a developmental psychologist, an ethicist, a Christian educator, or a cultural critic? Arguably, any of these might be used to describe Fowler's work in one or another of his books. Yet none accurately reflects the discipline in which Fowler has worked across his academic career, the discipline of practical theology. Indeed, it can be argued that his most important and lasting contribution across the past four decades is not primarily his theory of faith development, for which he is rightly famous. Rather, it his contribution to the new understanding of practical theology that emerged in the second half of the twentieth century. Fowler is one of a small handful of scholars who have reshaped our thinking about the nature and purpose of practical theology as a scholarly discipline. Indeed, his corpus as a whole is best viewed as a paradigm or exemplar of what practical theology can and should be. At times, he does work as an empirical researcher in psychology. At other points, he does offer action-guiding proposals for Christian education, family ministries, or pastoral counseling. Sometimes, he does serve as a critic of culture or a prophet of the church. But only when we see how these various sides of Fowler's work hang together in a comprehensive program of practical theology will we really grasp his importance as a scholar. Fowler has helped to redefine a field.

In order to see how this is the case, it is necessary to offer a brief summary of the new understanding of practical theology that has emerged over the past four decades and Fowler's contribution to the emergence of this new disciplinary understanding. Briefly put, contemporary practical theology is viewed as carrying out four distinguishable but mutually influential tasks: the *descriptive-empirical,* the *interpretive,* the *normative,* and the *pragmatic.* Attention to all four of these tasks allow practical theologians to construct *action-guiding theories of contemporary religious practice.* It is helpful to conceptualize the mutually influential relationship of these four tasks along the lines of a hermeneutical circle.[1] The circle can be entered at any point, but all four tasks must be attended to at some point in a comprehensive program of practical theological reflection.

In order to grasp Fowler's contribution to this new understanding of practical theology, we will briefly describe each of these tasks and point to examples of the way he has carried out each task across his various writings.

Figure 1: The Four Tasks of Practical Theology

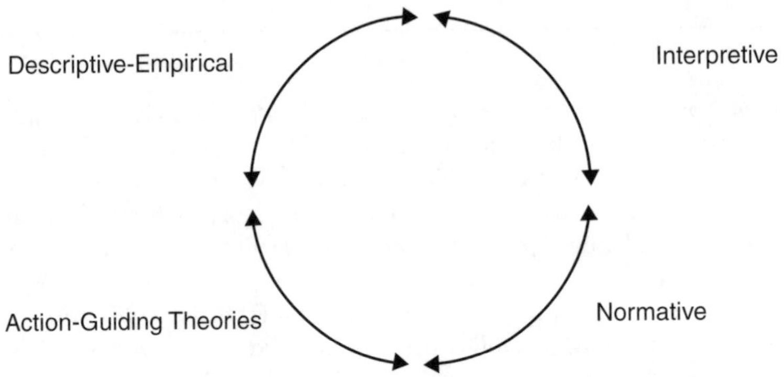

Descriptive-Empirical   Interpretive

Action-Guiding Theories   Normative

The *descriptive-empirical* task focuses on the actual, empirical state of some form of religious praxis in a particular social context. It asks: *What is going on?* What is the state of religious praxis in this particular sphere of life? It seeks to describe as fully and accurately as possible a particular field of experience. Sometimes, this sort of research can be taken over from other fields. In recent years, however, many practical theologians have come to recognize the importance of carrying out their own research.[2] Social scientists are often uninterested in the questions of greatest importance to contemporary religious communities and, sometimes, work with reductionistic understandings of religion.

Across his career, Fowler has carried out a variety of empirical research projects, including not only the research giving rise to his stage theory of faith development but also research on congregations and public schools.[3] The empirical research that culminated in Fowler's stages of faith is exemplary of the way this task is pursued in practical theology. It also clarifies certain confusions and criticisms that are commonly directed at his work. On the one hand, Fowler builds on the structural developmental tradition of psychology. He draws on a structuralist model to guide his empirical investigation, using a semistructured interview, transcribing and scoring interviews according to the protocols of a validated scoring manual, and so forth. On the other hand, he constructs his most important guiding concept, the domain of "faith," in dialogue with the comparative religionist Wilfred Cantwell Smith and the Christian ethicist H. Richard Niebuhr. Critics have typically failed to appreciate that Fowler is working in precisely the interdisciplinary fashion one would expect of a practical theologian. His interests–here, the domain of faith–are theologically motivated and defined. Yet his empirical research methods are those of any scholar working within the framework of structural development psychology.[4]

The *interpretive* task seeks to place empirical research in a more comprehensive explanatory framework. It asks the question: *Why is this going on?* Here, the findings of more focused research are located in a framework that provides an explanation of patterns of behavior, attitudes, and ideas. On the surface, it would seem that a sequencing of these tasks necessarily follows: first description, then interpretation. It would be a mistake to view them in this way, however. In recent years, researchers in many fields have come to acknowledge the various ways their interpretive commitments inform their empirical investigation, shaping what they "see." Interpretation interpenetrates description, and, in turn, description has the potential of opening up and correcting interpretation. Often, the anomalies of descriptive work–data not fitting the researcher's expectations–lead to revisions in an interpretive framework. While distinguishable, thus, the descriptive-empirical and interpretive tasks of practical theology stand in a mutually influential relationship.

One of the more remarkable aspects of Fowler's published work in the 1990s was his ability to move back and forth between the descriptive-empirical and interpretive tasks of practical theology. In *Faithful Change,* for example, he moves in two directions simultaneously.[5] First, he broadens his psychological account of faith development derived from his original empirical research, bringing it into dialogue with depth psychology. This enables him to describe more fully the place of the emotions in the religious life, particularly the relationship between shame, guilt, and faith. Second, he locates this broadened descriptive account of faith development in a comprehensive interpretive framework that focuses on the cognitive challenges of postmodern life. The importance of postconventional forms of religious and/or moral identity is explored, with a special eye to the Christian community's role in shaping public Christians, a theme to which we will return below.

The *normative* task of practical theology focuses on the construction of theological and ethical norms by which to critically assess, guide, and reform some dimension of contemporary religious praxis. It asks the question: *What forms ought religious praxis take in this particular social context?* Here, practical theology looks in two directions simultaneously. It looks to the resources mediating truth, goodness, and beauty in a particular religious tradition and to the problems and possibilities of contemporary religious praxis in the particular context under investigation. While it is primarily at this point that practical theology will enter into dialogue with other theological and ethical disciplines, the norms of praxis it develops are not merely the application of the normative proposals of these fields. This is because the norms it develops take into account the particularities of the context of praxis it is seeking to address. Norms of praxis in practical theology, thus, are context-dependent in a strong sense. They are informed by the outcome of empirical and interpretive work.

One of the best examples of Fowler's attention to the normative task of practical theology is found in his book *Weaving the New Creation: Stages of Faith and the Public Church,* his most extended constructive theological statement since his first book, *To See the Kingdom,* on the thought of H. Richard Niebuhr.[6] The book is a remarkable example of constructive practical theology. Its overriding goal is to offer theological patterns by which contemporary Christians can discern and participate in God's praxis in the world and to guide the church in helping to give shape to new forms of postmodern public life. To project contemporary theological norms for the church, Fowler weaves together three distinct activities: (1) a dialogue with other theologians, particularly Niebuhr and Sallie McFague; (2) an interpretation of the contemporary context, informed by his prior descriptive empirical work; and (3) the construction of various forms of theological discourse, including narrative, autobiography, and discursive exposition. The result is a normative theory of praxis that can help the church discern and act in the contemporary world in ways that are both faithful to their understanding of God and the specific challenges of their own time and place.

The *pragmatic* task of practical theology focuses on the development of *rules of art,* a concept first introduced by Friedrich Schleiermacher in his seminal description of this field.[7] Rules of art are open-ended guidelines that can assist those who are leading or participating in a particular form of religious praxis. This task asks the question: *How might this area of praxis be shaped to embody more fully the normative commitments of a religious tradition in this particular context of experience?* The primary focus at this point is on matters of "how to." How might a pastoral counseling relationship be structured over a number of sessions? How might families balance the needs of the young and the careers of parents in a fair and egalitarian fashion? How might the members of a religious community influence the policies of their government? When we pose questions like these, it becomes clear that rules of art are not guidelines that can be applied in a mechanical or rote fashion. They presuppose creativity and good judgment of a quasi-aesthetic nature, the discernment of a fitting course of action in a particular context of experience. Moreover, we would argue that religious praxis when carried out in a reflective fashion is *epistemic,* that is, it yields knowledge and insights that cannot be gained through empirical research, comprehensive interpretations, or normative reflection alone.[8] It is not difficult to think of examples of the epistemic role reflective practice has played in recent scholarship. In education, one need only recall the way Paulo Freire's critical pedagogy emerged out of his struggle to teach illiterate peasants in Brazil or the important ways Thomas Groome's theory of shared praxis is informed by his work in congregations and as a parochial school teacher.[9] In therapeutic psychology, one might think of the importance of clinical work to the theories of Sigmund Freud and Donald Winnicott or of pastoral counselors like John Pattern or Charles Gerkin who construct theories informed by clinical practice.[10] In each case, reflective participation in a field of practice is epistemic, yielding knowledge that cannot be gained in other ways.

Fowler has consistently given attention to the pragmatic dimension of practical theology. No doubt, the fact that his wife, Lurilene, is a first-rate

Christian educator has served as a living reminder that practical theology must ultimately provide guidance to those on the frontlines of leadership in the church. The final chapters of *Weaving the New Creation: Becoming Adult, Becoming Christian,* and *Faith Development and Pastoral Care,* as well as extended articles such as "Practical Theology and the Shaping of Christian Lives," all move in the direction of rules of art directed toward the critical assessment and guidance of concrete praxis in actual communities of faith.[11] Moreover, Fowler is one of the few contemporary Christian practical theologians with the ability to address a broader audience than the church. His writings and public lectures consistently strike a chord in persons on the margins of religious communities or unaffiliated with any religious community at all. Such people find their struggles and doubts taken seriously in Fowler's depiction of the journey of faith. They also commonly find his stage theory a helpful map with which to understand their own life story.

It is important to correct a possible misperception of this description of practical theology and Fowler's work in relation to its four core tasks. These tasks are not pursued in isolation from one another. What is distinctive about practical theology as a field is the way all four tasks are pursued in a mutually influential fashion. Pragmatic concerns guide empirical research; interpretations of contemporary life are influenced by both theological norms and empirical investigation, which, in turn, are shaped by such interpretation; and so forth. At any given time, a practical theologian may give primary attention to one or another of these tasks, but the others remain close at hand and often reappear in ways that are surprising to those who are unfamiliar with the way practical theologians work. No doubt, this is one of the chief reasons that contemporary interpreters of Fowler's work are often perplexed by his ability to move so adeptly between empirical, interpretive, theological, and pragmatic modes of discourse. Yet it is precisely this ability to hold together all four tasks of practical theology that has made James Fowler a paradigm or exemplar for a younger generation of practical theologians. He has helped redefine the very nature of this field, a contribution that may ultimately be his most important and lasting to theological scholarship.

This leads us to a second important theme of Fowler's work, which is signaled in the title of this book: his ongoing attention to the contribution of the church and practical theology to public life. Here, too, Fowler has helped to reshape the inherited understanding of practical theology as a discipline. Historically, this field has been oriented primarily to the tasks of the clergy or the life of the church, with little explicit attention to religious praxis beyond the church. Fowler has been at the forefront of these practical theologians who have broadened the subject matter from clergy functions (the so-called clerical paradigm) and church functions (ecclesiocentric models of practical theology) to religious praxis within the context of public life in its various dimensions. Not only has Fowler explicitly studied and treated public life as a theme in his theology, but more importantly, he has functioned as a public practical theologian. Here, too, he has helped redefine the nature of this field.

Today, practical theology strives to be fully public in several senses. By making the social sciences its partner in academic dialogue and by taking psychological, societal, and cultural factors into account, practical theology makes its claim to having a voice within the academic world beyond theology and the church. And by addressing issues of public interest and importance, practical theology strives to become involved with the social and political attempts of shaping the future of society or, thinking of current debates, even the future of our globalizing world.

In many ways, this public practical theology, as we have called it elsewhere, parallels the current interest in a public theology that is directed at a general audience beyond the church.[12] One of its main impulses concerns the role of religion within the public. Several analysts have pointed out the need for values and a moral education that rest upon a religious foundation. This is why they are highly critical of the widespread tendency to keep all matters of public interest clear from anything that could resemble a religious influence.[13]

While we agree with those who want to see a stronger acknowledgment of the need for a religious undergirding of moral values, we are not convinced that this need can be fulfilled by some kind of civil religion or by some type of minimalist consensus between the various denominations and religions. Models of the civil religion type are based on the expectation that religion can assume a public role only to the degree that it sheds its dogmatic dimensions in order to focus on its moral or ethical impulses. Dogmatic views or religious truth claims are considered divisive, while moral claims are expected to be inclusive and therefore able to pave an easier way toward mutual acceptance and joint action. It is easy to see that these models are based on the Enlightenment idea of taking over from traditional religion that (and only that) which is considered helpful for the future—that is, religion's moral influence—while leaving behind what is considered dated and traditionalist beyond hope—that is, dogmatic faith. In the meantime, however, it has become obvious that such reductionist views of religion are not able to do justice to religion and therefore, in the long run, are detrimental to religion, not only to religious faith but also to the moral attitudes supported by this faith. This is why we advocate a public practical theology that works toward true religious dialogue as a public endeavor, including conflicting religious truth claims as well as ethical perspectives.

Again, we consider it obvious that many of the concerns connected to a public practical theology have been addressed and advanced by the work of James Fowler. Building on his seminal *Stages of Faith* published in 1981,[14] Fowler continued his research by tracing the relationship of faith development to a number of public issues. Among his concerns, we find not only the challenge of moral education in a pluralist society but, more far-reaching, the question of restoring *paideia*, the education of the public, in order to prepare people for their responsibilities in public life. Moreover, Fowler has based his model for responsible life on the notion of "calling," which incorporates and combines both a religious view of the aims of one's life and a continued relationship to what traditional Christian language refers to as the "world" and what is now called public life.[15] Fowler's early appropriation of Martin Marty's notion of a "public church" also belongs in this context.[16] With this interpretation of this notion, Fowler has made an important contribution to convincing congregations and churches of the need to go beyond their traditional ecclesial focus.

Many will agree that, in the end, Fowler's most special contribution to a public practical theology arises at the intersection of a public Christian ethic and his psychological and educational research on personal development. Through this combination of ethical theology and social scientific research, he is able to set forth far-reaching critical analyses of the shortcomings of contemporary culture and religion as well as powerful perspectives for overcoming such weaknesses and defaults. This is why we think that faith development theory does indeed have to offer a unique contribution to the future of public life.

In closing, it may be helpful to provide an overview of the different parts of this book and the rationale for its organization along these lines. In a very real sense, the structure of the book reflects the various dimensions of Fowler's work as a practical theologian. Part One–Fowler's Contribution: Characterization and Contrast–provides both an introduction to and assessment of his theory. In chapter 1, Heinz Streib offers an extremely valuable overview of empirical and theoretical research that has built on Fowler's work. He demonstrates the importance of faith development theory especially in religious education in the United States and in many countries around the world during the 1980s and 1990s and points to promising new directions in the faith development paradigm that have begun to emerge in recent years. Streib's chapter certainly is the most comprehensive description of the research pertaining to faith development theory currently available. It shows that this theory has become an important foundation for many efforts in the fields of psychology, theology, counseling, and education.

In chapter 2, Gabriele Klappenecker provides a helpful introduction to various aspects of Fowler's work, including his stage theory. Her chapter introduces readers to some of Fowler's backgrounds in theology and in the social sciences. The kingdom of God, the notion of covenant, and the idea of vocation are identified as key symbols of his work and are explained in relationship to the challenges of public life.

In chapter 3, Sharon Parks develops a beautiful account of the dialectic of "making home" and "venturing forth" that lies at the heart of the religious life. She locates Fowler's stages of faith within the comprehensive metaphor of pilgrimage, correcting an overemphasis on separation or individuation (the pole of "venturing forth") that often characterizes theories of developmental psychology.

Part Two–Philosophical and Theological Issues Raised by Fowler's Work– takes up foundational issues in contemporary theology, locating Fowler's constructive theological work in relation to these issues. In chapter 4, Maureen Junker-Kenny examines issues of methodology in faith development research, of the understanding of morality, and of the rendering of the self in the context of recent debates within philosophical and theological ethics. Drawing on the work of Charles Taylor and Paul Ricoeur, Junker-Kenny suggests that faith development theory must be sensitive to the pluralism arising from different religions as well as to the different anthropological models guiding empirical research. This kind of sensitivity becomes mandatory, Junker-Kenny continues, once one includes the new philosophical insights into the continuing role of normative traditions of the good and the right that can also broaden our concepts of the self.

In chapter 5, Gordon Mikoski explores the theological foundations of Fowler's thought, giving special attention to Fowler's long-standing dialogue with the theological ethics of H. Richard Niebuhr. He raises important questions about the adequacy of Niebuhr's understanding of God, especially when viewed from the perspective of the recent renaissance of trinitarian theology, and indicates ways Fowler has moved beyond Niebuhr in his recent work.

In chapter 6, Michael Welker identifies three types of theology in order to shed light on moral and faith formation. The first type is often found in theological classics. It is characterized by an elaborate connection of theological thought and conviction. The second type is the theology that is entertained by the everyday believer. It comes close to what Fowler calls "faith." Welker's main interest, however, is the third type of theology, which mediates between the first two types. It is this mediating type that holds the three types of theology together in interaction and that should be pursued in academic theology. According to Welker, academic theology should understand itself as a "truth-seeking community" that carries out its mediating work in open and public communications and in dialogue with scripture that must be appreciated in its pluralistic texture and with its potential for shaping our cultural memory.

Part Three—Faith Development and Public Life as Practical Theological Matters—explores practical theology's contribution to contemporary public life, in critical dialogue with Fowler's work. In chapter 7, Karl Ernst Nipkow takes up Fowler's perspective on the public church and relates it to the role of the church within institutions of public education in several European countries. In his analysis, Nipkow shows that the church—as a public church—should also be seen as a public organization and that its public role goes beyond the limits of individual congregations. Moreover, Nipkow identifies and critically discusses various tendencies to be observed within the European context, among others, the tendency toward a spirituality that is not related to any particular religious tradition and the tendency toward reducing religious education to some kind of neutral moral education. According to Nipkow, only a religious education that faces up to the situation of multiculturalism and multireligious society and that is able to balance commitment and openness can do justice to the challenges of pluralism and of a public church as an organization in society.

In chapter 8, the editors of this volume, Richard Osmer and Friedrich Schweitzer, bring Fowler's stage theory into dialogue with a research project in which they are involved that explores the impact of globalization on adolescent faith. Fowler's theory is portrayed not only as providing help in interpreting the data emerging in this project but also as projecting a framework with which to understand the cognitive challenges of our multicultural and multireligious world. In chapter 9, Hyun-Sook Kim argues that the challenges of late modernity represent a social context in which "postconventional" forms of religious and moral identity are necessary for participation in public life. She brings Fowler's work into dialogue with Jürgen Habermas, Carol Gilligan, Lawrence Kohlberg, and others, noting Fowler's more positive valuation of the potential of religious symbols in evoking continued development across adulthood and "postconventional" forms of participation in the public domain.

Over the course of his career, Jim Fowler has served as the director of two important centers of research, education, and interdisciplinary collaboration: the Center for Faith Development at Candler School of Theology and, more recently, the Center for Ethics in Public Policy at Emory University. Noting Fowler's leadership of the latter, Duncan Forrester in chapter 10 reflects on his own involvement in the Edinburgh University Centre for Theology and Public Issues. He points to a long-standing Scottish tradition linking confessional affirmation and social transformation, a stance in which theology plays an important role in the formation of public life. In a very real sense, his own constructive contributions in the chapter parallel Fowler's interest in developing a public practical theology for the common good.

In chapter 11, Johannes van der Ven takes up one of the core questions concerning the future of public life and of democracy or freedom as it arises from the contemporary conflicts around religion, culture, and politics. September 11, 2001, has become the sad symbol of such conflicts, which are often associated with fundamentalism. Van der Ven raises the question of what Fowler's faith development theory can tell us about the transition from conventional to postconventional faith, which van der Ven sees as the presupposition for religious freedom. Based on this analysis, van der Ven suggests that the public church should not only strengthen and renew its commitment to peace and justice at an international level but should also set forth developmental programs aimed at interreligious perspective taking and exchange. Developing countries will only be willing to work toward the religious freedom that is traditionally associated with Western modernity, van der Ven says, if they experience that people in the affluent Western world are prepared to take account of their perspective as well.

At first glance, it might seem odd to include the final two chapters, which focus on the family, in this part of the book, which focuses squarely on public life. Here, we follow those who view the family as intimately connected to matters of public life—public policy, broader social trends, and the changing shape of a globalizing economy. In chapter 12, Thomas Groome offers a beautiful and personal account of the ways parents and children are mutually influential in faith formation. He draws on his own experience of becoming a parent late in life and describes the importance of moving beyond a schooling model of Christian education to one that takes more seriously the creative dance of interaction in the "domestic church." Drawing on his research as director of the Religion, Culture, and Family Project, in chapter 13 Don Browning explores various ancient and contemporary perspectives on the role of the family in moral and spiritual development. In so doing, he provides an extremely helpful overview of some of the most important perspectives on the family in contemporary ethics, locating Fowler's contribution within this framework.

The final part of this book gives James Fowler the opportunity to respond to the various essays written here in his honor. In his typically gracious but incisive style, he engages the contributors to this book as interlocutors with questions, challenges, and insights to offer him in his continuing work as a practical theologian. Almost all of the contributors to this volume have been Jim's colleagues and friends across the years. It is likely that we speak for all of them in offering him our heartfelt thanks for his work as a practical theologian, his insightfulness as a colleague, and his support as a friend. This volume of essays is offered in appreciation of his contribution to our lives, our church, and our world.

Richard Osmer,
Princeton, New Jersey

Friedrich Schweitzer,
Tübingen, Germany

Notes

[1]It is important to note that there are "circles within circles" in this model. The regulative cycle as described by Heitink, for example, has its own interrelated set of interpretive tasks, appropriate to the construction of knowledge in the pragmatic moment of practical theological reflection. Likewise, van der Ven describes the interrelated set of interpretive tasks appropriate to the empirical-theological cycle, appropriate to the construction of knowledge in the empirical moment. Similar cycles might be projected for the normative and interpretive moments as well.

[2]Dutch practical theologians, in particular, have drawn attention to the importance of empirical work in practical theology. See Johannes A. van der Ven, *Practical Theology: An Empirical Approach* (Kampen, The Netherlands: Kok Pharos, 1993); *Ecclesiology in Context* (Grand Rapids, Mich.: Eerdmans, 1993); *Formation of the Moral Self,* Studies in Practical Theology (Grand Rapids, Mich.: Eerdmans, 1998). See also Gerben Heitink, *Practical Theology: History, Theory, and Action Domains,* Studies in Practical Theology (Grand Rapids, Mich.: Eerdmans, 1999); Don Browning, Bonnie Miller-McLemore, Pamela Couture, Brynolf Lyon, and Robert Franklin, *From Culture Wars to Common Ground: Religion and the American Family Debate* (Louisville, Ky.: Westminister John Knox Press, 1997); Friedrich Schweitzer, Karl Ernst Nipkow, Gabriele Faust-Siehl, and Bernd Krupka, *Religionsunterricht und Entwicklungspsychologie. Elementarisierung in der Praxis* (Gütersloh: Gütersloher, 1995); Friedrich Schweitzer, Albert Biesinger et al., *Gemeinsamkeiten stärken—Unterschieden gerecht werden. Konfessionelle Kooperation im Religionsunterricht* (Freiburg/ Gütersloh: Herder/Gütersloher, 2002).

[3]The research on congregations was part of a collaborative project known as The Faith and Practice of Congregations project. See Fowler's discussion of this project in *Weaving the New*

Creation: Stages of Faith and the Public Church (San Francisco: HarperCollins, 1991), ch. 6. The research on public schools was carried out by the Center of Faith Development, of which Fowler was the director.

[4]It is quite helpful to view Fowler's empirical work in terms of van der Ven's empirical-theological cycle of research (*Practical Theology*). In this model, the various steps a practical theologian moves through in bringing theology and empirical research together are explored.

[5]James W. Fowler, *Faithful Change: The Personal and Public Challenges of Postmodern Life* (Nashville, Tenn.: Abingdon Press, 1996).

[6]Fowler, *Weaving the New Creation.* Idem, *To See the Kingdom: The Theological Vision of H. Richard Niebuhr* (Nashville, Tenn.: Abingdon Press, 1974).

[7]Friedrich Schleiermacher, *Brief Outline on the Study of Theology,* trans. Terrence Tice (Richmond: John Knox Press, 1966), par. 265ff. See also, idem, *Christian Caring: Selections from Practical Theology,* ed. James Duke and Howard Stone, trans. James Duke (Philadelphia: Fortress Press, 1988), 99ff.

[8]The cycle of reflection and action in reflective practice is complex and has been thematized in terms of the regulative cycle by a number of contemporary scholars. See, for example, P. J. van Strien, *Praktijk als wetenschap: Methodologie van het sociaal-weten-schappelijk handelen* (Assen: Van Gorcum, 1986); and Donald A. Schön, *The Reflective Practitioner: How Professionals Think in Action* (New York: Basic Books, 1983). See also Heitink's treatment of the regulative cycle in *Practical Theology.*

[9]Paulo Freire, *Pedagogy of the Oppressed,* trans. Myra Ramos (New York: Continuum, 1993). Thomas Groome, *Christian Religious Education: Sharing Our Story and Vision* (San Francisco: Jossey-Bass, 1999).

[10]Freud drew extensively on his clinical work to construct his theory. For one example, see Sigmund Freud, *The Interpretation of Dreams,* trans. James Stachey (New York: Avon, 1965). Donald Winnicott, *Playing and Reality* (New York: Basic Books, 1971). John Patton, *Pastoral Counseling: A Ministry of the Church* (Nashville, Tenn.: Abingdon Press, 1983). Charles Gerkin, *The Living Human Document: Re-Visioning Pastoral Counseling in a Hermeneutical Mode* (Nashville, Tenn.: Abingdon Press, 1984).

[11]Fowler, *Weaving the New Creation.* Idem, *Becoming Adult, Becoming Christian: Adult Development and Christian Faith* (San Francisco: Harper & Row, 1984); *Faith Development and Pastoral Care* (Philadelphia: Fortress Press, 1987); "Practical Theology and the Shaping of Christian Lives," in *Practical Theology: The Emerging Field in Theology, Church, and World,* ed. Don Browning (San Francisco: Harper & Row, 1983), 148–66.

[12]Richard R. Osmer and Friedrich L. Schweitzer, *Religious Education between Modernization and Globalization: New Perspectives on the United States and Germany* (Grand Rapids, Mich.: Eerdmans, 2003).

[13]To cite just one example, Parker J. Palmer, *The Company of Strangers: Christians and the Renewal of America's Public Life* (New York: Crossroad, 1981).

[14]James W. Fowler, *Stages of Faith: The Psychology of Human Development and the Quest for Meaning* (San Francisco: Harper & Row, 1981).

[15]See Fowler, *Weaving the New Creation,* also his *Becoming Adult,* as well as many of his articles.

[16]Martin E. Marty, *The Public Church: Mainline-Evangelical-Catholic* (New York: Crossroad, 1981).

PART ONE

Fowler's Contribution:
Characterization and Contrast

1

Faith Development Research at Twenty Years[1]

HEINZ STREIB

Within a relatively short time period of twenty years, the theory of faith development formulated by James W. Fowler[2] has attracted attention and inspired theoretical and empirical research in psychology, theology, religious education, and pastoral care. While the United States has been the main center of research, interest in faith development theory has spread steadily worldwide.

The growing reputation of faith development theory had its seismic focus in Emory University's Center for Faith Development; however, the Center in Atlanta never claimed to be the sole faith development research laboratory. The Center never sought to establish rigid research coordination or to propagate a sacrosanct theory and methodology. On the contrary, faith development theory has had a history of widespread dissemination from the very beginning, and, thus, it has experienced not only a great amount of both positive and negative critique but also a creative evolution in theory and research method.

This chapter intends to summarize these past twenty years of dissemination, while also providing an overview of the critique and creative evolution experienced by faith development theory. I will focus mostly on the last decade here, referring for a more detailed account of the earlier years to the reports by Sharon Parks,[3] H. J. McDargh,[4] and Nicola Slee.[5] I also will provide an account of my comprehensive search of the literature, while paying special attention to the more recent contributions in Fowler's own writings. We can distinguish three directions in the evolution of faith development theory: empirical research, theoretical reflection, and studies on practical application. This leads to the structure of the first part of this chapter. The second part deals with more recent developments and the perspectives for future research. I explicitly invite your critical comments about my portrayal of the last twenty years of faith development research, and I further would appreciate information about any literature that my efforts have not uncovered thus far.

1. Reception, Replication, and Responses, 1981–1999

1.1 Statistical Overview

Within the last twenty years, Fowler's faith development theory has inspired a great number of theoretical and empirical projects. A statistical survey of completed dissertations allows us to assess the influence of Fowler's faith development theory. In my search of the literature,[6] I found well over a hundred dissertations completed between 1976 and 1999, for which Fowler's faith development theory constituted at least a significant position. Out of this number, I have identified eighty-two dissertations focusing primarily or exclusively on Fowler's faith development theory ("Fowler dissertations"). Figure 1 shows the rise and decline of interest in faith development theory from the early years to the present, including an obvious peak four years after *Stages of Faith* was published. A slight decline in the number of doctoral students focusing exclusively on Fowler's theory also becomes evident in the 1990s.

Figure 1: Faith Development and Fowler Dissertations 1976–1999

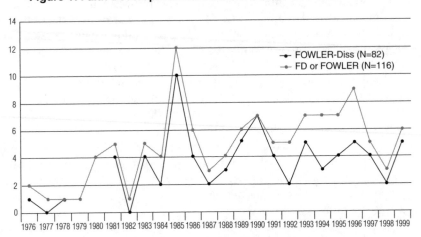

Within this time period, almost all of the dissertations on Fowler's theory and research were published in the United States, with the following exceptions: five dissertations in Canada, two in Germany, two in England, and one in Finland. Judging from the number of dissertation projects, European theology and European psychology of religion obviously do not appear to have developed an extensive interest in faith development research. To be sure, Fowler's theory of faith development awakened interest in Europe starting almost immediately after the publication of *Stages of Faith*.[7] This interest has increased over the years[8] and continues into the present;[9] however, most of the European contributions issue from the fields of theology and religious education and focus more on theoretical aspects than on research questions. European research on religion appears rather reserved regarding the inclusion of Fowler's theory.

The majority of dissertations dealing with Fowler's theory are empirical studies. As Figure 2 shows, out of the total of eighty-two studies that I have identified as Fowler dissertations, forty-four (53%) are empirical studies, of which twenty-five (30%) apply the classical Faith Development Instrument, fifteen (18%) apply a variation of the instrument, and four (5%) use a scale-type instrument to measure faith development; twenty-seven (34%) discuss Fowler's theory; and eleven (13%) deal with questions of applying faith development theory in religious education, pastoral care, and church work.

Figure 2: Dissertations Dealing with Fowler's Theory

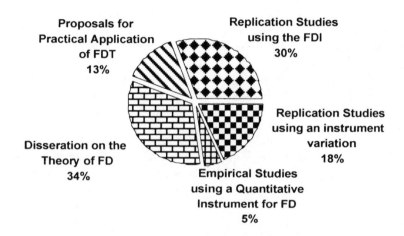

The books and the large number of journal articles on Fowler's faith development theory have not been evaluated statistically. It is interesting to note that all of the monographs focusing exclusively on Fowler's theory are dissertations. There are also several other thought-provoking monographs that dedicate at least a chapter or two to Fowler.[10] This means that most of the research on faith development theory is only accessible for a scholarly elite with the resources to locate and finally obtain the texts on paper, microfiche, or as computer files. I shall now go through the various fields in which research and reflection on Fowler's theory have been undertaken, beginning with a brief look into proposals for the practical application of faith development theory.

1.2 Practical Application Studies: Using Faith Development as a Perspective and Instrument in Practical Work, Especially in Religious Education

A statistical analysis of the most valued books–or "best-sellers"–in religious education, compiled by Woodrow Walter,[11] reached the surprising conclusion that the books on Fowler's theory are the absolute best-sellers in the United

States. Religious educators have rated three faith development books among the top four, namely Fowler's *Stages of Faith,* Dykstra and Parks's *Faith Development and Fowler,* and Stokes's *Faith Development in the Adult Life Cycle.*

In another dissertation completed in 1996, Nancy Vanlue[12] presents a meta-analysis of dissertations in English that she regards as highly relevant to adult faith development. Vanlue identified sixty such dissertations completed between 1980 and 1994. Twenty-six of the dissertations judged by Vanlue to be highly relevant for adult education are found in my sample of Fowler dissertations as well. This can be taken as another indicator of the special recognition Fowler's faith development theory has received in religious education in the United States.

Especially for the field of religious education, Fowler's theory seems to be a significant source of new insights. The focus on religious education is obvious in both the United States and Europe, even if on a considerably lower level for Europe. A significant number of European dissertations and other contributions address religious education from a faith development perspective,[13] some of them based on empirical studies. The German project on religious education and developmental psychology also should be mentioned in this context. Based on empirical research in the teacher-student interaction in the Tübingen area,[14] this project has provided an impulse for the further integration of a developmental perspective in religious education.[15]

Faith development theory also has been considered helpful for the field of pastoral work. The question of the "modal levels of development" of a congregation or religious group has received some attention in this context.[16] However, the focus on pastoral work and congregations has remained a minor focus for the application of faith development theory.

The case is different for the field of pastoral care, for which Fowler's book *Faith Development and Pastoral Care* has been inspiring.[17] If we include psychological counseling and psychoanalytic treatment, a line of research in faith development that appears very promising in terms of its practical application comes to light: the study of faith development in relation to psychological well-being, coping with crises, and dealing with stress factors. Early research already attempted to put the faith development instrument to work in pastoral assessment.[18] Detailed contributions on this topic have been made in the last decade, including the following: Dale Brown's work on "Doubt and Anxiety in Theological and Psychological Perspective with Implications for Pastoral Care and Pastoral Theology"[19] and Ronald Oliver's study on "Effects of an Acute Traumatic Crisis on Faith."[20] Furthermore, empirical studies have investigated the relation between faith development and AIDS,[21] the faith development of people recovering from chemical dependency,[22] the faith development of mothers of multihandicapped children,[23] and that of parents after the death of a child.[24] These studies suggest that research on religion and health, or religion and coping, could include at least a subdivision of research on the relation between faith development and health and/or coping. The advantage of including a developmental perspective lies in the possibility of obtaining a better differentiation between the stages or styles of religion in regard to their influence and effect on health and coping. This also provides a means of overcoming simplifying questions such as "Is religion good for your health?"[25] Most of these studies include an empirical research component and thus can be assigned to the group of empirical studies treated below. However, they also include thoughtful proposals for using the faith development perspective within the context of pastoral care and counseling. A theoretical dimension can also be discerned—the relation of faith development to personality theories and psychoanalytic perspectives in particular. This leads us to the next section, which surveys theoretical reflections on Fowler's theory.

1.3 Theoretical Reflection on Fowler's Theory

Many of the early critical contributions to the discussion of Fowler's theory are summarized in Parks's article on "The North American Critique of James Fowler's Theory."[26] Parks highlights five areas of concern in the North American critique of Fowler's theory: its definition of faith, its description of Stage 6, its adequacy in relation to particular religious beliefs, its account for the emotional and the unconscious, and, finally, its adequacy in terms of sociopolitical analysis, particularly gender analysis. I wish to highlight two realms of theoretical discourse about Fowler's faith development theory here: discussions, some of them highly critical, focusing mainly on faith development theory's theological adequacy and consistency; and contributions investigating contradictions and correlations of Fowler's theory with psychoanalytic perspectives on human development.

1.3.1 Theological Concerns with Faith Development Theory

Fowler's theoretical framework has been scrutinized and critically evaluated from different theological angles. The various theoretical reflections on the basic principles of Fowler's theory have led to quite a number of attempts to reconstruct Fowler's theory or at least to suggest significant modifications.

Theological reflection, with special focus on Fowler's own roots in H. Richard Niebuhr, is the characteristic of some contributions in the early years. With rather positive results, Mark Durrett[27] investigated Fowler's roots in the theology of H. Richard Niebuhr. Though he suggests a modification of Fowler's structural model so as to more adequately present Niebuhr's thought on faith as loyalty, his overall conclusion suggests an understanding of Fowler's theory as an agenda for the formation and transformation of faith in accordance with Niebuhr's triadic conception of human and Christian faith. With more critical conclusions, One Park[28] draws attention to a distortion of the theological dimension in faith development theory. According to Park, Fowler does not do justice to Niebuhr's discussion of the dark and inevitable side of human nature including meaninglessness and sin.[29] Park contends that this deficiency is due to Fowler's strong alliance with the structural-developmental model, which corresponds to Fowler's dependence on a highly optimistic view of the human being. "His theory would be more balanced and useful for Christian education," Park concludes, "if it paid more attention to the inescapably conflictual aspects of human being."[30]

Romney Moseley[31] already takes a critical standpoint in his dissertation. In his subsequent research, he has proposed a differentiation of the concept of religious conversion into *lateral* and *structural* conversion—an aspect that Fowler integrated to some extent in his 1981 book. In his later book *Becoming a Self before God,*[32] Moseley challenges the philosophical and theological foundations from a Kierkegaardian perspective and claims that Fowler's theory has missed the dialectical-paradoxical character of faith. We also meet the theme of conversion in Hancock's dissertation.[33] He focuses on conversion in the faith development theories of Fowler and James Loder, notes similarities and dissimilarities between them, and draws parallels to the identity development theories of Erikson and Marcia. Finally, Hancock draws conclusions for adolescent Christian education. Gregory Hunt[34] also investigates the theological foundations of faith development theory and presents a profound critique of Fowler's theory. After an extensive discussion of strengths and weaknesses in faith development theory, he concludes his dissertation by delineating "a set of foundational theological affirmations for a meaningful theory of faith development."[35]

A special focus of critique has been the structuralism of faith development theory. The problem of "structure versus content" is discussed in a fair amount of contributions. George Cristiano devotes special attention to this problem.[36] He analyzes Fowler's theory to determine how much it is influenced by and dependent on the theological works of Paul Tillich and H. Richard Niebuhr, which could be a reason for precluding faith development theory from public schools. He finds that "[B]y exorcising content out of accepted religious concepts Fowler effectively secularized his faith theory, thus opening the door for inclusion into public education."[37] According to Cristiano, Fowler's theory could qualify as an alternative, for example, to moral development theory, because of its sufficient exclusion of theological and religious content. Though Cristiano contends that there is a lack of clarity regarding faith development's application in public schools, the advantage of Fowler's theory is the more decisive inclusion of the affective domain. While Cristiano's conclusion appears rather critical and skeptical in regard to the content-structure relation, Randy Simmonds, in the dissertation he completed in the same year,[38] makes a strong case for an essential relation between structure and content in faith. Simmonds highlights the effect of the contents of faith assuming that "the contents of a person's faith...are embodied in the faith community to which the person belongs."[39] The results of Simmonds's empirical comparison of two congregations indicates that "the community modal level of faith was the determinative factor in the difference between the two groups."[40] Thus, Simmonds concludes that "the contents of the community's faith effects the structure of their faith."[41]

My own dissertation[42] also belongs in this group of critical-constructive contributions to the theory of faith development. I investigated the hermeneutics of faith development theory and formulated a critique of Fowler's conceptualization of faith, of faith development, and of the research methodology from the perspective of the French phenomenological philosophy of Paul Ricoeur. The conclusions are contextual modifications of the concept of faith and faith development and also constitute a proposal for a new methodological approach in faith development research that can better account for the narrative quality of faith trajectories. Norbert Hahn[43] develops an interpretation of faith development theory as a "liberation theology for the middle-class." Assuming that, in the context of U.S. congregations, the metaphor of development opens up much greater access to and potential for institutional transformation than the metaphor of liberation, Hahn aims at the formulation of a model of practical theological transformation. Faith development theory's descriptive, empirical focus thereby shifts from the individual to congregations.

Judging from the following two contributions, my European colleagues appear to be rather critical of the faith development perspective. Gabriele Bussmann,[44] in her dissertation at Münster, is highly critical of both Fowler's and Oser's theories; she concludes that both theories are incapable of delineating the foundations of Christian faith, which, from her perspective, would require inclusion of the dimensions of experience and function. As an alternative, Bussmann works out a concept of *Vertrauen* ("trust") that would be adequate for theology and religious education when facing the loss of faith in our times. In an equally critical approach, Lauri Oikarinen's dissertation,[45] completed in Finland, examines the consistency of faith development theory with respect to the philosophy of science and also with respect to its applicability in religious education. Fowler's concept of faith as universal human meaning making and its grounding in structural cognitive patterns is criticized for being inconsistent throughout the stages, especially in the definition of the sixth stage. Oikarinen concludes that "in defining faith and faith development, Fowler uses models based on different kinds of ontology, epistemology, and methodology simultaneously and in some respects without integration. In conjunction with the principles of progressivism and pragmatism Fowler tries to proceed from the immanent reality delineated by empiristic and rationalistic criteria to transcendent reality based upon revelation."[46] Furthermore, Oikarinen doubts that Fowler's structural approach does full justice to the affective, dynamic, and paradoxical features of the Christian faith tradition and the contextual dimension of faith development. Though finding some value in the faith development perspective, especially in the Stage 5 description, for its capacity to enrich the understanding and evaluation of religious education, Oikarinen concludes: "Fowler's theory is not able to offer a consistent and universal criterion for ideological and religious education."[47]

That European theology is not only critical toward faith development theory but also has some thoughtful new suggestions to offer can be seen in the most recent theoretical contribution, which is also the first monograph on Fowler's theory in theology in the German-speaking world—the reconstruction of faith development theory in Gabriele Klappenecker's dissertation, completed at Heidelberg.[48] On the basis of a thorough analysis of the theories of H. Richard Niebuhr, Kohlberg, and Erikson, Klappenecker reconstructs Fowler's faith development theory in terms of an ethics of responsibility that has implications for practical theology. Klappenecker suggests a reconstrual of Fowler's stages as "stages of responsibility."

This extensive survey of the critical reflections on faith development theory from various predominantly theological standpoints cannot be distilled into a harmonious synthesis. It resembles rather a dissonant orchestra. However, the articulated positions are similar in the seriousness with which they respond to the challenge of a theory that, without denying its roots in theology, adopts its basic principles from structural-developmental theory. Most of these researchers felt the need to both investigate their own theological roots and present various proposals for a reconstruction of faith development theory. This indicates above all that Fowler's theory has attracted attention from many theologians in both the United States and beyond, inspiring them to respond to the challenge it presents. Nevertheless, some common themes emerge: the call to attend to the contents of faith, the critical question of whether or not an optimistic structural logic of development diverts attention from the dark side of the human experience, and the proposal to account for the determinative influence of the context, especially the faith communities, to name but a few. From this variety of critical-constructive contributions, it is understandable that Fowler has engaged primarily in the theological grounding of his perspective. However, to the disappointment of many of these researchers, Fowler has not ventured into major theoretical revisions; rather, he has engaged in deepening and enriching the theological grounding of faith development theory,[49] proposing its application in pastoral care,[50] religious education, and the public church,[51] and finally explicates the implications of his perspective for practical theology and for the "public challenges of postmodern life."[52]

1.3.2 Theoretical Correlation of Faith Development Theory with Psychoanalytic Perspectives

From its early years, faith development theory has evoked reflection on its relation to psychoanalysis. The Jungian perspective was investigated in three of the earlier dissertations. The study completed by Gregg Raduka[53] focused on the differences and possible synthesis between Fowler's descriptions of stages of faith development and Jungian stages of personality development. Leonard Bradley's dissertation[54] investigated possible relationships between personality type as measured by the Myers-Briggs Type Indicator and faith development as measured by Fowler's "Faith Development Interview." Finally, Mary Ford-Grabowsky[55] suggests a concept of the Christian faith developed from the works of Hildegard of Bingen and C. G. Jung as a "critical alternative to Fowler." Ford-Grabowsky[56] has continued to elaborate upon her critical view on faith development. H. J. McDargh[57] investigates the relationship between object relations theory and the faith development paradigm. It is very likely due to the fact that Fowler himself has drawn a connection to the psychoanalytical perspective of Ana-Maria Rizzuto[58] that the correlation of faith development theory with Rizzuto's psychoanalysis has been discussed increasingly over the years. M. Thompson's thesis[59] on Fowler and Rizzuto is an example of this type of work. However, we also have the dissertation completed by Renee Penticoff,[60] who investigated Rizzuto's concept of the God representation as it arises dynamically in early childhood and possibly plays a role in the process of faith and self-becoming. With respect to therapeutic assessment and intervention, Penticoff suggests applying both perspectives in therapeutic assessment and intervention: the God representation in Rizzuto's terms and faith development. Recently, Fowler himself[61] intentionally has included Rizzuto's perspective for his description, especially in reference to the early stages of faith development. Even more recently, the discussion about the relevance of Rizzuto's psychoanalytical perspective has intensified, for example, in her response[62] to a series of papers[63] presented in an American Psychological Association (APA) symposium on "Faith Development beyond the Modern Paradigm" held in Boston in 1999. The studies show that a correlation between psychoanalytic perspectives and faith development theory is not only plausible, but that both sides gain from such a correlation. For faith development theory, it promises to balance out some of the cognitive-structural limitedness and thereby lead to a more comprehensive account of faith development. However, this correlation requires further clarification and still remains one of the desiderata inviting further research.

1.4 Empirical Studies

Criticism of Fowler that maintains he had little interest in providing more empirical evidence for his theory[64] may appear justified, since he has worked more extensively on the theological grounding of faith development theory. However, his texts not only have a theological and practical focus but also contain some advancements and modifications of faith development theory. Finally, this criticism voiced against faith development theory is no longer justified in view of the large number of qualitative replication studies using the faith development instrument. I shall first provide an overview before going into more detail.

1.4.1 Empirical Studies on Faith Development–An Overview

According to Nicola Slee,[65] eleven empirical studies in faith development qualify as "replication studies" of Fowler's research,[66] and another eight as what she calls "correlational studies." In contrast, I have identified thirty Fowler replication studies completed before the turn of the century. Twenty-six of them used the classical Faith Development Interview[67] in their research,[68] and four of them used a variation of the faith development instrument. The empirical studies in faith development using some kind of creative qualitative method variation based on Fowler's instrument amount to a total of sixteen.[69] In my opinion, only four of them can be termed replication studies. The qualitative studies, taken together, add approximately 1,000 Faith Development Interviews to the sample of 359 upon which *Stages of Faith* was based. There have also been some attempts to develop a shorter research instrument, a Fowler Scale or Faith Development Scale, and to use it in part in combination with other measurements.[70] Figure 3 presents a statistical overview.

Figure 3: Empirical Studies in Faith Development

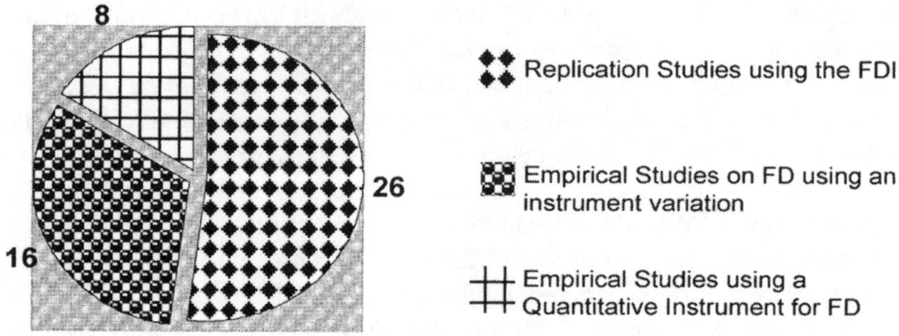

8

26

16

✦✦ Replication Studies using the FDI

▦ Empirical Studies on FD using an instrument variation

╫ Empirical Studies using a Quantitative Instrument for FD

Only a lengthy chapter or a book could portray adequately the studies and present an overview—or, to the extent that this is possible, a comparison—of the results. This task still awaits another hard-working and excellent doctoral student. What I can do here is highlight some results that speak to specific foci of research.

1.4.2 Research Focus: Correlation of Faith Development with Personality Development

The interest in research on the relation between faith and moral development that was so important in the first decade of faith development research has decreased.[71] There are few new results to report that have not been presented already in earlier searches of the literature. Correlations of faith development with other dimensions of human development have become more interesting—for example, psychoanalytic aspects of the person as they relate to faith development. This, of course, takes up a line of studies that has been mentioned previously. However, with the exception of the dissertations dealing with the correlation of faith development and Jungian psychology, the dialogue has tended toward a theoretical discussion about this correlation and has not yet been put to work and tested in empirical research. This has changed in recent years with two empirical studies that I will mention here.

Victor Clore's study "Faith Development in Adults: Scale of Measurement and Relation to Attachment"[72] suggests that we understand development as "the progressive appropriation of self and other."[73] He assumes that faith relates to attachment, and thus he proposes a new and different model of development, for which he refers to John Bowlby[74] and to Bartholomew and Horowitz.[75] Clore reports that "[T]he analysis of the data suggested that faith development, rather than a linear progression of one stage succeeding another, is better conceived as a continuous two-dimensional process of self and other appropriation."[76]

Another recent empirical study has been completed by John Canavan on "Oedipal Resolution and Locus of Control as Determinants of Stage of Faith Development."[77] Canavan examined the impact of psychosexual development on faith development and hypothesized specifically that less adequate levels of Oedipal resolution would be related to lower levels of faith development, and that more adequate levels of Oedipal resolution would be related to higher levels of faith development. Canavan also examined the locus of control construct to determine how it relates to faith development. His sample consisted of eighty-three women and fifty men from western Ireland. The results led Canavan to the conclusion that faith development theory has the potential both to enhance the understanding of human development and also to provide a framework enabling clinicians to intervene effectively with religiously oriented clients.[78]

These studies are promising in the sense that they test the relation between psychodynamics and faith development, an aspect that has been hypothesized by quite a number of researchers in the field, including Fowler himself, but that has not been tested empirically in an adequate manner. This line of research could have the capability to test what I have discovered in more recent developments in Fowler's work (see below, 2.1) and in the discussion on faith development.

1.4.3 Research Focus: Women's Religious Development

Some *theoretical* studies (that I could also have mentioned in section 1.3) can be understood as opening perspectives on concepts of faith and faith development capable of accounting for women's faith development. Discussions about imagination and the self can be mentioned within this context.[79] Theresa Sallnow, in her critical exploration of Fowler's theory with special reference to personalist philosophy,[80] poses serious questions to the basic framework of faith development theory from the perspective of human development, which according to her should account for the "mystery and uniqueness of persons as the essential foundation for any exploration of human faith life."[81] Therefore, Sallnow seeks to highlight the role of "imagination and responsibility," but concludes that a developmental theory must account for the "paradox and ambiguity in human experience" and also for "the distinctiveness of personal rather than linear time."[82] Referring more explicitly to feminist theory, but also to psychoanalytic theory, Carol Pitts's investigation "The Self as a Metaphor"[83] examines and compares Fowler's, Kegan's, and Kohut's concepts of the self and Keller's feminist theory. She develops the metaphor of the self as a pluriform self, honoring its potential oneness and manyness, which may help not only to improve pastoral care and counseling–her focus is women with Dissociative Identity Disorders–but also to advance feminist and postmodern conceptualizations of the self.

The *empirical* studies in faith development of women present a strong proposal for revising the definition of faith to include a relational perspective, especially with regard to Individuative-Reflective faith (Stage 4). Based on theoretical reflection on the nature of faith and also on the interpretation of interviews with twelve women ministers, Nancy Devor[84] highlights the relational character of women's faith and suggests that Fowler's stages and logic of development be reworked to include a much more prominent relational perspective. In a parallel perspective, but more focused on a very specific sample, Janice Leary[85] found in her study of twenty-one mothers of multihandicapped children an ethics of care and responsibility as the outstanding pattern of faith. She maintains that this ethics of care is not valued appropriately in faith development theory, thereby depressing women's scores onto Stage 3.

Two more recent empirical studies on women's faith development confirm these accounts but do not agree with their conclusions. Pamela Morgan[86] has studied the faith development of women in crisis. Fowler's theory and research instrument were tested in a marginal population of women experiencing mental health crises. Twenty-four women living in an urban halfway house setting were interviewed. Morgan reports that seventy-five percent of the women operate from the Synthetic-Conventional stage of faith development and that all of the women shared stories in which they retold or expanded their Faith Development Interview, focusing on their experiences. Rather than questioning the foundation of faith development theory to do justice to these women, Morgan concludes that the ultimate challenge is that development be the aim of therapy. Margaret Cowden's study "Faith Development in Women: A Comparison of the Moral Development Theories of Carol Gilligan and Lawrence Kohlberg and the Faith Development Theory of James Fowler"[87] examined Kohlberg's and Gilligan's moral development theories and Fowler's faith development theory in order to determine their implications for a better understanding of faith development in women. From an analysis of in-depth interviews with ten American Baptist clergywomen, Cowden reports that five women showed evidence of a predominant moral orientation toward care, four showed an orientation toward justice, and one an integration of those two. Cowden concludes:

> The results of this research suggests that a starting point for future research lies in further analysis of the possible interrelatedness of Gilligan's theory of moral development and Fowler's theory of faith development...[N]either model alone is sufficient to explain the process of faith development in women...[I]n order to obtain a fuller understanding of the dynamic process of faith development in women, Fowler's theory would have to accommodate insights from Gilligan's theory of moral development in order to adequately portray the faith development process in women's experience.[88]

Robin Smith[89] has studied the professional and faith development of female religious leaders using a qualitative method of narrative analysis. Smith aims at developing a grounded theory about the faith and professional development of women in religious leadership and concludes that, although there are thematic similarities found in James Fowler's faith development theory and this research, women do not move vertically and permanently through specific stages of faith development. Rather, women experience what Smith describes metaphorically as a whirlpool experience of faith.

It is obvious that most of the studies on women's faith development conclude with a clear proposal to revise the concept of faith and faith development, especially for the Individuative-Reflective stage of faith, as they regard Fowler's description of this stage to be inadequate for women's faith and faith development. In the foreword to the German translation of *Stages of Faith*,[90] Fowler responded to this critique and suggested a revision of the Stage 4 description to include a concept of relational knowing.[91] The 1993 revised edition of the *Manual for Faith Development Research*[92] includes "provisional insights and revisions"[93] in the form of a contribution by Karen DeNicola, but this revision was not worked into the Manual itself.

1.4.4 Research Focus: Cross-cultural Research

In addition to the cross-cultural studies comprising a major portion of empirical research, there are also theoretical studies that interpret Fowler's faith development theory from the perspective of other faith traditions and cultural contexts. Jose Plackal undertook "A Dialogical Inquiry into the Theory of James W. Fowler from the Cultural Context of India."[94] U. M. A. Majmudar's[95] East-West interfaith study interprets the "structures" of Mahatma Gandhi's selfhood and spirituality in the light of James Fowler's theory. Fowler's Western theory is employed as a heuristic guide for examining and interpreting an Eastern man and his spiritual growth. Majmudar's conclusion provides overall support for Fowler's fundamental thesis that faith is a generic and universal feature of human living and meaning making. However, he also sees the need for modifying some stages that he considers somewhat too pro-Western. Though modest, this evaluation also raises questions about the cross-cultural applicability of faith development theory.

On the basis of the three cross-cultural faith development studies[96] that were available when she completed her article, Slee concludes: "These few studies provide some fascinating, but as yet inconclusive, evidence regarding the universality of Fowler's theory, as well as demonstrating some of the difficulties of translating Fowler's methodology to a non-Western milieu, and highlighting the need for more systematic research using cross-cultural samples."[97]

Some additional cross-cultural research has been completed since then. There is the study of forty Baha'i, a sample of twenty in Canada and another sample of twenty in India, which confirmed the "general validity of the Fowler instrument when applied to the Indian sample; however specific problems arose with the construction of Stage 3 descriptors," indicating that faith development theory is not entirely free of cultural bias.[98] Two other recently completed research projects[99] using the faith development interview method in Korean and Romanian contexts only need to be mentioned in passing. While both studies had a rather small sample, they report general usefulness and applicability of the faith development instrument within their contexts. Thus, we can report some progress here in terms of the cross-cultural validity and applicability of the faith development instrument. Nevertheless, I agree with Slee that the research is not yet sufficient to provide empirical evidence of Fowler's universality claim, a claim that Fowler has not revoked but also has not repeated lately.[100]

1.4.5 Advancement of the Method to Measure Faith Development

As already mentioned, there have been some attempts to develop and implement a shorter research instrument, partially alongside other measurements.[101] The instrument used by Green and Hoffman[102] in their research project for measuring the faith stage of their subjects was a newly formulated series of questions that reflected what the authors assumed to be compatible with the questions in the Fowler research tradition. In my opinion, these questions do not meet the standards of faith development research because, on the one hand, they fall back into a closed Christian worldview and, on the other hand, they pose very sophisticated and self-reflective questions. To my knowledge, their instrument has never been used in research again.

The "Fowler Scale" by Barnes, Dole, and Johnson[103] was the first scale to receive some attention and be used again in research.[104] The "Fowler Scale," a nine-item measure, was constructed for Fowler's Stages 2 through 5. The scale does not measure development in the sense of movement through these stages but allows for a differentiation of Fowler's faith styles (as the authors label the stages). For this scale, we only have initial evidence of validity. It is also not clear what the scores really mean, because we have no construct validity results.[105] In addition, I have the same judgment about Barnes et al.'s "Fowler Scale" as about Green and Hoffman's scale: It cannot be used among non-Christians. Thus, some work and perhaps revision would be required before it can be called *the* Fowler Scale.

For their empirical study about the impact of terminal cancer on the lives of patients and their spouses as a function of the stage of religious faith, Swensen, Fuller, and Clemens[106] have developed the "Stages of Faith Scale" as an instrument for measuring faith development. This scale is taken up by Canavan[107] in his dissertation, which I have already described. The "Stages of Faith Scale" is a very brief five-question selection from the *Manual of Faith Development Research*.[108] In my judgment, this series of questions leaves out important dimensions of the *Manual* entirely, such as the section on relationships (significant others, parents), the openness of value commitment beyond the individual, specific dimensions of religion (prayer, death, sin), and, finally, crises and peak experiences beyond the, nonetheless important, question of hope and faith. I regard this scale as too brief. Furthermore, I could not find any validity testing.

Clore's study[109] has been mentioned as a fresh approach to faith development in terms of a relationship between self and other (attachment). However, Clore also introduced a new methodological approach in his study: an original psychometric measure that he constructed and tested in a rather large sample of 509 subjects. This is a thirty-item scale and is more comprehensive than the "Stages of Faith Scale," but it is, nevertheless, a new measure rather independent from the classical faith development instrument. It still requires validity and reliability testing.

The "Faith Development Scale" (FDS) developed by Gary Leak and his group[110] is probably the most recent development of a brief instrument for the quantitative evaluation of faith development. Leak et al. present results of studies to evidence validity. This short eight-item scale would be well-suited for research with larger samples in respect to time limitations. However, the FDS created by Leak and his group has a narrow focus on the institutional environment of Christian churches, family, friends, and belief systems. Here, I voice again the critique of narrowing the focus so that the instrument cannot include non-Christian faith orientations. Persons with a non-Christian new religious orientation would not find themselves represented well. Furthermore, the FDS has a strong focus on formal-operational reflection (Stage 4 competencies), and the style of the questions elicits rather self-reflective statements.

My conclusion about the quantitative instruments for measuring faith development is not positive. While we need a good quantitative instrument, we also need considerable time and energy to revise the instruments that have been developed so far—or to invent new ones—and put them through thorough testing for reliability and validity before going on to design larger research projects.

However, there has been some experimentation with and advancement of qualitative instruments for analyzing faith development. The methodological proposals for including a narrative approach in the analysis of interviews[111] are interesting, as is the invention of an instrument to use a written narrative in essay form as an instrument. Research strategies for presenting stories to the interviewee have been developed and used.[112]

The following empirical research projects have taken a narrative approach. Smith's[113] project has been described above. E. Morgan[114] presents "A Narrative Theological Study of Religious Autobiographical Quests" and describes four "journeys in faith" in a local Episcopal Church. Morgan looks at the narrative structure of these reports and attempts to elucidate the "model" or framework in them. Morgan also asks for the ways in which these journeys in faith are integrated with, and contrasted to, developmental stage and faith theories. Caitlin Anderson's[115] study explores the role of religion, spirituality, and faith in the lives of three college women. Anderson has used, instead of the Faith Development Interview, descriptive narrative research as a form of interpretive inquiry. For this kind of approach, Anderson derives support from critics of Fowler's theory who suggest the adoption of a narrative lens. In terms of analysis, Anderson looks for narrative structures[116] in the participants' stories.

Sogol Nahavandi[117] investigates the process of psychospiritual development and attempts to establish a narrative model of personality development. Anderson presents two case studies, using a new interview protocol that was compiled from two existing interview models—that is, Dan McAdams's "Identifying Personal Myth Interview Protocol"[118] and Fowler's Faith Development Interview. The results confirmed that, in the later years of life, there is a shift in perspective with regard to one's personal mythology. Moreover, Anderson concludes that Fowler's theory and research instrument are universal and applicable, not only to people within Christian or Protestant religious backgrounds. He maintains that the Faith Development Interview can gather scorable and analyzable information even if conducted in a different language and given to people of different ethnicities, belief systems, and cultures.

The narrative approach adopted in these studies is suggestive and appears to yield, according to narrative analysis, in-depth interpretations and comprehensive case studies. Unfortunately, the very small numbers of subjects included in these projects indicate that this procedure consumes even more time and resources than the classical faith development instrument. Such a decided qualitative approach has its price. However, in my opinion, this could be a good way to continue. Looking for a briefer objective measure than the lengthy Faith Development Interview, David Rose[119] developed an interesting new method to investigate faith development in large samples—a four-story instrument. The instrument presents four stories that raise issues of faith, and the subjects then respond to belief statements regarding the stories. Finally, David Hoffman[120] has developed a "Faith Development Essay Instrument" (FDEI), for which she claims reliability, validity, and good agreement with the classical Faith Development Interview.

2. Recent Developments and Perspectives for the Future

2.1 Faithful Change and Postmodern Challenges—Recent Developments in Fowler's Work

Fowler's style of reflecting, modifying, and expanding the faith development theory of *Stages of Faith* has not changed significantly. To the disappointment of some empirically oriented researchers, he has not reconstructed major aspects of the theory, which a great number of theoretical and empirical studies would suggest, nor has he engaged in revisions of the faith development methodology. Rather, not long after *Stages of Faith* was written, Fowler engaged in theological, philosophical, and social-scientific clarification of the faith development perspective in search of correlations with other theories and in explicating the value of the faith development perspective for the predicaments in church and society.[121] However, some modest changes can be identified in these contributions, especially in the more recent ones. I would like to bring three of these new developments to your attention.

First, it is possible to identify developments in Fowler's work that incorporate a psychoanalytic perspective. In his interpretation of the interview with Mary,[122] the psychosocial perspective already plays a decisive role, emphasizing the psychodynamic, life history, and also the life world as resources in Mary's journey of faith. Here, Fowler has given theoretical and empirical prominence to Erikson's work, which, as critics say, was not sufficiently worked into the theoretical and methodological core of the faith development theory of 1981. In 1987, Fowler took a significant step toward more seriously integrating psychodynamic models by correlating his own stages of faith with those of Robert Kegan.[123] Now, in his book *Faithful Change*,[124] Fowler has adopted, at least for the early stages of faith, a more psychodynamic perspective. He gives extensive reference to psychoanalytic contributions about infancy and early childhood that offer a rich description of Primal faith and Intuitive-Projective faith. He maintains that a more detailed reference to Erikson's psychosocial description of infancy yields deeper insights into the origin of faith and basic trust. Daniel Stern's[125] work on the interpersonal world of the infant also allows a more detailed and more precise account of imagination, ritualization, symbolization, and participation in faith as they emerge in infancy. And finally, a more explicit reference to Rizzuto's work results in a detailed perspective on key religious symbols as they emerge and develop in infancy and early childhood. Here, in the fresh description of Primal faith and Intuitive-Projective faith, the "profoundly relational"[126] character of faith is brought into the foreground. Child development as "a profoundly *interactive* matter"[127] is unfolded, focusing on emotional, psychodynamic, and interpersonal characteristics. In other words, in this new portrait of faith development focusing on the first stages in infancy and early childhood, Fowler integrates more fully some of the basic dimensions of religion/faith that pure structural-developmental theory has bracketed—*experience, function,* and *content.*

While I agree with this portrait of the origin of faith in early childhood, I suggest that it be expanded to include the other stages or styles of faith. For I believe that the expansion of the psychodynamic and, even more, of the interpersonal perspective, which has yielded better insights in the origin and early development of faith, would substantially change our perspective on adolescent and adult development. Perhaps then, faith development theory could provide a more profound answer to Rizzuto's questions: "What are the interpersonal and psychodynamic conditions for the emergence of a particular style? What are the narratives, affects, conflicts, defenses, fears, satisfactions that organize to form a particular style?"[128]

A second advancement in Fowler's 1996 book deserves attention. Fowler expands his developmental differentiation between Stages 3 to 5 to an analysis of modern or postmodern societies. This can best be captured in Fowler's own figures.[129]

While he parallels the Synthetic-Conventional faith stage with the orthodox, hierarchical, and external authority structure of society, the Individuative-Reflective faith stage parallels the progressive, social contract type of societal structure, which allows and requires an internal locus of authority and also a rational mediation in public discourse.

Figure 4: Stages of Faith and Organizational Structures (Fowler)

Faith Stage/ Temper	Faith Con- sciousness	Religion	Politics	Organization
Synthetic-Conventional; rooted in pre-Enlightenment; *orthodox*	Tacit; interpersonal; non-critical; external locus of authority	"Some of my best friends are…"; assumed superiority; *mystery-mastery*	Reduced to personal qualities of leaders or reference groups; *organic society*	Hierarchical authority; information control
Individuative-Reflective; rooted in Enlightenment; *progressive*	Explicit; autonomous; critical-reflective; internal locus of authority	Dichotomous; competing truth claims; either exclusive truth or relativism; *demythologizing*	Ideological; claim chosen political and economic philosophy as defining self; *social contract*	Specialization; differentiation of function; rational-bureaucratic organizaiton

Figure 5: Stages of Faith and Organizational Structures (Fowler)

Faith Stage/ Temper	Faith Con- sciousness	Religion	Politics	Organization
Conjunctive; emerging post-Enlightenment outlook; practical postmodern	Multiple perspectives and systems; second naivete; commitment in embraced pluralism	All reality outlooks are constructed; God's reality exceeds our constructs; integrate conscious and unconscious	Multiple realities; multiple systems; beyond ideology; ecological interdependence; covenant	Ecological networks; multi-related project orientation; information-driven; flexibility

The Conjunctive Faith stage's parallel, in what Fowler calls a postmodern societal structure, indicates a way beyond the culture of warlike tension between the orthodox and the progressive model. Of course, this analysis of society leads primarily to the proposal "to claim and model Conjunctive faith in American society" and to call for leaders in the public who "alter the environments of debate and dialogue."[130] However, this analysis also leads Fowler to an inquiry into theology's potential response to postmodern challenges. What is said only between the lines here, but should be regarded as a major advancement of faith development theory, is its application as a means of understanding social bodies and social conflicts and as a possible and promising answer to the predicaments of modernity. This potential for faith development theory to provide a model for understanding social differentiation and conflict in society and religious communities should not be underestimated and should be elaborated in methodological terms. If we succeed in making use of this perspective for research in social milieus, it could provide a major contribution to social-scientific analysis.

A third related development in Fowler's thought is reflected in his Boston paper[131] at the APA symposium on "Faith Development beyond the Modern Paradigm." There, Fowler not only engages in an extensive review of the history of faith development theory, he also sketches some answers to the postmodern challenges that have not been addressed by the faith development framework so far–this assumption remained unquestioned in *Faithful Change*– and still require a rethinking of some of the theory's basic principles. If it is true, as I maintain,[132] that the fundamentalisms of our time are the outstanding incidences to which the project of modernity is exposed, and that these grave disturbances call into question the smooth teleological metastory of modernity[133] and the respective metastory of development obliged to it, then faith development theory has a problem as well. Can we still maintain the logic of development consisting of structural stages that are understood as structural wholes, as invariant, sequential, and hierarchical? Fowler responded to these challenging questions in a far-reaching remark:

> The most vulnerable feature of formalist stage theories such as Piaget's, Kohlberg's and F[aith] D[evelopment] T[heory] lies in the tendency to over trust the structuring power of the formally describable opera-tions of knowing and construing that constitute the stages. In this paper I have said in several different ways that the formal structuring of the stages is, at best, only half the story as regards the shaping and maintaining of a person's (or a group's) worldview. There is both structuring and deconstructing power in the cultural environment with its social and media "surround."[134]

It is this deconstructing power of cultural environment, consisting of such factors as media influences and pluralistic fragmentations, that jeopardizes the achievement of a coherent self. Thus, this could affect not only research results but also the very foundations of the theory itself:

> For all these reasons, it is not surprising that interviewers may find fewer adolescents and young adults who show the qualities of synthetic-conventional faith, or construct the coherent critical com-mitments that go with individuative-reflective faith. It seems that there is a need for an "average expectable environment" of sponsorship support that children and youth need in order to form coherent selfhood and faith. There is a logic to Streib's (1999) turn toward "off-road religion" and toward relinquishing concern with "stages."[135]

To be sure, Fowler did not announce here an inclination to relinquish concern with his stages of faith, but he has proposed to distinguish the stages by including a differentiation of four types cutting across the stages: Totalizing, Rational Critical, Conflicted or Oscillating, and Diffuse Types. This has initiated an interesting discussion that has not yet reached a conclusion but indicates that there is motion in Fowler's conceptualization of faith development.

Taken together, these advancements in the faith development perspective indicate that Fowler's theory is still in motion, especially with regard to a reaction to the challenges in culture and society and the attempt to provide answers to these challenges. However, the precision work on theoretical revisions of faith development theory, and on research strategies and methodological details in faith development research in particular, are future tasks. In this context, I can locate my own proposal for a revision that I will now set forth briefly.

2.2 Proposed Revision: The Religious Styles Perspective

Based on James Fowler's faith development theory, I proposed a new perspective of structural-developmental theory of religion in a recent article, "Faith Development Revisited: The Religious Styles Perspective."[136] A first portion of this proposal for modification was published in 1997 in an article in the *Archiv für Religionspsychologie* entitled "Religion als Stilfrage."[137]

In my opinion, it is time not only to call into question the primacy of cognitive development as the motor and guideline of religious development, but also to propose a new model, which I call the typology of religious styles. This revision is aimed at accounting more fully for the life-history and life-world relatedness of religion at its principal interactive, interpersonal origin and shape. Thus, the phenomenologists Maurice Merleau-Ponty and Paul Ricoeur, who provide philosophical perspectives, Gil Noam's developmental perspective that is based on interpersonality, as well as Ana-Maria Rizzuto's view of the psychodynamic development of religion play a significant role for the reformulation. In the article, I present an overview of styles and illustrate this perspective in a figure.[138]

The religious styles perspective, I contend, is able to provide an explanation of fundamentalism that the structural-developmental theories of religious or faith development have not been able to provide, because their framework cannot account for regression, or the kind of partial regression onto, or revival of, earlier rigid styles.[139] The cognitive-structural theories of development in their traditional form of structural, hierarchical, sequential, and irreversible logic of development result from an all-too-optimistic interpretation of the project of modernity. If left unchanged, they cannot provide us with an explanatory framework for understanding fundamentalism and individual fundamentalist revivals. The modification of the developmental model takes account of the fact that the project of modernity is exposed to disturbances. I am thus sketching out the developmental psychology variant of a fundamental problem of modernity: namely, as already mentioned, that the teleological metastory of modernity is challenged by disturbances that include individual and global fundamentalisms.

2.3 Perspectives for the Future of Research in Faith Development

The future of faith development research, as already indicated above, lies primarily in the adaptation of the qualitative instrument. From my point of view, the leading edge in method development lies in the inclusion of narrative approaches and the accounting for content dimensions. A number of empirical studies already have moved in this direction and included a narrative approach; others also have searched their data for content dimensions in the various aspects of faith. We would need a consistent methodology to integrate these innovative approaches. This would be the methodological counterpart to the more comprehensive inclusion of life history into the model of religious development, at which the religious styles perspective aims as well. These are some tasks to be completed as we proceed in future research.

Second, for future research with larger samples, it would be helpful to have a shorter faith development research instrument that would be able to yield valid and reliable results. The quantitative instruments that have been developed and tested so far have shown insufficient validity for comprehensively covering the dynamics of the development of faith in cross-cultural research. I doubt that they can be applied in research on new religions within our Western societies. However, if we take on the task of investigating milieus in society and religious communities, such a shorter instrument would be useful. Much work also lies ahead of us in this area.

Third, I suggest adding another dimension of innovation in methodology. The attempt to account more fully for the life world, which the religious styles perspective tries to promote, invokes the inclusion of the sociological research tradition on lifestyles.[140] If we avoid the trap of focusing mainly on leisure activities, fashion, and consumer attitudes, a trap into which part of lifestyle research has fallen, lifestyle research can provide an inspiring new dimension in faith development research, as it calls to our attention the simultaneity of *distinction* and *milieu formation.* Thus, it could take up the question of "modal levels of development" that has remained rather marginalized despite some good attempts to address it. In this way, research in faith development could venture further out of its niche and contribute its gift for investigating religious, and religious community, milieus. Such research has already begun in Germany with a study on *Milieus in the Church.*[141] Unfortunately, this study lacks a developmental perspective. The rapid generational changes in religious orientation in our times also require an adequate methodological response in faith development research method.

Notes

[1]Revised version of a paper presented at the 14th Conference of the International Association for the Psychology of Religion, September 28–30, 2001, in Soesterberg, Netherlands.

[2]James W. Fowler, *Stages of Faith: The Psychology of Human Development and the Quest for Meaning* (San Francisco: Harper & Row, 1981).

[3]Sharon Parks, "The North American Critique of James Fowler's Theory of Faith Development," in *Stages of Faith and Religious Development*, ed. James W. Fowler, Karl Ernst Nipkow, and Friedrich Schweitzer (New York: Crossroad, 1991), 101–15.

[4]H. J. McDargh, "Faith Development Theory at Ten Years," *Religious Studies Review* 10 (1984): 339–43.

[5]Nicola Slee, "Further on from Fowler: Post-Fowler Faith Development Research," in *Research in Religious Education*, ed. Leslie J. Francis, William K. Kay, and William S. Campbell; (Leominster, Engl.: Gracewing, and Macon, Ga.: Smyth & Helwys, 1996), 73–96.

[6]Though the information about the relatively large number of dissertations has been compiled from my own files and also using other resources including Internet databases, I cannot claim that the statistics are perfect and also cannot exclude the possibility that some contributions may be missing.

[7]See Karl E. Nipkow, *Grundfragen der Religionspädagogik, Bd.3: Gemeinsam leben und glauben lernen* (Gütersloh: Gütersloher, 1982).

[8]See Hans-Jürgen Fraas et al., eds., *Religiöse Erziehung und Glaubensentwicklung. Zur Auseinandersetzung mit der kognitiven Psychologie* (Göttingen: Vandenhoeck & Rupprecht, 1986). Friedrich Schweitzer, *Lebensgeschichte und Religion. Religiöse Entwicklung und Erziehung im Kindes- und Jugendalter* (Gütersloh: Kaiser; Gütersloher, 1987). Karl E. Nipkow et al., eds., *Glaubensentwicklung und Erziehung* (Gütersloh: Gütersloher, 1988). Michael Utsch, "Glaubensentwicklung als Thema der Psychologie. James Fowlers 'Stufen des Glaubens,'" *Wege zum Menschen* 42 (1990): 359–66. Heinz Streib, *Hermeneutics of Metaphor, Symbol, and Narrative in Faith Development Theory* (Frankfurt: Peter Lang, 1991). Jeff Astley and Leslie J. Francis, eds., *Christian Perspectives on Faith Development: A Reader* (Leominster, Eng.: Gracewing; Grand Rapids, Mich: Eerdmans, 1992).

[9]Karl E. Nipkow, Friedrich Schweitzer, Gabriele Faust-Siehl, and Bernd Krupka, "Developmental Research in the Classroom: An Empirical Study of Teaching-Learning Processes," in *Research in Religious Education*, ed. Leslie J. Francis, William K. Kay, and William S. Campbell (Leominster, Engl.: Gracewing; Macon, Ga.: Smyth & Helwys, 1996), 113–28. K. H. Reich, "Relational and Contextual Reasoning in Religious Education: A Theory-based Empirical Study," in *Research in Religious Education*, 129–44. Gabriele Klappenecker, *Glaubensentwicklung und Lebensgeschichte: Eine Auseinandersetzung mit der Ethik James W. Fowlers, zugleich ein Beitrag zur Rezeption von H. Richard Niebuhr, Lawrence Kohlberg und Erik H. Erikson* (Stuttgart: Kohlhammer, 1998). Heinz Streib, "Faith Development Theory Revisited: The Religious Styles Perspective," *International Journal for the Psychology of Religion* 11 (2001): 143–58.

[10]Walter Conn, *Christian Conversion: A Developmental Interpretation of Autonomy and Surrender* (New York: Paulist Press, 1986). David G. Creamer, *Guides for the Journey: John Macmurray, Bernhard Lonergan, James Fowler* (Lanham: University Press of America, 1996). Romney M. Moseley, *Becoming a Self before God: Critical Transformations* (Nashville, Tenn.: Abingdon Press, 1991). Sharon Parks, *The Critical Years: The Young Adult Search for a Faith to Live By* (San Francisco: Harper & Row, 1986). Schweitzer, *Lebensgeschichte und Religion.*

[11]Woodrow J. Walter, Jr., "Books in Religious Adult Education Valued by Professional Religious Adult Educators" (Ed.D. diss., University of North Texas, 1996). Walter's list of the top ten books includes: (1) Fowler, *Stages of Faith*; (2) Nancy T. Foltz, ed., *Handbook of Adult Religious Education* (Birmingham, Ala.: Religious Education Press, 1986); (3) Craig Dykstra and Sharon Parks, eds., *Faith Development and Fowler* (Birmingham, Ala.: Religious Education Press, 1986); (4) Kenneth Stokes, ed., *Faith Development in the Adult Life Cycle* (New York: W. H. Sadlier, 1982); (5) R. E. Y. Wickett, *Models of Adult Religious Education Practice* (Birmingham, Ala.: Religious Education Press, 1991); (6) John L. Elias, *The Foundations and Practice of Adult Religious Education* (Malabar, Fla.: R. E. Krieger, 1982); (7) Sharon Parks, *The Critical Years*; (8) John M. Hull, *What Prevents Christian Adults from Learning?* (Philadelphia: Trinity Press International, 1991); (9) Leon McKenzie, *The Religious Education of Adults* (Birmingham, Ala.: Religious Education Press, 1982); (10) Kenneth O. Gangel and James C. Wilhoit, eds., *The Christian Educator's Handbook on Adult Education* (Wheaton, Ill.: Victor Books, 1993).

[12]Nancy S. Vanlue, "A Meta-Analysis of the Concepts, Characteristics, and Variables Addressed in Sixty Doctoral Dissertations Highly Relevant to Adult Faith Development [1980–1994]" (Ed.D. diss., Ball State University, 1996).

[13]Selectively, I refer to some contributions in the last decade: Jeff Astley, ed., *How Faith Grows: Faith Development and Christian Education* (London: National Society and Church House Publishing, 1991). John H. Bolen, "Faith Development and Higher Education" (Ph.D. diss., Iowa State University, 1994). Aubrey P. Hancock, "An Investigation of the Element of Conversion in the Faith Development Theories of James Loder and James Fowler with Implications for Adolescent

Christian Education" (Ed.D. diss., New Orleans Baptist Theological Seminary, 1992). Lauri A. Oikarinen, "Development of Human Faith: An Analysis of the Consistency of James W. Fowler's Theory" (Th.D. diss., Helsingin Yliopisto [Finland], 1993). Richard R. Osmer, "James Fowler and the Reformed Tradition: An Exercise in Theological Reflection in Religious Education," *Religious Education* 85 (1990): 51–68. Daniel J. Srinivasan, "Mentoring for Faith Development" (Ed.D. diss., Union Theological Seminary in Virginia, 1996).

[14]Friedrich Schweitzer et al., "Religious Development and the Praxis of Religious Education," *Journal of Education for Teaching* 8 (1995): 5–23. Nipkow et al., "Developmental Research."

[15]Friedrich Schweitzer et al., *Religionsunterricht und Entwicklungspsychologie. Elementarisierung in der Praxis* (Gütersloh: Kaiser; Gütersloher, 1995).

[16]Randy J. Simmonds, "Content and Structure in Faith Development: A Case Examination of James Fowler's Theory" (Ph.D. diss., The Southern Baptist Theological Seminary, 1986). See also Clyde E. Lansdell, "Religious Convictions and Interpersonal Relations in a Christian Community" (Ed.D. diss., University of Toronto [Canada], 1980).

[17]James W. Fowler, *Faith Development and Pastoral Care* (Philadelphia: Fortress Press, 1987).

[18]Steven S. Ivy, "The Structural-developmental Theories of James Fowler and Robert Kegan as Resources for Pastoral Assessment" (Ph.D. diss., The Southern Baptist Theological Seminary, 1985). Carl D. Schneider, *Faith Development and Pastoral Diagnosis, Faith Development and Fowler* (Birmingham, Ala.: Religious Education Press, 1986), 221–50.

[19]Dale J. Brown, "Doubt and Anxiety in Theological and Psychological Perspective with Implications for Pastoral Care and Pastoral Theology" (Ph.D. diss., Southwestern Baptist Theological Seminary, 1994).

[20]Ronald C. Oliver, "Effects of an Acute Traumatic Crisis on Faith" (Ph.D. diss., The Southern Baptist Theological Seminary, 1993).

[21]Michael A. Backlund, "Faith and AIDS: Life Crisis as a Stimulus to Faith Stage Transition" (Ph.D. diss., Pacific Graduate School of Psychology, 1990). Susan M. Driedger, "Relationships among Faith Development, Ego Development, and Religious Orientation in HIV+ Individuals: A Construct Validation Study" (Ph.D. diss., Simon Fraser University [Canada], 1998).

[22]Nina M. Chychula, "Recovery as an Activity of Faith or Meaning-Making: A Study of the Faith Development of Males Recovering from Chemical Dependence" (Ph.D. diss., Temple University, 1995).

[23]Janice P. Leary, "The Relationship of Coping with Chronic Stress and Faith Development in Women: Mothers of Multihandicapped Children" (Ph.D. diss., Boston College, 1988).

[24]Oliver, "Acute Traumatic Crisis."

[25]See Harold G. Koenig, *Is Religion Good for Your Health? The Effects of Religion on Physical and Mental Health* (New York: Haworth Pastoral Press, 1997).

[26]Parks, "North American Critique."

[27]Mark E. Durrett, "The Triad of Faith and Faith Development: A Study in the Thought of H. Richard Niebuhr with Special Reference to the Work of James W. Fowler" (Ph.D. diss., Duke University, 1987).

[28]One H. Park, "A Study of Anthropology in James Fowler's Faith Development Theory" (Ed.D. diss., Presbyterian School of Christian Education, 1989).

[29]Ibid., 204; see also 189f.

[30]Ibid., 204.

[31]Romney M. Moseley, "Religious Conversion: A Structural-developmental Analysis" (Ph.D. diss., Harvard University, 1978).

[32]Moseley, *Becoming a Self.*

[33]Hancock, "Element of Conversion."

[34]Gregory L. Hunt, "Toward Theological Foundations for a Faith Development Theory with Special Attention to James Fowler" (Ph.D. diss., The Southern Baptist Theological Seminary, 1985).

[35]See ibid., ch. 6; quotation is taken from the Abstract, 307.

[36]George Cristiano, "An Analytical Assessment of the Faith Development Theory of J. W. Fowler: An Approach to Moral Education" (Ed.D. diss., Rutgers, State University of New Jersey at New Brunswick, 1986).

[37]Ibid., Abstract, i.

[38]Simmonds, "Content and Structure."

[39]Ibid., 207.

[40]Ibid., 221.

[41]Ibid., 208.

[42]Streib, *Hermeneutics.*

[43]Norbert F. Hahn, "Developing Faith–Liberating Faith: Towards a Practical Theology of Congregational Faith Development as a Liberation Theology for the Middle-Class" (Ph.D. diss., Emory University, 1994).

[44]Gabriele Bussmann, "Vertrauen als Handlungskompetenz: Vorüberlegungen zu einer religiösen Entwicklungstheorie dargestellt in Auseinandersetzung mit den religiösen Entwicklungstheorien von F. Oser und J. W. Fowler" (Dr.theol. diss, Katholisch-theologische Fakultät, Westfälische Wilhelms-Universität, Münster, 1990).

[45]Oikarinen, "Analysis of Consistency."

[46]Ibid.

[47]Ibid.

[48]Klappenecker, *Glaubensentwicklung und Lebensgeschichte.*

[49]See James W. Fowler, *Becoming Adult, Becoming Christian* (San Francisco: Harper & Row, 1984).

[50]Fowler, *Pastoral Care.*

[51]James W. Fowler, *Weaving the New Creation: Stages of Faith and the Public Church* (San Francisco: Harper & Row, 1991).

[52]James W. Fowler, *Faithful Change: The Personal and Public Challenges of Postmodern Life* (Nashville, Tenn.: Abingdon Press, 1996). Idem, "Faith Development Theory and the Postmodern Challenges," *International Journal for the Psychology of Religion* 11 (2001): 159–72.

[53]Gregg G. Raduka, "An Investigation of Hypothesized Correspondence between Fowlerian Stages of Faith Development and Jungian Stages of Personality Development" (Ph.D. diss., University of Maryland, College Park, 1980).

[54]Leonard R. Bradley, "An Exploration of the Relationship between Fowler's Theory of Faith Development and Myers-Briggs Personality Type" (Ph.D. diss., Ohio State University, 1983).

[55]Mary Ford-Grabowsky, "The Concept of Christian Faith in the Light of Hildegard of Bingen and C. G. Jung: A Critical Alternative to Fowler" (Ph.D. diss., Princeton Theological Seminary, 1985).

[56]Mary Ford-Grabowsky, "What Developmental Phenomenon Is Fowler Studying," *Journal of Psychology and Christianity* 5 (1986): 5–13. Idem, "Flaws in Faith Development Theory," *Religious Education* 82 (1987): 80–93. Idem, "The Fullness of the Christian Faith-Experience: Dimensions Missing in Faith Development Theory," *Journal of Pastoral Care* 41 (1987): 39–47.

[57]H. J. McDargh, *Psychoanalytic Object-Relations Theory and the Study of Religion: On Faith and the Imaging of God* (Washington, D.C.: University Press of America, 1983).

[58]Ana-Maria Rizzuto, *The Birth of the Living God: A Psychoanalytic Study* (Chicago and London: University of Chicago Press, 1979).

[59]M. Thompson, "Fowler and Rizzuto: Making Sense of Life and Ourselves" (M.Ed. thesis, University of Birmingham [U.K.], 1988).

[60]Renee M. Penticoff, "The Dynamic God Representation and Faith Development: Considering Religious Information in Psychotherapy" (Psy.D. diss., Widener University Institute for Graduate Clinical Psychology, 1996).

[61]Fowler, *Faithful Change.*

[62]Ana-Maria Rizzuto, "Religious Development beyond the Modern Paradigm–Discussion: The Psychoanalytic Point of View," *International Journal for the Psychology of Religion* 11 (2001): 201–14.

[63]James M. Day, "From Structuralism to Eternity? Re-Imagining the Psychology of Religious Development after the Cognitive-Developmental Paradigm," *International Journal for the Psychology of Religion* 11 (2001): 173–83. Fowler, "Postmodern Challenges." H. J. McDargh, "Faith Development Theory and the Postmodern Problem of Foundations," *International Journal for the Psychology of Religion* 11 (2001): 185–99. Streib, "Religious Styles Perspective."

[64]See C. E. Nelson, "Does Faith Develop? An Evaluation of Fowler's Position," in *Christian Perspectives*, 62–76; C. E. Nelson and Daniel Aleshire, "Research in Faith Development," in *Faith Development and Fowler,* 180–201; Derek H. Webster, "James Fowler's Theory of Faith Development," *British Journal of Religious Education* 7 (1984): 14–18. See also Slee, "Post-Fowler Research."

[65]Slee, "Post-Fowler Research," 75–81, 82–86.

[66]As "replication studies," Slee's review mentions: Backlund, "Faith and AIDS"; Perry E. Bassett, "Faith Development and Mid-Life Transition: Fowler's Paradigm as It Relates to Personality Profile" (Ph.D. diss., Baylor University, 1985); Terry R. Hamrick, "Transitional Factors in the Faith Development of Middle Adults" (Ed.D. diss., University of Georgia, 1988); Elizabeth W.

Howlett, "Entering the Unitive Life: A Study of Fowler's Faith Stages 5 and 6 and the Intervening Transition" (Ed.D. diss., University of Massachusetts, 1989); T. P. Kalam, "The Myth of Stages and Sequence in Moral and Religious Development" (Ph.D. diss., University of Lancaster [U.K.], 1981); Lansdell, "Interpersonal Relations"; Eugene J. Mischey, "Faith Development and Its Relationship to Moral Reasoning and Identity Status in Young Adults" (Ph.D. diss., University of Toronto [Canada], 1976); Moseley, "Religious Conversion"; Sharon Parks, "Faith Development and Imagination in the Context of Higher Education" (Ph.D. diss., Harvard University, 1980); Richard N. Shulik, "Faith Development, Moral Development, and Old Age: An Assessment of Fowler's Faith Development Paradigm" (Ph.D. diss., University of Chicago, 1979); Simmonds, "Content and Structure."

[67]Romney M. Moseley et al., *Manual for Faith Development Research* (Atlanta: Center for Faith Development, Emory University, 1986); or, Romney M. Moseley et al., *Manual for Faith Development Research* (Atlanta: Center for Research in Faith and Moral Development, Candler School of Theology, Emory University, 1993).

[68]Backlund, "Faith and AIDS"; Bassett, "Mid-Life Transition"; Bradley, "Fowler's Theory and Myers-Briggs"; Stacy N. Broun, "An Analysis of Ego Development and Religious Development" (Ph.D. diss., University of Texas Southwestern Medical Center at Dallas, 1984); Chychula, "Males Recovering"; Paula A. Drewek, "Cross-cultural Testing of James W. Fowler's Model of Faith Development among Baha'is" (Ph.D. diss., University of Ottawa [Canada], 1996); Driedger, "HIV+ Individuals"; Eunice A. Farc, "A Pilot Case Study of Fowler's Faith Interview in the Romanian Context" (Th.M. thesis, The Southern Baptist Theological Seminary, 1999); Randall Y. Furushima, "Faith Development Theory: A Cross-cultural Research Project in Hawaii (Ed.D. diss., Columbia University Teachers College, 1983); Maria R. Gardin, "Wisdom and Faith: An Empirical Analysis of Deirdre Kramer's and James Fowler's Models of Development" (Ph.D. diss., Fuller Theological Seminary School of Psychology, 1997); Barbara R. Grossman, "Faith Development and Psychosocial Accomplishment: Trends in Adult Intimacy Growth and Higher Faith Stages" (Ph.D. diss., School of Theology at Claremont, 1991); Dennis A. Haggray, "A Description of the Faith Development of Five Students Attending a Church-related College" (Ph.D. diss., Iowa State University, 1993); Hamrick, "Middle Adults"; Emily W. Hitchens, "Stages of Faith and Values Development and Their Implications for Dealing with Spiritual Care in the Student Nurse-Patient Relationship" (Ed.D. diss., Seattle University, 1988); David A. Hoffman, "Nurturing Spirituality: An Assessment of the Cognitive, Moral Judgment, and Faith Development of First-Year College Students Participating in a Developmental Retreat Program" (Ph.D. diss., University of Maryland, College Park, 1994); Howlett, "Unitive Life"; Linda M. H. Johnson, "Psychotherapy and Spirituality: Techniques, Interventions, and Inner Attitudes" (Ed.D. diss., University of Massachusetts, 1989); Kalam, "Myth of Stages"; Leary, "Coping and Faith Development"; Soon K. Lee, "Fowler's Faith Development Interview Questions in a Korean Context" (Ph.D. diss., Trinity Evangelical Divinity School, 1999); Mischey, "Moral Reasoning"; Shulik, "Old Age"; John Snarey, "Faith Development, Moral Development, and Nontheistic Judaism: A Construct Validity Study," in *Handbook of Moral Behavior and Development*, ed. William M. Kurtines and Jacob L. Gewirtz, (Hillsdale, N.J.: L. Erlbaum, 1991); 279–305; Gary A. Spencer, "A Study of the Founders at Suntree United Methodist Church" (D.Min. diss., Princeton Theological Seminary, 1996); Augustine R. Vanden Heuvel, "Faith Development and Family Interaction" (Ph.D. diss., The Union for Experimenting Colleges and Universities, 1985); Voncile M. White, "Faith Stages, Affiliation, and Gender: A Study of the Faith Development of Catholic College Undergraduates" (Ed.D. diss., Boston University, 1985).

[69]Caitlin L. Anderson, "'How Can My Faith Be So Different?' The Emergence of Religious Identity in College Women" (Ph.D. diss., Indiana University, 1995); Bolen, "Higher Education"; John T. Chirban, *Human Growth and Faith: Intrinsic and Extrinsic Motivation in Human Development* (Washington, D.C.: University Press of America, 1981); Margaret A. Cowden, "Faith Development in Women: A Comparison of the Moral Development Theories of Carol Gilligan and Lawrence Kohlberg and the Faith Development Theory of James Fowler" (Ph.D. diss., Temple University, 1992); Lansdell, "Interpersonal Relations"; D. J. Loomis, "The Relationship of Imagination to Religious Faith among Presbyterian Church Elders, Considering the Mediating Influence of Intuition" (Ph.D. diss., University of Maryland, 1987); E. F. J. Morgan, "'Journeys in Faith': A Narrative Theological Study of Religious Autobiographical Quests" (Ph.D. diss., Ohio University, 1990); Pamela A. Morgan, "The Faith Development of Women in Crisis: A Constructivist Window to Intervention" (Ed.D. diss., University of Houston, 1990); Sogol S. Nahavandi, "On the Process of Psychospiritual Development, Old Age, and the Narrative Theory Model of Personality Development" (Psy.D. diss., The Wright Institute, 1999); Nipkow et al., "Developmental Research"; Roselyn H. Rael, "Una Vida Buena Y Sana: The Development of

Faith among Older Indo-Hispanic Women" (Ph.D. diss., University of Utah, 1995); David B. Rose, "An Instrument to Measure Four of James Fowler's Stages of Faith Development" (Ph.D. diss., California School of Professional Psychology, Fresno, 1991); Robin L. Smith, "Professional and Faith Development in Women Religious Leaders" (Ph.D. diss., The Claremont Graduate University, 1997); Eric K. Sweitzer, "The Symbolic Use of Religious Language among Evangelical Protestant Christians from the Perspective of James Fowler's Faith Development Theory" (Ph.D. diss., Boston University, 1984); Edwin F. Tulloch, "A Study of Faith Stage Transition in Adults" (Ph.D. diss., East Texas State University, 1985); Sherry K. Watt, "Identity and the Making of Meaning: Psychosocial Identity, Racial Identity, Womanist Identity, Self-esteem, and the Faith Development of African-American College Women" (Ph.D. diss., North Carolina State University, 1997).

[70]Michael Barnes et al., "The Formulation of a Fowler Scale: An Empirical Assessment Among Catholics," *Review of Religious Research* 30 (1989): 412–20; John F. Canavan, "Oedipal Resolution and Locus of Control as Determinants of Stage of Faith Development" (Ph.D. diss., New York University, 1999); Victor Clore, "Faith Development in Adults: Scale of Measurement and Relation to Attachment" (Ph.D. diss., Wayne State University, 1997); C. W. Green et al., "Stages of Faith and Perceptions of Similar and Dissimilar Others," *Review of Religious Research* 30 (1989): 246–54; Charles D. Hammond, "The Relationship of Faith Development Stages and the Type and Degree of Irrational Beliefs in Adult Church Attendants" (Ed.D. diss., University of Arkansas, 1993); Dennis W. Hiebert, "Schools of Faith: The Effect of Liberal Arts, Professional, and Religious Education on Faith Development" (Ph.D. diss., University of Manitoba [Canada], 1993); Gary K. Leak et al., "Development and Initial Validation of an Objective Measure of Faith Development," *International Journal for the Psychology of Religion* 9 (1999): 105–24; Clifford H. Swensen et al., "Stage of Religious Faith and Reactions to Terminal Cancer," *Journal of Psychology and Theology* 21 (1993): 238–45.

[71]For example, in dissertations from 1979 to 1992: Cowden, "Faith Development in Women"; Hoffman, "Nurturing Spirituality"; Kalam, "Myth of Stages"; Lansdell, "Intepersonal Relations"; Shulik, "Old Age"; Snarey, "Nontheistic Judaism"; Vanden Heuvel, "Family Interaction."

[72]Clore, "Faith Development in Adults."

[73]Ibid., 157.

[74]John Bowlby, *Attachment and Loss,* vol. 1, *Attachment,* and vol. 2, *Separation* (New York: Basic Books, 1969).

[75]Kim Bartholomew et al., "Attachment Styles among Young Adults: A Test of a Four-Category Model," *Journal of Personality and Social Psychology* 61 (1991): 226–44.

[76]Ibid., 157–58.

[77]Canavan, "Oedipal Resolution."

[78]I agree with this conclusion and find Canavan's empirical work a major contribution—despite the critique I voice below about his use of the Stages of Faith Scale of Swensen et al., "Reactions to Terminal Cancer."

[79]See also Parks, "Faith Development and Imagination."

[80]Theresa Sallnow, "Faith in Persons: A Critical Exploration of James Fowler's Theory of Faith-Development, with Special Reference to Personalist Philosophy" (Ph.D. diss., University of Lancaster [U.K.], 1989).

[81]Ibid.

[82]Ibid.

[83]Carol B. Pitts, "The Self as a Metaphor: Empirical, Psychological, and Theological Approaches" (Ph.D. diss., Emory University, 1995).

[84]Nancy G. Devor, "Toward a Relational Voice of Faith: Contributions of James Fowler's Faith Development Theory, Psychological Research on Women's Development, Relational Feminist Theology, and a Qualitative Analysis of Women Ministers' Faith Descriptions" (Ph.D. diss., Boston University, 1989).

[85]Leary, "Coping and Faith Development."

[86]P. Morgan, "Women in Crisis."

[87]Cowden, "Faith Development in Women."

[88]Ibid., 143.

[89]Smith, "Women Religious Leaders."

[90]James W. Fowler, *Stufen des Glaubens. Die Psychologie der menschlichen Entwicklung und die Suche nach Sinn* (Gütersloh: Kaiser, 2000), 18–19.

[91]Mary F. Belenky et. al., *Women's Ways of Knowing: The Development of Self, Voice, and Mind* (New York: Basic Books, 1986).

[92]Moseley et al., *Manual.*

[93]Ibid., Appendix H.

[94]Jose C. Plackal, "Indian Culture and Developmental Stages of Faith: A Dialogical Inquiry into the Theory of James W. Fowler from the Cultural Context of India" (D.Min. diss., Colgate Rochester Divinity School, Crozer Theological Seminary, 1990).

[95]U. M. A. Majmudar, "Mahatma Gandhi's Trajectory in Truth and Fowler's Theory of Stages of Faith: A Mutually Critical Correlational Developmental Study" (Ph.D. diss., Emory University, 1996).

[96]Kalam, "Myth of Stages"; Furushima, "Project in Hawaii"; Snarey, "Nontheistic Judaism."

[97]Slee, "Post-Fowler Research," 88.

[98]Drewek, "Testing among Baha'is," Abstract.

[99]Farc, "Romanian Context"; Lee, "Korean Context."

[100]Fowler, "Postmodern Challenges."

[101]Barnes et al., "A Fowler Scale"; Canavan, "Oedipal Resolution"; Clore, "Faith Development in Adults"; Green et al., "Perceptions of Others"; Hammond, "Irrational Beliefs"; Hiebert, "Schools of Faith"; Leak et al., "Development and Validation"; Swensen et al., "Reactions to Terminal Cancer."

[102]Green et al., "Perceptions of Others."

[103]Barnes et al., "A Fowler Scale."

[104]B. J. James et al., "High Stress Life Events and Spiritual Development," *Journal of Psychology and Theology* 27 (1999): 250–60.

[105]See Leak et al., "Development and Validation," 106.

[106]Swensen et al., "Reaction to Terminal Cancer."

[107]Canavan, "Oedipal Resolution."

[108]Moseley et al., *Manual.*

[109]Clore, "Faith Development in Adults."

[110]Leak et al., "Development and Validation."

[111]Anderson, "Identity in College Women"; Nahavandi, "Psychospiritual Development"; Smith, "Women Religious Leaders"; E. Morgan, "Religious Autobiographical Quests."

[112]Rose, "Measure Four Stages."

[113]Smith, "Women Religious Leaders."

[114]E. Morgan "Religious Autobiographical Quests."

[115]Anderson, "Identity in College Women."

[116]See Jerome Bruner, "Life as Narrative," *Social Research* 54 (1987): 11–32; George Lakoff and Mark Johnson, *Metaphors We Live By* (Chicago: University of Chicago Press, 1980).

[117]Nahavandi, "Psychospiritual Development."

[118]Dan P. McAdams, *The Person: An Introduction to Personality Psychology* (San Diego: Harcourt Brace Jovanovich, 1990); idem, "Biography, Narrative, and Lives: An Introduction," in *Psychobiography and Life Narratives,* ed. Dan P. McAdams and Richard L. Ochberg (Durham, N.C.: Duke University Press, 1988), 1–18.

[119]Rose, "Measure Four Stages."

[120]Hoffman, "Nurturing Spirituality."

[121]See Fowler, *Becoming Adult, Becoming Christian*; James W. Fowler, "Stages in Faith Consciousness," in *Religious Development in Childhood and Adolescence,* ed. Fritz K. Oser et al. (San Francisco: Jossey-Bass, 1991), 27–45. Idem, "The Public Church: Ecology for Faith Education and Advocate for Children," in *Faith Development in Early Childhood,* ed. Doris A. Blazer (Kansas City: Sheed & Ward, 1989), 131–54. Idem, "Practical Theology and the Shaping of Christian Lives," in *Practical Theology. The Emerging Field in Theology,* ed. Don S. Browning (San Francisco: Harper and Row, 1983), 148–66. Idem, "Pluralism and Oneness in Religious Experience: William James, Faith-Development Theory, and Clinical Practice," in *Religion and the Clinical Practice of Psychology,* ed. Edward P. Shafranske (Washington: American Psychological Association, 1996), 165–86. Idem, "The Vocation of Faith Development Theory," in *Stages of Faith and Religious Development,* ed. James W. Fowler et al. (New York: Crossroads, 1991, 1987), 19–36. Idem, "Strength for the Journey: Early Childhood Development in Selfhood and Faith," in Blazer, 1–36.

[122]Fowler devotes an entire chapter to reproducing and interpreting this interview with a young woman (Fowler, *Stages of Faith,* ch. 22); compare also the evaluation of Nelson and Aleshire, "Research in Faith Development."

[123]Robert Kegan, *The Evolving Self: Problem and Process in Human Development* (Cambridge, Mass: Harvard University Press, 1982).

[124]Fowler, *Faithful Change.*

[125]Daniel N. Stern, *The Interpersonal World of the Infant* (New York: Basic Books, 1985).

[126]Fowler, *Faithful Change,* 72.

[127]Ibid., 52.

[128]Rizzuto, "Beyond the Modern Paradigm," 205–7.

[129]Fowler, *Faithful Change,* 165, 174.

[130]Ibid., 177.

[131]Fowler, "Postmodern Challenges."

[132]See Streib, "Religious Styles Perspective"; Heinz Streib, "Is There a Way beyond Fundamentalism? Challenges for Faith Development and Religious Education," in *The Fourth R for the Third Millennium: Education in Religions and Values for the Global Future,* ed. Leslie J. Francis et al. (Dublin: Lindisfarne Books, 2001), 177–99.

[133]See, for instance, Jean F. Lyotard, *Postmodern Fables* (Minneapolis: University of Minnesota Press, 1997, 1993) and his designation of this megastory as "negative entrophy" in idem, *The Difference: Phrases in Dispute* (Minneapolis: University of Minnesota Press, 1988).

[134]Fowler, "Postmodern Challenges," 169.

[135]Ibid.

[136]Streib, "Religious Styles Perspective."

[137]Heinz Streib, "Religion als Stilfrage. Zur Revision struktureller Differenzierung von Religion im Blick auf die Analyse der pluralistisch-religiösen Lage der Gegenwart," in *Archiv für Religionspsychologie,* ed. Nils G. Holm et al. (Göttingen: Vandenhoeck & Rupprecht, 1997), 48–69. An English translation of this article has been accepted for publication in the *International Journal of Practical Theology*

[138]Streib, "Religious Styles Perspective," 150.

[139]I have illuminated this in more detail in Streib, "Is There a Way beyond Fundamentalism?"

[140]See Annette Spellerberg, "[Review of] Peter H. Hartmann: *Lebensstilforschung,*" *Kölner Zeitschrift für Soziologie und Sozialpsychologie* 53 (2001): 170–71; Heinz Streib, *Religion und Lebensstil. Die Erlebnisgesellschaft als neuer Horizont der Religionspädagogik?* (forthcoming); Peter H. Hartmann, *Lebensstilforschung. Darstellung, Kritik und Weiterentwicklung* (Opladen: Leske & Budrich, 1999); Friederike Benthaus-Apel, "Religion und Lebensstil. Zur Analyse pluraler Religionsformen aus soziologischer Sicht," in *Religion in der Lebenswelt der Moderne,* ed. Kristian Fechtner et al. (Stuttgart: Kohlhammer, 1998), 102–22.

[141]Michael Vester et al., eds., *Kirche und die Milieus der Gesellschaft, Bd. 1: Vorläufiger Abschlußbericht der Studie, Bd. 2: Dokumentation der Tagung* (Loccum: Evangelische Akademie, 1999).

2

The Development of Public Responsibility in James William Fowler's Theology and Psychology

GABRIELE KLAPPENECKER

1. Introduction

James W. Fowler's theory begins with the observation that the act of investing the heart in a transcendent point of reference that structures relationships to other beings and objects is a universal human characteristic. Members of religious communities communicate with one another by means of the common reference points in their traditions, which in turn regulate and define their relationships to one another—thus forming a triadic relationship. While the symbols and people involved are variable, the act of investing the heart in a transcendent point of reference is the universal characteristic of the triadic relationship.

Fowler defines this act as "faith." He also defines the Christian faith within this general framework. But the point of reference in the relationship does not necessarily come from one specific religious tradition. Fowler is interested not only in the Christian "faith" but also in all ways of creating meaning—that is, the methods by which human life is structured regarding that which is of "ultimate concern." In Fowler's theory, the structuring of life unfolds consciously or unconsciously in stages.

Stages of Faith describes the development of relationships.[1] It begins with the smallest nonverbal signs and rituals of closeness and moves towards the acceptance of responsibility for one's home—or in the broadest sense, for the whole threatened planet earth. To nurture faith development is to nurture public life. The future of political decisions, institutional values, and cultural life depends on the way humanity has learned to build relationships, especially those centered on ultimate concern.

Theology has always had a tradition of working with stage models of human development. Many examples of this theological tradition can be seen in mysticism and in the history of the Reformation, or in the works of Ignatius of Loyola, John Bunyan, and John Wesley. These traditions serve as sources for the models developed in psychology and related disciplines.

In the following discussion, I will summarize three traditions of decisive importance to Fowler's work (2). Then I will discuss the complex term *faith* (3), followed by the stages of faith development and their theology (4). Only on this basis is it possible to analyze their importance for the future of public life (5). I will do this with reference to three central symbols of Fowler's theology: the kingdom of God, covenant, and vocation. I will conclude with a discussion of the significance of Fowler's approach for the future of religious education in public schools (6), and a critique and assessment of his method (7).

2. The Traditions of Faith Development Theory

2.1 H. Richard Niebuhr, Lawrence Kohlberg, and Erik H. Erikson

Fowler wrote his doctoral dissertation on H. Richard Niebuhr (1894–1962), his professor at Yale Divinity School.[2] Niebuhr's understanding of faith is relational. Moral acts and judgments involve not only the character of the person who is acting but also God. The individual participates in a community of faith. This participation operates under the presupposition that the revelation of God in Jesus Christ becomes part of the structure of the self. The self responds to God. By responding to God in all life situations, the self reveals itself as a responsible self.

In this line of reasoning, Niebuhr draws on confessional phenomenology. Like Martin Luther and Friedrich Schleiermacher, he understands "God" and "faith" as being constantly in close relationship with each other. He refers to this as *radical monotheism*, which stands behind the sharp juxtaposition between faith and belief/religion. *Radical monotheism*, on the one hand, describes the intensity and loyalty basic to the Christian faith. On the other hand, belief, or religion, is an everyday, nonexistential, or purely institutional mode of relationship. There are two basic ways in which God and faith can be separated. Niebuhr refers to them as *henotheism* and *polytheism*. In *henotheism*, life is oriented toward one person, object, or idea that takes the place of God. In *polytheism*, a person divides the self through total capitulation to the various "gods" of the industrial and postindustrial age, resulting in a complete loss of personal identity.

The central characteristic of faith is connection to, and therefore identification with, the God of Jesus Christ. This understanding of faith is linked to an ethic of value. One can summarize Niebuhr's ethics in the following way: There are no ethics without relationship, and there can be no value without awareness of the center of all value and being. The experience of being valued by an absolute source of value is the basis of Niebuhr's understanding of responsibility. Christian faith defined as relatedness to God does not allow a person to withdraw from cultural life or to avoid responsibility for society. Human culture is a reality in which God came into being and in which God remains involved through Jesus Christ.

Without Lawrence Kohlberg (1927–1987), Fowler could not have developed his theory of faith development. The significance of Kohlberg's theory for Fowler's approach consists in its capacity to recognize structures. The variety, abundance, and complexity of faith experiences can be organized and understood through the recognition of structures.

The structures in Kohlberg's theory can be characterized as "hard" (as opposed to the "soft" structures of faith development). Kohlberg's cognitive structuralism isolates moral judgments from the developmental process. His six-stage structure depicts the pattern of what remains when moral judgments are studied without taking into account the personal motivations for moral action and their cultural and religious environments. Kohlberg's only interest is in the general or universal expressions of moral judgment.

In contrast, faith development theory is based on, and expects, an authentic correlation to practical experience, because the purpose of the theory is to expose the unique character of every life story. This is not compatible with the universalism proposed by Kohlberg. That is, Kohlberg's approach to moral development stands in a theoretical tradition rooted in Jean Piaget and his reception of the principle of categorical imperative developed by Immanuel Kant.

In assimilating the philosophy of the Enlightenment, Kohlberg's theory claims autonomy from theology and religion. Although this claim also has become popular in contemporary theology, particularly liberation theology, Kohlberg considers autonomy to be possible only outside the sphere of religion. Religion becomes the basis for formulating moral judgments only at the seventh stage of his system. This religious stage can be achieved only if the other six stages have been transcended. Kohlberg conceptualizes the first six stages as within the boundaries of a purely rational ethic. They are the structural reorganization of the manner in which moral judgments are generated in light of the goal of universal justice.

Autonomous moral judgment is achieved at stage six. Equality and reciprocity are the decisive principles of justice. Although these principles of justice serve as main insights to be communicated in religious education,[3] Kohlberg's understanding of autonomous moral judgments always leads to an exclusion of religious images, symbols, and stories, as well as the emotions tied to them via their embeddedness in individual life stories.

Kohlberg's stages describe a gender-specific moral development. His student Carol Gilligan has demonstrated empirically that women's moral decisions tend to be oriented toward the social structure of the small group, while men's decisions are oriented toward institutions and the urge to fulfill responsibilities. In Kohlberg's model of progressive hierarchical stages, women's ethics of care are interpreted as belonging to the third stage, while male ethics belong to the fifth stage, the point at which autonomous decisions of justice begin to occur. This clearly indicates a discrimination against women as well as a depreciation of an ethic of care and solidarity.

Fowler's theory can offer some illuminating insights regarding women's faith, but it needs to account more adequately for the relational character of women's faith consciousness.[4] "Connectedness" is a typical way for women to reach decisions of faith, including moral decisions. Even if this form of decision-making were not gender-specific, it could not be valued enough in an era of alienation, isolation, and solipsism. The principal openness to valuing connectedness in faith development theory contradicts the low value it receives in Kohlberg's theory. Faith does not and cannot exist on the basis of solipsistic decisions.

Like Niebuhr's confessional phenomenology, Erik H. Erikson's (1902–1994) social-developmental theory also explains the development of a sense of responsibility with respect to the self, the individual personality. Erikson is interested particularly in the development of the body and the interconnectedness of social functions. The development of identity is the result of a process consisting of eight phases. The harmony or disharmony between the patterns of bodily development and the structure of social institutions can be described in terms of these eight stages. The life cycle, comprising the phases, proceeds through crises. Every crisis contains the potential for new developments in identity and marks the entrance to a new phase.

Erikson's understanding of identity is compatible with Christian thought. The motivation underlying his interpretation of the development of responsibility is his desire to ensure world democracy. This includes the struggle to secure democratic conditions as the developmental environment for every child. The fight against autocracy, exploitation, and injustice in this world begins with the realization that the first occurrence of injustice in the life of a human being is the one experienced in the relationship between the child and its parents. Erikson's therapeutic ethos seeks to heal and transform the energies trapped by the individual's anxieties into a capacity for commitment to intimate relationships and to work. Like Fowler, Erikson's concept of identity is relational. However, the achievement of the third phase of Erikson's model, "initiative," is ascribed exclusively to male development.

"Faith" is the result of successful reciprocity between the child and the first person responsible for its upbringing. According to Erikson, faith originates in regularly repeated expressions of mutual recognition between the child and its caregiver. In this sense, faith carries connotations of trust, loyalty, and hope. The need to be welcomed by a mighty Other, whose friendly countenance shines upon us, survives into adulthood. This need is satisfied through the institutionalization of faith. Rituals of public institutions can deliver a periodic collective renewal of trust and thus a renewal of faith, if they are not abused as instruments of power and manipulation.

2.2 The Influence of Niebuhr, Kohlberg, and Erikson on Fowler

Fowler adopts Niebuhr's distinction between faith as a universal human characteristic and the Christian faith as trust in, and loyalty to, God in Jesus Christ. This distinction allows him to study faith empirically as a universal dimension of human life while at the same time discussing the ways in which the Christian community turns the general phenomenon of "human faith" into the specific "Christian faith."

Niebuhr's theology of a God who is the center toward which all human values should be directed provides the normative framework for Fowler's main point of interest–that is, the reconstruction of life stories in light of the eschatological history of the kingdom of God. Within human values and decisions, not outside of them, one discovers that which is of ultimate value. Moral development and moral education can transpire only through the sharing of life stories, not through the imposition of abstract norms. Like Niebuhr, Fowler listens to the reasoning of the heart, a phenomenon that cannot escape the necessity of the search for patterns and meaning in life relationships.

In adopting Niebuhr's ethics, Fowler cannot incorporate Kohlberg's theory without ambivalence toward Kohlberg's neo-Kantianism. Fowler utilizes the structural developmental tradition as a research program. Yet he cannot accept Kohlberg's definition of moral development as a process by which the individual moves towards a universal principle of justice through structures emptied of their contents. The development of faith, especially in the case of children, can be described only in "soft" structures, that is, images, symbols, and stories, as well as the emotions tied to them.

Fowler summarizes the significance of Erikson's approach for his own as follows: "Erikson's influence...has touched me at convictional depths that the structural developmentalists have not addressed. As unsystematic and unsatisfactory as it may seem, I simply have to say that Erikson's work has become part of the interpretative mindset I bring to research on faith development."[5] Erikson's theory allows Fowler to outline the development of human identity. In this regard, he has a much broader focus on human cognition than Piaget's, as an individual's ability to trust and hope, as well as to fail, is brought into view. Body, mind, and soul and their interrelatedness cannot be overlooked in faith development research. Moreover, Fowler's later appropriation of Robert Kegan's understanding of the evolving self indicates that he has a much richer notion of an individual's development than Piaget or Kohlberg. (Kegan was a member of the research team that helped carry out and interpret the research that provided the foundation for Fowler's theory of the stages of faith.)

3. "Faith"

Fowler interviewed people of various ages, cultures, denominations, and religious or agnostic convictions, both during his time at "Interpreter's House" and also later, with the help of teams, while teaching at universities. The interviews provide the empirical base material for his stage model. Interviewees were encouraged to reflect on the past and present constructions of meaning that have sustained their lives. Questions concerning the individual's religion only occurred in the last part of the interview. Throughout the interviews, Fowler and his team abstained from any judgments.

In my opinion, Fowler's model is based on pastoral psychology, although he never admits this himself. It is obvious in all of his writings that he intends a recognition and "reading" of the Christian tradition in and between the lines of biographies, and, vice versa, a recognition of the images and symbols in scripture that support biographical development. His approach represents a hermeneutic of life in the service of counseling. That is, it attempts to connect the individual's story to God's eschatological story.

What does Fowler exactly mean by the term *faith?* Faith is a process of structuring life in a meaningful way. It is a universal human characteristic. The development of faith is dependent on the child's earliest environment and, at later stages, on institutions. Christian faith, as one expression of the human characteristic of "faith," is connected to, and derives its power from, the traditions and scriptures of a religious community. For Fowler, a decisive criterion in distinguishing "faith" from "belief" is—similar to Niebuhr and Paul Tillich—the question of intensity and loyalty to that which is of "ultimate concern." To have "faith" means to invest one's heart in a person or thing of utmost importance. "Belief" does not have this intensity and, today, often describes secular assumptions that do not have an existential character—for example, the statement, "I believe I've missed the bus."

Fowler offers many definitions of the term *faith.* I will quote two that seem to be the most representative: (1) "Faith is the process of constitutive-knowing underlying a person's composition and maintenance of a comprehensive frame (or frames) of meaning;"[6] and (2) "faith is the forming of images of, and relation to, that which exerts qualitatively different initiatives in our lives than those that occur in strictly human relations."[7] Through involvement with symbols, narratives, and rituals, modes of relationship are discovered that help give answers to the questions of ultimate concern and, on this basis, help us structure our relationships to other people, places, and things in our environment.

Although Fowler feels deeply connected to the Christian church and its theology, his definition of faith differs from Niebuhr's in that it also allows a description of non-Christian modes of relationship. In the formula, "the universality of the particular," Fowler summarizes his attempt to conceptualize Christianity as just one of many possibilities leading to common life-sustaining values. Universality cannot be expressed in "hard," abstract structures, but rather within the rich language of the particular tradition in which one lives. Thus, Fowler's stage model expresses the intention to discover, to point out, and to describe constructions of normative images within life history that create meaning for public life in an age of pluralism.

4. The Stages

4.1 Description

Stage 0: Undifferentiated faith/Primal faith[8] –

Faith begins with a pre-language disposition of trust and loyalty toward the environment that takes shape in the mutuality of one's interactive rituals of relationship with those providing consistent primary care. This rudimentary faith constructs pre-images of powerful and trustworthy ultimacy, in order to offset the anxiety that results from the separations and threats of negation that occur in the course of infantile development.[9]

Stage 1: Intuitive-Projective faith–Along with the ability to explore the surrounding environment and the objects within it, the ability to make conscious efforts to give meaning to experiences occurs at this stage. There remains a lack of stable logical operations. This is coupled with a limited capacity to differentiate and coordinate one's own perspective from and with other viewpoints. The visual and sensual world can be expressed symbolically through the use of language.

Further, power becomes a part of the repertoire of social acting. Punishment by, and obedience toward, authorities determines moral behavior. The experience of God as *fascinosum et tremendum* has its origin in this stage. Deep and long lasting images can be formed. This can result, for better or worse, in impressing a permanent mold on the emotional and cognitive foundation of faith. On the positive side, these images can be supportive in the process of struggling with power, death, and taboos.

Stage 2: Mythic-Literal faith–The previous stage's store of images gets "sealed over," and its episodic, intuitive forms of knowing are subordinated by the cognitive construction of a world in terms of a new "linearity" and predictability. This stage typically relies on the external structures of simple fairness. It most frequently constructs an ultimate environment with the analogy of a ruler or parent who is caring and just. Goodness is to be rewarded, while badness is to be punished. If the child realizes that the world does not always follow this scheme, the so-called "eleven-year-old-atheism" results. The child remains largely concrete and literal in the use of concepts and symbols.

Stage 3: Synthetic-Conventional faith–In early adolescence, the dominant characteristic for structuring one's identity is "mutual interpersonal perspective taking." "I see you seeing me; I see me the way I think you see me." One's own identity and the identity of others become an absorbing concern. Selfhood is derived from important relationships and role models. Self-worth is keyed heavily to the approval and affirmation of those considered important. God is the One who knows us better than we can know ourselves, and in being connected deeply with others, we are linked somehow with the depth, or height, of ultimacy. Any attempt to approach religion analytically or scientifically for the purpose of "demythologization" is seen as an attack on faith. Similarly, the ultimate environment is constructed in personal terms. At this stage, it still remains difficult to reflect and live faith as a meaningful relatedness within social, economic, and political structures.

Stage 4: Individuative-Reflective faith–Faith roles and relationships, once constitutive of identity, now are placed under a critical process of selection. The term *system* becomes a generative metaphor for this stage, and its goal is control. In its drive to bring the self, others, and the world under critical scrutiny and presumed control, this stage is vulnerable to a self-deception that denies any form of mystery, including the mystery of the unconscious. The earliest, generally naïve attitudes toward symbols are terminated. In this stage, one relates to symbols with a strategy of demythologization. Symbols are experienced as "broken" (Tillich). They are examined critically, and their "meanings" are converted into rationally formulated concepts, with little awareness that much is lost in this process.

Stage 5: Conjunctive faith–This stage arises from the diametrically opposed tensions within the self. A paradox in the nature of truth is acknowledged. One seeks to unify that which is experienced or conceived as opposites. God is both transcendent and immanent. God is not to be reduced to anthropocentric categories; nevertheless, God can be the subject of personal experience.

A type of "second naïveté" in which symbols are symbols again is developed, as is an epistemological humility in recognition of the intricacy and richness of the mystery of life. The stranger is valued as one from whom new truths can be learned or who can serve as a catalyst toward liberation from self-deception. Multiple names and metaphors for the Holy are used in order to avoid idolatry and to honor paradox. Christ is seen as the one suffering with the poor and the marginalized. This empowers one to engage in compassionate, liberating practices in the service of those in need.

Stage 6: Universalizing faith–The structure of this stage is based on the completion of a radical process of decentralizing the self as the assumed epistemological and moral point of reference for constructing the world. One's affections are drawn beyond the finite centers of value and power that offer meaning and security. Participation in, or identification with, the Ultimate brings a transformation that causes the individual to love and make value judgments from a focal point of identity located in the ultimate reality. It is possible to struggle for the realization of the absolute imperatives of love and justice, and even to love the enemy, in a way that can be described as ascetic and disciplined.

Fowler's description of this stage is based not so much on personal interviews concerning faith, but rather on the biographies of "great men" such as Mahatma Gandhi, Martin Luther King, Jr., and Dietrich Bonhoeffer. This stage, therefore, has a tendency to be artificial and gender-biased.

4.2 The Aspects

The aspects of the stages can be compared to various windows through which a person's faith development is observed. One can study, for example, the social competence of an individual–the way he or she structures moral judgments, or uses and interprets symbols. In *Stages of Faith,* there is a faith interview with a young woman called Mary (see the chapter "Mary's Pilgrimage"). Her answers to questions, with the help of categories provided by certain aspects of the stages, create a description of her life pilgrimage.

Through this process, her level of faith development can be evaluated for the purpose of counseling and reconstructing her life story.

Seven aspects are evaluated on the basis of the research interviews. Each aspect has six levels of development corresponding to the faith stages. In each aspect, a person may have a different level of development. The levels then are averaged in order to establish a composite estimate of the stage of faith development. The aspects allow not only a genetic and historic analysis of an individual's faith biography but also an identification of the individual's competence in reference to each aspect in the given stage of development.

The first aspect (A), "form of logic," is related to Piaget's cognitive development theory. It focuses on the capacity to increase reasoning skills. Analyzing an individual's capacity to assume another's point of view is the task of aspect B, "role taking," adopted from Robert Selman's research. Aspect C, "form of moral judgment," is derived from Kohlberg.

The next four aspects have their origin in Fowler's own work. Aspect D, "bounds of social awareness," refers to the persons, groups, and classes involved in an individual's formulation of images and meanings. Aspect E, "locus of authority," examines the criteria used for the approval and sanction of values. Aspect F, "form of world coherence," represents the pattern of meaning by which a person portrays his or her world. Finally, aspect G, "symbolic functioning," studies the contents of images and metaphors, and the meanings given to them, through the process of interpretation.

4.3 Central Symbols

It is necessary to discuss Fowler's interpretation of three symbols–kingdom of God, covenant, and vocation–in reference to competence in public life.

To begin, every stage contains traces of the kingdom of God and represents movement toward it. Such traces can be seen in the attitude of trust, the search for justice, and solidarity with the marginalized. According to Fowler, the faith of Stage 6 most represents faith understood as an answer to God's liberating, healing, and redeeming love.

The kingdom of God is the normative content of faith development. Normative contents are to be understood in general as symbols, rituals, and narratives of an ethnic group or a religious tradition that has power to create structures. The kingdom of God is a symbol of relationship. It empowers individuals in their search for meaning and allows them to express the depth and transcendence of that which is of ultimate concern. The symbol of the kingdom has integrating power, sustaining a person during conflicts of personal and, depending on the stage level, public relevance.

As an eschatological symbol, the kingdom of God sanctions an interpretation of human development within the perspective of God's open future. The kingdom is already present wherever the values it represents are cherished and wherever liberation from sin, war, violence, and homelessness is implemented. The symbol, kingdom of God, facilitates the conscious discovery of traces of redemption, reconciliation, and renewal in the world.

It is important to note that the universality of the stages of faith and their central symbols are not to be understood in terms of cognitive structuralism. In cognitive structuralism, "universality" indicates a parity of structures that are emptied of content. For Fowler, however, universality is achieved through an explicit creation of meaning with the assistance of specific life-sustaining content.

Unfortunately, one can get the impression that the "kingdom-of-God-tendency" becomes more intense at higher levels. Not only his critics but also Fowler himself recognizes the potential danger that the stages might get interpreted, and applied with pressure, as a ladder of success to be climbed. He thus emphasizes how the kingdom breaks into life stories. The progression from stage to stage is an unfolding of the biographical experience of justification. This progression is the answer to God's preceding revelation. In other words, the stages describe how a person can participate in God's act of redemption and can anticipate justice in Jesus Christ—that is, the stages offer the means to follow the call to take responsibility for creation.[10]

However, there remains an irritating contradiction between the general theory of human development in stages and the use of language tied to the Christian concept of the kingdom of God. Once again, when Fowler postulates the kingdom of God as a universal goal of faith development on the one hand and describes it in Christian theological language on the other, he does not see this as a contradiction because he is working with an understanding of universality that has to be distinguished from the cognitive-structuralist, neo-Kantian models. Whereas cognitive structuralists such as Kohlberg define universal justice in structures emptied of contents—such as personal motivation, emotions, or specific religious socialization—the sociopsychological (Erikson) and confessional (Niebuhr) models make these contents a condition for the proper description of, and precondition for, faith development. Fowler incorporates these models and believes that the universal can be discerned only through the particular. Therefore, Stage 6 can be described in Christian terms, but the terminology of other traditions is applicable as well. On the basis of religious comparisons conducted in the field of religious science, Fowler assumes a parity of central Christian moral ideas and those of other religions. One example would be the concept of Dharma in Buddhism and the Christian kingdom of God.

Second, the triadic structure of faith is connected intimately to the symbol of the covenant. A covenantal relationship to an ultimate reality—the very core of faith—is defined by Fowler as "a centering affection, an organizing love, a central object of loyalty and trust."[11] Here, Fowler employs Niebuhr's concept, defining a special form of relatedness as a covenantal relationship insofar as it includes a common state of trust in a shared center of ultimate value and being.

According to Fowler, covenant is the basic structure that constitutes the precondition for establishing successful relationships within any group or community. Any form of relationship, when directed toward a transcendental center, can be a covenantal relationship if it shows structural parallels to the way the covenant is described in the Old Testament. If public or private trust is damaged, not only are the covenant partners demeaned, but the central points of supraordinate value—which represent the values held in common and thereby create a structure for the relationship—are called into question. For individuals living in the United States, the term *covenant* connotes the memory of the pilgrim fathers and mothers—an important element of educating the young for public life. The covenantal partnership established by their ancestors expresses responsibility not only for family members but also for friends and humanity in general.

In light of Fowler's covenant theology, it becomes clear, once again, that faith development is not an ascent through structures emptied of content, but rather, it is a model that enables one to recognize an order to the phenomena of life. This order has a sustaining effect through the help of the "soft" structuring power of symbols. The Old Testament covenant is a symbol of the structuring and life-sustaining power and providence of God. It offers ways of responding to all situations in public and personal life. Further, Fowler's covenantal view of the self and human community leads him to appreciate the human capacity to establish relationships in ways not accounted for by Kohlberg's neo-Kantian notion of autonomy. There is an echo of Fowler's covenantal theology in Gilligan's postulate to value this capacity.

Third, according to Fowler, self-discovery is the precondition for pursuing one's vocation or calling. He claims that there is no reason to identify vocation with self-denial, as was the case throughout much of the history of Christianity. However, Fowler's theology of vocation prevents the identification of self-discovery with pure satisfaction of the ego. He emphasizes that self-discovery is the presupposition for a responsible self. Life in vocation is compared with a dance into the *Heilsgeschichte* ("salvation history"). Faith development theory functions as an aid for developing the self—that is, "toward a point of maximum individuation of the self and corresponding minimization of the personal ego as the standpoint from which evaluations are made."[12]

Vocation is not to be identified completely with a profession or job, because in doing so, invalids, the unemployed and retired, and homemakers (men and women) would be excluded from the possibility of answering with their whole being God's call to partnership. Yet Fowler does not express adequately the fact that women, in particular, often experience a painful gap between the certainty of their calling and the inability to fulfill their calling due to sexist barriers. Women's faith experience can be characterized by powerlessness, alienation, and dead ends.[13] As far as public life is concerned, the task of faith development theory, in my opinion, is to change political and institutional structures for the purpose of liberating women from the dilemma of experiencing a conflict between their vocations as professionals in highly qualified jobs and as partners or mothers. The present political and educational structures still force women to choose between their professional, public vocations and their private, familial vocations.

To summarize, in Fowler's theory, the concept of vocation points to the contents of a life of responsibility in partnership with God. There is no area of life so unimportant or "secular" that it could not be used by an individual as a means of response to God's call for partnership with God and God's people.

5. The Meaning of Faith Development Theory for the Future of Public Life

5.1 The Public Church

The concept "public church" was coined by Martin E. Marty.[14] The public church fulfills the mission of counseling, educating, and empowering people to achieve their vocation in a pluralistic age. The public church is connected with social, ecological, and political networks. The shaping of the public sphere is a goal of every democracy. However, public life has lost its meaning through the radical division of the private and public spheres. The "tyranny of intimacy" also leads to a privatization of religion. For this reason, Fowler admonishes the church to reestablish an awareness of the public sphere as a point equally accessible to all people, where reason reigns instead of temptations, violence, and betrayal.

The public church is characterized by public involvement. The stage model is a dimension of practical theology, a theological discipline that, according to Fowler, has an ecclesiological foundation. The stage model is one dimension of his idea of church life, which he characterizes as an "ecology of care and vocation."[15] His use of this term encourages church members to express their faith in a variety of ways in churches where a culture of honest, open discussion is nurtured. Faith development derives from a context of pluralism, and it contradicts solipsistic withdrawal at the expense of others, individual seclusion, shallow harmony, and an undifferentiated homogeneity.

5.2 Public Education

One of the educational challenges in the United States, according to Fowler, is the division between the church, which is responsible for religious education, and institutions within the political/public sphere, which are responsible for public education without "religious bias."

The responsibility for education in values, he argues, does not begin within educational institutions. The very first steps toward establishing relationships are also the first steps toward establishing responsibility, that is, "faith." Due to the significant impact of culture and religion on the establishment of relationships, there is an early interdependence between the family circle and the public sphere. Thus, the dichotomy between the church's religious education and the nonreligious moral education of public schools is false. It neglects the fact that moral and religious awareness begins long before an individual reaches school age. Moreover, the state cannot deny its responsibility for faith education, because the structure of faith is a human universal.

A set of norms relevant for the individual's competence in public life can be developed if the symbol of the covenant is offered as the ultimate point of reference in the triadic faith relationship. The political and social vision of the first colonists of New England was a community held together by a covenant, which also includes a commitment to the goal of ensuring the well-being of every community member. As far as German theologians are concerned, the misuse of community symbols of biblical origin for the purpose of celebrating National Socialist myths comes to mind immediately. However, a responsible and critical use of developmental myths and symbols can have the positive effect of encouraging the individual to assume public responsibility. Education with the purpose of building the individual's capacity to establish covenantal relations can renew public culture.

Sharon Parks's argument offers a fitting summation: First, Fowler's concept of education offers the possibility of keeping traditional religious symbols in mind without inhibiting the discussion of ultimate values and relations in a pluralistic setting. Second, Fowler's approach expresses faith as the centering basis of human trust during every life transition. Third, it illuminates the relationship between the needs of the individual and those of the larger community.[16]

6. The Future of Faith Development Theory

In Germany, religious education occurs in public schools, in contrast to the United States, where it occurs exclusively in religious congregations or private schools. The church in Germany is responsible for the content of this Religious Education. As one of many other subjects, "Religion" is part of general education.

As someone who has taught nearly one thousand hours of Religious Education in public schools, I consider Fowler's theology of "faithful change" to be a particularly adequate answer to the questions of personal and public life with which I am confronted as an individual person responsible both for my students' faith development and for values education within the public sphere. According to my interpretation of this twofold task, the subject "Religion" must support the individual-biographic quest for meaning as well as offer the richness of that which is of ultimate concern from a Protestant perspective. Religious education has a public dimension insofar as the church is founded on the redeeming and liberating work of God in Jesus Christ. In particular, siding with the least of our brothers and sisters (Mt. 25:40) is a public task of the church.[17]

In the third chapter of his book *Faithful Change*,[18] Fowler discusses "Faith and the Challenges of Postmodern Life." He integrates public policy issues into his analysis with the assumption that they are deeply connected to faith development, theology, and the church. He applies his faith development theory to the theological analysis of culture.

> Here Fowler suggests (1) a correlation between the movement from the Conventional to the Reflective and historical transition of cultural consciousness of pre-Enlightenment (orthodox, pre-critical) to Enlightenment (progressive, critical), and (2) a further correlation

between the movement from the Reflective to the Conjunctive and the transition from Enlightenment modes of consciousness to postmodern modes. Fowler...affirms practical postmodern consciousness as necessary for today's reflective person. This may be an orderly and helpful way of understanding the relationship between premodern, modern and postmodern (Conjunctive) consciousness.[19]

Fowler derives from faith, as an essential human element, the necessity to offer the richness and wisdom of our particular tradition as a resource for guidance and courage in facing collective changes in the new millennium.[20] I now will discuss this approach toward Religious Education as a relevant task for future public education in my context, the Federal Republic of Germany.

Two federal churches have been responsible for establishing the curricula for "Religion" in the federal state of Baden-Württemberg (South Germany). An analysis of these curricula by theologians at the University of Heidelberg reveals a tendency to reduce the existential dimension of theology to a quest for superficial harmony that avoids all forms of paradoxical insight and limits theology to a type of secularized moralism. The curricula also tend to banalize and secularize[21] Christianity.[22] As stated by a newspaper journalist, the church "comes under pressure to justify its very own matter of religious education."[23] As a result, it seems as though the subjects of philosophy or ethics easily can replace religion.

The analysts of the curricula note the tendency to decrease the significance of specifically Christian contents. This reduction has four aspects: (1) Reference to transcendence is eliminated; (2) the concepts of sin and the power of evil are avoided; (3) the depth of the concept of God is concealed; and (4) eschatology is neglected.

Faith development theory opposes these secularizing tendencies, because it describes meaning as the quest for the existential dimension of the holy. The triadic faith structure always includes the element of transcendence. Fowler interprets *faith* in accordance with Tillich. The person "who enters the sphere of faith enters the sanctuary of life. Where there is faith there is an awareness of holiness...The awareness of the holy is the awareness of the presence of the divine, namely of the content of our ultimate concern."[24] So the stage development theory is a hermeneutic tool that enables us to become aware of religious styles of life[25] and to interpret them as different variations on the quest for the holy.[26]

We could juxtapose the inability to develop curricula that expresses or helps to express the different aspects of the *fascinosum et tremendum*, on the one hand, and the religious lifestyles of young people, in particular, in their quest for the holy, on the other. The German Catholic theologian Georg Hilger has conducted an empirical study entitled "What is holy/sacred to youth" ("Was Jugendlichen heilig ist"). He presented an incomplete sentence, "Holy to me is..." ("Heilig ist mir..."), to nearly one thousand teenagers and asked them to complete it in writing. An analysis of the responses resulted in a list of priorities ranked as follows: "Holy to me is..." (1) family; (2) friends; (3) stereo, computer, telephone, vehicles, or objects (of reminiscence); (4) values (reliability, health, love, friendship); (5) explicitly religious subjects (God, praying, church); (6) places (one's own bedroom, meeting points for young people); (7) animals; (8) my life.[27] These results reveal some astonishing parallels with the issues addressed in Fowler's faith interviews.

The general human quest for the holy has many faces. And, of course, "the ambiguity of the holy is its demonic possibility. Our ultimate concern can destroy us as it can heal us. But we can never be without it."[28] Fowler's stages offer a way to relate to the holy in a healthy way and to value the objects of our everyday life in like manner, that is, in relation to that which is of ultimate value. Trust, reliance, and hope (Stage1), significant relationships (Stage 4), and the care and struggle for the rights of oppressed minorities (Stages 6 and 7) can be inspired by the ultimate concern.

I have observed a special affinity to Niebuhr's thought in Fowler's *Faithful Change.* Not only does Niebuhr discuss faith development on the basis of the sociological analysis of the phenomena of culture, but he also emphasizes the revealing act of the sovereign God in Jesus Christ. Fowler looks at faith development not only from the vantage point of experience, but also from the vantage point of God's providence, which is revealed in God's acts of liberation, redemption, creation, and sovereignty. Through this double perspective, Fowler avoids a reduction of the holy to human needs or to a secularization of the "ultimate concern." At the same time, he acknowledges the possibility of recognizing the kingdom within human experience, development, and the struggle for a life in the public sphere that takes the side of the least of our brothers and sisters. Conjunctive faith as the faith stage in a postmodern age may help us "to eschew *relativism,* while acknowledging *relativity.*"[29]

7. Critique and Appreciation

Fowler generalizes central contents of the Christian tradition and the so-called cultural heritage of the West as universal categories of the life cycle. Sometimes, he does not pay enough attention to the fact that both he and Erikson, one of his primary sources, do not consider in depth the patriarchal background of their heritage (the covenant) or the patriarchal reinterpretation of originally female virtues (for example, the wisdom tradition). Likewise, in the postmodern situation of radical plurality with its corresponding lifestyles, the question of defining a successful life still needs to be thought through more critically. In order to emphasize the process of faith development as a gift of grace, the stage model could be structured under a cyclical concept of development or as a spiral, as in the Christian liturgical calendar. Further, Luther's theology of a *fides infantium* reminds us that growth in faith is not only a gain of maturity but also a loss of innocence, unconcern, and ease.[30] So once again, a difference is illuminated between the content of faith and the structure of the stage.

Nevertheless, Fowler has given us commendable reasons for appreciating a perspective in which a set of norms, established through the relatedness to symbols and through the orientation of human life toward them, can be considered only if there is an explicit inclusion of the relationship to God. Fowler's stages offer a way to relate in a healing way to the holy and a way to value the objects of our everyday life in a healthy manner and in relation to that which is of ultimate concern.

In conclusion, the relevance of Fowler's approach can be summarized as follows: *Public responsibility is the result of biographical developmental processes of relatedness. It is structured by perceptions of, and reflections on, an ultimate environment.*

Notes

[1]James W. Fowler, *Stages of Faith: The Psychology of Human Development and the Quest for Meaning* (San Francisco: Harper & Row, 1981). Many parts of this essay summarize my doctoral dissertation on Fowler: Gabriele Klappenecker, *Glaubensentwicklung und Lebensgeschichte. Eine Auseinandersetzung mit der Ethik James William Fowlers, zugleich ein Beitrag zur Rezeption von H. Richard Niebuhr, Lawrence Kohlberg und Erik H. Erikson* (Stuttgart: Kohlhammer, 1998). I would like to thank Brigitte Hilsenbeck and Martin Dorn for professional assistance in the translation of this summary.

[2]James W. Fowler, *To See the Kingdom: The Theological Vision of H. Richard Niebuhr* (Nashville, Tenn.: Abingdon Press, 1974).

[3]Lisa Kuhmerker, Uwe Gielen, and Richard L. Hayes, *Lawrence Kohlberg. Seine Bedeutung für die pädagogische und psychologische Praxis* (München: Kindt-Verlag, 1996).

[4]Nicola Slee, "Some Patterns and Processes of Women's Faith Development," *Journal of Beliefs and Values* 21, no. 1 (2000): 5–16, esp. 14.

[5]Fowler, *Stages of Faith,* 110. Fowler might think of Robert Kegan in a similar way. See Robert Kegan, *The Evolving Self* (Cambridge, Mass.: Harvard University Press, 1982).

[6]James W. Fowler, "Faith and the Structuring of Meaning," in *Faith Development and Fowler,* ed. Craig Dykstra and Sharon Parks (Birmingham, Ala.: Religious Education Press, 1986), 14–42.

[7]Fowler, *Stages of Faith,* 33.

[8]In my dissertation, I refer to the stage "Undifferentiated faith" as Stage 1 because there is no reason to refer to it as Stage 0.

[9]James W. Fowler, "Pluralism, Particularity, and Paideia," *Journal of Law and Religion* 3 (1985): 263–307, quotation from 296.

[10]Fowler, *Stages of Faith,* 208–11.

[11]James. W. Fowler, "Faith Development and the Aims of Religious Socialization," in *Emerging Issues in Religious Education,* ed. Gloria Durka and Joanmarie Smith (New York: Paulist Press, 1976), 187–208, quotation from 191.

[12]James W. Fowler, "Stages in Faith Consciousness," in *Religious Development in Childhood and Adolescence,* ed. Fritz W. Oser and W. G. Scarlett (San Francisco: Jossey-Bass, 1991), 27–45, quotation from 27.

[13]Slee, "Women's Faith Development," 5–16, quotation from 14.

[14]Martin E. Marty, *The Public Church* (New York: Crossroad, 1981). See also Richard Sennett, *The Fall of Public Man* (New York: Paulist, 1976) and William J. Everett, *God's Federal Republic* (New York: Alfred A. Knopf, 1988).

[15]James W. Fowler, *Faith Development and Pastoral Care* (Philadelphia: Fortress Press, 1987), 25, 97.

[16]Sharon Parks, "James Fowlers Theorie der Glaubensentwicklung in der nordamerikanischen Diskussion–Eine Zusammenfassung der Hauptkritikpunkte," in *Gaubensentwicklung und Erziehung,* ed. Karl Ernst Nipkow, Friedrich Schweitzer, and James William Fowler (Gütersloh: Gütersloher, 1988), 91–107, esp. 92.

[17]Wolfgang Huber, *Kirche und Öffentlichkeit* (Stuttgart: Klett, 1973), 50, 242, 461.

[18]James W. Fowler, *Faithful Change: The Personal and Public Challenges of Postmodern Life* (Nashville, Tenn.: Abingdon Press, 1996).

[19]Walter E. Conn, "Review of Fowler: *Faithful Change,*" *Horizons* 24 (Fall 1997): 326–28, quotation from 328.

[20]See Fowler, *Faithful Change,* introduction.

[21]See Wolfgang Huber, *Kirche in der Zeitenwende* (Gütersloh: Gütersloher, 1998), 10.

[22]Hartmut Rupp and Heinz Schmidt, eds., *Lebensorientierung oder Verharmlosung? Theologische Kritik der Lehrplanentwicklung im Religionsunterricht* (Stuttgart: Calwer, 2001), preface.

[23]Heike Schmoll, "Selbstbanalisierung im Religionsunterricht. Die Lehrpläne für Evangelische Religionslehre in Baden-Württemberg unter theologischer Perspektive," trans. G. Klappenecker, in *Frankfurter Allgemeine Zeitung*, 11 July 2001.

[24]Paul Tillich, *Writings on Religion/Religiöse Schriften*, ed. Carl Heinz Ratschow, vol. 5, *Dynamics of Faith*, ed. Robert P. Scharlemann (Berlin, New York: De Gruyter, 1988, orig. 1957), 231–38, quotation from 237–38.

[25]"Styles of religion" are "modes of access to and the involvement with religion in their narrative, symbolic and ritual ways of expression, being generated by multiple factors, namely by life environment and life history" *("Modi des Zugangs zu und Umgangs mit Religion in ihren narrativen, symbolischen und rituellen Ausdrucksformen, die multifaktoriell, nämlich lebensweltlich und lebensgeschichtlich generiert sind")*. Heinz Streib, "Religion als Stilfrage. Zur Revision struktureller Differenzierung von Religion im Blick auf die Analyse der pluralistisch-religiösen Lage der Gegenwart," in *Archiv für Religionspsychologie* 22, ed. Nils G. Holm et al. (Göttingen: Vandenhoeck & Ruprecht, 1997), 48–69, esp. 66.

[26]This topic will be further developed in my *Habilitation:* Gabriele Klappenecker, *Religionspädagogik im Anschluss an Otto Friedrich Bollnow.*

[27]See Georg Hilger, "'Heilig ist mir...'," in *Katechetische Blätter* 6 (1999): 411–12.

[28]Tillich, *Writings on Religion*, vol. 5, 238.

[29]Fowler, *Faithful Change*, 175.

[30]See Dieter Seiler, "Frühe Schicksale des Glaubens. Überlegungen zur Fides Infantium," in *Wege zum Menschen* 48 (1996): 70–95.

3

To Venture and to Abide:

The Tidal Rhythm of Our Becoming

SHARON DALOZ PARKS

We dwell in a time when fast-paced technologies have plunged all of us into a sense of being swept up in the motion of life. The new sciences and especially a growing ecological awareness are awakening in us a consciousness of the dynamic interrelatedness of the universe in which we dwell. Simultaneously, the fact of a "shrinking planet" brings cultures together in ways both promising and perilous. In this context, one of the great gifts of James Fowler's work (as a theologian, an ethicist, a psychologist, and a theorist with deep pastoral commitments) is his invitation to "seculars" and "believers" alike to imagine "faith" as a verb. Faith, he has shown, is not bound into creedal forms as something we do or do not "have"–fixed, static, and irrelevant in a world of dramatic change. Rather, "faith" is something we do and are as human beings in the daily process of making meaning in an ongoing dialogue between self and world–between trusting and fearing, belonging and alienation, power and powerlessness, hating and loving, despairing and hoping.

This dynamic character of faith has been compellingly illumined in conversation with constructive-developmental psychology, and Fowler has been the primary pioneer–staking out the scope of the terrain and providing sturdy and gracious leadership into a horizon that challenges the religious, educational, and ethical imagination, while at the same time inviting social psychologists into a larger discourse. All of us who have moved into this terrain have increasingly recognized that while notions of "development" have captured important dimensions of the dynamic evolution of the soul/psyche, the developmental paradigm has been dominated by an imagination of differentiation, a story about moving away and beyond.

This imagination has power, in part, because it is deeply resonant with established cultural images of human becoming. The mythic journey of the pilgrim from ignorance to enlightenment and from lowly beginnings to noble accomplishment is marked by fierce testings, great losses, and adventures of all kinds as dramatized in both the classic and contemporary imagination from *Beowulf* and Dante to *Star Wars* and *Lord of the Rings.* The journey of the pilgrim pervades the religious imagination—the story of the Buddha's venturing forth and discovering the reality of suffering, the story of the Jewish pilgrimage from Egypt to the promised land, the Christian's seven stages of the cross and *Pilgrim's Progress,* and the journey of Muhammad to the mountain—all bespeak the power of the human capacity to venture, and in that venturing, to undergo transformations of meaning and purpose and to become more faith-full. Moreover, we live in a society that tells us we must be on the move in an economy prepared to pass us by; busyness is a hallmark of success; and travel signifies freedom, importance, and a privilege not to be missed.

Yet in this time of an enhanced consciousness of dynamic motion and travel opportunities available on an unprecedented scale (including space exploration), there is a corresponding longing for "home." Some months after the events of September 11, 2001, I was reflecting with an American professor on his recent conversation with a student. Remarking on her experience of seeing the film clips of some Palestinians celebrating the attack on the World Trade Center, this young woman said that after she got over the shock, she realized, "They associate us with their pain." As the professor listened to this empathic response, he knew that he, too, would grant to others everywhere (including Israel and Palestine) what he would claim for himself—the right to want and to love a homeland. The United States—his homeland—had been wounded in a new way. We have all been hurt, and "homeland security" has emerged in our public vocabulary. This set of thoughts and feelings is complex and requires us to hold many perspectives, stories, and tensions all at once. At the core of this complex web dwells an ancient hunger—for place, home, and the practices of abiding.

This longing for homeland is one of the two great pulls in the tidal ebb and flow that powers the development of meaning and faith. "Faithing" seems to ask us again and again to go forth, to risk letting go, to reach beyond the familiar, and to practice the way of a pilgrim. But there is another powerful sensibility that pulls as deeply and truthfully at the core of the human soul— the call to dwell, to stay, to abide, to return home.

The compelling essence of this call has become difficult to hear in contemporary society. Yet we recognize it in the words of Thomas Kelly, the Quaker philosopher, teacher, and mystic who wrote:

> Simplification comes when we "center down,"
> when life is lived with singleness of eye,
> from a holy Center
> where the breath and stillness of Eternity
> are heavy upon us and
> we are wholly yielded to God.
> Some of you know this holy,
> recreating Center of eternal peace and joy

and live in it day and night.
Some of you may see it over the margin and
wistfully long
to slip into that amazing Center
where the soul is at home with God.
Be very faithful to that wistful longing.
It is the Eternal Goodness calling you to return Home.[1]

And we glimpse it in the meditation mantra suggested by Thich Nhat Hanh:

I have arrived.
I am home.

In a world of competing fragments and systematic distractions, the desire to experience ourselves in that centeredness within which we know we are at home in the universe is a primary point of orientation for the formation–the development–of a faith to live by. Wilfred Cantwell Smith, the historian of religion whose distinction between faith and belief has significantly informed faith development theory, has placed this capacity to be "at home in the universe" at the heart of his definition of faith:

Faith, then, is a quality of human living. At its best, it has taken the form of serenity and courage and loyalty and service: a quiet confidence and joy that enable one to feel at home in the universe and to find meaning in the world and in one's own life, a meaning that is profound and ultimate and is stable no matter what may happen to oneself at the level of immediate event. Men and women of this kind of faith face catastrophe and confusion, affluence and sorrow, unperturbed; face opportunity with conviction and drive; and face others with a cheerful charity.[2]

1. The Power of Place

As human beings in modern and postmodern societies, we are relearning that a faith that yields an experience of centeredness and "at home-ness" is intimately related with the experience of "place." And "place" is not an abstraction.

Place (too often described merely as "social location") both forms and conditions our perceptions of reality. While it necessarily places limitations on our capacity for comprehensive and universally adequate thought, a consciousness of place, grounded in the "land" that constitutes "homeland," cannot be dismissed as mere provincialism. A consciousness of place is an essential element of human strength and a primary feature in the formation of a sturdy faith. A consciousness of place, most profoundly understood, is the gift of a relationship between the human and the more-than-human world.

In his book *Weaving the New Creation,* Fowler has recognized that the formation of viable forms of faith in our time requires a recognition of "the fundamental participation of everything in *process*...the ecological interdependence of all systems, including systems of thought and consciousness."[3] And bearing witness to his own faith he writes: "I have deep confidence that a creative, saving, and sustaining God is involved integrally in the process of our increasingly complex and richly dangerous project of interdependence on planet Earth."[4]

That we are now having to become conscious of being involved in a "complex and richly dangerous project of interdependence on planet Earth" reflects the overdifferentiation from place and loss of consciousness that we have suffered and continue to suffer in today's societies. Our capacity to know ourselves as an intimate part of the vast tissue of life, an integral feature of the fabric of landscape, has been obscured by ideologies of individualism and their consequent economies of consumerism. These conditions require faith to be composed as a private heroic gesture and ask us to spin "stuff" and "cumber" into meaning in ways that are exhausting the more-than-human world and ourselves.

In his extraordinary book *The Spell of the Sensuous: Perception and Language in a More-Than-Human World,* David Abram describes the experience of the Australian Aboriginal person whose traditional culture taught that all elements of the landscape—rocks, trees, water sources—were the embodiments of the Ancestors who had in prior forms chanted their way across the continent, crisscrossing the land with thousands of meandering "songlines." Now, after a man has "prepared" a woman for conception, the actual conception is assumed to occur much later, when the already pregnant woman is out on her daily round of gathering food and she happens to step on or near a song couplet left by the Ancestor. It is then that the "spirit child" lying beneath the ground at that spot slips into her, impregnating the fetus with song, and the woman feels the *quickening*—the first kick within her womb. She notes the precise *place* in the land where the quickening occurred and reports this to the tribal elders who examine the land, discerning which stanzas of a particular Ancestor's song will belong to the child. "In this manner every Aboriginal person, at birth, inherits a particular stretch of song as his private property, a stretch of song that is, as it were...title to a stretch of land, to his conception site...it is that place on the earth where he most belongs, and his essence, his deepest self, is indistinguishable from that terrain."[5]

Such an intimate relationship to place, set at the heart's core, is available to very few in today's societies. At the Whidbey Institute, where we seek to prepare people to practice creative and committed leadership for Earth, Spirit, and the Human Future, we often pose the question, *Where is your soul's landscape?* We find that most people—though sadly, not all—find within them some meaningful response to that question. They know that they are most at home in shimmering desert sands, or among the grasses of the prairie, or on a craggy coast. Some are most at home on the water. Earth offers an almost infinite variety of places for anchoring the soul in the fabric of life.

The conversations that ensue are animated, reflective, wistful, and complex. Some discover that their birthplace is not necessarily their soul's homeplace. Others discover that they reside in an alien habitat. Still others realize that they have just stepped into a horizon of reflection in which they are initially simply lost, with few points of orientation. What we discover over and over again is that most people have taken a sense of place into account only marginally, if at all, in their composing of life and meaning in the most comprehensive dimensions we name "faith." They have put their trust in the assumed rightness of following the route of work-jobs-career and sometimes have factored in the location of family and friends. But they have most typically ignored or deferred the primacy of "place"–their relationship with landscape– in choosing their life partners, location of work, residence, and even play. They have been swept up in the currents of social, economic, and political expectation. They reflect an understandable mix of satisfaction and alienation, a tenuous grip on meaning and purpose, and it is not difficult to discover beneath the surface of certain forms of success a longing for another quality of knowing, belonging–and a more adequate faith.

It has been observed that the knowledge of homeplace is "hardwired" into every species and has survival value.[6] When one's need for "place" remains unhonored, the kind of deeply grounded trust of self, world, and "God" that is intimately associated with faith is impoverished. Further, if, as many religious traditions affirm, the revelation of God–Spirit–The Holy is mediated through all of the relationships of one's life, and that revelation is distorted when key relationships are absent or abusive (as psychosocial perspectives have shown), we must posit that when faith is composed without the distinctive forms of revelation that may occur within an intimate relationship with the soul's landscape, then faith is in some important sense bereft. The psalmist wrote, "The heavens are telling the glory of God; and the firmament proclaims his handiwork" (Ps. 19:1).

This same conviction of the revelatory power of the more-than-human world and the particularity of place in the formation of faith is captured by Thomas Berry when he writes:

> The world of life, of spontaneity, the world of dawn and sunset and starlight, the world of soil and sunshine, of meadow and woodland, of hickory and oak and maple and hemlock and pineland forests, of wildlife dwelling around us, of the river and its well-being–all of this some of us are discovering for the first time as the integral community in which we live. Here we experience the reality and the values that evoke in us our deepest moments of reflection, our revelatory experience of the ultimate mystery of things. Here...we receive those larger intuitions that lead us to dance and sing, intuitions that activate our imaginative powers in their most creative functions. This, too, is what inspires our weddings, our home life, and our joy in our children. Even our deepest human sensitivities emerge from our region, our place, our specific habitat, for the earth does not give itself to us in a global sameness. It gives itself to us in arctic and tropical regions, in seashore and desert, in prairielands and woodlands, in

mountains and valleys. Out of each a unique shaping of life takes place, a community, an integral community of all the geological as well as the biological and the human components. Each region is a single community so intimately related that any benefit or any injury is immediately experienced through the entire community.[7]

One of the contributions of faith development theory is that it has dramatized the ways in which the human mind is not a mere transmitter but a great transformer, an active composer of knowledge—and even of faith. At the same time, the social conviction of the constructive-developmental paradigm has illumined the power of the social environment in the formation of faith, recognizing that the self is formed in the self-other relation. That is, we come to faith in the faith of others. The "other" has most typically been assumed, however, to be the world of human relationships.[8] What has not been recognized within developmental models is that the "other" includes the more-than-human world, and our understanding of the adequacy of faith must take our relationships within the whole Earth community into account. As we do so, the locus of agency is reconfigured, and we recognize more adequately that the human is not only composing faith, but is simultaneously being composed in the ongoing work of creation. The poet writes:

Look: Underneath our hurriedness
The Earth moves, time is eons.
Rock bends,
Folds back upon itself,
Washes clean in long flowing water.
She was made before you
Lies deep beneath the forest floor
Bears all of us with sweet support.
Linger here a very long time.
See?
She moves grain by grain
Washed away, set down again.
Mountain becomes plain,
Plain is cut to gorge,
Sea floor rolls, folds, pushes,
Births mountains.
Tired of your hurriedness?
Go home.
Stay put.
Earth will be there
Still flowing
Like solid rock.
If only we stayed still
Long enough to be so carved,
Settled down grain by unique small grain

And hardened by pressure long endured,
Yet soft enough to be formed
By sacred water and wind exposing our essence,
Then washed away in utter silence.[9]

The poet has glimpsed the long view and another dimension of motion and habitation in the rich and dangerous project of our interdependence with planet Earth. We act, yes, but we are also acted upon. We create and are created. We are composers and are composed. Faith becomes less an act of personal heroism and more an act of participation in a relationship. We become participants within the more-than-human world rather than mere consumers of it. We are dependent and interdependent within a larger frame. The imagination of faith is invited home.

2. The Heart of a Place Is a Home

Whatever may be our soul's landscape, we human beings require shelter, nourishment, community, and familiarity. We are physical beings who desire and depend on both residence and routine. Within the landscape, we create houses to shelter us, and we long for them to become homes. A home is woven from the consequences of need and choice.

Because developmental theories feature sequential stages, they are often characterized as captives of linear time and are best understood through the metaphor of *journey*. Thus, developmental theories, including theories of faith development, have been critiqued as being, indeed, too linear, celebrating discontinuity while obscuring continuity—revealing how we move beyond and leave behind while masking how we stay and keep.

Seeking to address this distortion in recent years, I have often invited various groups of people to "draw a series of circles that represent your *home(s)*, beginning with the home you were born into and continuing until the present." I have encouraged them to be aware that "home" may or may not coincide with "residence." I have offered follow-up questions for reflection such as: Which homes did you create, and which ones were created for you?

Initially, I confess, I imagined that people would draw a series of separate circles stretching in a line across the page! Not so, of course. The circles often overlap, spin out in various twists and turns, and finally suggest another, nonlinear metaphor. A series of concentric circles presents itself, an image that recognizes that "everything remains" in the ongoing spiral composing and recomposing of our consciousness. Our faith evolves from a Center that we learn to know also as Self. At the same time, our boundaries of consciousness, both inner and outer, are continually being enlarged—always invited to account for more, to embrace more.[10]

Within this enlarging consciousness of "homeplace" and its gifts and challenges to faith, the particularity of one's own "home" plays a vital role. For example, using the lens of Fowler's stages,[11] we know that the quality of the composing of "Primal" faith is dependent on the degree to which the mother and father and other primary caregivers are themselves held and nurtured within their own experience of homeplace. The warp of the life tapestry of which Fowler speaks is laid down in the seamless bonds of attachment between the depth of trust or mistrust that the parent(s) embody and the capacity for trust in the life of the child.

In the formation of the Intuitive-Projective faith of early childhood, the familial home environment continues to play an essential role, determining whether or not the young child has access to life-bearing experiences of trust and also the room to venture safely and explore with pride as the child is learning to "stand on one's own two feet." A homeplace that essentially says "yes" rather than "no, don't touch, shame on you" serves as sturdy ground for the formation of faith.[12] In this and other ways, the child is dependent on the protection of trustworthy others and the home they craft to provide safety, comfort, and continuity when the child can only hold reality in episodic forms. Recognizing this, one mother, whose community commitments required her to attend many evening meetings when her child was very young, made a point of providing in each setting the continuity of key elements of "home"–the same blanket, the same song, the same mom–wherever her child lay down to sleep.

Indeed, in the early years of every childhood, homeplace is "nest." Gaston Bachelard has written that "when we discover a nest, it takes us back to our childhood or, rather, to *a childhood*; to the childhoods we should have had."[13] Gary Paul Nabhan observes that "Balchelard is speaking of an emotion deeper than nostalgia. He is touching upon a more ancient animal notion encoded within us: the simple comfort of the nest." Reflecting then upon his own experience as a father, he remembers how his son Dustin and his daughter Laura Rose, "were born, raised, and baptized in the solar fire and cactus-strippled basins of the Sonoran Desert." Dustin, "seven going on fifteen, and Laura Rose, pushing age five," were sent out to play in wildness but admonished not to go any further than the ridge line from where they would still be able to see the house. He learned, however, that they were most likely to end up in the brush across the road from the house, where a densely vegetated wash meandered "not fifty yards away."

> "Papa!" Laura cries. "Come over and see the hideout we made be-neath a tree over there. See if you can walk down the wash and find us. I bet you won't even be able to figure out where we are!"
>
> She takes my hand, leads me to the wash, makes me close my eyes, until both yell, "Ready?" I proceed down the open gravel bed until I hear giggling coming from a concealed corner where a hack-berry tree's canopy sweeps down to touch the ground. They have decorated a small opening with a wreath of wildflowers, and have made stools of pieces of wood found nearby.
>
> "Let's see if you can fit in too, Papa," Laura suggests. "We've found the perfect place for eating cookies."[14]

Environmental psychologist Mary Ann Kirkby believes that there is a developmental basis for the way young children "take refuge in natural and simply constructed, concealed settings. Such refuges extend the sphere of safety that children sensed earlier while still within the constant parental care they knew during their postnatal development."[15] Providing both concealment and "lookouts," these early forms of homemaking play a dramatic role in the dialogue between fear and trust. "Nest"–and the many forms that it takes throughout life–serves as a "holding environment" for the composing and recomposing of the relationship of self and world, the composing of a sturdy faith.[16]

When Mythical-Literal faith emerges (early childhood and beyond), episodic meaning making gives way to the capacity to see the connections among things, to place things in order and sequence (albeit in concrete forms). Consciousness of place expands as the child can not only venture out but also find the way back home. Thus, homeplace is enlarged to include neighborhood. Faith can now begin to be composed by story–narratives mediated by the values and norms of home-neighborhood. The stories of my place and my people–whether mediated by TV or grandparents or schoolbooks or movies– story the self into "place" and "home" for better and for worse. The stories that one is given "to grow up on" are a part of the way that one learns to become (or learns to fear to become) at home in the world. Gina O'Connell Higgins, who has studied the lives of adults who were significantly abused in childhood but who are able to love well in adulthood, was surprised to discover that many of them had been nourished by "fifties television"–family sitcoms that portrayed another, more viable, pattern of home and family life.[17]

In the adolescent years and beyond, Synthetic-Conventional faith can take form as the pull of hormones combines with enhanced perspective taking, and reflective thought emerges. "Home" can be enlarged once again to include the wider community beyond family, home, and neighborhood. Though the terms of belonging are initially experienced as tenuous at best and terrifying at worst, the newly reflective self now seeks a wider belonging. In our study of adults who are able to sustain commitment to the common good when they are not naïve about the complexity, diversity, and moral ambiguity of the contemporary world, we found that in the adolescent years good initiation into place and tribe, combined with invitations to venture into wider circles of participation, bode well for the capacity, later in life, to transcend narrow self-interest and commit to the common good.[18] Notably, when adolescent youth were given meaningful recognition in their homeplace, good work to do, and could safely travel (venture) throughout a city or region *and return home to people prepared to hear their story*–a deepening trust of self and world were forged.[19] Adolescent youth long for a place that is "theirs"–individually (*my* room) and collectively (*our* hangout). Honoring that longing is a critical contribution to the evolution of the self-world-God relation and the maturing of faith, as the self ventures into new realms and seeks to abide in a deepening interiority and an enlarged field of belonging.

I have described elsewhere and in depth the vital role that mentoring environments can play in the postadolescent, young adult years.[20] As young adults move into the world of first job, early career, partnership, marriage, and parenthood, they are wrestling quite literally with the questions of homeplace—where will I live, who will I live with, where will I place my stake in the ground and invest my life? If young adults have been initiated into critical thought, they are no longer dependent in the same way on either parents or peers for self-definition. Yet young adults remain appropriately dependent on recognition, support, challenge, and inspiration as they are keenly attuned to what will be asked and allowed, critically aware that they must now join the adult work of asking what is real and meaningful and good—and what is not—in a world of partial knowledge. Faith has become "adult" because it can now have a doubt of itself.

We are beginning to observe that for many young adults in today's culture, it is in becoming at home within the more-than-human world that a faith can be formed that does not have to disavow the insights from science, yet can be decidedly and consciously "spiritual." "Who am I among these stars?" is now asked in an informed and urgent way.[21] The childhood attraction to nest is now joined by the adult's capacity for vista—an attraction to the "big picture." Fowler's Individuative-Reflective faith (young adulthood and beyond) harbors the capacity to think systemically and thus more spaciously. Though this era of faith is vulnerable to a reach for consistency at the cost of caring (as Gilligan has shown), it can prompt a yet more profound sense of participation in the fabric of life itself—and compose new loyalties and commitments. An enlarged consciousness and an enhanced potential for commitment to justice signal the development of expanded notions of belonging and homeplace.

In the subsequent stage that Fowler describes as Conjunctive faith (early mid-life and beyond), there emerges a capacity to hold the truth of life's paradoxes that in the earlier stages seemed to beg for a false resolution. Thus, it becomes possible to know and hold in a more conscious way the soul's tidal rhythm of venturing and abiding, journeying and homemaking—not as either/or options, but as a single motion of the soul-in-relation, continually giving rise to a heightened and deeper, more expansive and more centered, more complex and more simplified sense of life and faith.

Recently, a man now in his sixties who lives a few hundred miles away dropped by our office to write a check—a faithful donation we have learned we can count on. When I thanked him, he responded simply, "I haven't worked for two years, but it seems important to care for the *anchoring places*." I asked him what he meant. He told me that when he was in his mid-forties and moving through transition on many levels of his life, he recognized the need for stability (abiding) in the midst of change (venturing) and began to identify four places that ground his life: (1) his family's ancestral lands in Montana; (2) Priest Lake—"a beautiful, moist, cool, *nurturing* environment"—where there is a cabin that served as a haven and provided comfort when he was going through great pain; (3) the Selway, a wilderness area in Idaho that, in contrast, is filled with extremes (a cold glacier river and 105 degrees of heat in the valley), where everything is "big, sensual, powerful, demanding, and *challenging*"–a place he now returns to annually for a hike with his brother; and (4) the "most western place," our Chinook lands–one hundred acres of forest and meadow land–where in that time of midlife "gateway," sitting in the "Farmhouse," he was asked, "How do you want your life to be?" This heartplace continues to be for him, he says, "a place of integration"–spiritual, intellectual, and physical. "It serves as a lens that has helped me focus." In this account, we hear the adult capacity to hold the complex features of adult faith in meaning-full paradoxes anchored by the powers of "place."

In Fowler's description of the last stage of faith development, Universalizing faith (midlife and beyond), he suggests that the achieved competency of Conjunctive faith seeks "completion."[22] We might describe this movement of faith as the emergence of a further refinement of paradox, or perhaps a consciousness in which the elements of a paradox become so deeply integrated as to lose their identifiable distinctions, where, as T. S. Eliot captured it, "the fire and the rose are one."[23]

3. Venturing and Abiding

It may have become evident to the reader that when the metaphors of venturing and abiding are employed to illumine the dynamics of the formation of faith, venturing need not mean dramatic physical movement. Sometimes, for example, the great venture is into new intellectual territory, or back into our home to become reacquainted with our spouse, or down into the long unexplored cellar of one's own psyche. Sometimes, the venturing is only across town rather than across continents.

"Homebuilding" paradoxically might tug us out of our houses and into a more intimate relationship with our bio-region, restoring waterways and discovering in the process that our personal energies are necessarily woven into a wider communal fabric and that we have become more "at home." As Belenky, Bond, and Weinstock have described so elegantly, we may be beckoned out of our private homes to become a part of creating "public homeplaces"–organizations dedicated to goals that have been confined to private life and "women's work." Public homeplaces (for example, centers for cultural and community development, "schoolhomes," community art centers) manifest the values of a healthy home, functioning in ways that nurture the development of everyone–especially the most vulnerable.[24]

This ironic play with metaphors must not, however, eclipse a fundamental observation: The effort to achieve the realization of self and the formation of a viable faith through the imagination of the journey of differentiation alone leaves both individuals and cultures impoverished and weak. A journey may be endless. A pilgrimage, in contrast, requires a return home. The story of the development of faith can be told as the account of an ongoing Journey–the pull of the tide into the sea. It can also be told as the call to return Home to the shore of the authentic self, to the Center–to the Spirit that dwells within as well as beyond. If a good life is an elegant mix of both venturing and abiding, then throughout our entire lives, as a primary need of our species and our souls, we must reclaim the need for pilgrimage—venture and return—over and over again. In today's culture, this requires the renewal and legitimation of our vital need for home, homemaking, homesteading, homeplace—a participation in the power of place as an integral feature of our hunger for a more adequate and bolder faith.[25]

4. The Practices of Abiding

To reclaim the significance of the role of homeplace in the formation of faith will require a conscious attention to "practices." Practices are ways of life, things we do with and for one another to make and keep life human.[26] We act, and thus we habituate ourselves into trusting, feeling, thinking, knowing, and believing. The practices we keep form the grounding, centering motion of life in which faith is birthed and sustained. Our hunger for homeplace invites renewed attention to the "practices of abiding." Consider, for example, the practices of walking and learning, eating and meeting, mending and fixing, resting and dreaming.

4.1 Walking and Learning

In our time, growing numbers of people live, as Cornel West has suggested, in a "hotel culture" where we simply move from one context to another with a minimal sense of attachment.[27] We are significantly insulated from the soul's landscape as we speed about, encapsulated in cars and planes; even children's play*grounds* are covered with asphalt. The practice of walking, however, awakens us to another kind of motion and re-presences us to our surroundings for the ongoing composing of meaning and faith.

Consider a distinction between road and path.

The difference between a path and a road is not only the obvious one. A path is little more than a habit that comes with knowledge of a place. It is a sort of ritual of familiarity. As a form, it is a form of contact with a known landscape. It is not destructive. It is the perfect adaptation, through experience and familiarity, of movement to place; it obeys the natural contours; such obstacles as it meets it goes around. A road, on the other hand, even the most primitive road, embodies a resistance against the landscape. Its reason is not simply the necessity for movement, but haste. Its wish is to *avoid* contact with the landscape; it seeks so far as possible to go over the country, rather than through it; its aspiration, as we see clearly in the example of our modern freeways, is to be a bridge; its tendency is to translate place into space in order to traverse it with the least effort. It is destructive, seeking to remove or destroy all obstacles in its way. The primitive road advanced by the destruction of the forest; modern roads advance the destruction of topography.[28]

As I write, my husband also is sitting at his computer and writing. As I pass by his study on my way to a cup of tea, he exclaims how much he is loving what he is doing, and I know it is because he has fallen in love with a landscape. His imagination is not in his study, confined by the frame of the screen. This morning, his imagination is dwelling in the land he has been walking in for the past five years, the Chinook lands of the Whidbey Institute, the conference and retreat center where we teach. He is passionately working to recover our relationship with the land as "teacher" by creating with other colleagues a guided walk through the forest that will assist us alienated humans in discovering a lost relationship and our place within the larger story of the landscape. He has discovered that the word *path* shares the same root as *find,* and, thus, embedded in *path* is a sense of discovery.

This morning, he is meditating on "sunlight," and he invites me to notice how I might recognize that the clearing where we walk the labyrinth is an old clearing because the "crowndepth" (the foliage of the surrounding trees) extends all the way to the ground, revealing that sunlight has been present for the entire life of those trees—douglas fir, hemlock, and red cedar.

I, too, am walking and learning when I walk rather than drive the asphalt of my neighborhood. I smell, hear, and discover my connections among things in a dramatically different fashion. My body learns the pitch of the hill. I am exhilarated by the sting of the wind. I discover that my neighbor has aged considerably in the past six months, and I need to become more aware and available. The practice of "walking in place" is a mode of learning that invites the soul to be composed within yet wider dimensions of knowing and into a more powerful dance of faith.

Gary Paul Nabhan, quoted earlier, recalls the day he and his daughter Laura Rose were taken through Utah canyon country by Caroline Wilson, who with her sister had grown up in Arches National Park, where their father had been superintendent. As children, the Wilson girls had spent hours, alone or together, "back in the rocks," acting out dramas, mounting expeditions, or watching clouds roll by. A quarter of a century later, Caroline escorted Laura Rose through their fantasyland—"the Indian Cave...The Princess's Bedroom, the Train, the Deer Pond. The scale of these little puddles, niches, crawl spaces, shelters, and passages fit Laura...to a tee."[29] Caroline has become a ranger-interpreter for the National Park Service, and her sister has become a physical therapist in the city. They both have "a healthy perspective about human kind," writes Nabhan, and "their social graces are not unrelated to their feeling at home in the wild"—to the confidence the girls gained themselves while exploring the terrain behind their house in Arches.

> There was a moment on the tour of their childhood playground that stands out above all others. Caroline led Laura...into the Ballroom, a slightly sloping bench of creamy Navajo sandstone overlooking the rock house. It was surrounded by nearly animate rockforms and a dozen floral fragrances. "This, Laura Rose," Caroline exclaimed, "this

is where we danced!" She shut her eyes. Then, feeling the tilt of the sandstone beneath her feet, Caroline spun around and danced us up an image that she had carried with her from childhood.

"I *remember* these rocks!" Caroline whispered, somewhat astonished by the sudden upwelling of tears in her eyes. "They are as familiar to me as the freckles on my arm."

I glanced down at Laura Rose, at my side. Her eyes grew wide. I closed mine and hoped that I would be around one day when, as a fully grown woman, Laura Rose will dance herself in place.[30]

4.2 Eating and Meeting

A central practice of abiding within a homeplace is the practice of the table—practices of eating and meeting. In a society of "fast food," this practice is under siege. Yet it is at the family dinner table where key patterns of trust, meaning, and faith are laid down early and recomposed again and again throughout life. Douglas Meeks has said that, in the practice of the table, "you know there will be a place for you, what is on the table will be shared, and you will be placed under obligation." In the daily, dependable ritual of the table, we come together around our common vulnerability—our need to eat—and we receive the nourishment that sustains both body and soul.[31]

Reflecting on his early boyhood, a man recalled how keenly he had experienced the family dining table as a dependable center of trust. Each week when his mother moved the dining table to sweep the floor beneath, he was quite anxious until she would return the table to its place—and his world felt centered, stable, and whole again. The family table functioned as an orienting center of power, value, and affection, an anchor of faith.

The table, through the practice of hospitality, also offers the practice of "meeting." When we gather for eating, we meet other members of our family and tribe and are nourished by the bonds of friends and relations. The table is a place for bonding. It can also be a place for bridging.[32] As our planet homeplace becomes smaller and cultures collide, one of the big questions of our time is, Can we all dwell together in the small planet home we share? Positive, constructive encounters with those who are "other" are essential if we are going to have the capacity to transcend the perils of tribalism and wars of retribution. The sharing of a common meal, spiced with genuine dialogue, can serve to open the soul to the other's landscape.[33]

It has been observed that communities of faith who are able to resist either declining or moving, and who can adapt to changing neighborhoods and demographics, regularly and often gather around tables laden with coffee and food. They "create opportunities for different constituencies to eat together. They have after-church potlucks, holiday picnics, and well-attended coffee hours. Just as they intentionally alter their styles of worship, so they also pursue the informal, interpersonal sharing that occurs in the context of a common meal. Both are instrumental in building the new culture [and the faith] necessary for an adapted congregation."[34] In the practices of eating and meeting, we may discover and recompose the connections among us, ritually acknowledging with gratitude the grace of a yet wider dependence and belonging–and the gifts of staying and abiding.

4.3 Fixing and Mending

Place and Home are often associated with stasis in contrast to motion. The practices of abiding do not court stagnation. Rather, in the practices of abiding, homebuilding, and homemaking, we participate in another kind of movement that along with venturing also serves the composing of meaning and faith. Scott Russell Sanders captures this sense of dynamic motion-in-place in his book *Staying Put: Making Home in a Restless World.* He writes: "What do I hope for? Eternal life, I suppose...The eternal life I seek is not some aftertime, some other place, but awareness of eternity in this moment and this place. What I crave is contact with the force that moves and shapes all there is or has been or will be."[35]

Sanders knows something of that creative force coursing through his own body in his practices of staying and fixing. Having lost irretrievably the childhood landscapes he loved (because of the damming of a river), he has become all the more committed to the place he has come to as an adult. Early on, he and his wife bought a "fixer-upper" and assured each other that they would give swift attention to a list of essential projects from roof to foundation.

> We moved in almost twenty years ago, and we are still working on that list...For every job completed, two new jobs arise. Reglaze a broken window, and before you've put away your tools a gutter sags or a switch burns out...Things fall apart–and not only in politics and religion. Pipes rust, nails work loose, shingles crumble, wood warps...A house is a shell caught in a surf that never stops grinding...How has this box, this frame of possibilities, come to fit me so exactly? By what alchemy does a house become a home?
>
> The short answer is that these walls and floors and scruffy flower beds are saturated with our memories and sweat...After nearly two decades of intimacy, the house dwells in us as surely as we dwell in the house.[36]

> I carry slivers of wood under my fingernails, dust from demolition in the corners of my eyes, aches from hammering and heaving in all my joints...A house is a garment, easily put off or on, casually bought and sold; a home is skin. Merely change houses and you will be disoriented; change homes and you bleed. When the shell you live in has taken on the savor of your love, when your dwelling has become a taproot, then your house is a home.[37]

Sanders discovers that staying and fixing becomes a spiritual practice that serves as a taproot of meaning and faith, and Gunilla Norris similarly finds that the practice of homemaking opens into meditation and prayer. She writes about "mending."

One garment cannot be fixed–
into the rag bag it goes!
But another can be stitched together again.
As I sort and mend I think of the larger fabric,
the fabric of life. I think about relationships
that tear apart...
Help me to realize when my busy needle
will do no good...
Beyond knowing
what is torn apart breathes
in its own way with You,
mends if it can, when it can.
Let me accept the frayed.[38]

Fixing, mending, washing, cleaning–these are fundamental motions integral to our vocation as humans. In a distracted, throw-away, consumer culture, such practices are increasingly rendered marginal, if not irrelevant. When these practices of abiding are demeaned or carried out in a state of "absent mindedness," we have failed to pay attention to fundamental, informing features of our participation in the ongoing weaving of creation. Ungrounded in the tangible practices of maintaining the daily, immediate, physical, and emotional fabric of our lives, we are less prepared to imagine and lead the mending and restoration of the body politic.

4.4 Resting and Dreaming

The longing for home is most deeply anchored in the longing for sanctuary, for a sheltered, safe place where we can truly rest. The practice of resting is difficult in a world gone busy, where many are homeless and where others, even within their houses, do not find themselves at home. This is a perilous state, because a time of dramatic change calls for new creation, for the participation of the human imagination in the ongoing work of Creator Spirit.

The work of the imagination (not fantasy, but rather the highest power of the mind) requires times of "pause," when the active mind is still, while the deep master currents of the soul are at work. We have known from ancient times that practices of "Sabbath" are essential to faithful living.[39] The practice of sabbath rest invites us home, to ourselves, to each other, to the earth.

Resting gives way to dreaming. Bachelard has written, "If I were asked to name the chief benefit of the house, I should say: the house shelters day-dreaming, the house protects the dreamer, the house allows one to dream in peace."[40]

We live in a time when we need to dream new, more life-bearing dreams. It is said that approximately 57 percent of all children born in "developing" countries will grow up in urban slums, and a quarter of the children born in the United States in this next generation will start their lives in such slums.[41] "Slum" as homeplace betrays the promise of Life. In this and other ways, our planet home is endangered by economic practices that tear at the fabric of ecological systems everywhere.[42] Now threatened by new terrors, we have awakened to discover that one-fifth of the world's peoples are Muslim, yet two-thirds of the world's refugees–the world's homeless–are Muslim.[43]

Wendell Berry has prophetically observed "a division that is rapidly deepening in our country: a division between people who are trying to defend the health, the integrity, and even the existence of places whose values they sum up in the words *home* and *community,* and people for whom those words signify no value at all."[44] In a world in which these essential values are, therefore, regularly assaulted and rendered invisible, reclaiming the practices of abiding can carry us into vital aspects of what Fowler points toward as "the gestalt of divine praxis," that transforming and reconfiguring power within history.[45] The formation of the scope of the soul that is required for building the structures of love and justice in today's world depends, in part, on strengthening our capacity to stay, to "stay with," in spiritual solidarity and practical hope. The development of a worthy faith for our time invites us to recover the ancient tidal rhythm of both venturing *and abiding.*

Notes

[1]Thomas Kelly, quoted in Catherine Whitmire, *Plain Living: A Quaker Path to Simplicity* (Notre Dame, Ind.: Sorin Books, 2001), 21.

[2]Wilfred Cantwell Smith, *Faith and Belief* (Princeton: Princeton University Press, 1979), 12.

[3]James W. Fowler, *Weaving the New Creation: Stages of Faith and the Public Church* (San Francisco: HarperSanFrancisco, 1991), 24.

[4]Ibid., 25.

[5]David Abram, *The Spell of the Sensuous: Perception and Language in a More-Than-Human World* (New York: Vintage Books, 1991), 167.

[6]See Tony Hiss, *The Experience of Place* (New York: Vintage Books, 1991).

[7]Thomas Berry, quoted in *The Sacred Earth: Writers on Nature & Spirit,* ed. Jason Gardner (Novato, Calif.: The New World Library, 1998), 75.

[8]From the beginning, a key girder in Fowler's structure of faith has been the "bounds of social awareness." See James W. Fowler, *Stages of Faith: The Psychology of Human Development and the Quest for Meaning* (San Francisco: Harper & Row, 1981), 244–45.

[9]Sam Magill, "Earth Homework, Summer '95." Copyright held by author; used with permission.

[10]See Laurent A. Daloz, James P. Keen, Cheryl H. Keen, and Sharon Daloz Parks, eds., *Common Fire: Leading Lives of Commitment in a Complex World* (Boston: Beacon Press, 1996), ch. 2.

[11]For a recent statement of Fowler's classic six stages of faith, see James W. Fowler, *Faithful Change: The Personal and Public Challenges of Postmodern Life* (Nashville, Tenn.: Abingdon Press, 1996), 54–74.

[12]See Fowler, "Faith and the Fault Lines of Shame," *Faithful Change,* Part 2.

[13]Gaston Bachelard, *The Poetics of Space* (Boston: Beacon Press, 1969), 93.

[14]Gary Paul Nabhan and Stephen Tremble, *The Geography of Childhood: Why Children Need Wild Places* (Boston: Beacon Press, 1994), 6–7.

[15]Quoted in ibid., 8.

[16]See Clare Cooper Marcus, *The House as a Mirror of Self: Exploring the Deeper Meaning of Home* (Berkeley, Calif.: Conari Press, 1995).

[17]See Gina O'Connell Higgins, *Resilient Adults: Overcoming a Cruel Past* (San Francisco: Jossey-Bass, 1994).

[18]See Daloz et al., *Common Fire,* esp. ch. 2.

[19]See Sharon Daloz Parks, "Home and Pilgrimage: Deep Rhythms in the Adolescent Soul," in *Growing Up Postmodern: Imitating Christ in the Age of "Whatever"* (Princeton, N.J: Institute for Youth Ministry, Princeton Theological Seminary, 1999), 53–65.

[20]See Sharon Daloz Parks, *Big Questions, Worthy Dreams: Mentoring Young Adults in Their Search for Meaning, Purpose, and Faith* (San Francisco: Jossey-Bass, 2000).

[21]Parks, *Big Questions, Worthy Dreams,* ch. 3.

[22]Fowler, *Faithful Change,* 66.

[23]T. S. Eliot, "Little Gidding," in *The Complete Poems and Plays, 1909–1950* (New York: Harcourt Brace, 1958), 145.

[24]Mary Field Belenky, Lynne A. Bond, and Jacqueline S. Weinstock, *The Tradition That Has No Name* (New York: Basic Books, 1997), 164.

[25]See Sharon Daloz Parks, "Home and Pilgrimage: Companion Metaphors for Personal and Social Transformation," *Soundings* 72, no. 2–3 (Summer/Fall 1989).

[26]See Craig R. Dykstra, *Growing in the Life of Faith: Education and Christian Practices* (Louisville, Ky.: Geneva Press, 1999), and Dorothy C. Bass, ed., *Practicing Our Faith: A Way of Life for a Searching People* (San Francisco: Jossey-Bass, 1997).

[27]See Cornel West, *Race Matters* (Boston: Beacon Press, 1993).

[28]Wendell Berry, "A Native Hill," in *At Home on Earth: Becoming Native to Our Place– A Multicultural Anthology,* ed. David Landis Barnhill (Berkeley and Los Angeles: University of California Press, 1999), 49.

[29]Nabhan and Tremble, *Geography of Childhood,* 12–13.

[30]Ibid., 13–14.

[31]See Sharon Parks, "The Meaning of Eating and Home as Ritual Space," in *Sacred Dimensions of Women's Experience,* ed. Elizabeth Dodson Gray (Wesley, Mass.: Roundtable Press, 1988).

[32]Robert D. Putnum, *Bowling Alone: The Collapse and Revival of American Community* (New York: Simon & Schuster, 2000), 22–23.

[33]See Daloz et al. *Common Fire,* chs. 3 and 4.

[34]Nancy Tatom Ammerman, *Congregation and Community* (New Brunswick, N.J.: Rutgers University Press), 338.

[35]Scott Russell Sanders, *Staying Put: Making Home in a Restless World* (Boston: Beacon Press, 1993), 54.

[36]Ibid., 23.

[37]Ibid., 33–35.

[38]Gunilla Norris, *Being Home* (New York: Bell Tower), 66–67.

[39]See Dorothy Bass, "Keeping Sabbath," in *Practicing Our Faith,* ch. 6.

[40]Bachelard, *Poetics of Space,* 6.

[41]Nabhan and Tremble, *Geography of Childhood,* 11.

[42]See Sharon Daloz Parks, "Household Economics," in *Practicing Our Faith,* ch. 4.

[43]Diana L. Eck "Forming the Next Generation: Muslim in America," *Christian Century* (June 6–13, 2001): 20.

[44]Wendell Berry, *Home Economics* (New York: North Point Press; Farrar, Straus & Giroux, 1987), 53.

[45]Fowler, *Faithful Change,* 193–94. See Peter Hodgson, *God in History* (Nashville, Tenn.: Abingdon Press, 1989).

PART TWO

Philosophical and Theological Issues Raised by Fowler's Work

4

Moral Development, the Good Life, and Faith

Continuity or Conflict?

MAUREEN JUNKER-KENNY

The task of supplementing James Fowler's long-established research on faith development is quite difficult. Many insights from the practical theological and ethical debates of the last twenty years already seem to have been anticipated in his circumspect adaptation of stage theories of moral development to the religious dimension of humanity. On a philosophical level, Fowler attests to the constructive nature of stage theories: "The most revealing aspect of any theory of human development is the character of the last stages. What vision of completion, of fullness of being, of maturity informs the research on and definitions of stages or phases of development?"[1] On an ethical level, his implicit recognition that we are dealing with a "crisis of values" even more than with a "crisis of norms" leads him to favor an ethical "model" over against a "precept ethics."[2] Here, stories are more significant than rules; the biblical tradition is appreciated first in its narrative character before any moral commands are highlighted. Fowler's early sympathetic presentation of Carol Gilligan's critique of Lawrence Kohlberg[3] spares him the objections leveled against the predominantly male bias of existing theories of development. Finally, his cultural analysis accounts for the changes that have made the vocational ideals, for example, of small-town communities, irretrievable and accounts for the pluralistic conditions necessary for the formation of moral and religious identity.

All these features testify to the critical and discerning manner in which Fowler utilizes research from the social sciences, especially developmental psychology, in order to trace steps in religious maturation. In this regard, his theory escapes the suspicion that has accompanied practical theology since its turn to interdisciplinary debate with the social sciences: that it has exchanged its ancillary status to dogmatics by way of a unilateral dependency on secular sciences, a movement "from applied dogmatics to applied psychology." In Fowler, the interdisciplinary dialogue is bidirectional. Insights and questions generated in research on religious development are posed to the original theories of Erik Erikson, Jean Piaget, Daniel Levinson, Lawrence Kohlberg, and Carol Gilligan.

In light of the benefits of the past two decades of debate within and between philosophical and theological ethics, I would like to pursue three questions regarding the manner in which Fowler builds his research on stage theories of morality. My questions focus on: (1) Fowler's methodology; (2) key concepts in the "parent" theories of Piaget and Kohlberg, such as "autonomy" and the definition of morality as justice; and (3) the need to delineate the psychological concept of self used in life-cycle theories in light of a philosophical analysis of the self. From this discussion, I conclude, among other things, that the social sciences need to dialogue with the disciplines of philosophical and theological anthropology and ethics in order to situate their research and key concepts within a broader academic context.

1. Methodology

Two main objections voiced against Fowler's methodology deal with the differences between the disciplines of psychology and theology. The first objection is interested in the integrity of theology as the reflective theory of faith, while the second is concerned with the integrity of social scientific research. The theological critique questions whether "concepts like 'faith' [do not] obtain different meaning when put in a psychological versus a theological frame of reference."[4] This perceptive question becomes even more acute when one analyzes the specific moral-psychological approach utilized by Fowler. How suitable is a theory whose stages presuppose a definite goal of maturity that delimits a person's relationship to God?[5] Fowler recognizes that the "stages 'are not to be understood as stages of soteriology'" and that no "person must have constructed a given stage of development in faith or selfhood 'in order to be saved.'"[6] Still, as Nipkow observes, "notwithstanding all safeguards, a stagelike sequence, whether made up of 'hard' or 'soft' stages, does articulate a normative hierarchy."[7] It leads to the question, How can a faith that is based on redemption, that is, on a liberating act of God, fit into a framework of growth in moral competence? The question about which concept of morality Piaget and Kohlberg drew on as the model for their original theories will be pursued further in the next section of this chapter.

In its most positional form, however, this theological critique is directed against any "psychological understanding of faith as human activity."[8] It is critical of reflecting on the anthropological presuppositions of revelation, rather than on God's revelation itself. Such a fundamental theological opposition needs to be discussed with regard to its general assumptions about the divine-human relationship. As a critique of Fowler though, it is mistaken. The problem is not that Fowler overly emphasizes faith as a human activity; indeed, his attribution of the genuine response of human freedom to God's self-revelation, to "synergy with the Spirit,"[9] makes even the believer's own faithful answer ultimately a joint venture between human and divine activity. This merging, however, invites the suspicion leveled against Karl Rahner that divine action and human action are identified with each other in his theology of grace (*gnadentheologisches Identitätsdenken*[10]), to the detriment of human freedom. Against Rahner's and Fowler's attribution of the human response to God, to God's grace, or to God's Spirit, it is decisive to acknowledge it as a free and grateful personal human self-commitment. Only then is it the answer that God would require and hope for in the history of creating a counterpart for God's love.

Many Christian critics believe that "the formalization of the fundamental theological assumptions lacks theological clarity,"[11] which creates a second objection to Fowler's methodology. Should a stage theory that parallels cognitive, moral, and religious development not be regarded as a generic account of the growth of human competence, and a theory of faith development as the specific historical explication unique to each religious community? Is it not a misunderstanding to categorize psychological and religious stages on an equal universal level and thereby ignore the particulars of individual religions? Karl Ernst Nipkow suggests that a "general *psychological* theory of faith *development*" should be complemented by a "*theological* theory of faith *history*."[12] In response, Fowler denies the difference in epistemological status between these. He also underlines the thoroughly scientific character of faith development research, which is not compromised by its inherent theological nature: "It is a principal thesis of this chapter that the acknowledgment and rational explication of these broadly theological foundations do not jeopardize the theory's claim to scientific integrity. In this regard, there are parallels to the conviction-laden philosophical rationales for normative and descriptive theories of cognitive development and for developmental theories of moral and religious reasoning."[13]

Nipkow's critique of Fowler parallels recent contributions to interfaith dialogue that are significant because of Fowler's reliance on Wilfred Cantwell Smith. Instead of trying to establish general traits of religious traditions–by neglecting, for example, the christological difference and focusing on the one God to whom all religions are deemed to respond, as advocated by the defenders of the "theocentric paradigm"–the alternative is to develop a theory of religious pluralism from *within* a particular religion. This option enables us to remain within the parameters of a particular religion both for hermeneutical reasons and reasons of faith. Rather than formalizing traits inherent in one's own faith community, an adherent of a self-conscious "christocentric inclusivism" would explicate concepts of the human person, society, history, ethics, and so forth from within the religion's image of God. The individual then could converse with adherents of other religions, treating their faith tenets as different paths to (a different?) salvation. This approach seriously considers the hermeneutical insight that one's point of departure in a particular religion is significant.[14]

While Nipkow's proposal to distribute the task of tracing faith development between two disciplines, a general psychological discipline and a particular theological discipline, makes sense, it is important to anchor both disciplines in a more encompassing framework. Both psychology, however generic, and a theory of historical and contemporary Christian self-understanding and praxis operate as individual empirical sciences. Both inquiries need the broader framework of elaborated philosophical and theological anthropologies against which the guiding hypotheses of empirical research can be checked and into which the perspectives of different disciplines can be integrated. Only then can incompatibilities be discovered between different frameworks.

Fowler admits the difficulty of fitting important markers of Christian anthropology, such as "concepts of personal and corporate sin, distortion, defensiveness, and self-deception into the theory...when the faith stages are too quickly assimilated to the enlightenment, rationalist framework of the Piaget-Kohlberg tradition."[15] Yet the elements through which he chooses to describe the human-divine relationship lend themselves to understanding faith not only as a religious, but also as an intellectual and moral, process of growth. According to the editors of *Stages of Faith and Religious Development,* the

> degree of compatibility of theology and psychology depends also on the quality of the theology employed. It appears that in the domain of theological anthropology, a theological model such as Fowler's, which leans towards the Reformed tradition and stresses the Old Testament idea of covenant, the concept of vocation and human partnership with God, is much more receptive than other theologies to the psychological understanding of faith as human activity.[16]

The discovery of the human person as a partner of God in late medieval nominalism and the regnocentric interpretation of human agency can be appreciated for avoiding the notion of competition between human and divine freedom, a notion that discredited theology in modernity. But further qualifications are needed—for example, the human mandate to follow the self-limitation of God's power by God's love, or to measure one's actions by the praxis and proclamation of Jesus, which contributed to the interpretation of God as unconditional love. Otherwise, the emphasis on God's human partners as co-creating the reign of God would leave theology defenseless against an uncritical endorsement, for example, of techniques for the genetic enhancement of human beings, in the name of co-creation. To be less prone to such ideology, the harmonizing alignment of Stage 6 convention-free autonomy and a personal call from God should be reexamined. There are other theological approaches besides the emphasis on covenant and vocation that are vulnerable to ideological abuse in order to support the respective *Zeitgeist.* Each of these theologies needs content-related safeguards that specify what types of relationships deserve to be qualified as anticipating or exemplifying "the reign of God."

Charles Taylor's critique of Piaget, whose theory has influenced both Kohlberg and Fowler, illustrates the potential critical role of philosophical anthropology for individual sciences. Taylor questions, from the perspective of a philosophical anthropology, certain interpretations made by Piaget, namely the role he accords to play with regard to the ability for perspective taking and thus of moving from "egocentrism" to an intersubjectively shared horizon. Taylor summarizes how Piaget assigns playacting, or pretending,

> a role in the development of the symbolic function. Play represents the supremacy of assimilation over accommodation; it is "la pensée égocentrique à l'état pur." It arises because the subject cannot yet make a balanced adaptation to reality, where accommodation and assimilation are in equilibrium, and hence his grasp on things is an objective one. It is destined to merge more and more into constructive activity, on the one hand, and socialized competitive games with rules, on the other, as the child matures.[17]

Taylor's alternative interpretation recognizes playacting as an appropriate activity and goes on to suggest two types of objectivity, one related to objects, the other interpersonal:

> But it is possible to take another view of the nature and function of this kind of symbolic play. Piaget sees it in the context of growth towards objectivity which is itself defined in terms of reversibility. But we can see it in another light. Make-believe can be seen as a function which is complementary to language. If speech is the vehicle of a disengaged awareness of what surrounds us, pretending or make-believe is a way of disengaging in another sense, by lifting oneself out of one's situation...A child may act out with her doll a dramatic scene she has just had with her mother...It is tremendously valuable to be able to step out of the situation...in order to be able to live it from another vantage point; not, in other words, to remain inextricably trapped in the primary experience...This is how I would interpret the behavior of the child who reenacts the emotional scene with her mother with her doll. The powerful emotion is worked through again in the make-believe situation in which the little girl even takes the other role, and in this way the child can come to terms with it...[P]lay acting...allows us to see our predicament from a different vantage point, and it builds up a capacity to live on several levels, which the adult normally has...The life of the imagination is thus in part the successor activity in adult life of the play acting of the child; it continues to feed the ability to extend the situation in which we live.
>
> In this view, play acting is not an early inadequate substitute for objectivity in Piaget's sense; it is not a deforming assimilation destined to be replaced by a properly balanced one. On the contrary, it may help us to come nearer to an objective understanding of our

emotions and our relations with others...[P]retending and symbolic play...can help this process along (but there is no necessity in this; it can also feed our egocentric fantasies). It can also help the child to achieve the articulated understanding of distinct points of view of the world, that is, to overcome egocentrism in Piaget's sense.[18]

Therefore, the "disinvolved" type of objectivity marked by "reversibility," which Piaget emphasized, is not the only one. A second type of objectivity can be distinguished from it. This objectivity is concerned with "understanding our relations with others."[19] It "cannot achieve disinvolvement, and strives rather to achieve a truer perspective...and 'play it back' from a different vantage point...Where we cannot loosen the affective link with our situation, we can still live it through play in another perspective."[20]

This early critique of certain anthropological assumptions in Piaget's 1968 study has been endorsed by subsequent contributions to the theory of education. Ursula Peukert's summary confirms that Piaget employs a one-sidedly instrumental concept of agency.[21] To distinguish this from the capability for interpersonal "objectivity" clearly has significance for ethics. Yet the interpretation of play should be relevant for theology in other respects as well. If one of the constitutive theories in the interdisciplinary project of establishing stages of faith is unable to give a full account of the ontogenetic significance of imaginative "pretend" play for children, and consequently of the anthropological dimension of playfulness and imagination, what repercussions are likely for a theory of religious faith and its practice? Such a theory must make sense of symbolic representation, (re-)enactment, ritual, the drama of the history of salvation, the hope for the eschatological resolution of the story of God and creation. Being developmentally destined merely for participation in competitive games with rules seems to be a poor vision of human flourishing. Analogous to Friedrich Schleiermacher's attempts, we now need to recover the "nonreductionist anthropology and education over against a rationalist philosophy and culture," which, as Friedrich Schweitzer demonstrates, forms part of the enlarged definition of development in Fowler's stages despite his "rationalist methodology."[22]

While Kohlberg does not expand on play apart from marking out the differences between boys' rule-oriented group games and girls' twosome structure of play, he seems to share Piaget's assumption that the first stage ought to be regarded as self-centered and that subsequent stages gradually include the perspective of the other. In this crucial question for the origin of morality, Peukert points out that the concept of young children as "egocentric" has not accounted for the difference between performance and competence.[23] This gap leaves the observed behavior further open to interpretation and, therefore, at the mercy of researchers and their gift for, or lack of, sensitivity and empathy.[24]

It seems as if the only solutions to this methodological difficulty are (1) to check both hypotheses guiding empirical research and the anthropological models behind them, and (2) to place their basic assumptions in dialogical comparison with other anthropologies. The need to base one's theory of morality in anthropology is recognized increasingly in philosophical ethics, due to the impact of approaches such as the communitarian critique of proceduralist ethics, Paul Ricoeur's hermeneutical philosophy of the self, and Hans Krämer's proposal of an "Integrative Ethics."[25] These philosophies are linked by their interest to rehabilitate the Aristotelian ethics of striving for a flourishing life within a modern framework of autonomy and pluralism, while equally recognizing the need for normative ethics.

Fowler's theory shows affinities to some of these philosophical and ethical concerns. His critique of "self-realization" concurs with Taylor's cultural analysis that an engrossing interest in self-realization ultimately endangers political liberty as well as personal autonomy:

> A society of self-fulfillers, whose affiliations are more and more seen as revocable, cannot sustain the strong identification with the political community which public freedom needs...The "triumph of the therapeutic" can also mean an abdication of autonomy where the lapse of traditional standards, coupled with the belief in technique, makes people cease to trust their own instincts about happiness, fulfillment, and how to bring up their children. Then the "helping professions" take over their lives.[26]

Taylor is careful, however, not to succumb to the "antisubjectivist readings" of antimodernists who reduce the multifaceted cultural challenges to merely one cause. He writes: "Bellah et al....write as though there were not an independent problem of the loss of meaning in our culture, as though the recovery of a Tocquevillian commitment would somehow also fully resolve our problems of meaning, of expressive unity, of the loss of substance and resonance in our man-made environment, of a disenchanted universe."[27]

A stage theory of moral and religious development needs to consider possible sources for any type of commitment beyond the self. Fowler's theological qualification of maturing to higher stages by the idea of "conversion" indicates his awareness that linear progress is an inappropriate ideal. He realizes that identity cannot be directly achieved, that human dignity is more than agency, and that faith, though a component of humanity in general and even part of human biological-genetic makeup, still remains a gift. Here, Fowler parallels Ricoeur's analysis of the self and its receptivity and his reflections on the "economy of the gift." Elements of Krämer's "ethics of counseling" are paralleled in the role Fowler designates to congregations as partners in individuals' life journeys. Despite these shared views, however, there is no denying that the central thrust of theories of moral development is toward a deontological sixth stage of convention-critical autonomy. My thesis (in sections 2 and 3 below) is that several of the ambiguities and missing links within Fowler's theory could be solved if he incorporated certain distinctions achieved in the critique of proceduralist deontological ethics throughout the last twenty years.

2. Autonomy and Solidarity: Deontological or Teleological Ethics, the Logic of Moral Development, and Cultural Traditions as Resources of Meaning

Since the 1980s, societal development and ethical debates have revealed that the hopeful assumption of simultaneous growth in personal "autonomy" and social "solidarity" has not materialized.[28] The endpoints of both Piaget's and Kohlberg's theories of moral development, however, presuppose the lived unity of both goals. The lower stages are judged in light of the ideal of a free, socially responsible, democratic subject whose autonomy is expressed by distinguishing universally binding rules from existing moral conventions. If the attainability of this combination has become doubtful today, the question is how the "*terminus ad quem* of successful development" can be conceptualized and what stages progress toward it. Taylor reminds us that "[c]oncepts of successful maturity are the basis for arguments of how we should live."[29] What type of obligation does this "should" stand for?

Recent ethical and political debates regarding what motivates and sustains self-determination toward solidarity instead of self-interest have rediscovered important distinctions–distinctions between a teleological and a deontological orientation in ethics, or between the goals of "authenticity" and "autonomy." As a result of these discussions, a number of mediating concepts have been proposed–for example, "strong evaluations" on what makes life worth living, cultural traditions as resources of meaning and motivation for normative ethics, and the element of "self-respect" that creates common ground between the good life and morality, according to Taylor and Ricoeur.

How can theories of moral-religious development be interpreted in the light of these categories? My thesis is that having been oblivious to the need to base their research on an explicitly philosophical anthropology and to the importance of the difference between the teleological and the deontological approaches, Piaget and Kohlberg misconstrued the logic of moral development. They failed to recognize inherent problems that have been "felt with a vengeance" since the development of their theories. If the *terminus a quo,* the first stage, cannot be regarded simply as egocentrism into which the perspective of interpersonal respect must be introduced from without, then the logic of development must be more complex.[30] The construal of the *terminus ad quem* is marked by distantiation from conventional morality. This amounts to a sanguine dismissal of normative traditions of the good and the right, which forces the theory to make an ill-prepared jump from Stage 5 to an heroic sixth stage–the moral agent who has it all (the standpoint of universal obligation, motivation, and resources of meaning) within him.

The rationalistic confidence in the self-motivating power of the moral agent and the disdain for "conventions" result in neglecting both the cultural and the personal sources of the good, such as traditions and moral communities, as well as "self-respect" and the "strong evaluations" mentioned above. The Enlightenment critiqued tradition and defined freedom as distantiation much more than critical reappropriation. This view of the progress of history from authoritarianism to liberty, however, is self-mutilating when, as Ricoeur points out, the Enlightenment itself has become a tradition and, moreover, one rooted in the Jewish and Christian understanding of history as salvation history. In the following sections, I have examined (2.1) the relationship between teleological and deontological elements, (2.2) the logic of moral development, and (2.3) the mediating role of cultural traditions as resources of meaning.

2.1 Teleological and Deontological Elements

Life-cycle theories originated by establishing developmental stages of operative intelligence. They were applied to the moral sphere, which was construed in a deontological framework and thereby oriented toward universalization as the criterion for the right. In a theory of moral judgment, this focus on normative ethics is expected. Fowler, however, moves from the level of moral judgments about hypothetical dilemmas to real life. The individual life stories of congregation members are taken seriously, and the question about how to conduct one's life moves to the foreground. In terms of ethical theory, this means that "teleological" goals of self-realization (in faith) enter the picture. Since it is not possible to flag any vision of the good as the last stage of development, in contrast to the deontological framework, the theory turns "soft."[31] Therefore, different images of maturity can be offered:

> In Moran's own vision neither development towards "autonomy" nor "the way up" can be the final word, but "the way inward" and the "communion" of all living creatures and life forms. This, however, turns out to be another normative image of a developmental goal. Therefore, it appears most appropriate to the current state of this discussion to remain open to various images of mature faith. Then the existing psychological images of a highest stage represent only one possible descriptive attempt.[32]

If this stance is not to be judged as a cop-out (as an option for noncommitment where a decision about the adequacy of different views would be needed), but rather accepted as an appropriately "nonjudgmental" attitude, it is because the framework has been switched from a universalistic moral orientation to a plurality of equally valid life goals. The plurality of visions regarding the religious dimensions of the flourishing life originates from within each individual striving for personal authenticity.

Even if Kohlberg's theory remains at the level of judging constructed dilemmas, are there tacit overlaps between morality and the good life? Despite the deontological conception of the final stage,[33] the need to distinguish between both ethical orientations—that is, neo-Kantian and neo-Aristotelian—could remain neglected in life-cycle theories. The first five stages could be valid for both the teleological and the deontological approach. Kohlberg's description of his Stage 2, "Right is serving one's own or other's needs and making fair deals in terms of concrete exchange,"[34] with its ability to distinguish between and recognize one's own and others' legitimate interests, fits both bills. This also is true of his Stages 3 and 4 at the conventional, Stage 4 at the transitional, and even Stage 5 at the principled and postconventional level. "Moral decisions are generated from rights, values, or principles that are (or could be) agreeable to all individuals composing or creating a society designed to have fair and beneficial practices." [35] Contributing to this kind of society also is in one's individual self-interest. The goals of self-realization and respect for others are not envisaged as conflicting. This is evident from the parallel concern to "protect their own rights and the rights of others," and from the construal of the "social contract" one has made and the friendships one has entered into as equally free and self-motivated decisions. It is further evident from the fact that the principle of universalization appears in its utilitarian form as the "rational calculation of overall utility: 'the greatest good for the greatest number.'" [36] Therefore, moral subjects at Stage 5 must believe that their own individual happiness and that of others do not conflict.

It is only at Stage 6 that the moral agent expresses an ethical principle as a naked obligation without any trade-off. "This stage assumes guidance by universal ethical principles that all humanity should follow...The perspective is that of any rational individual recognizing the nature of morality or the basic moral premise of respect for other persons as ends, not means." [37] Here, a switch has taken place: from inclination and enlightened self-interest as sufficient motivation to accepting principles that respect the rights of others as binding, to a new self-determination as a "rational individual." For the sake of her rationality, specified as the ability to "recognize the nature of morality," the moral subject will be ready to sacrifice goals of mere self-realization if they conflict with the needs of others or if they use human beings as means to another end. It is only here that a possible conflict between "virtue" and "happiness" comes into view. In Stage 5, "a rational individual aware of values and rights prior to social attachments and contracts...integrates perspectives by formal mechanisms of agreement, contract, objective impartiality and due process." In contrast to Stage 6, the main conflict occurs between "the moral...and the legal point of view," rather than between desires of personal self-fulfillment and the demands of morality.

2.2 The Logic of Moral Development

Once this divergence is admitted and not too quickly bypassed by an appeal to the "rationality" of the self that suddenly constitutes its exhaustive definition, one has to choose between alternative conceptions of morality–intrinsic or extrinsic.

> The point under dispute is whether normative claims with moral import arise out of designs of identity (*Identitätsentwürfen*), thus regarding the perspective of the flourishing of one's life as coinciding with the moral perspective in the stricter sense (intrinsic conception), or whether its difference to the subjective perspective of happiness

and striving is inevitable and only to be reconciled subsequently (*sekundär*) by integrating the moral perspective into one's existential conduct of life (extrinsic conception).[38]

How one answers this question determines how one will construct the logic of development. Taylor's approach assumes a basic harmony and continuity between personal striving for a flourishing life and the moral imperative for equal rights and justice for all. He therefore does not envision a radical antinomy between happiness and virtue, as does Kant. The mediating categories of "strong evaluations" and "self-respect" do not have to bridge a total abyss between self-realization and morality. The human person is oriented toward the good, at least in the subjective sense. This good, teleological insofar as it forms the goal of one's self-project, supplies the motivational force for distinguishing between expendable short-term and essential long-term fulfillment, and for sacrificing the former in order to achieve an identity congruent with one's "strong evaluations."

Yet, it is exactly with regard to these "strong evaluations" that a problem arises representative of Taylor's entire analysis of ethical subjectivity–that is, the lack of clarity on whether they are subjectively or universally morally binding and whether they refer to moral or nonmoral goods.[39] According to Hille Haker, this ambiguity obfuscates "the tension-filled back and forth movement (*spannungsgeladenes Wechselspiel*) between individual self-realization and subjective obligation on the one hand, and an intersubjective obligation that can be argued for, on the other hand." In some passages, this tension is one-sidedly resolved in favor of self-realization.[40] Haker's analysis further criticizes Taylor's for failing to distinguish clearly between both perspectives, thereby resulting in an insufficient concept of free recognition and making it impossible to draw the normative conclusions needed for a theory of justice.[41]

> [The] normative claim to recognize others arises from the need for a value perspective in order to develop individual identity which ultimately needs a social mediation and a moral sphere of validity...In the final analysis, the normative claim does not go beyond the psychological insight that a conception of self cannot succeed if recognition by others is lacking...This justification is too weak to be able to serve as a foundation of morality.[42]

This basic weakness of Taylor's conception can be explained by the "lack of a sufficient methodological distinction between the hermeneutical and the normative levels of ethics."[43] Positively, however, he unites several features that are important for any stage theory of moral development: (1) a "comparative model of biographical learning"; (2) a "cognitive moral theory without leaving the hermeneutical frame of reference"; and (3) an illustration of how the "tension between integration and rupture, continuity and discontinuity, unity and fragmentation of the individual life are the motor of the dynamics of development."[44]

Some of Taylor's weaknesses can be remedied by Ricoeur. Ricoeur delineates the limit between the two types of ethical orientation much more precisely. The recognition of the reality of evil necessitates the move from the level of striving to the level of normative ethics. The reason for returning to the ethics of striving on the third level is similar to Taylor's—that is, "to give the point of the rules" for the second level in instances of conflicting norms. Although Ricoeur places the "ethical intention as *aiming at the 'good life' with and for others, in just institutions*"[45] at the first level of orientation toward a flourishing life, his approach is extrinsic. The "sieve of the norm,"[46] through which the first-level orientations must pass, is an independent forum. Morality is not simply an extension of the good life. The question of motivation for moral development that remained unanswerable in Kohlberg is resolved by the notion of "self-respect." Without this bridging category, the "recognition of moral claims practically can not be mediated with the concept of one's personal conduct of life."[47]

According to Ricoeur, the logic of development does not begin from a self-centered first stage and then proceed gradually toward a commitment to universal justice. Rather, it has self- and other-related aspects at every stage. Ricoeur and Gilligan both accord great significance to "solicitude" or "care" for the other. Ricoeur links this to "equality" and "justice" at the societal level:

> *Equality...is to life in institutions what solicitude is to interpersonal relations.* Solicitude provides to the self another who is a face...Equality provides to the self another who is an *each*...[T]he sense of justice takes nothing away from solicitude; the sense of justice presupposes it, to the extent that it holds persons to be irreplaceable. Justice in turn adds to solicitude, to the extent that the field of application of equality is all humanity.[48]

In contrast, Gilligan introduces "care," instead of "justice," as an alternative realization of Stage 6. Its inscription into a purely deontological sixth stage is misleading, however. It makes much more sense to understand "care" in Ricoeur's and Taylor's frameworks, which mediate between spontaneous striving and a moral obligation accepted as one's ideal of self-respect.

Do the "stages of faith" follow the extrinsic or the intrinsic model? Is there continuity or conflict between the good life, morality, and faith? Overall, Fowler's depiction is one of continuity. The tensions held together at the sixth stage of "conjunctive" faith are explained as being, for example, old and young, well-meaning and destructive, or relating to the immanence and transcendence of God.[49] Even the "conversion" featured at this sixth stage is explained in terms of regaining the believer's designation as a partner of God. Fowler aims at the

> integration of development in faith, as illumined in stage theory, with conversion, understood as the disjunctive and redirecting encounter with God's grace as a liberating expression of God as the power of the future..."Conversion means a realignment of our affections, the

restructuring of our virtues, and the growth in lucidity and power of our partnership with God's work in the world."[50]

Perhaps Fowler is appealing implicitly to a Christian sense of self-respect. Yet there is no explicit recognition of a possible conflict between morality and the quest for self-fulfillment, a recognition that would necessitate the development of categories to bridge the gap, as does "self-respect."

At Stage 7, discontinuity is expressed most clearly, even if it is still portrayed as "the radical completion of a process of decentration from self that we have been tracing throughout the sequence of stages."[51] The description of "kenosis,"[52] where "the self is no longer the prime reference point from which the knowing and valuing of faith are carried out" but is itself "relinquished as epistemological and axiological center,"[53] is similar to Emmanuel Levinas's ethics of a decentered selfhood. While Levinas's philosophical model has inspired contemporary theology and ethics, particularly Ricoeur's interpretation of the "self as another," its insertion into Fowler's final stage is problematic. It has not been formed by the anthropology implied in former stages. The fact that "universalizing faith" rarely is achieved, of course, could be interpreted as an exceptional calling that ought not to be included in the regular stage sequence. Yet even if there is a stage marked by prophet-like experiences of vocation, Fowler's theological explanation of such "extraordinary openings that come occasionally with 'saving grace'" by "the initiatives of the Transcendent of Being, of God, or of Spirit"[54] is unsatisfactory. The possibility for achieving each stage should be contained and accounted for in the basic anthropology and not attained by a leap from psychological considerations into steep theological assumptions that appear fideistic due to their lack of antecedents.

Similarly, Taylor's and Ricoeur's analyses of moral identity feature a move away from egocentrism, but they honor as legitimate one's own conception and striving for a flourishing life. They emphasize the

> interrelationship between self-respect, the good life and morality insofar as the ideals of the good life have to satisfy the moral demands of universal reciprocal respect. The insight into this connection is founded on self-respect that is a necessary condition (*unerläßlich*) for forming and maintaining identity. From this link strong evaluations or ideals both in the individual and political-ethical realms arise.[55]

The attention they give to the supporting and motivating force of cultural traditions can play a corrective role in relationship to the bias against "convention" that Piaget and Kohlberg share with neo-Kantian philosophers such as Habermas.

2.3 The Role of Cultural Traditions as Resources of Meaning

An aspect of communitarianism's well-known critique of liberalism is that it does not account for the historical mediation of its principles and procedures.

In the name of abstract reason, they are proposed as universals. Even if liberalism correctly points out the difference between origin and validity, and even changes the status of its approach, as John Rawls did between "A Theory of Justice" and "Political Liberalism," they do not dwell on questions of motivation, socialization, and resources of meaning for normative ethics in the same manner as communitarians. Taylor's catchphrase "High standards need strong sources"[56] is exemplified by the connection between the Jewish and Christian religious traditions and the norm "equal dignity of every human being." The purpose of his genealogical project on the values and norms of modernity is to uncover the silted sources of this view of humanity within its originating theistic framework(s). Taylor illustrates the difference it makes in one's perception and moral motivation as to whether the human person is connected ontologically to God's affirmation of creation, "And God saw that it was good (Genesis 1),"[57] or whether she must impose her own self-made structures of meaning on a questionable world.

Ricoeur's critique of the jaded view of tradition in some neo-Kantian accounts, such as Jürgen Habermas's account, is more immanent. It questions the internal presuppositions of these evaluations—for example, the interpretation of "convention." Convention holds the place attributed to "inclination" by Kant, something in need of purification:

> I attribute the rigorousness of the argumentation to an interpretation of modernity almost exclusively in terms of breaking with a past thought to be frozen in traditions subservient to the principle of authority and so, by principle, out of the reach of public discussion. This explains why, in an ethics of argumentation, convention comes to occupy the place held by inclination in Kant. In this manner, the ethics of argumentation contributes to the impasse of a sterile opposition between a universalism at least as procedural as that of Rawls and Dworkin and a "cultural" relativism that places itself outside the field of discussion.[58]

One consequence he notes as "amusing" is that Habermas, following Kohlberg, regards the golden rule as belonging to the stage of convention:

> In this regard, the recourse to L. Kohlberg's model of developmental psychosociology reinforces the antinomy between argumentation and convention, to the extent that the scale of development is marked by preconventional, conventional, and postconventional stages. Thus it is amusing to observe that, following this model, the Golden Rule belongs to the conventional model and the rule of justice does not reach the higher level of the postconventional stage.[59]

Ricoeur's second point is "communitarian" or hermeneutical in that it reveals the inescapability of tradition. If the Enlightenment itself is a tradition, then the concept must be differentiated, and its principal opposition to self-reflection and self-determination must be questioned.

Elsewhere, I suggested distinguishing three uses of the word "tradition": the *style* of traditionality, innovation being one of its somewhat antagonistic components; the *traditions* of a people, a culture, a community, which can be living or dead; and the *Tradition,* as an antiargumentative authority. It is only in the last sense that the antitraditionalist crusade of the ethics of argumentation is acceptable. We touch here, as in connection with the idea of convention, on a sensitive point of the ethics of argumentation, namely its tendency to overevaluate the break of modernity, to confirm secularization not only as a fact but as a value, to the point of excluding from the field of discussion, either tacitly or openly, anyone who does not accept as a prior given the Nietzschean profession of the "death of God."[60]

In contrast to following "Habermas' continually pejorative use of the idea of tradition, following his long-standing confrontation with Gadamer,"[61] the task is to distinguish between traditions that negate and that rescue freedom. Ultimately, what is at stake is the link between tradition and utopia as represented in Habermas's ideal of repression-free communication. Since the transcendental object has been deconstructed, Ricoeur inquires about the basis and starting point for the critique of ideology:

[F]rom where do you speak when you appeal to *Selbstreflexion,* if it is not from the place that you yourself have denounced as a non-place, the non-place of the transcendental subject? It is indeed from the basis of a tradition that you speak...*Aufklärung...*is a tradition nonetheless, the tradition of emancipation rather than that of recollection. Critique is also a tradition. I would even say, it plunges into the most impressive tradition, that of liberating acts, of the Exodus and the Resurrection...[N]othing is more deceptive than the alleged antinomy between an ontology of prior understanding and an eschatology of freedom...As if it were necessary to choose between reminiscence and hope![62]

By questioning the liberal views of "convention" and tradition, Ricoeur shows that the alleged alternative between tradition and modernity cannot account for important elements of individual and political life—for example, the narrative generation of continuity in the identity of individuals and communities, and the connection between remembering and forgetting, including its political dimension. In an age marked by individualization, the discontinuation of traditions, and immediate exposure to the market, transforming the orientation toward autonomy into a "postconventional identity" is counterintuitive.

If the double orientation toward autonomy and solidarity is not to remain a counterfactual ideal, traditions and institutions that are able to create the conditions for their realization must be identified. Francis Schüssler Fiorenza has highlighted churches' potential to become "communities of public discourse," because they incorporate normative traditions of both the good and the right. While there are other such communities–for example, universities–he suggests the following:

> [C]hurches have a special role insofar as religious communities have at their core religious traditions that bring to the fore normative traditions not only of the good life, but also of justice. As religious institutions and communities, they also provide a locus for the discussion of the affective and expressive spheres of human life. In this regard the church keeps alive the utopian dimension that has been central to critical theory.[63]

The need to connect deontological morality, the justification of the "right," to subjective goals of flourishing–that is, a teleological ethics of (justified) desire–is fulfilled in a religious tradition that bases its moral demands of discipleship on the redemptive experience of God's prior and unconditional love in Jesus Christ. Differences in religious and moral conceptions of the human self will be explored now in conclusion.

3. Concepts of the Self

Three short remarks are sufficient at this point: (1) the need to distinguish between two different aspects of the self, (2) the programmatic understanding of identity as "narrative," and (3) the relationship between moral and religious identity.

Fowler's psychological concept of the self employed in his empirical research needs philosophical explication. Notions he presupposes, such as continuity, distantiation, and reflexivity, need to be anchored in a philosophical anthropology. Ricoeur's theory of the self with the distinction between *idem* and *ipse* is a philosophical framework that provides the necessary categories to interpret the results of Fowler's empirical research. These two aspects of the self capture both the given temporal continuity of a person's bodily existence and the task of creating an ongoing notion of the self in its identity despite changes over time. Without this distinction and the ability to reflect on the self in its two aspects, the individual subject could not grasp as her own all the discontinuities, changes, and transformations that are nevertheless stages of "development." This capacity presupposed by life cycle theory needs to be clarified by distinctions such as *idem* and *ipse* in Ricoeur's hermeneutical framework, or by distinctions between transcendental and empirical, formal and concrete freedom, as in transcendental anthropologies.

If "the stability of an individual identity is the presupposition of moral competence,"[64] then we must consider seriously the manner in which identity is constructed. Due to our temporality, this construction occurs solely in a "narrative" form. According to Ricoeur, the "temporal dimension of human life binds the self-reflection of the self in the manner of her life story to the form of narrative."[65] This story may include a religious dimension.

On the one hand, the compatibility of moral and religious attitudes to life should be evident. On the other, a significant difference between these attitudes is whether morality becomes the defining feature of human personhood, or whether "the human person's greatest distinction is his/her need for redemption," as insisted by Søren Kierkegaard and Schleiermacher. The demoralizing effect of moralizing is overcome by the individual's insight into her need and capacity for redemption.

I question whether Fowler distinguishes sufficiently between the deontological and the teleological understandings of the moral life, and whether their relationship to faith is one of continuity or conflict. Instead of simple continuity, their connection should be conceived as a historically rooted interrelation. F. Schüssler Fiorenza reveals that the link between "justice," autonomy, and solidarity is not automatic. This link was forged historically via faith formation in which the ethics of obligation ("justice") were joined to individual and communal hopes for a fulfilled life in light of the promise of salvation.

> Whereas justice deals with the equal freedom of individual persons, solidarity relates to the common welfare of consociates as well as the integrity of common life...The interrelation among the notions of equal rights, solidarity, and common welfare is not simply a formal logical or ethical interrelation, but it is an interrelation historically rooted in a religious tradition and history with their vision of the individual's value in relation to a community and to God.[66]

If there is no natural but only a historically mediated connection, then the stages of moral and religious development have to be reconstructed in a theological ethical framework that distinguishes the levels of desire, vision, self-project (teleological), and obligation (deontological). Further, the framework for the stages of moral development must include the limit questions of their conflict, which Kant, for one, expressed in the antinomy of practical reason. In a theological perspective of hope permitted and required, on a subjective level, by Kant, two more dimensions emerge: (1) what human beings are enabled to do (*Können*) by being redeemed, and (2) what only God can fulfill for them.[67] The *Ethik des Könnens* (Dietmar Mieth) encompasses the sheer imperative of the "ought." And where even the best of human ability reaches the limits of finitude, divine agency fulfills its intentions. This, at last, could be the place to speak of "synergy with the spirit."[68]

Notes

[1]James W. Fowler, *Becoming Adult, Becoming Christian* (San Francisco: Harper & Row, 1984), 20.

[2]See Dietmar Mieth, *Moral und Erfahrung. Bd. 1, Beiträge zur theologisch-ethischen Hermeneutik* (Freiburg i.Ue./Freiburg i.Br: Universitätsverlag/Herder, 1977), 6.

[3]Fowler, *Becoming Adult*, 37–47.

[4]James W. Fowler, "Introduction," in *Stages of Faith and Religious Development: Implications for Church, Education, and Society*, ed. James W. Fowler, Karl Ernst Nipkow, and Friedrich Schweitzer (New York: Crossroad, 1991), 9.

[5]See Karl Ernst Nipkow, "Stage Theories of Faith Development as a Challenge to Religious Education and Practical Theology," in *Stages of Faith,* ed. Fowler, Nipkow, and Schweitzer, 82–98, esp. 90–96.

[6]Ibid., 92, quoting James W. Fowler, *Faith Development and Pastoral Care* (Philadelphia: Fortress Press, 1987), 80.

[7]Ibid., 93.

[8]Fowler, "Introduction," 8.

[9]Fowler, *Becoming Adult,* 74.

[10]See Thomas Pröpper, *Erlösungsglaube und Freiheitsgeschichte,* 2d ed. (München: Kösel, 1988), 272.

[11]Fowler, "Introduction," 9.

[12]Ibid., 7.

[13]Ibid., 33.

[14]See Jacques Dupuis, *Toward a Christian Theology of Religious Pluralism* (Maryknoll, N. Y.: Orbis Books, 1997).

[15]Fowler, "Introduction," 30.

[16]Ibid., 8.

[17]Charles Taylor, "What Is Involved in Genetic Psychology?" in *Philosophical Papers 1, Human Agency and Language* (Cambridge: Cambridge University Press, 1985), 139–63, quotation from 157.

[18]Ibid., 157–60.

[19]Ibid., 160.

[20]Ibid., 161.

[21]Ursula Peukert, *Interaktive Kompetenz und Identität* (Düsseldorf: Patmos, 1979), 71–75.

[22]Friedrich Schweitzer, "Developmental Views of the Religion of the Child: Historical Antecedents," in *Stages of Faith,* ed. Fowler, Nipkow, and Schweitzer, 67–81, quotation from 79.

[23]Peukert, *Interaktive Kompetenz,* 127–43.

[24]Ibid., 141.

[25]Hans Krämer, *Integrative Ethik* (Frankfurt: Suhrkamp, 1992).

[26]Charles Taylor, *Sources of the Self: The Making of Modern Identity* (Cambridge: Cambridge University Press, 1989), 508.

[27]Ibid., 509.

[28]When Habermas insists that "justice" and "solidarity" are not just "complementary moments but rather two aspects of the same matter," it is stated in the mode of a postulate: "Justice understood in a deontological way demands as its other solidarity" ("Gerechtigkeit und Solidarität. zur Diskussion über 'Stufe 6'," in *Erläuterungen zur Diskursethik* [Frankfurt: Suhrkamp, 1991], 70). But what makes this solidarity possible and real? The potential for solidarity arising from shared traditions cannot be tapped into, since for him, such particular traditions need to be overcome toward a posttraditional identity, a universal perspective as life-form. And as to the motivation for adopting the moral standpoint of justice "even when what is morally required conflicts with their interests," the question is posed but then given short shrift: Questions of motivation do not belong to moral theory; it is up to processes of socialization to supply motivational strength (*Justification and Application,* trans. Ciaran Cronin [Cambridge: Massachusetts Institute of Technology Press, 1993], 127–28). At this stage, as Haker astutely remarks, particular traditions have to be reintegrated because morality is, as Habermas recognizes, in need of supporting life-forms (*entgegenkommende Lebensformen*) (Hille Haker, *Moralische Identität* [Tübingen: Francke, 1999], 67–68). What is shown, therefore, is the relevance of the existence of both justice and solidarity, but not their reality. Thus, the problems of the realizability of morality and its resources remain.

[29]Taylor, "Genetic Psychology?" 162.

[30]See, for example, Colwyn Trewarthen's research into the development of infant subjectivity and relationality: "Communication and Cooperation in Early Infancy: A Description of Primary Intersubjectivity," in *Before Speech: The Beginning of Human Communication,* ed. M. Bullowa (London: Cambridge University Press, 1979), 321–47; idem, "The Concept and Foundation of Infant Intersubjectivity," in *Intersubjective Communication and Emotion in Early Ontogeny* (Cambridge: Cambridge University Press, 1998), 15–46.

[31]See F. Clark Power's critique, "Hard versus Soft Stages of Faith and Religious Development: A Piagetian Critique," in *Stages of Faith,* ed. Fowler, Nipkow, and Schweitzer, 116–29.

[32]Fowler, "Introduction," 9.

[33]Lawrence Kohlberg's later distinction between two aspects of his Stage 6, "justice" and "benevolence"–that is, care for the well-being of the concrete other–which he developed in

response to Carol Gilligan and other critics, still remains at the deontological level. See Habermas, *Erläuterungen zur Diskursethik,* 63.

[34]Lawrence Kohlberg, *The Philosophy of Moral Development: Moral Stages and the Idea of Justice* (San Francisco: Harper & Row, 1981), 409.

[35]Ibid., 412.

[36]Ibid.

[37]Ibid.

[38]Haker, *Moralische Identität,* 153.

[39]Ibid., 98 n. 131.

[40]Ibid.

[41]Ibid., 96 n. 126.

[42]Ibid., 78, 92, 96 n. 126.

[43]Ibid., 96 n. 126.

[44]Ibid., 95.

[45]Paul Ricoeur, *Oneself as Another* (Chicago: University of Chicago Press, 1992), 172.

[46]Ibid., 170.

[47]Haker, *Moralische Identität,* 78.

[48]Ricoeur, *Oneself as Another,* 202.

[49]See James W. Fowler, *Faith Development and Pastoral Care* (Philadelphia: Fortress Press, 1987), 71–74.

[50]Fowler,"Introduction," 28–29, with a quote from Fowler, *Becoming Adult,* 140.

[51]Fowler, *Faith Development and Pastoral Care,* 75.

[52]Ibid., 76.

[53]Ibid., 75.

[54]Fowler, *Becoming Adult,* 73–75.

[55]Haker, *Moralische Identität,* 273.

[56]Taylor, *Sources of the Self,* 516.

[57]Ibid., 515.

[58]Ricoeur, *Oneself as Another,* 286.

[59]Ibid., 286 n. 78.

[60]Ibid., 287 n. 79.

[61]Ibid., 286.

[62]Paul Ricoeur, *Hermeneutics and the Human Sciences,* ed. and trans. by John B. Thompson (Cambridge: Cambridge University Press, 1981), 99–100.

[63]Francis Schüssler Fiorenza, "The Church as a Community of Interpretation: Political Theology between Discourse Ethics and Hermeneutical Reconstruction," in *Habermas, Modernity and Public Theology,* ed. D. Browning and F. Schüssler Fiorenza (New York: Crossroad, 1992), 66–91, quotation from 87.

[64]Haker, *Moralische Identität,* 273.

[65]Ibid., 76.

[66]Francis Schüssler Fiorenza, "The Works of Mercy: Theological Perspectives," in *The Works of Mercy,* ed. F. Eigo (Philadelphia: Villanova Press, 1992), 31–71, quotation from 60.

[67]See Maureen Junker-Kenny, "Ethik und Praxis," in *Interdisziplinäre Ethik. Grundlagen, Methoden, Bereiche* (Festschrift Dietmar Mieth), ed. A. Holderegger, J. P. Wils (Freiburg i. Ue.: Universitätsverlag, 2001), 185–212.

[68]See Fowler, *Becoming Adult,* 74.

5

H. Richard Niebuhr and Fowler's Evolution as a Theologian

GORDON MIKOSKI

> Nearly all the wisdom we possess, that is to say, true and sound wisdom, consists of two parts: the knowledge of God and of ourselves. But, while joined by many bonds, which one precedes and brings forth the other is not easy to discern.[1]

This opening sentence of Calvin's monumental *Institutes of the Christian Religion* seems a good place to begin a consideration of the influence of H. Richard Niebuhr on the thought of James W. Fowler. Both of these thinkers would celebrate the conviction to which Calvin gave classic expression: namely, that there can be no fundamental separation of theological reflection from anthropological reflection.[2] They would agree with Calvin that the conception of God and the conception of the self are mutually constituting. To be sure, Niebuhr and Fowler, though, would further nuance Calvin's statement by subdividing knowledge of self into the knowledge of self and the knowledge of the neighbor or neighbors.[3] The larger point that we must keep clearly in view is that, in the Niebuhr-Fowler trajectory, theological reflections always have implications for human self-understanding and practice, even if such implications are implicit and indirect. Likewise, for both Niebuhr and Fowler, knowledge of all things human is always incomplete if it does not take into account the often implicit theological dimensions of the various renderings of human experience.[4] While both Niebuhr and Fowler are conversant with speculative philosophical and theological discourse, their primary constructive energies have been directed toward the dual task of interpreting and changing both church and society in the direction of the reign of God.

In this chapter, we will examine only one side of the complex divine-human correlation operative in the Niebuhr-Fowler synthesis: namely, the way in which the doctrine of God impacts the normative constitution of the self. Along these lines, it will be important for us to bear in mind Elizabeth Johnson's assertion in her book *She Who Is* that "the symbol of God functions."[5]

This means that the way in which the mystery of God is conceived has direct bearing on the conceptualization of selves and communities. The way in which the knowledge of God is rendered has enormous personal, communal, and political implications.

Niebuhr's doctrine of God shines through much of James Fowler's work. Inasmuch as this is the case, we must begin with a consideration of Niebuhr's doctrine of God and the way in which it impacted his approach to anthropology if we want to gain insight into Fowler's constructive theological anthropology. Following a brief consideration of Niebuhr's doctrine of God and the way in which it functions anthropologically, we will turn in the middle section of this chapter to a look at some of the ways in which Fowler has appropriated and modified the Niebuhrian approach to the doctrine of God as it functions in the conceptualization of selfhood in community. The third and final section will offer some suggestions whereby the promise of the divine-human correlation in both Niebuhr and Fowler might be advanced and, in some sense, fulfilled within the framework supplied by a radically relational trinitarian doctrine of God.

1. H. Richard Niebuhr's Doctrine of God and Its Function in His Anthropology

Niebuhr's doctrine of God is complicated and not entirely consistent across the body of his work. One can detect at least three strata or moments in his thought on the doctrine of God. These aspects of his doctrine of God are not simply chronological phases, each one superceding the previous. Rather, one can detect multiple aspects of his doctrine of God functioning together at the same time, often in the same book.

One aspect of Niebuhr's doctrine of God has much in common with classical Neoplatonist notions of the One who is utterly transcendent. In this view, all things in the cosmos are what they are by virtue of their relation to and dependency on this undifferentiated One. This One is beyond all categories of being and existence. It is the "One beyond the many."[6] It is the supremely unconditioned that conditions everything else.

Early on, Niebuhr grew uncomfortable with this particular notion of radical transcendence.[7] When he compared this conception of the radically transcendent One with the God of the Bible, Niebuhr noticed that the latter was not passive.[8] In fact, the one God of the Bible is active–*the* active force– in all of history. The biblical One is the creator and the governor of all things. This God is the biblical "One beyond the many" lesser gods of polytheism and henotheism. Only this One is ultimate. Further, this one God revealed "himself" to Moses and the prophets. Niebuhr found the fullest revelation of this conception of radical monotheism in Jesus. Jesus functioned for Niebuhr as the authoritative pointer to the One through the example of his life and the content of his teachings.

In good neo-Kantian[9] fashion, Niebuhr was very wary of going too far into the murky and unreliable realm of the metaphysical; instead, his doctrine of God was oriented to the ethical. Niebuhr quite clearly and consistently expressed a definite preference for practical reason over against the undisciplined claims of speculative reason. In keeping with this emphasis on the primacy of practical reason, Niebuhr characteristically equated the ontological with the axiological in his doctrine of God: That is, he routinely emphasized the inherent and indissoluble connection between being and value.

Though we might be tempted to argue that Niebuhr was merely an undifferentiated monotheist in his doctrine of God, we can see that Niebuhr was actually something of a binitarian. He seemed willing to affirm at several points that Jesus was not only human but also divine. Niebuhr was willing to affirm the two-natures christology of Chalcedon,[10] though reframed in the mode of neo-Kantian concerns about historicity. Jesus was both man-in-God and God-in-man. In the posthumously published *Faith on Earth,* Niebuhr writes:

> The three persons who are involved in the community of faith are Father, Son and this poor human self which has by creation and re-demption been lifted into the unbelievable privilege of communion with the Father and Son and with all those other persons into whom God has breathed his Spirit...We are thus led to a kind of binitarian formula; God is Father and Son in two persons.[11]

We will return to the complicated issue of the Spirit in Niebuhr's thought in a moment. For now, let us observe that, at points, Niebuhr moved beyond the solitary Subject to a form of Augustinian-tinged binitarianism.[12] Niebuhr eventually reconciled his thought to the claims of scripture and tradition (especially the Council of Chalcedon) with respect to the divinity of Jesus.

It is a very interesting question as to whether or not Niebuhr's doctrine of God was actually trinitarian and, if so, to what extent. James Gustafson, in his introduction to *The Responsible Self,* asserted that Niebuhr was, in fact, trinitarian.[13] Likewise, Hans Frei, in an essay on Niebuhr's theology, discussed some of the unique features of his trinitarian approach to the doctrine of God.[14] But a close look at Niebuhr's writings raises questions about whether these judgments are completely warranted.

To be sure, Niebuhr made a number of references to the doctrine of the Trinity throughout his writings. He even once wrote a powerful diagnostic article on the three Unitarian tendencies in Christianity using the doctrine of the Trinity as a hermeneutical tool.[15] Niebuhr was dissatisfied with the christomonistic tendencies of emerging Barthianism and saw that the doctrine of the Trinity made possible an effective linkage between creation and culture with redemption and the church.[16] Niebuhr was familiar with the complexities of trinitarian discourse and the challenge to rethink it in terms that would make sense to modern thinkers.[17]

Even with a number of pithy trinitarian references sprinkled throughout Niebuhr's writings,[18] one is hard-pressed to argue conclusively that he was, in fact, fully trinitarian with respect to his doctrine of God. At most, one can say with certainty that he struggled at some length with the tension created by the witness of the tradition and his own theological commitments and experiences on the matter. For instance, Niebuhr had no effective or consistent way of speaking about the Holy Spirit.[19] He quite candidly stated that the Spirit is not a person in the same way that the Father and the Son were persons. In laudable honesty and struggle, Niebuhr wrote:

> We also say that in our life in faith we know that God is Spirit, that the Lord is Spirit, that the spirit in the human being proceeds from the Father and the Son, that the Spirit proceeds from the Father and the Son, that the Spirit which proceeds from the Father and the Son is interpersonal reality. We can attach great significance to the statement that the Spirit is consubstantial with Father and Son. *What we cannot say for ourselves is the Spirit is not the Father, that he is not the Son, and that he is equal to Father and Son—as a power or a person like them but distinct from them.* But those of us who speak in this fashion are not in a position to deny that the classic formulation is true. We can believe it; it is not an expression of our trust in God, however, and not an oath of loyalty to him but only an expression of our lower trust, our secondary but real loyalty to the community of faith which has so expressed its trust in God and so made its vow of fidelity. I believe that there is a Holy Spirit.[20]

One can observe quite readily in this passage Niebuhr's struggle with what to do with the claims of church tradition about the Holy Spirit and, by extension, the doctrine of the Trinity. About the integrity and the depth of the struggle of this theologian with the doctrine of God as Trinity there can be no doubt. What is in doubt, however, is whether his doctrine of God was, in the end, fully trinitarian. Though he called for a rethinking of the results of the classically formulated doctrine of the Trinity issuing forth from the councils of Nicaea (325 C.E.) and Constantinople (381 C.E.), he does not seem to have engaged in the task himself beyond some important beginnings. Perhaps the most that can be concluded with reasonable certainty is that Niebuhr's doctrine of God was tentatively or provisionally trinitarian.[21]

We must now turn to a brief consideration of the ways in which Niebuhr's doctrine of God functioned with respect to the constitution of human personhood or selfhood. The reader can discern a tension within Niebuhr's thought with regard to the correlation between the doctrine of God and the constitution of the self. One side of the tension is most clearly represented by his argument in *Radical Monotheism and Western Culture.* There, Niebuhr argued that the unity of God is the basis for the integration of the human self. Niebuhr argued persuasively that there is a fundamental correlation between the object of one's trust and loyalty and the constitution of the self. Niebuhr argued that functional polytheists lack any fundamental and deep-level integration of selfhood. Their lives are essentially fragmented and incoherent. It is only by means of trust in and loyalty to the one God beyond the many gods that one may achieve integration of personhood:

As revelation so considered means the event in which the ultimate unity is disclosed as personal or faithful, so the human response to such revelation is the development of integrated selfhood...Integration of the self in the presence of the First Person is not only an affair of the practical understanding of all events that happen to the self or its community. The elicited trust and loyalty of radical monotheism express themselves in the positive response to such events.[22]

The disclosure of God as unified Self becomes the basis upon which human beings move from disoriented confusion resultant from adherence to several centers of value or to one penultimate center of value toward a coherent and integrated pattern of theocentric life. The triadic nature of human faith that includes self, other/community, and a shared center of value finds its fulfillment in relation to the one living God witnessed to by the scriptures.

The marks of an integrated theocentric selfhood are the development of a sensibility in which all things that exist can be affirmed in their created goodness, openness to all living things, a stance of objective and committed relativism, and the commitment to engage in ongoing effort to transform all things in the direction of the reign of God. Encounter with the divine Self, in other words, leads to a life of permanent revolution or ongoing *metanoia* in which one moves by steps and degrees (one might even say "stages") toward fundamental resonance or alignment with the universal divine Subject. Jesus, as the one who brings God to humans and also the one who brings humans to God, is the exemplar of that life of faith.

The other side of the tension in Niebuhr's divine-human correlation can be seen in a consideration of the central theme of *The Responsible Self.* In this book, Niebuhr explores human selfhood in terms of radical relationality and responsiveness. In this work, the mature, faithful human being is less like an iron filing that is being aligned to the magnetism of divine sovereignty and is more like a flexible and interactive intersection of forces and intentionality in a web of relationality. The God who is revealed in the burning bush of Exodus 3 and in the example and teachings of Jesus engages in relationship with human beings. God is a "Thou" who enters into dialogue with each human "I." This dialogical relationality of the divine reality becomes for Niebuhr the foundation of a *homo dialogicus* anthropology[23] in which humans are flexibly responsive to the panoply of interactions with other selves.

In this posthumously published work, we can see Niebuhr's partial rejection and reworking of the Neoplatonic One in the direction of a biblically engaged and responsive "Thou" in its fullest expression. Here, the Absolute Subject is personal and is the guarantor of authentic human relationality on both the vertical and horizontal planes. But herein lies an enduring problem: The divine guarantor of radically relational anthropology is still the Absolute Subject of Enlightenment modernism. There is in this a kind of disconnect between the doctrine of God and the theological anthropology that issues from it. The radical relationality of the anthropology is continually, if subtly, undercut by its anchorage in a doctrine of God that, for all of its modifications in the direction of dialogue, is monarchical, male, and, finally, solitary.[24]

2. James W. Fowler's Appropriation of and Modifications to Niebuhr's Doctrine of God as It Is Brought to Bear on the Conceptuality of Human Selfhood

The above treatment of Niebuhr's doctrine of God and its relation to theological anthropology is not exhaustive. This is clearly seen when we turn to a consideration of the work of James W. Fowler. Fowler's doctoral dissertation focused on the interrelationship between the doctrine of God and anthropology in Niebuhr's work. In many ways, the central chapter of the dissertation is "Chapter 3: Radical Faith." A look at Fowler's interpretation of Niebuhr's correlation between the doctrine of God and theological anthropology in that section of the dissertation will prove useful in a consideration of the unfolding of Fowler's own constructive work across the past three decades. The central Niebuhrian themes that Fowler features in this chapter of his doctoral writing figure prominently throughout Fowler's subsequent works.

Fowler attempted in the "Radical Faith" chapter of the dissertation to make explicit what was implicit in Niebuhr's writings on the doctrine of God and its impact on theological anthropology.[25] Fowler's struggle to unlock the inner logic of his theological mentor's various writings yielded the central conviction of the sovereignty of God. According to Fowler, the sovereignty of God for Niebuhr was expressed in terms of three interrelated metaphors: namely, God the creator, God the governor, and God the redeemer-liberator. Fowler discerned that Niebuhr was profoundly influenced in his doctrine of God by Alfred North Whitehead's metaphorical description of the process of one's journey by stages into deeper relationship with God. Whitehead had argued that one moves from the conception of God as void, to God as enemy, to God as companion. Fowler's observation is that Niebuhr developed a similar cluster of metaphors, albeit more biblically based, which describe the changing aspects of our evolutionary and revolutionary experiences of the one God and of ourselves.

Fowler saw quite clearly that, for Niebuhr, the three root metaphors that depicted the one God's sovereign activity in the world implied three co-metaphors for the human creature. Humans were seen as partners with God in the work of creation, governance, and redemption-liberation. Actually, there are two versions of the three human co-metaphors: one set of co-metaphors that described the natural evolutionary development of human life, and a transformed or transfigured set that represents the three co-metaphors in light of the revolution brought about by the in-breaking of Jesus Christ into a person's and a community's life. Fowler's complex model renders explicitly what is implicit and unvarying in Niebuhr's mature thought:

> [This] suggests the direction of evolutionary development in the individual religious consciousness. And it depicts the dramatic

transformations in faith-knowing that issue from ongoing encounters with revelation event and revelational person. Despite the dangers of oversimplification and reification, this action model does seem to take us "inside" Niebuhr's thought and to put us in the midst of the tensions, polarities, and movement that give it its life and power.[26]

Fowler's understanding of the way in which the doctrine of God functions for theological anthropology in Niebuhr is expressed here in compressed and potent form. This complex model of three interrelated metaphors for the various aspects of the activities of the sovereign God and the attendant human co-metaphors (both in their evolutionary and in their revolutionary or conversionistic forms) will show up again and again at critical moments in the arguments of Fowler's subsequent works.[27] The *Ur*-ground of Fowler's deep indebtedness to Niebuhr's doctrine of God and the way that the doctrine of God impacts anthropology is to be found here. Faith development theory owes its origins to Fowler's attempt to bring Niebuhr's mature theological vision into constructive dialogue with the rich and textured accounts of human experience provided by Erik Erikson, Jean Piaget, and Lawrence Kohlberg. Another way to say this is that, in faith development theory, Fowler attempted to describe how persons might attain the theological vision of the reign of God found in Niebuhr's work in the course of their unfolding and potentially transformed lives.

We can see in the unfolding of Fowler's subsequent work two tendencies with regard to the doctrine of God. On the one hand, Fowler reaffirms, extends, and variously modifies the Niebuhrian conviction of the sovereignty of God as depicted in the previously mentioned three co-metaphors. From *Stages of Faith* to *Faithful Change,* the Niebuhrian doctrine of God shows up at crucial junctures and provides the normative impetus for Fowler's theological anthropology.

One of the most important modifications Fowler has made within the Niebuhrian framework pushes the doctrine of God a step beyond divine openness to dialogue with the human other. More than simply entering into Buberian "I-Thou" dialogue with humanity, in Fowler's view God now suffers with humanity. Especially in his more recent works, Fowler rejects any notion of a God who is unable to suffer with, and on behalf of, humanity. Fowler has further chipped away at the Absolute Subject of Enlightenment–inspired theology by insisting that God is not impassible. To love means to be open to suffering on behalf of the beloved. For Fowler, a God who is unable to suffer is a God who is both distant and unable to love. Worst of all, this kind of God would be incapable of meaningful personal relationships. Fowler pushes further than did Niebuhr in the direction of a radically relational doctrine of God.

On the other hand, we can also trace a trajectory of movement away from Niebuhr with regard to both pneumatology and the doctrine of the Trinity. With respect to the Spirit, Fowler appears to start out with the same theological reticence to talk about the Spirit as was found in Niebuhr. As his work unfolds, however, Fowler begins to talk more and more about the work of the Spirit. Fowler increasingly links human evolution and revolution with pneumatology. Curiously, there is an alternation in several of Fowler's texts between "spirit" and "Spirit" in reference to pneumatology.[28] While we would not want to overinterpret this inconsistency, it does seem to point to a certain incoherence with respect to pneumatology on Fowler's part. He does, to be sure, incorporate pneumatology into his discussions much more so than Niebuhr ever did; yet the reader is unclear at points as to Fowler's working conception of the Spirit. Upon reflection, it appears that, along the way, Fowler has gradually moved away from the neo-Kantian aversion to pneumatology in Troeltsch and Niebuhr and has appropriated dimensions of Hegelian pneumatology into his work.[29] Interestingly, in his more recent work, Fowler has discussed the praxis of God (a term for Niebuhr's sovereignty of God purged of its connotations of the Enlightenment male, executive Ego) in dialogue with the Hegelian pneumatology supplied by Peter Hodgson.[30] It seems that themes in Hegelian discourse provide Fowler with a richer and more meaningful way to talk about the presence of grace in both human evolution and revolution and in their linkage than was the case for Niebuhr. It appears to provide Fowler with a more flexible grammar for describing the nearness and immanence of the transcendent God in human life. Yet for all that, Fowler appears not to have finally resolved the crucial pneumatological question as to whether the Spirit is a force (cultural mood?) or a divine Person, the third member of the Trinity.

From a consideration of Fowler's pneumatology, we can easily move to an investigation of the role of the doctrine of the Trinity in his work. In general, it can be said that, while not always the dominant theme, the treatment of God as triune is at least a major subtheme in several of his works, including *Becoming Adult, Becoming Christian, Faith Development and Pastoral Care,* and *Weaving the New Creation.* In fact, in *Weaving the New Creation,* one might well argue that the doctrine of God as Trinity is the predominant theological theme.[31]

How does Fowler treat the doctrine of God as Trinity? With respect to the doctrine of the Trinity, one can trace a similar trajectory away from Niebuhr in Fowler's still-unfolding corpus. Early on, Fowler demonstrated that he was aware of and interested in working with a trinitarian doctrine of God. As early as *Becoming Adult, Becoming Christian,* Fowler writes: "And we learn in the primal fellowship of Being, we are dealing with an inner-trinitarian fellowship, a threeness in oneness that already represented a profound unity in differentiation."[32]

Here, it can be seen quite clearly that Fowler has made an attempt, via the work of Gabriel Fackre, to speak about Niebuhr's radical monotheism in a trinitarian key. Fowler goes on to say that it is the inner fellowship of the Trinity that makes possible human relationality and partnership. But almost immediately upon the heels of an interesting trinitarian discussion of the knowledge of God and of ourselves, Fowler returns to the theological grammar of Niebuhr's undifferentiated monarchical monotheism as depicted in the dissertation.[33]

The pattern of alternation between increasing explorations into the doctrine of the Trinity and continuing commitment to the metaphors of the providence of God identified in the dissertation can be traced through all of Fowler's writings up to the present. Perhaps it is most instructive to compare three of his most recent writings. *Weaving the New Creation* is perhaps Fowler's boldest and most sustained attempt to incorporate a thoroughgoing doctrine of God as Trinity into his work. He turns to another Niebuhrian, Sallie McFague, to help him further explore trinitarian territory. He also finds the theological poetry of Brian Wren to be of great help in appropriating key features of contemporary trinitarian discourse such as *perichoresis*. In his next book, *Faithful Change,* the treatment of the doctrine of God in trinitarian terms is simply and mystifyingly AWOL. Instead, Fowler has returned to a modified (that is, less male, rational, and distant) form of the Niebuhrian emphasis on the action of God in human life and history. But in a more recent unpublished paper entitled "How Can We Speak of the Providence of God?"[34] trinitarian language and concepts are ubiquitous. Here, we see perhaps Fowler's clearest attempt to reframe Niebuhrian themes in a trinitarian key:

> What we have been considering, however, is that the sovereign Godhead, that dynamic relational Trinity of Father, Son, and Holy Spirit, sets Himself the task of nurturing people and movements who can be partners in shaping and fulfilling the glory of God's divine vision. In doing so, God takes the risk—and keeps on taking the risks—of placing the fulfillment of the Divine dream, in significant part, in the hands of finite men and women. He entrusts partnership to finite churches and groups, and frequently to persons and organizations whom God trusts, not because they are church members of even Christians, but because they are able and they are accessible to the Spirit of God.[35]

It is clear here that Fowler has moved a step closer to integrating the powerful Niebuhrian thematics of the doctrine of God (as modified by Fowler) and theological anthropology into a trinitarian modality.

What are we to make of this interplay of Niebuhrian and trinitarian doctrines of God in Fowler's work? At one level, it might be argued that Fowler has simply attempted to laminate a veneer of trinitarian discourse onto the modified Absolute Subject view of God found in Niebuhr's work. At a deeper level, however, it seems that something else is taking place. There is something of a subterranean struggle occurring across the course of Fowler's work. It appears that he has been attempting in various ways to bring the compelling power of the Niebuhrian vision into a meaningful synthesis with the dynamism of recent trinitarian thought. Based on a careful attentiveness to the unfolding of his work thus far, we would have to conclude that this remains an unfulfilled vocation for Fowler. Based on the trend that began in *Becoming Adult, Becoming Christian* and includes the radical critique of appropriated Niebuhrian doctrine of God as found in *Faithful Change,*[36] it would be reasonable to expect that Fowler's next major work may well push further and sustain a deep appropriation of major trends in contemporary trinitarian theology. Perhaps Fowler will take up Niebuhr's challenge to do what he himself did not accomplish: namely, a rethinking of the doctrine of God as Trinity in terms that make sense in light of contemporary experience and thought.

We have already seen above how the Niebuhrian doctrine of God functions in Fowler's theological anthropology as a source of the cluster of metaphors for partnership with God in working toward the realization of the commonwealth of love and justice. A few more words of explication on the way in which the doctrine of God functions in Fowler's anthropology need to be said before we move to a consideration of possible ways to further the Niebuhr-Fowler synthesis in a thoroughly trinitarian key.

For Fowler, as for Niebuhr, faith is a human universal. Both thinkers affirm the long lines of Augustinianism, which stress that God has created human beings with an innate capacity and longing for God. Fowler appropriates the Niebuhrian insight that faith is not just a matter between the individual and the center of value and power. It is fundamentally a communal matter. That is, faith has a triadic, covenantal structure that includes the believer, the neighbor(s), and the shared center of trust and loyalty. As with Calvin, Fowler asserts not only that there is a *sensus divinitatum* within each person that can only finally be realized in a vital and rightly ordered relationship with the biblical God, but also that humans can direct their faith and loyalty to a seemingly inexhaustible array of penultimate goods along the way to that alone which satisfies the longing heart. Human faith has a teleological quality to it that ultimately points to the only One in whom our hearts may find their proper rest.

One of Fowler's doctoral students, Heinz Streib, noticed that Fowler used the language of faith when referring to universal human experience and the language of vocation with respect to the shape and character of the specifically Christian response to God's praxis in history.[37] Vocation for Fowler is the rubric that he habitually uses to describe the various interrelated aspects of human participation in God's activities in creation, governance, and redemption-liberation. In later works, Fowler has broadened his way of talking about vocation such that it is no longer focused only on the church and the church's engagement with public life, but it is instead a Christian perspective on the general human call of God to partnership toward the realization of the divine commonwealth. Because God has created, continues to be involved in governing, and is working for the transformation of the world, Fowler's anthropology is never strictly ecclesiological in scope; there is always a wider, public dimension to his thinking about the human vocation to partnership.

3. Toward a Trinitarian Reframing of the Niebuhr-Fowler Synthesis

If judging the worth of an enterprise by its fruits is in any way reliable, then it would have to be said that the respective contributions of Niebuhr and Fowler have been quite successful over time. Their work has born much creative fruit in theory and in practice. Their analytical concepts and creative contributions have become part of the working vocabulary of many, even of those who disagree with them on key points. Perhaps one of the greatest honors that can be paid to such thinkers is to take their work seriously enough to engage in constructive criticism of it. The critique offered here aims to do just that.

This chapter began with the assertion that both Niebuhr's and Fowler's constructive works hang on the correlation between the conception of the Divine and the conception of the human. It is this correlation that has made it possible to categorize their work as "theological ethics" or "practical theology," respectively. In the present discussion, we have limited our investigation to only one side of the correlation: namely, the ways in which the doctrine of God functions in the formulation of theological anthropology. We briefly treated the doctrine of God in Niebuhr's work and its impact on his understanding of theological anthropology. Following this, we embarked on an investigation of the ways in which Fowler both appropriated and modified the Niebuhrian inheritance with respect to the doctrine of God and its influence on theological anthropology. Some overall analysis of the Niebuhr-Fowler synthesis will now provide the basis for suggestions as to ways to bring this theological corpus into harmony with recent trinitarian thought.

Both Niebuhr and Fowler appropriated and struggled with the theological framework provided by nineteenth-century German liberal thought, particularly neo-Kantianism. Fowler chronicled in some detail in his doctoral dissertation the development of Niebuhr's doctrine of God from a kind of passive Neoplatonic monism to the active and responsive Father of Jesus Christ. The root metaphor that lay behind much of Niebuhr's doctrine of God was the Absolute Subject of German theology and philosophy of the nineteenth century.[38] To be sure, this framework was stretched and reformulated by Niebuhr to include an increasingly divine Jesus and a dialogical openness to the human person in community. Even with some modifications, however, it was still the Moral Monarch that carried the day in Niebuhr's doctrine of God.

We can detect a certain tension within Niebuhr's theological anthropology that is based on his doctrine of God. On the one hand, Niebuhr's conception of God as Supreme Self or Subject provided the model and the basis for the integration of human selfhood. The selfhood Niebuhr had in mind in *Radical Monotheism* looked a lot like the male, executive ego of the Enlightenment.[39] This self is well differentiated and autonomous, if theocentric.

On the other hand, Niebuhr was not satisfied with a God who was self-contained and uninterested. He embraced a conception of the Divine that was active and open. This God cared and was involved in human lives and human history. This was a "Thou" that corresponded to an "I." Similarly, Niebuhr's conception of humanity was also one of dialogical openness or responsiveness. In *The Responsible Self*, we see quite clearly a conception of humanity that is thoroughly relational in character. But the constitutional relationality is not simply that of one person with another person; no, it is one person in dialogue with a community of other persons and with the divine Person.

Fowler has tended to follow Niebuhr in the doctrine of God as Absolute Subject, yet he went further than Niebuhr in reframing and reshaping it. It is quite evident from a close reading of Fowler's works that while he begins within the contours of Niebuhr's doctrine of God, he moves increasingly toward an understanding of God that is more radically relational and less wedded to the assumptions of God as Absolute Subject. Fowler replaces Niebuhr's "providence of God," with all of its connotations of distant monarchy, with "the praxis of God," which allows for an engaged and passible God. We increasingly have the sense that in his more recent discussions of the suffering of God and the relational openness and responsiveness of God to human persons, he is only a half-step away from the social doctrine of the Trinity that is most often associated with Jürgen Moltmann.[40] In fact, Fowler has made various forays into the trinitarian thicket in his writings, in the classroom, and in recent conversations. He is likely in the future to return to the challenge of updating his Niebuhrian commitments by further reworking his doctrine of God in a trinitarian direction.

Fowler's theological anthropology echoes Niebuhr's evolutionary and revolutionary experience with God conceived of as partnership in the actions of God in creation, governance, and redemption-liberation. All people are, in a sense, "hard-wired" for triadic faith, and all are called by the One beyond the many to participate in the transformation of church and society in the direction of the commonwealth of love and justice. Though Fowler's anthropology is thoroughly responsive and responsible, it has not been decisively grounded in or derived from a doctrine of God that is radically relational. To the extent that this is true, there is a certain internal tension in Fowler's work, as with Niebuhr's, in the correlation between the knowledge of God and the knowledge of ourselves as human.

We might well ask ourselves at this point what difference it makes to ground theological anthropology in a thoroughgoing doctrine of God as Trinity versus a doctrine of God derived from the Absolute Subject. Jürgen Moltmann is very helpful to us at this point. In his highly influential work *The Trinity and the Kingdom,* Moltmann draws our attention to the argument of Erik Petersen that the doctrine of God as Absolute Subject or undifferentiated Moral Monarch leads inexorably to the justification of oppressive hierarchies in church and state.[41] In radical contrast, Petersen (and Moltmann) argues that a relational doctrine of God as Trinity leads to an anthropology in which loving and egalitarian fellowship, liberation, and solidarity figure prominently. This means that the tension inherent in the way in which the doctrine of God functions in the Niebuhr-Fowler synthesis may only resolve itself in a trinitarian framework. Perhaps Dan Migliore put it best:

> Christian social ethics is thus grounded in trinitarian theology. The Christian hope for peace with justice and freedom in community among peoples of diverse cultures, races, and gender corresponds to the

trinitarian logic of God. Confession of the triune God radically calls in question all totalitarianisms that deny the freedom and rights of all people and resists all idolatrous individualisms that subvert the common welfare. The doctrine of the Trinity seeks to describe God's "being in love" as the source of all genuine community, beyond all sexism, racism, and classism. Trinitarian theology, when it rightly understands its own depth grammar, offers a profoundly relational and communal view both of God and of life created and redeemed by God.[42]

Put another way, the promise of the relational anthropology of *The Responsible Self* and Fowler's descriptions of human vocation as partnership may best come to fruition in the theological context of a God who is radically relational, responsive, and dynamic. The relational ontology of the Cappadocian fathers[43] (and mother[44]) seems more compatible with the radically relational thrust of both Niebuhr and Fowler than with the often problematic inheritance of Augustine.[45] In this view, personhood, whether divine or human, is radically relational. Fowler's future work would profit greatly from a thick and nuanced treatment of human beings as *imago trinitatis.*[46]

Lest we think that this reframing is a one-way street, let it also be said that while Fowler's work could be strengthened by pushing even deeper into trinitarian territory, contemporary trinitarian theology would be strengthened considerably by the kind of serious engagement with the human sciences that we see in Fowler's work. While it is true that a good bit of recent trinitarian theology is moving in the direction of practice, praxis, and practical theology, something is seriously lacking in virtually the whole discussion: namely, engagement with rich and textured descriptions of individual and collective human experience. Catherine Mowry LaCugna may be called on to speak for many recent trinitarian theologians when, in the opening lines of her "magnum opus" *God For Us,* she wrote, "The doctrine of the Trinity is ultimately a practical doctrine with radical consequences for Christian life."[47] Many trinitarian theologians today make the argument that a proper understanding of the doctrine of God as Trinity leads to practice, but very few of them actually get their feet on the ground. The absence of serious engagement with human sciences leaves much of the trinitarian talk about practice idealistic and platitudinous. Contemporary trinitarian theologians would do well to become thoroughly conversant with the perspectives and the resources in the human sciences. Fowler's work certainly provides a clear model of the way in which theology and human sciences can be in fruitful conversation. Fowler's sustained theological conversation with the human sciences can help to keep trinitarian reflection close to human experience and may help to avoid the perennial problem of getting stuck in the highly technical and abstruse theological verbiage for which this branch of theology is famous.

In closing, a number of questions present themselves that may help to point the way forward in bringing the Niebuhr-Fowler synthesis into deeper discussion with recent trinitarian thought:

1. What role do communal practices play in the formation of persons? More specifically, what role do religious practices play in giving rise to our knowledge of God and or ourselves? How might the trinitarian practices of baptism and eucharist effect the formation of both the notion of God as Trinity and the conception of human beings as radically relational beings? What are the political implications of participation in the mystery of God as Trinity through these religious practices?

2. What is the nature of the analogy between divine and human personhoods? What are the points of similarity? of difference?

3. How might the concept of human personhood be reconceived if we were to derive it from the concept of divine personhood as found in the trinitarian theology of the Cappadocians or of more contemporary trinitarian theologians who have been influenced by them?

4. While sharing a common human "essence," might the development and shape of human personhood be multiple and differentiated?

5. What resources might a doctrine of God as Trinity provide for thinking about how to form faithful persons who have a well-developed sense of religious identity and who are radically open to the human "other"?

6. What resources are there in the doctrine of the Trinity for furthering the Niebuhrian stance of "committed relativism" in the context of growing multiculturalism and religious diversity?

These questions and many more like them are offered to James W. Fowler in sincere gratitude for many conversations about the possibilities and the importance of the development of trinitarian practical theology over the course of the past four years. May these questions serve as down payment on several more years of such fruitful conversation on the subject of a thoroughly trinitarian approach to the correlation between the knowledge of God and the knowledge of ourselves.

Notes

[1]John Calvin, *Institutes of the Christian Religion* I.1.i., ed. J. T. McNeill, trans. F. L. Battles, The Library of Christian Classics (Philadelphia: Westminster Press, 1960), 35.

[2]See Niebuhr's discussion of this passage from Calvin in his Cole Lectures, "The Next Steps in Theology," in H. Richard Niebuhr, *Theology, History, and Culture,* ed. W. S. Johnson (New Haven, Conn.: Yale University Press, 1966), 10–12. See also this statement: "What is knowable in theology is God in relation to self and to neighbor, and self and neighbor in relation to God. This complex of related beings is the object of theology," in H. Richard Niebuhr's *The Purpose of the Church and Its Ministry: Reflections on the Aims of Theological Education* (New York: Harper & Brothers, 1956), 112.

[3]Niebuhr, *Purpose of the Church,* 113.

[4]Theologically speaking, this is a fundamental and profound insight, which is found in the work of St. Augustine. See *The Confessions,* I.1. Wolfhart Pannenberg's *Anthropology in Theological Perspective* (Philadelphia: Westminster Press, 1985) provides a more recent example of a fundamentally Augustinian approach to anthropology. See also David Pacini's *The Cunning of*

Modern Religious Thought (Philadelphia: Fortress Press, 1987) for a highly insightful Augustinian treatment of the religious thought of modernity.

[5]Elizabeth A. Johnson, *She Who Is: The Mystery of God in Feminist Theological Discourse* (New York: Crossroad, 1992), 4.

[6]H. Richard Niebuhr, *Radical Monotheism and Western Culture in the Library of Theological Ethics,* ed. R. W. Lovin et al. (1943; reprint, Louisville: Westminster John Knox Press, 1993), 32.

[7]See James W. Fowler, *To See the Kingdom: The Theological Vision of H. Richard Niebuhr* (Lanham, Md.: University Press of America, 1974), 68–69.

[8]H. Richard Niebuhr, *The Meaning of Revelation* (New York: Macmillan, 1941), 183.

[9]Neo-Kantianism began as a late nineteenth-century movement in German philosophy and theology that sought to "go back to Kant" in the wake of recognition of the excesses and failures of German Idealism, particularly with respect to the growing disenchantment with Hegel. Such neo-Kantian figures as Ernst Troeltsch (the focus of Niebuhr's doctoral dissertation), Rudolph Otto, and Ernst Cassirer clearly exerted significant influence on the development of Niebuhr's thought, including his doctrine of God.

[10]See, for example, H. Richard Niebuhr, *The Responsible Self: An Essay in Christian Moral Philosophy* (New York: Harper & Row, 1963), 163.

[11]H. Richard Niebuhr, *Faith on Earth: An Inquiry into the Structure of Human Faith,* ed. R. R. Niebuhr (New Haven, Conn.: Yale University Press, 1989), 105.

[12]There is an unmistakable Augustinian influence in Niebuhr's doctrine of God throughout. See below (n. 21) for further discussion of the Augustinianism in Niebuhr's doctrine of God.

[13]James M. Gustafson, "Introduction," in H. R. Niehbuhr, *Responsible Self,* 40.

[14]Hans W. Frei, "The Theology of H. Richard Niebuhr" in *Faith and Ethics: The Theology of H. Richard Niebuhr,* ed. P. Ramsey (1957; Gloucester, Mass.: Peter Smith, 1977) 94–104.

[15]H. Richard Niebuhr, "The Doctrine of the Trinity and the Unity of the Church," in *Theology, History, and Culture* (New Haven, Conn.: Yale University Press, 1966 [orig. in *Theology Today* 3 (1946): 371–84]), 50–62.

[16]Ibid., 58; and H. Richard Niebuhr, *Christ and Culture* (New York: Harper & Brothers, 1951), 114–115.

[17]Niebuhr, *Purpose of the Church,* 45.

[18]See, for example, Niebuhr, *Christ and Culture,* 81; and idem, *Purpose of the Church,* 20–21 and 31.

[19]We can speculate that in the background of Niebuhr's references to the Spirit, the neo-Kantian reaction against the excesses of Hegelian Idealism along with an enduring suspicion of sectarian groups is operative.

[20]Niebuhr, *Faith on Earth,* 108; italics mine.

[21]Niebuhr's struggle with the doctrine of the Trinity is notable in its candor with regard to the characteristic problems posed by the approach to the Trinity in the Latin (Western Church) Christian tradition. Among the tendencies in this theological tradition are the emphasis on the unity of God to the point of slipping into monarchical modalism, treatment of the "Father" and the "Son" as divine persons in dialogical love relation, and conceptualization of the Holy Spirit as impersonal force or "bond of love" between the two divine persons. Even when Niebuhr employs fairly traditional trinitarian language, one always gets the feeling that he is not quite comfortable with it. See, for example, "…certain implications of the historic and *apparently* necessary Trinitarian understanding of the divine reality on which the Church depends may be called to attention as important for the reorientation of theological education" (Niebuhr, *Purpose of the Church,* 21; italics mine).

[22]Niebuhr, *Radical Monotheism,* 47–48.

[23]Niebuhr, *Responsible Self,* 160.

[24]In Niebuhr's defense it might be said that in his treatment of the biblical one God, Niebuhr is simply working out of the Augustinian teaching on appropriations. The notion of appropriation as applied to the doctrine of the Trinity asserts that while each member of the Trinity is involved in creation, redemption, and transformation—such that the work of the triune God toward the cosmos (*ad extra*) is unified—particular activities in the divine economy are appropriated to one of the divine persons. The problem, however, is that the predominant emphasis in Niebuhr's writings is placed on the work of the Father of Jesus Christ in creation and redemption. There is very little talk, for instance, of a divine Logos involved in creation or of the ongoing work of the Spirit in creation and governance of the creation.

[25]See Fowler, *To See the Kingdom,* 146.

[26]Ibid., 151.

[27]See James W. Fowler, *Stages of Faith: The Psychology of Human Development and the Quest for Meaning* (San Francisco: Harper & Row, 1981), 302–3; idem, *Becoming Adult, Becoming Christian: Adult Development and Christian Faith* (San Francisco: HarperSanFrancisco, 1984), 84–92; idem, *Faith Development and Pastoral Care,* ed. Don Browning (Philadelphia: Fortress Press, 1987), 37–51; and idem, *Faithful Change: The Personal and Public Challenges of Postmodern Life* (Nashville, Tenn.: Abingdon Press, 1996), 205–15.

[28]For example, see Fowler, *Faith Development and Pastoral Care,* 115.

[29]Sometimes one can faintly detect themes from Hegel's "phenomenology of spirit" running just below the surface of Fowler's treatment of spirit or Spirit.

[30]Fowler, *Faithful Change,* 193–94.

[31]This represents a major shift from the Niebuhrian "tone deafness" to the full-blown doctrine of the Trinity that can be seen in the verbatim of the interview with the elderly monk in James W. Fowler and Sam Keen, *Life Maps: Conversations on the Journey of Faith,* ed. Jerome Berryman (Waco, Tex.: Word, 1978), 90ff. The monk and the interviewer appear to be working out of two different theological frameworks with respect to the doctrine of God.

[32]Fowler, *Becoming Adult, Becoming Christian,* 82.

[33]See ibid., 85ff., for a return to the three metaphors that describe the aspects of the providential work of the biblical One in human life and history.

[34]James W. Fowler, "How Can We Speak of the Providence of God?" (paper presented at the University of Edinburgh, summer 2000).

[35]Ibid., 10.

[36]See Fowler, *Faithful Change,* 192.

[37]Fowler, *Weaving the New Creation,* 118.

[38]In this part of the discussion, I am borrowing from the work of Jürgen Moltmann in *The Trinity and the Kingdom: The Doctrine of God* (San Francisco: Harper & Row, 1981), 13–16.

[39]For further discussion, see Catherine Mowry LaCugna, *God For Us: The Trinity and Christian Life* (New York: HarperCollins, 1991), 250–55.

[40]See especially Moltmann, *The Trinity and the Kingdom.*

[41]Moltmann, *The Trinity and the Kingdom,* 191–202.

[42]Daniel L. Migliore, *Faith Seeking Understanding: An Introduction to Christian Theology* (Grand Rapids, Mich.: Eerdmans, 1991), 70.

[43]See John D. Zizioulos, *Being as Communion: Studies in Personhood and the Church* (Crestwood, N.Y.: St. Vladimir's Seminary Press, 1985), 40ff.

[44]On the testimony of Gregory of Nyssa, we must also include his older sister as one of the Cappadocian trinitarians. He maintained that she was the real theological teacher of her younger brothers Basil and Gregory.

[45]See, particularly, Colin Gunton, *The Promise of Trinitarian Theology* (Edinburgh: T & T Clark, 1991), 31–57, for an extended discussion of the perpetual problems and pitfalls of Augustinian approaches to the doctrine of the Trinity.

[46]Jürgen Moltmann, *God in Creation: A New Theology of Creation and the Spirit of God [The Gifford Lectures, 1984–1985]* (Minneapolis: Fortress Press, 1985), 241–43.

[47]LaCugna, *God For Us,* 1.

6

Theology, Truth, and Scripture

MICHAEL WELKER

The following chapter offers a contribution to two topics raised by James Fowler in his more recent publications: how to support what he terms "the moral and faith formation" in social and cultural environments that, by their very texture, do not seem to welcome this enterprise?[1] How to engage "the Christian story in a new key" in this attempt?[2]

1. THEOLOGY, theology, and Theology

"Theology"–in history and in the contemporary situation–meets us in an overwhelming wealth of forms, a vast array of methods, topics, interests, and goals. In the midst of all these appearances of "theology," it seems advisable to distinguish three basic and general forms of theology. For the sake of a comfortable overview and cognitive control, I would like to speak, first, of maximalist theologies (let's name them *THEOLOGY* written in capitals), second, of minimalist theologies (*theology* written with no capitals), and third, of theologies moving between maximalist and minimalist theologies (*Theology* written with a capital "T"). These forms of "theology" must interact if theological reflection and existence are to remain vibrant and valid.

By THEOLOGY, written in capitals, we understand an elaborate interconnection of thought and conviction related to God and God's workings. When we speak, for instance, of the THEOLOGY of Augustine, Luther, or Schleiermacher, the THEOLOGY of the reformed confessional writings, or the THEOLOGY of a specific biblical book, we refer to such a THEOLOGY. THEOLOGIES written large can be, but need not be, theological classics. We can speak of the THEOLOGY of a dogmatics, a congregation, or a church tradition, without necessarily praising or even accepting it. Many THEOLOGIES written large can be unconvincing for us or can even appear dead. The elaborated interconnection of theological thought and conviction is the point of THEOLOGIES written large. Such an elaborated interconnection can be a blessing or a curse. Schleiermacher warned against trying to press on people theologies that cultivate modes of thought and

117

imagination "in which nobody really thinks any longer." On the other hand, THEOLOGICAL voices from the past, written large, are constant challenges to investigate and reshape our own theological thinking. Such elaborated THEOLOGIES rarely arise outside communities of faith. They presuppose religious movements, congregations, and churches, as well as church and academic education, and, in all this, tradition and intense spiritual exchange. Not only do they presuppose other THEOLOGIES written large, but THEOLOGY written large presupposes the other two basic forms of theology.

We refer to theology, written without capitals, when we claim that every pious person, every member of a religious community is enabled to theological utterances and contributions. As I have argued in more detail elsewhere,[3] not every remark about God is theological. Not even every pious utterance can be considered theological. The sigh directed to God and the silent prayer are no more theological utterances than the cynical remark about God or the presentation that makes clear that it is talking about a religion that is spiritually and profoundly foreign to the speaker.

Although a theological utterance about God or matters religious does not have to evidence a well-developed faith (a task, the fulfillment of which is expected of THEOLOGY written large), it must show *a minimum of conviction and a minimal degree of having been existentially influenced.* No matter what the reflective distance may be at which faith appears in theological utterances, if those utterances do not evidence a minimum of certainty shared or valued by the speaker, if they do not at least evidence the search for spiritual reliability and truth or the need to believe, then these statements about God and matters religious can not be considered theological. But this is only the first of two conditions to qualify an utterance as theological. The second presupposition is no less demanding. *A theological utterance must be formulated in words and must be comprehensible. It must be such that others can follow its logic, and it must be capable of material development.* In order to reach the level of *theological propositions,* religious utterances must express certainties that are communicable, comprehensible, and open to development with respect to their object and content. Although academic theology sometimes finds this side underdeveloped in individual piety and church life, we should not operate with a cliché that leaves conviction and existential involvement to the church and comprehensibility as well as material development to the academy. By its very commitment to teaching and research, the academy can not avoid reaching out for existential commitment, personal certainty, and conviction. Academic theology decays when it simply administers THEOLOGIES written large, treating them, more or less, as interesting museum pieces.

2. Theology in Truth-Seeking Communities

This observation leads us to the third basic form of Theology, written with a large "T." This Theology navigates and mediates between THEOLOGIES written large and theologies written small. This Theology–characteristic for a sound academic Theology–is exercised in "truth-seeking communities" (I am indebted to John Polkinghorne for this expression[4]). Truth-seeking communities are not to be confused with groups that announce more or less loudly that they have found the truth and now possess it. *Truth-seeking communities are groups of human beings that indeed raise truth claims, but that, above all, develop and practice open and public forms and procedures in which these truth claims are subjected to critical and self-critical examination.* The academy, active in research and education, is one such truth-seeking community.

On the one hand, truth-seeking communities advance processes in which certainty and consensus can be developed, interrogated, and heightened. In doing so, they are to guard against reducing truth to certainty and consensus. On the other hand, truth-seeking communities advance processes in which complex states of affairs can be made accessible in repeatable and predictable ways. In doing so, they are to guard against reducing truth to the repeatable, predictable, and correct investigation of the subject under consideration.

In my view, the path of the search for truth is characterized adequately only by the reciprocal relation between, on the one hand, the interrogation and heightening of certainty and consensus and, on the other hand, the repeatable, predictable, and correct investigation of the subject under consideration. This path can be traveled only in open and public critical and self-critical communication.

We ought not make light of the accomplishment, worth, and blessing of truth-seeking communities, even though we must account self-critically for the fact that these communities are always guided by other interests. For example, they also are guided by the search for maximum cultural resonance and for moral and political influence, as well as by vanity and the desire for power and control. The sober recognition that there are no pure and perfect truth-seeking communities can help us to balance appreciation and self-critique. It helps us to be very careful about the blind self-privileging of academic work. We must not attach lesser value to "justice-seeking communities" or to communities that aim at "physical and psychic therapy and the restoration of health." We also have the obligation to respect communities that seek "political loyalty and a corresponding exercise of influence," communities that seek "economic and monetary success," and communities that seek to maximize "public attention and resonance." It is characteristic of pluralistic societies that truth-seeking communities do not absolutize themselves, but that they recognize and delineate their important and indispensable contributions to the entire society and enable them to be perceived in other contexts as well.

Why is scripture so crucial for Theology in truth-seeking communities? Although theologies written small are by their very nature on the path of truth—namely, by their simultaneous insistence on individual certainty, cognitive communication, and progress in insight—they can easily settle with mere certainty and some reductionistic truisms. So they have to be challenged, time and again, to move on from certainty and correct and defendable insight toward truth, thus reaching higher levels of certainty and consensus, higher levels of mediating complexity and coherence in the knowledge of faith. But not only do theologies written small have to be challenged. Convincing and successful THEOLOGIES written large are held in esteem and are interpreted in the church and the academy over long spans of time. They are quite likely to have been born out of the search for truth. But great THEOLOGIES can prove to be ignorant in respect to crucial issues of faith. In extreme cases, THEOLOGIES written large can degenerate into dangerous religious ideologies, for example, when they cease to stimulate the theologies written small in their search for truth and even block or suppress these searches. Now we see why all three forms of "theology" have to interact. Only in their interaction do we aim at utmost coherence, existential relevance and plausibility, and orientation toward validity and truth. When the three forms are shattered and falling apart, the dangers of creating religious ideologies, pious and moral simplification, self-righteousness, and mere academic procedure arise. Here, the third topic of our enterprise comes into perspective.

3. The Canonic Texture of Scripture

Not all, but many religions on this planet center on holy scriptures. Some of them try to develop THEOLOGIES written large and theologies written small in truth-seeking communities. Without making a judgment on the holy scriptures of other religious traditions, I would like to claim that the *canonic texture* of the Hebrew Bible and the Christian Bible, containing the Old and New Testaments, is of the utmost importance for a critical and self-critical lively Theology in the move from certainty and shared insight to truth. The canonic texture of the biblical tradition, rightly understood, is a continuous stimulus and challenge for the development of vibrant theologies in truth-seeking communities. The canonic texture of the biblical traditions continuously invites and challenges them to search for encompassing concepts, images, figures of thought, and narratives. It is, however, also a challenge to examine and question those encompassing concepts, images, figures of thought, and narratives. The canonic texture of the biblical traditions continuously challenges theologies written small and THEOLOGIES written large not to settle with minimalist certainties and reductionistic insights on the one side or with grand worldviews and all-encompassing religious or academic ideologies on the other.

It is crucial for this insight to acknowledge that the biblical canon, grown over a millenium, has a thoroughly *pluralistic texture.* By pluralistic and pluralism, I do not mean vague plurality, diffuse diversity, and chaotic polyindividuality. I have argued in several places against this confusion that, in my view, is the most devastating intellectual plague of our time.[5] Pluralism, rightly understood, is neither chaos nor constant combat. It is a rich textured form of our societies, of our academy, of the biblical canon, and of other precious religious and cultural forms and achievements. The fact that many people have great difficulty in moving beyond monistic, dual or dualistic forms of thinking, understanding, and orientation should not stop us from rising to the challenge of clearly understanding structured pluralism over against vague and relativistic plurality. The very texture of the biblical canon can help us in this endeavor.

With two seminal insights, the Heidelberg Egyptologist Jan Assmann and my junior colleague Andreas Schüle have helped me in my understanding and appreciation of the pluralistic texture of the biblical canon. In a lecture given on the occasion of an honorary theological doctorate at the University of Münster, Assmann reconstructed "five steps on the way to a canon."[6] The desire for canonization arises, he argues, when human beings are haunted communally by radical ruptures, discontinuations of their lives. For Israel, the loss of the land, the deportation, and the exile were such experiences of radical historical discontinuity. For the New Testament community, the crucifixion of Christ is such a shattering of foundations.

These experiences of radical discontinuity, disruption, and the threat of chaos become textured in potentially canonical texts. The radical discontinuity requires interpretation. For the process of canonization, it is crucial that a limited *multiplicity* of exemplary interpretations is developed in order to explain and to bridge the catastrophe of discontinuity. Different worldviews—views of history, of ultimate norms, and of possible futures—condition a specific multiplicity of interpretations. Only when a small "pluralistic library," as Heinz Schürmann put it, only when a structured pluralism of different interpretations becomes textured and coded, is the substance of a canon guaranteed. The canon can operate with several centers, but it also draws and negotiates boundaries. We still have to explore the complex theological reasons for the boundaries of the biblical canon. I would be prepared to argue that in respect to many deuterocanonic texts, we could show why theologians and councils were rightly insecure whether they should include them or not. An alternative view to Assmann's was proposed recently by Schüle in his second doctoral dissertation.[7] Schüle's proposal is that the postexilic experience of a discontinuity now overcome made possible a pluralism of interpretations, many of which, possessing complementary potential for knowledge, could no longer be suppressed. As the Jewish community—meaning, the early church—grew in multiple contexts, it, too, could not do without this pluralistic potential for theological knowledge. Thus, scripture acquired its canonical weight.

This canonical weight was acknowledged by Karl Barth and other theologians with the phrase that the canon "imposed itself on the church."[8] I have argued elsewhere[9] that the canonical weight is grounded in the theological weight of scripture, namely, in God and God's workings to which it gives a complex polycontextual witness. The canonical weight is also connected with an enormous historical and cultural weight radiating in a great existential, moral, and symbolic richness. The often rightly bemoaned fact that scripture was used to spread suppressive ideologies and even suppressive THEOLOGIES written large, the suspicion that it even contains dangerous theologies written small and written large, should not blur the great blessing of its canonic texture.

4. Canonic Memory and Truth-Seeking Theology

In his book *Das kulturelle Gedächtnis,*[10] Assmann offers an impressive examination of the cultural shaping power of communal memory. Taking up ideas from Maurice Halbwachs,[11] Claude Lévi-Strauss,[12] and other theorists of the culture of memory, he shows that memory is not just an individual or a communal mental phenomenon. It is the power to construct a common world. Assmann differentiates "communicative memory," which always remains fluid, which is continually being enriched, and which also continually is disappearing, from formed, stabilized, and organized memory, which he calls "cultural memory."[13] Events such as the French Revolution, the Civil War, and those of September 11, 2001, mark our cultural memory, giving it enduring contents, bases for orientation, and directions for learning.

Taking up these insights and the insights in the genesis of the biblical canon, I have proposed to discover and to investigate a third type of memory, namely, the "canonic memory," a living cultural memory that should be of the greatest interest to Theology. When a cultural memory is codified in a specific plurality of different interpretations, I have argued, the cultural memory potentiates itself and becomes a "canonic memory." A structured and bounded pluralism of interpretations leads to a necessarily restless memory that continually opens itself to its content and source and that calls forth new interpretations without losing its centering. Communal memory is challenged to stay in a constant search for truth without losing its focus. The sustenance of truth claims and self-critical, communicative evaluations of certainties and insights go together in this type of memory.

The Christian faith affirms the vitality and inexhaustibility of the canonic memory of the risen Christ by desiring to cultivate this memory until Christ's *parousia.* Recently, David Tracy has rightly emphasized that the theme of the *parousia* should by no means be left to fundamentalism. Living cultural or canonic memory is oriented toward a future that remains beyond its control because it moves toward that future out of many temporal contexts that are concentrated on it. An anti-ideological and antitriumphalistic power lies in this canonic memory as it grows ever anew out of many testimonies. It is a communicative, critical, and self-critical memory. Canonic memory seeks certainty and growth in certainty. At the same time, it examines, relativizes, and corrects certainty in an ever-renewed quest for truth. Christian Theology referred to God's Spirit when it spoke of the processes we have just taken into view. Classic but intriguing topics such as the inspiration of scripture and the relation of Spirit and truth could and should be reexamined in light of what we have just explored.[14] But, this would lead us beyond our topic "Theology, Truth, and Scripture," which is already vast enough.

Notes

[1]See James W. Fowler, *Weaving the New Creation: Stages of Faith and the Public Church* (San Francisco: HarperSan Francisco, 1991), esp. 172–97; idem, *Faithful Change: The Personal and Public Challenges of Postmodern Life* (Nashville, Tenn.: Abingdon Press, 1996), esp. 221–36. I am very grateful to William Schweiker for his comments on an earlier version of this chapter.

[2]See Fowler, *Weaving the New Creation,* 117–42.

[3]John Polkinghorne and Michael Welker, *Faith in the Living God: A Dialogue* (London: SPCK; Minneapolis, Minn.: Fortress Press, 2001), ch. 9; see also Welker, "Theology in Public Discourse outside Communities of Faith?" in *Religion, Pluralism, and Public Life: Abraham Kuyper's Legacy for the Twenty-first Century,* ed. Luis E. Lego (Grand Rapids, Mich.: Eerdmans, 2000), 110–22.

[4]John Polkinghorne, *The Faith of a Physicist: Reflections of a Bottom-up Thinker* (Minneapolis, Minn.: Fortress Press, 1996), 149; idem, *Faith, Science, and Understanding* (London: SPCK, 2000), 29–30; Polkinghorne and Welker, *Faith in the Living God,* esp. chap. 9.

[5]See Michael Welker, "'...And Also upon the Menservants and the Maidservants in Those Days Will I Pour Out My Spirit.' On Pluralism and the Promise of the Spirit," *Soundings* 78 (1995): 49–67; idem, *Kirche im Pluralismus,* 2d ed. (Gütersloh: Kaiser, 2000).

[6]Jan Assmann, *Fünf Schritte auf dem Weg zum Kanon* (Münster: Lit, 1999).

[7]Andreas Schüle, *Israels Sohn, Jahwes Prophet. Ein Versuch zum Verhältnis von Religionsgeschichte und kanonischer Theologie anhand der Bileam-Perikope (Num 22–24),* Altes Testament und Moderne 17 (Münster: Lit, 2001).

[8]See Karl Barth, *Church Dogmatics* vol. I/2 (New York: Harper, 1961), 473ff and 597ff.

[9]Michael Welker, "Sola Scriptura? The Authority of Scripture in Pluralistic Environments," in *A God So Near: Essays on Old Testament Theology in Honor of Patrick D. Miller,* ed. Brent A. Strawn and Nancy R. Bowen (Winona Lake, Ind.: Eisenbrauns, 2003).

[10]Jan Assmann, *Das kulturelle Gedächtnis. Schrift, Erinnerung und politische Identität in frühen Hochkulturen* (München: Beck, 1992, 2d ed. 1997).

[11]Maurice Halbwachs, *Das Gedächtnis und seine sozialen Bedingungen* (Frankfurt: 1985; *Les cadres sociaux de la mémoire,* Paris: F. Alcan, 1925); idem, *Das kollektive Gedächtnis* (Frankfurt 1985; *La mémoire collective,* Paris: Presses universitaires de France, 1950).

[12]Claude Lévi-Strauss, *La pensée sauvage* (Paris: Plon, 1962).

[13]See ibid., 48ff.

[14]See Michael Welker, *God the Spirit,* trans. John Hoffmeyer (Minneapolis, Minn.: Fortress Press, 1994).

PART THREE

Faith Development
and Public Life as
Practical Theological Matters

Public Church and Public School Systems in Pluralistic Contexts

A European Perspective

KARL ERNST NIPKOW

1. Extending the Issue: Public Church and Public Education

In the chapter "The Church and the Future: Images of Promise and Peril" in his inspiring book *Weaving the New Creation: Stages of Faith and the Public Church,* James W. Fowler describes "a *revival of religion and the pluralism of faiths*"[1] as "a sixth cluster of promising possibilities" for the twenty-first century. The issue of pluralism has two sides. On the one hand, it relates to the *individual* and the process of personal maturation. People today should be enabled to respond constructively to social, ethnic, cultural, religious, and ideological diversity. On the other hand, pluralism means the multiplicity of *social institutions.* These institutions need to be studied as well: Are they ready to react favorably to a pluralistic world? In his many well-known publications, Fowler has focused on both dimensions of pluralism—the spiritual journey of the individual believer and the growth of congregations. His overall theological intention is to trace God's Spirit in history and to take seriously the vocation of Christians as "pioneers of the kingdom of God."[2] In this dynamic historical context with an eschatological outlook on a "divine commonwealth of love and justice,"[3] he offers the following "bold hypothesis": "We are experiencing in our time the emergence of a new paradigm that has the power to address many of the anomalies of our present patterns of living,"[4] in particular the church's challenge of coping with religious diversity.

At this point, *stage theory* enters the picture in relation to an interpretation of modern history. In Fowler's view, the eighteenth-century Enlightenment created a paradigm shift in cultural consciousness, which led to the development of the Individuative-Reflective style (Stage 4).[5] Our current movement into the new century and new millennium may propel, or require, the strengths of Conjunctive faith (Stage 5), that is, the power of mutual understanding in religious pluralism. Stage theories develop not only descriptive-analytic instruments but also normative "levels of aspiration"[6] that are meant to guide church leadership, pastoral care, and Christian adult formation. It is interesting to note how, for Fowler, the stages of faith in the individual's life seem to correlate to evolutionary historical "stages" of humanity as a species.[7] Today, Stage 5 seems to be the level that mirrors and promotes those new gifts demanded in the local congregation as a "public church," gifts that are needed to cope with radical pluralism.

In the following, an attempt is made to extend Fowler's approach in a direction typical of most European countries, *the role of the church as a public church within public educational institutions.* In exploring this field, Fowler's main focal points, the tasks of individual and "congregational formation or transformation in faith,"[8] can be complemented. What Fowler calls "ecclesiogenesis," that is, "forming personal and public faith,"[9] envisaging primarily *local congregations,* will be related to the possible role the church can play in public life as a *public organization.*

In entering this broader sphere, we will confront factors that reveal the difficulties churches face in becoming acknowledged allies in striving for justice, peace, and tolerance in public life. In Europe, churches are looked to not only with certain expectations, but also with mistrust. Furthermore, politicians tend to instrumentalize religion by utilizing it as a sort of "civil religion." They select what is useful to them publicly and thereby separate useful religious values from their roots in faith. In following Fowler,[10] we distinguish sharply, however, between the idea of a public church and that of civil religion.

To give a rough impression of the complexity of the issue, the following questions will have to be raised:

What are *state schools* in Europe concerned about today, and where on their agenda does religion appear? If it does appear, are churches embraced, or are religion and spirituality detached from the churches as institutions?

A complementary question is posed with regard to the *churches.* Do they understand themselves as a public church? And if so, how do they try to accomplish this mandate theologically? Do they feel urged, as Fowler hopes, "to respond to the Spirit as weaver in the process of awakening and nurturing the new creation"?[11]

To sum up: Which educational and theological criteria will meet both the understandable interests of the public school system as well as the indispensable principles of Christian theology? What solutions are compatible to both sides?

2. State School Problems in Europe and the Interest in Religion in the Context of Public Tolerance

Education is a major issue in public debate, but only as a result of challenges that have little to do with the churches. In European countries, one new educational crisis follows another. By way of illustration, I will focus initially on the situation in Great Britain.

One significant issue is *standards of learning achievement.* Progress is being made especially in primary schools, and less so in secondary schools, where "grade inflation" creates questions about the value of the latest examination results from summer 2001. International economic pressures chase headmasters and staff and frighten parents. What counts is the level of standards to be achieved in math, science, and modern languages. Required literacy and numeracy hours have been introduced in hopes of improving standards among younger students. But singling out a five-year-old who is reluctant to read and write can cause him or her to feel as if there is something wrong with him or her. This experience might create a new problem, one of motivation.

Another issue of broad public interest is the *shortage of teachers.* Many highly qualified teachers are leaving to take new jobs. Salary is not the main reason that so many disenchanted teachers are washing out of the profession in waves long before retirement. Rather, it is the cohort change that motivates teachers to leave their profession. That is, in contrast to the 1950s and early 1960s, teachers receive significantly less respect from students, parents, and the media.

Related to this issue is the growing *problem of discipline.* Some claim that the primary problem is students' poor behavior. In many places, disciplinary issues escalate to new forms of violence among pupils and aggression toward teachers who lack training as social workers. Many parents do not want (or are not able) to discipline their children. Therefore, when teachers discipline their students, some children react negatively.

A rather new and frustrating development in Europe is related to *privatization.* Private sector firms are becoming involved in public school administration (not to be confused with private schools such as church schools). This private involvement is motivated by the desire to elicit more value from public money. Many individuals are disgusted by the fact that the private sector can make money in this manner. Parents, however, are not overly concerned, because they understandably are seeking the best schools for their children. Much more than in former years, parents are turning to church-related schools to educate their children.

One might ask, Do religion, faith, and churches enter our discussion about public education at this point? The answer is no, or only in a restricted sense. One study in Germany indicates that, while some parents are attracted to church schools for religious reasons, most appreciate them primarily for educational reasons. Parents are interested in church schools because they combine a friendly school climate, high teaching standards, and good learning outcomes.[12]

We might expect that, besides general contributions to social cohesion, the churches in Europe promote *religious tolerance.* Waves of immigrants, mostly Muslim, have poured into the United Kingdom, the Netherlands, and France, due to the heritage of colonialism. Great Britain has experienced an influx of Hindus, Sikhs, and Buddhists as well. In the meantime, the economic and political situations in their home countries, specifically wars in Bosnia, Kosovo, and other parts of Africa and Asia, drive millions of refugees and asylum-seekers to Europe.

In this context, the label "multicultural society" is controversial. Conservative voices tend to think that the new situation might be getting out of control. Their language reveals a defensive posture. For example, they refer to the borders of Western countries as "under siege." They caution against accepting more migrants than necessary, and they argue that the West must consider incentives for would-be migrants to stay at home. While left-wing elites and green parties welcome a multicultural society, with a corresponding serious approach to interreligious education, the nationalist elite together with the majority of the indigenous population harbors, and even fuels, anxieties toward the growing influence of strangers. In Germany, Islam is the largest non-Christian minority, with approximately 750,000 Muslim pupils in state-run schools. Xenophobia is widespread and deeply rooted in human beings. To label a society "multicultural" solely based on demographics is inaccurate or, at least, a shallow interpretation of multicultural. Liberal values in public rhetoric mask deep reservations in attitudes toward multiculturalism. In situations of ruthless economic competition and unemployment, the facade crumbles, and naked hostility toward migrants reveals its ugly face. For example, since September 11, 2001, the paramount issue for domestic policy in Germany has been the connection between immigration and inner security.

It is important to note as background for this context that *religion and tolerance* were placed *on the agenda of the European Council* ten years ago. In 1993, the Assembly of the Council of Europe published its Recommendation No. 1202 on "Religious Tolerance in a Democratic Society." It goes without saying that any nation has the right to demand tolerance from religions that are living on its soil. The earlier declarations point to the same basic requirement: Recommendation No. 963 (1983) on "How to Reduce Violence," Recommendation No. 885 (1987) on "The Jewish Contribution to European Culture," Recommendation No. 1086 (1988) on "The Situation of the Church and Freedom of Religion in Eastern Europe," Recommendation No. 1162 (1991) on "The Contribution of the Islamic Culture to European Culture," and Recommendation No. 1178 (1992) on "Sects and New Religious Movements."

In each of these declarations, the Council expressed its conviction that all great religions in Europe–Judaism, Christianity, and Islam–can deliver a positive contribution to the development of tolerance as a necessary ingredient of human culture. Evidently, the Council has searched for the constructive potentials of religion. Yet it is also clear that European politicians are concerned deeply about the destructive potential of religion. Throughout history, religion has been two-faced, exercising the powers of both reconciliation and conflict, love and hate, respect and disregard of human dignity, both granting and stifling religious freedom.

3. The Church's Decline in Reputation within Public Education in Great Britain

The public is interested in religion because it has the potential to destabilize or to help maintain a society's coherence. Every society needs a value system that can hold diverging interests together (Émile Durkheim). Throughout Europe, the public has different expectations of the church. While many individuals in England and Wales expect the church to promote individual human rights and tolerance as cohesive powers in a multinational setting, conservatives tend to call for an established set of national values. These conservatives question even the idea of a "multicultural society." They claim that this is a contradiction in terms, which dissolves society into competing fragments. The concept of a "multicultural society gives people nothing to identify with or hold in common with each other. It creates a culture of grievance in which minorities present themselves as victims."[13]   In regard to Religious Education (RE) as a subject in state-maintained schools, the liberal standpoint has led to a nonconfessional "multifaith approach," whereas their conservative opponents plead for a much stronger emphasis on the national Christian heritage in the curriculum.

What about *the role of the church*? Does the church have an opportunity to contribute as a "public church"? In England and Wales, RE is based on two pillars—educational principles and religious studies—and no longer on Christian theology. The curriculum includes world religions rather than biblical studies. Teachers identify themselves as professional, not confessional. In recent decades, this phenomenological approach, which was intended to reduce and overcome the former approach of Christian nurture, has been supplemented and criticized.[14] Yet as Denise Cush recently remarked, "It is important to remember the joy and relief with which it was greeted by those trying to teach Religious Education in the late 1960s and early 1970s, who were no longer expected to promote confessional beliefs amongst their reluctant pupils."[15] Consequently, the connection of Religious Education to the church, be it the Church of England, the Roman Catholic Church, or Free Church traditions, was abandoned. Hence, the project of a "public church" cannot properly "work" in this context. From the very onset, the project is, in a sense, inappropriate. The only place where the churches can exert their public educational commitment is within their own church schools. In the language game of the "multifaithers" (as advocates of the multifaith approach are sometimes called), the very word *theology* (or *theological*) is avoided because it implies a connection with church doctrines that might be imposed on teachers.

The commitment to the impartial, phenomenological approach is so deep among Religious Education professionals that several were shocked to read in the new *Standards in Secondary Religious Education* that trainee teachers will be expected by inspectors to demonstrate that they can interpret contemporary social and religious issues "from a theological standpoint" and that they are aware of "the stages of faith development and how these relate to theological and pedagogical issues."[16]

Although Fowler uses the term "faith development" in a broad, inclusive sense, explicitly speaking of "human faith" rather than merely Christian faith,[17] there is resistance against terminology that seems to be associated with the church as a more or less authoritarian and obsolete institution.

The same type of aversion is evident in the replacement of the term *religion* with the term *spirituality.* For Religious Education in public schools, and, even more, as a guideline for the future of religion as such, *spirituality* is the only word that embraces all searches for meaning that transcend concrete reality. Thus, experts such as John Drane are recommending that attention be given to "New Age spirituality" in the "popular culture," particularly in the realm of postmodern art and music. According to Drane, the future of religion exists in this field, if at all.[18]

Such predictions about the future of religion are made in light of a steady decline in membership in the mainline churches and a growing revival of a highly individualized "religiosity." However this individual religiosity is expressed, it is not merely cognitive habitus, but something holistic. It is not just a Western phenomenon, but also an Asian one (or, more exactly, an assimilation of Asian spirituality and Western thinking). Further, this individual religiosity no longer follows the dichotomy between body and soul, or earlier divisions between right and wrong, good and evil, but rather, it displays new values such as freedom, individuality, and spiritual development. What is most important is that which engenders "spiritual unfolding" in individual lives. Similar to Fowler's reference to "a revival of religion"[19] and Peter L. Berger's description and reflection upon "the desecularization of the world,"[20] John Drane depicts the future of religion in terms of "spirituality" instead of religious "institutions." Drane concedes that his view of spirituality is not disconnected necessarily from institutions in fact, but certainly in principle. He simply does not recognize that the possibilities suggested by Fowler for the spiritual development of local congregations in North America also exist for Europe, or, at least, for Britain.

While I have some questions about the general validity of Drane's analysis, I have even more questions regarding a desirable plan of response. To put it very simply: Why not try to do whatever is possible to help develop spiritual life *within* religious institutions instead of leaving them *aside* as something that is no longer of any importance?

4. The Pattern of Cooperation between Public Education and a Public Church in Germany

As mentioned above, the religious situation in Europe is multifaceted. Therefore, I now will focus on religion in Germany. In Germany, the separation of church and state after World War I (1919), in contrast to the still existing state-churches in England and in Scandinavian countries, provided a new historical opportunity for churches to develop an independent pattern of participation in public life, a participation based on internal theological grounds. The German churches' commitment to the system of public education also slowly changed, especially during the second half of the last century. The former paradigm of Christian *nurture* as the rationale for Religious Education (the classroom envisaged as a congregation *in nuce* with praying, hymns, and instruction teleologically oriented toward the proclamation of the gospel) was transformed into the new paradigm of Religious Education in Christian *responsibility*. Now, the classroom provided a forum for an open-ended clarification and interpretation of the Christian tradition, including an unobtrusive, nondogmatic handling of truth claims. The Basic Law of the Federal Republic of Germany (1949, Art. 7.3) describes RE on denominational lines "in accordance with the principles of the religions" (not only the churches), but as far as Protestant RE is concerned, the German Protestant churches do not regard their theological principles as dogmatic doctrine in the Catholic sense.

In spite of this last point, the development of an experience-oriented, open-minded, and interpretive approach gradually has changed the former configuration of Religious Education. An increasing portion of the curriculum is devoted to world religions beside Christianity. There is room for interreligious education, which is necessitated additionally by the fact that 30 to 50 percent of Muslim children attend RE. Additionally, in the eastern parts of Germany (the former German Democratic Republic) with their atheist history between 1989 and 1994, nearly 60 percent of students are not affiliated with any church at all. Hence, *in spite* of the confessional emphasis described above, and, more importantly, *because of* the new interpretation of the goals of RE in an increasingly pluralistic context,[21] the churches' commitment to public education must be maintained on new terms.

In Germany (and also in Austria and in Switzerland, in modified form), the church does serve as a public church, in Fowler's terms. The church functions as a public church not only in local congregations outside of the state-school system (as in the United States) but also within the public system of state-maintained educational institutions, beginning at the elementary level (kindergarten), through the university level, and beyond. Thus, Cush's comparison of German Religious Education with the decline of the role of theology in RE in England and Wales is quite adequate. She writes:

> In Germany, Finland, Austria and Italy...religious education is more closely related to Christian theology. Thus Nipkow (1996), working within a university Theological Faculty in Germany, sees religious education as a "sub-discipline" of practical theology. However, he does not see this as contradicting the free investigation of religion identified with Religious Studies, but as supplementing phenomeno-logical description and historical explanation with critical assessment and spiritual formation.[22]

Since the role of theology is receiving new attention in the United Kingdom as well, Cush adds: "Those working within schools and colleges with a Christian foundation in the UK are thinking through the implications of Christian theology not only for Religious Education, but Education *per se* (see Astley and Francis 1996, Francis and Thatcher 1990 and Thatcher 1996 for many examples)."[23]

In the following sections, I would like to comment on three observations made by Cush regarding the focus of Protestant RE in Germany: (4.1) the task of "critical assessment," (4.2) "spiritual formation," and (4.3) German and British theologians' interest in the contribution of a public church to "education per se."

4.1 The Task of Critical Assessment

In Germany, reference to "critical schools" began at the end of the 1960s. During this time, many university students protested and demanded a definitive democratization of the postwar political system in reaction to established hierarchical authorities, ossified bureaucratic structures, moral hypocrisy of Western societies, and social injustice in the so-called Third World. The lack of democratic participation was experienced in schools and in RE as well. Moreover, the growing consciousness of worldwide misery, racism (specifically in South Africa), and the need for reconciliation among churches via participation in the ecumenical movement prompted Christian religious educators to change the old paradigm. At the same time, the "critical theory" of the Frankfort School (Theodor W. Adorno, Max Horkheimer, Jürgen Habermas) criticized the self-understanding of capitalist German society. The new strand of "political theology" (Jürgen Moltmann, Johann B. Metz) supported the reassessment of theological methodology. As a consequence, a third pillar in methodology, besides the *hermeneutical* (since the 1950s and 1960s) and the *empirical* (starting in the late 1960s), was established—that is, *ideological critique.*

Since then, it has been important to continue this threefold line of reflection on the practice of RE in state-maintained schools for several reasons, particularly in order to counterbalance the ever threatening danger of watering down the substantial contents of the prophetic traditions of the Bible. While our critical voices may be inconvenient for governmental interests, our Constitution (*Grundgesetz*) provides for a relative independence of RE. Although formally implemented and supervised by state authorities, RE is responsible, with regard to its goals and curriculum units, to none other than the "principles" of the churches (see above).

In moving toward a "public church" model, it is difficult to avoid the instrumentalization of religion. Protestant RE is mandated to express Christian freedom of faith and moral judgment without becoming judgmental in the process. In recent decades, the issues of peace and war, exploitation of natural resources, social injustice, the "corrosion of character"[24] by the rule of a "money-culture,"[25] and many others have been added to the curriculum. A self-critical RE addresses the situations in which the church itself failed in the past or is still failing in the present. Christian theology and education are challenged by the sufferings of the poor and miserable in the world. If a Christian RE forgets this, it will fall prey to self-contradiction by a false consciousness.

4.2 The Contribution of Spiritual Formation to the Development of an Open-minded Religious Identity

In order to help students develop an appropriate understanding of Christian faith, three aspects of Religious Education need to be related to one another—that is, exploring biblical and other faith traditions, studying culture and society, and examining the development of children and youth. The Tübingen concept of "elementarization" comprises five dimensions of education–"elementary structures," "elementary experiences," "elementary comprehension," "elementary truth claims," and "elementary forms of learning." The third dimension, which focuses on biographical and developmental factors, is indebted to insights from Fowler's stages of faith development.[26]

Religious Education in Germany is interested in contributing both to responsible life in church and society and to "spiritual formation" (see Cush above). In this short chapter, the concept of "spirituality" cannot be defined in depth. The term is used much less in Germany than in the Anglo-Saxon world. In England, "spirituality" can refer to almost anything related to the individual search for transcendent meaning, as Trevor Cooling recently remarked. In the practice of German Religious Education, the meaning of "spirituality" designates the promotion of an *elementary awareness of religion by using symbols, arts, music, and meditation.*

The question is, How might spiritual formation appear in a *pluralistic context*? How can it occur in classrooms composed of students from different religious backgrounds? Is it possible to make children familiar with spiritual formation in one heritage of faith without disconcerting children from other religious traditions? In my view, "spirituality" presupposes in-depth experiences in a particular faith context. Such experiences hardly could be actualized simply by describing and exploring multiple faith traditions in an "objective" juxtaposition. On purely logical grounds, a so-called "multi-faith approach" that purports to address several faith traditions simultaneously and adequately will have to limit the field of instructional contents in quantity with a possible impact on quality as well. Properly speaking, spirituality is incompatible with superficiality, and when used only in a broad sense, vague language devalues the meaning of the term.

Besides the difficulties mentioned above, there exist both principle and institutional aspects of the issue of spirituality. The first refers to the *relationship between religious identity and openness.* Fowler touches on this general aspect of spirituality in a remarkable statement that deserves to be quoted in full length.

> Public church Christians can relate non-defensively to persons and groups of other or no religious backgrounds in the larger public because of an openness born of identity and conviction. My colleague Walter Lowe once reminded us that "openness" is a second-level virtue. Often we speak of openness as though it were a primary virtue like faith, hope, love, prudence, or courage. But it is not; it is derivative. When you have only openness you don't have much. A window stuck *open* is as useless as a window stuck *shut.* In either case you have lost the use of the window. Openness is an attribute of a system or organism that has significant structure and integrity in itself. Openness is possible for persons or communities who know who they are. When the spine of identity is well established, it is possible to risk

relating in depth to those who are different from the self. Public church exhibits a principled openness in the midst of pluralism, born of its clarity about its convictional grounding and its own practice of inclusiveness.[27]

Roman Catholic and Protestant religious educators, who are in the majority in Germany, as well as Jewish and Muslim religious educators, who are in the minority, can agree with Fowler's statement. Somewhat unexpectedly, however, those in the minority sometimes respond ambivalently to *religious identity and openness*. On the one hand, when feeling suppressed by the majority, minority religious groups may develop rigid forms of identity that inherently are counterproductive to religious openness. On the other hand, Fredrik Barth has argued, from an ethnological point of view, that "ethnic distinctions [and for that matter, religious ones] do not depend upon an absence of social interaction and acceptance, but quite to the contrary, are often the very foundation of social systems"[28] (my interjection).

Identity formation must not be misunderstood as an isolated process. The same distinctions that serve as *boundaries* are generated by interethnic (and interreligious) *contact*. "Boundary maintenance" in multiethnic and multireligious settings includes religious affiliation and identity-building over against others. But it does not follow necessarily that boundary maintenance takes place in, or leads to, narrow-minded exclusion. Rather, it depends upon contact and interaction with others. "The persistence of ethnic groups in contact implies not only criteria and signals for identification, but also a structuring of interaction which allows the persistence of cultural differences."[29] In other words, the "nurture" of public church Christians for the purposes of fostering "a clear sense of Christian identity and commitment" and taking "joining and assimilation seriously"[30] is related *dialectically* to experiencing the otherness of others. This process ought to be valid, of course, for each religion involved, so that there is a bidirectional crossing of boundaries, be it the dialogue between Protestants and Catholics, Christians and Jews, Muslims and Christians, Muslims and Jews, and so forth. Hence, a "public church balances nurture and internal group solidarity with accountability in work and public life beyond the walls of the church."[31]

In my view, the *institutional* implementation of Religious Education in multifaith and multiethnic state-maintained schools ought to provide opportunities for an *analogous balancing* in concrete forms. The Evangelische Kirche in Deutschland (EKD) as the umbrella institution of all Protestant regional churches (*Landeskirchen*) has suggested the establishment of a "learning area" (*Lernbereich*) that would consist of a group of *cooperating* subjects (*Fächergruppe*)—Protestant RE, Roman Catholic RE, Moral Education (or Philosophical Ethics), Jewish RE (although only in few towns), and Islamic RE (in preparation). The basic idea is to promote (1) religious identity through learning in *differentiated* groups in respective phases, and (2) interreligious understanding through systematic religious interaction across boundaries in *integrating* phases or projects. It is important to stress the systematic character of the second aspect.

I do not deny the *limits* of this institutional solution. It hopefully can work (and does so far) in the German situation, but it will face difficulties in countries with hundreds of different denominations and religions, such as the United States. In these contexts, this institutional solution simply may not be feasible. Furthermore, the less Christian churches are open to ecumenical cooperation, the less substantive a shared learning can occur among students in the integrated phases or projects. In the present situation in Germany, Protestant religious educators have attempted to come to terms with both the Catholic Church and secular teachers of Moral Education.

Initial empirical investigations into the practice of a "Cooperative Confessional RE" (*konfessionell-kooperativer Religionsunterricht*) in primary schools shows that the hypothesis introduced above seems to be valid. Knowledge of, and mutual discussion about, confessional characteristics enable students (and teachers!) to become aware of their own denominational identities. At the same time, this process may lead them effectively toward a deeper ecumenical understanding and shared spirituality, particularly in the realm of rituals and symbols. *Shared spirituality* is not to be found *beyond,* but to be discovered in the journey *through* specific faith traditions.

4.3 Contributing to the School as a Whole and the Public Function of Church Schools

Institutionalized cooperation in modern schools is important on a broad scale. Step by step, schools are engaging in interdisciplinary cooperation among different subjects—for example, history, civic and intercultural education, biology, physics, arts, literature, and others. In many of these subjects, RE is involved officially in instances where topics have religious implications. For example, in scientific research, interdisciplinary inquiry is a well-known, long-standing practice. By participating in cooperative projects across subject boundaries, RE serves the educational goals of *the school as a whole.* Christian reflection that is directed beyond the specific tasks of Religious Education fulfills what Cush refers to as the contribution to "education per se." There is a long tradition of churches in Germany raising a Christian voice for the benefit of education. The term "religious education" is too narrow and therefore insufficient in expressing the broader range of the church's public commitment to education. What matters is an unobtrusive, but nevertheless comprehensive, "co-responsibility" of the church for public education.

The constitution of the Federal Republic of Germany provides for such a co-responsibility on all levels of the educational system. To a limited degree, *church schools* as private schools (though with considerable financial support by the state) add to the diakonia of the church in the realm of public education. In this context, the problems elicited by our analysis recur as well. These problems are of international interest. One of the most prominent issues is how to balance religious identity versus religious openness in pluralistic societies (see above).

The concept of a "public church," including the role of church schools in public life, is dependent on the general climate among church members. Thus, this concept faces several impediments. Empirical studies in England and Wales reveal "a dogged resistance" against a multicultural approach that Christian parents fear will invade church schools. These parents would like the church schools, at least, to be free of individuals from foreign cultures and religions.[32] I do not think that the church should yield easily to such interests, which are suspect of darkening the theological vision of the church as a public church. Yet the church still has to consider these perspectives.

Another empirical study cautions churches against placing too much hope in the recruitment effect and in the spiritual expectations of church schools. Representatives of the *Anglican schools* in the United Kingdom admit the failure to actualize former expectations. They assumed that Anglican schools would "produce the Anglicans of the future—and they have not."[33]

Further, comparative studies in several countries indicate a gap between self-concept and reality in *Catholic schools*. In studies in England, Leslie Francis and J. Egan demonstrate "that non-Catholic pupils attending Catholic schools record a less sympathetic attitude toward Christianity than Catholic pupils...[T]hese findings place a caveat against the policy of recruiting a significant proportion of non-Catholic pupils, even from churchgoing backgrounds."[34] In other words, the idea of a Catholic school as "faith community" can be achieved only at the cost of plurality, that is, by denominational isolation. This, however, would be a severe hindrance to establishing a public church.

Through a study undertaken in Wales, Francis and Egan reveal "that the most serious disaffection with the Catholic school is attributable not so much to the non-Catholic pupils as to the non-practicing Catholic pupils."[35] Therefore, they suggest "that if Catholic schools are to exercise an effective ministry among Catholic pupils from non-practicing backgrounds, these schools need consciously to abandon the assumption that all pupils can be treated as if they are part of the faith community characterized by practicing Catholics."[36]

Francis and Egan summarize studies in the *United States*: "By catering to pupils with three different backgrounds—practicing Catholic, non-practicing Catholic, and non-Catholic—the Catholic school vitiates the claim to be a faith community."[37] The last two classifications of students are (1) not supportive of the intentions of the school, (2) not disposed positively toward attending a Catholic school, and (3) not sharing Catholic values. This plurality works against the Catholic intent to nurture all students regardless of their religious backgrounds. "It is difficult to maintain that these schools represent a true community of faith." Hence, according to Francis, "it is considerably more realistic to modify the theory underpinning the Catholic school system to take into account the presence of non-Catholic pupils, pupils from non-practicing Catholic backgrounds, and non-practicing Catholic pupils, than to attempt to redefine enrollment policies to ensure that Catholic schools more truly represent a community of faith."[38]

To summarize, we can state that Fowler's concept of a "public church" is fully applicable in European countries. Since the Reformation, state-maintained schools have kept Christian Religious Education in the curriculum. Furthermore, church-run or church-related schools—foundations of Christian parents or groups—have added to the church's co-responsibility in public education. Today, these schools are highly attractive to a growing number of parents, primarily for educational rather than denominational reasons.

In a pluralistic context, however, a significant new "balancing" (Fowler) is required, as indicated by data regarding the heterogeneous composition of students in both public school RE and church schools. In contrast to the official Catholic stance, this plurality is not disconcerting or a factor of resentment from a Protestant perspective. There is no regret about the existence of pluralism, since Protestantism is the cradle of open-minded plurality. The concept of church schools and Protestant RE in public schools as forming a "faith community" was more or less a guideline in the past. During the last forty years, this concept has been transformed. Now, we are endeavoring to communicate the *Christian faith in dialogical patterns.*

Catholic educators join this new theological and educational vision on their own grounds. Interdenominational cooperation is increasing. Mostly due to religious indifference, the dialogue with secular education professionals is limited and sometimes difficult, but not in vain. New bridges are being built, particularly in areas in which religious education, moral education, and philosophy now overlap. More recently, the dialogue with Islam has broadened. Although different European countries are traveling different roads, the similarities between their approaches seem greater than their differences. At any rate, the future of European churches depends on a public church that, without reservation, affirms its educational vocation in a pluralistic world.

Notes

[1]James W. Fowler, *Weaving the New Creation: Stages of Faith and the Public Church* (San Francisco: Harper & Row, 1991), 13.

[2]Ibid., 115; see also James W. Fowler, *To See the Kingdom: The Theological Vision of H. Richard Niebuhr* (Lanham, Md.: University Press of America, 1986).

[3]Fowler, *Weaving the New Creation,* 85.

[4]Ibid., 21.

[5]See James W. Fowler, "The Enlightenment and Faith Development Theory," *Journal of Empirical Theology* 1 (1988): 29–42.

[6]James W. Fowler, *Faith Development and Pastoral Care* (Philadelphia: Fortress Press, 1987), 97.

[7]For discussion, see Karl Ernst Nipkow, "Stage Theories of Faith Development as a Challenge to Religious Education and Practical Theology," in *Stages of Faith and Religious Education: Implications for Church, Education, and Society,* ed. James W. Fowler, Karl Ernst Nipkow, and Friedrich Schweitzer (New York: Crossroad, 1991), 82–98, esp. 83–86.

[8]Fowler, *Weaving the New Creation,* 178; see also, 162–70, 179–95.

[9]Ibid., 172.

[10]James W. Fowler, "Öffentliche Kirche und christliche Erziehung in *Bildung, Glaube, Aufklärung. Zur Wiedergewinnung des Bildungsbegriffs in Pädagogik und Theologie,* ed. Reiner Preul, Christoph Th. Scheilke, Friedrich Schweitzer, Alfred K. Treml (Münster: Comenius Institut, 1998), 253–69.

[11]Fowler, *Weaving the New Creation,* 173.

[12]For the situation in Germany, see Karl Ernst Nipkow and Friedrich Schweitzer, eds., *Zukunftsfähige Schule–in kirchlicher Trägerschaft?* Die Tübinger Barbara-Schadeberg-Vorlesungen (Münster: Waxmann, 2001).

[13]Melanie Phillips in *Sunday Times* (London), Sept. 2, 2001.

[14]See, among others, Robert Jackson, *Religious Education: An Interpretive Approach* (London: Hodder & Stoughton, 1997), 7–29.

[15]Denise Cush, "The Relationship between Religious Studies, Religious Education, and Theology: Big Brother, Little Sister, and the Clerical Uncle?" *British Journal of Religious Education* 21, no. 3 (1999): 137–46, quotation from 138.

[16]Ibid., 140; the quotation refers to: Office for Standards in Education, ed., *Teaching Standards in Secondary Religious Education. Subject Guidance of Teacher Training* (London: Ofsted, 1998).

[17]James W. Fowler, *Stages of Faith: The Psychology of Human Development and the Quest for Meaning* (San Francisco: Harper & Row, 1981), ch 1.

[18]John Drane, "Truth in Conflict" (paper presented at the European Forum of Teachers for Religious Education [EFTRE] Conference 2001 in Edinburgh, August 30, 2001).

[19]Fowler, *Weaving the New Creation,* 13.

[20]Peter L. Berger, ed., *The Desecularization of the World: Resurgent Religion and World Politics* (Washington, D.C.: Ethics and Public Policy Center; Grand Rapids, Mich.: Eerdmans, 1999).

[21]Karl Ernst Nipkow, *Bildung in einer pluralen Welt:* vol.1, *Moralpädagogik im Pluralismus,* vol. 2, *Religionspädagogik im Pluralismus* (Gütersloh: Gütersloher, 1998).

[22]Cush, "Religious Studies, Religious Education," 143; with reference to Karl Ernst Nipkow, "Pluralism, Theology, and Education: A German Perspective," in *Christian Theology and Religious Education: Connections and Contradictions,* ed. Jeff Astley and Leslie J. Francis (London: SPCK, 1996), 38–59.

[23]Ibid., 143; with reference to Astley and Francis, eds., *Christian Theology and Religious Education;* Leslie J. Francis and Adrian Thatcher, eds., *Christian Perspectives for Education* (Leominster: Gracewing, 1990); Adrian Thatcher, "Theology of Education and Church Schools," in *Church Schools: History and Philosophy,* ed. W. W. Kay and L. J. Francis, (Leominster: Gracewing, 1996).

[24]Richard Sennett, *The Corrosion of Character* (New York: W. W. Norton, 1998).

[25]John M. Hull, "Money, Modernity, and Morality: Some Issues in the Christian Education for Adults," *Religious Education* 95, no. 1 (2000): 4–22.

[26]Friedrich Schweitzer, Karl Ernst Nipkow, Gabriele Faust-Siehl, Bernd Krupka, eds., *Religionsunterricht und Entwicklungspsychologie. Elementarisierung in der Praxis* (Gütersloh: Gütersloher, 1995, 2d ed., 1997).

[27]Fowler, *Weaving the New Creation,* 156.

[28]Fredrik Barth, ed., *Ethnic Groups and Boundaries* (Bergen/Oslo/Tromso: Universitetsforlaget, 1969), 9; quotation from Bernd Krupka, "Interkulturelles Lernen–Handeln im Zusammenhang von Kulturdifferenz, Macht, Diskriminierung, und Fremdwahrnehmung" (Ph.D. diss., Faculty of Social and Behavioural Sciences, Department of Education, University of Tübingen {Germany], 2001), 123.

[29]Barth, *Ethnic Groups,* 16.

[30]Fowler, *Weaving the New Creation,* 155.

[31]Ibid., 158.

[32]Wendy Ball and Barry Troyna, "Resistance, Rights and Rituals: Denominational Schools and Multicultural Education", in *Christian Perspectives on Church Schools,* ed. Leslie J. Francis and David W. Lankshear (Leominster: Gracewing, 1993), 397–409, quotation from 398.

[33]Alan Brown, "Aided Schools: Help, Hindrance, Anachronism, or Trailblazer?", in *Christian Perspectives on Church Schools,* ed. Francis and Lankshear, 163–68, quotation from 166.

[34]Leslie J. Francis, "The Catholic School as Faith Community: An Empirical Enquiry", in *Christian Perspectives on Church Schools,* ed. Francis and Lankshear, 429–43, quotation from 431.

[35]Ibid.

[36]Ibid.

[37]Ibid.

[38]Ibid.

8

Globalization, Global Reflexivity, and Faith Development Theory

The Continuing Contribution of Fowler's Research

RICHARD R. OSMER AND FRIEDRICH L. SCHWEITZER

In this chapter, we will explore the continuing importance of James Fowler's theory of faith development to new research and theorizing about the nature of globalization. We will draw on a collaborative book project in which we compare religious education in Germany and the United States over the course of the twentieth century and our participation in a research project exploring the effects of globalization of adolescent faith.[1] In the latter, research teams in Japan, the United States, Germany, Ghana, South Africa, Russia, India, Argentina, and Paraguay have conducted interviews with adolescents between the ages of fifteen and seventeen, exploring topics such as the young people's interaction with the media, their attitudes toward certain facets of globalization, the ways their religious communities help them understand and respond to globalization, and a variety of related matters.

Over the course of this research project, it has become apparent to a number of the researchers that Fowler's model of faith development provides important insights at two levels. First, it helps explain certain differences found across the interviews, which can be interpreted in terms of the different cognitive capabilities of persons in his stages of Synthetic-Conventional and Individuative-Reflective faith. Second and more central to this chapter, his theory provides help in conceptualizing the cognitive challenges globalization poses to young people and religious communities generally today. We will begin with a brief overview of globalization theory, introducing the concept of global reflexivity as a way of conceptualizing the interaction of psychological and sociological factors. We will then examine the ways Fowler's theory helps us conceptualize the challenge of global reflexivity in light of our research in the globalization project mentioned above. Finally, we will indicate some of the guiding perspectives on religious praxis in our globalizing context that faith development theory opens up.

1. Globalization and Global Reflexivity

What is at stake in using the conceptual framework of globalization to understand the context of contemporary religious praxis? Perhaps this is best illumined by way of contrast with the use of the conceptuality of modernization, which is quite widespread in contemporary practical theology and the social sciences.[2] Modernization and globalization can be viewed as historical-interpretative frameworks that point to key developments taking place during distinct eras. In the West, early modernization began to occur in the aftermath of the Reformation and Renaissance with the rise of the modern nation-state and the first impulses toward the creation of *national* cultural identities, political and judicial systems, and, to a lesser extent, economies. These early impulses were given their peculiarly modern form with the rise of modern science and the industrialization of the economy over the course of the nineteenth and twentieth centuries. Science served not only as the basis of the technological innovation driving the industrialization of the economy but also as a cultural ideal of modern life, the very epitome of a humanity "come of age." As a historical-interpretive framework, thus, modernization can be viewed as focusing on those social processes closely associated with the emergence of the modern nation-state, the rise of modern science, and the industrialization of the economy in the nineteenth and twentieth centuries.

Globalization, as a historical-interpretive framework, points to a markedly different set of social processes.[3] It brings into focus the diminishment of the nation-state as the center of cultural, political, and economic activity and a movement away from heavy industry as the driving force of the economy. Three closely related "revolutions," beginning during the final half of the twentieth century, can be seen as driving globalization to this point: (1) the technological revolution of the electronic media, emerging largely out of the invention of microprocessors for computers but also related to advances in other forms of electronic and satellite communications; (2) the emergence of a global economy, based on this technological revolution in the media; and (3) the collapse of the Soviet Union and the bipolar structuring of interstate relations characterizing the Cold War, leading to the emergence of new forms of political organization and cultural identity with multiple allegiances.

Obviously, modernization did not stop one day and globalization begin the next. Nation-states are still important centers of cultural, political, and economic activity. Scientific research and technological innovation continue to be important dimensions of contemporary life. But a significant shift has begun to take place. It is like the reconfiguration of colored pieces of glass that takes place when the end of a kaleidoscope is turned. The same colors are there, but they are arranged in a different pattern. We are in the very early stages of globalization. While it is apparent that the institutional and cultural patterns of modernity are changing, it is unclear at this point exactly what new configurations will emerge.

One of the most important by-products of the interconnections created by globalization at many levels of life is the emergence of "global reflexivity."[4] It can be defined succinctly as follows: a heightened awareness of and reflection on cultural "others" and the construction of diverse images of the global whole. This means that globalization must be viewed not only in terms of the interlocking systems that now connect most parts of the world but also in terms of consciousness of the global whole. This consciousness is shaped in two directions simultaneously. It involves the relativization of local traditions, on the one hand, and a renewed interest in these traditions as providing resources by which to understand and respond to the forces of globalization, on the other.

Perhaps the most important relativizing feature of globalization has to do with the cultural flows it has created across national and local boundaries. As we found in our research in the globalization project, young people today are deeply aware of cultural "others." They are studying other cultures and languages in school; interacting with people from other countries on the Internet; making friends from other cultures through exchange programs; interacting with media that communicate news, programming, and music from other countries; and traveling abroad themselves. All of these intensify and complicate the accounts of relativization associated with modernization. The sheer density and scope of global flows around the world today expose young people as never before to values, lifestyles, and gender roles that are quite different from those of their parents. They are deeply aware that the cultural identities and life paths of their parents are only one of many options available in a multicultural world. Local cultures remain important forces of socialization, to be sure. But they are now relativized, experienced as one of many possible life paths. More of the freedom and burden is placed on individuals to knit together a meaningful life project in the face of their experience of the cultural flows of globalization.

One of the most powerful relativizing forces of local culture in our present context is the pressure that globalization exerts toward cultural homogenization.[5] Three aspects of this trend are pertinent: (1) the emergence of a global consumer culture based on a globalized economic system and advertising; (2) the spread of rational approaches to life in conjunction with the increased administrative needs of modern states, transnational organizations, and multinational corporations; and (3) the communication of idealized, Western lifestyles through the global media, including television, movies, and music. Benjamin Barber aptly refers to these as the spread of "McWorld."[6] Especially among those who can participate successfully in the global economy, the cultural flows of globalization appear to be making cultures more and more alike. This has the effect of exposing young people to values, beliefs, and forms of life that, often, are quite different from those of their parents and their local cultural traditions generally.

This does not tell the whole story, however. While globalization has clearly created many new interconnections across national and local borders, this does not necessarily mean that this is leading to a world that is more fully integrated.[7] In many instances, it has led to the reaffirmation of ethnic, religious, national, and civilizational (e.g., "Western civilization") identities in direct response to the various forces of relativization. Cultural homogenization, often, is viewed as the importation of Western hedonism and materialism. It is a mistake, thus, to view the Western image of globalization—the inexorable movement of humankind toward a secularized, capitalistic, rationalized, and democratic end-state—as the only form global reflexivity can take. Already, the early stages of globalization have seen the emergence of a wide range of cultural and civilizational responses. Three fairly pervasive patterns of response can be identified: resurgent tribalism, cosmopolitanism, and postmodernism.

Resurgent tribalism takes a variety of religious and secular forms. At the heart of this response is the reassertion of the authority of local cultures and traditions in the face of global flows and cultural "others" who are viewed as threatening the well-being of a particular community. One of the most important forms of this sort of response is religious fundamentalism. The growth of fundamentalism on a worldwide scale seems to indicate that this phenomenon is a response to a set of global conditions that, increasingly, is all-pervasive.[8] Resurgent tribalism responds to the cultural flows of globalization defensively. Individual and corporate identity is defined over against cultural "others" who are construed as the enemy or as morally contaminated. In its most extreme religious expressions, it takes the form of jihad or crusade, which makes "slaughter of the 'other' a higher duty."[9] A sense of victimization or potential harm by cultural "others" provides moral legitimization for viewing them as a threat to be eradicated or brought under control. When viewed along these lines, the Islamic fundamentalism of the Cairo ghettos and the upwardly mobile fundamentalism of Jerry Falwell's Moral Majority can be viewed as having much in common. What they share is a defensive response to global flows that are viewed as corroding traditional values and patterns of life. It is the reassertion of these values and patterns in the context of new forms of community, which explicitly define themselves over against threatening others, that allows us to view them as variants of a common type of global reflexivity.

This is not the only form global reflexivity takes, however. Some social commentators identify a trend toward what they call the "new cosmopolitanism."[10] This, too, has begun to emerge on a worldwide basis, especially among those participating most successfully in the global marketplace.[11] Cosmopolitans are loosely connected to local and national communities. They focus their energies on competing successfully in the global economy and use the financial gains this affords to construct lifestyle enclaves centering on personal preference and taste. It is not difficult to discern such enclaves in Seoul, outside of Capetown, and in many gated communities across the United States. Among these groups, there are signs of a reduced sense of responsibility for those who have been "left behind." Concretely, this takes the form of a lack of care offered to desperate relatives or to the racial and ethnic groups to which the individual belongs. More broadly, it takes the form of a diminished sense of the common good, a lessened sense of responsibility for the institutions that make public life possible and contribute to the well-being of the social whole. Religious communities sometimes provide legitimization for the "new cosmopolitanism" by offering a highly individualized view of salvation, by associating economic success with divine blessing, and by keeping the religious life safely ensconced within the boundaries of the private sphere. In effect, they accommodate this form of global reflexivity by failing to address the social conditions that have brought it into being, perpetuating a highly privatized view of the religious life.

Still a third form of global reflexivity has emerged in recent decades: postmodernism. This weaves together three basic elements: (1) a recognition of pluralism, (2) a heightened awareness of the risks attending scientific research and technological innovation, and (3) a highly processive view of life.[12] In our research on adolescents in the United States and Germany in the globalization project, we have found various combinations of these elements in the thinking of a large number of adolescents. Perhaps most pervasive is a newfound awareness of pluralism. Adolescents today are deeply aware of cultural "others." This often leads many to affirm the positive value of encounters with these "others." Such encounters are viewed as "expanding" their understanding of life's possibilities–the music, dress, food, and customs that give life its richness and texture–and helping them move beyond the limitations of their own local cultures.

The second element of postmodernism also was apparent in our research. Many adolescents view the "manufactured risks" of scientific research and technological innovation in concert with the interconnectedness of globalization. They realize that problems in one part of the world spill over to other parts of the world. The meltdown of the Chernobyl nuclear plant in the former Soviet Union was a potential disaster, not only for the persons located in the immediate vicinity of the plant but also for many parts of Europe. Global warming, the spread of AIDS, global terrorism, the use of genetically-altered foods, and many similar problems are viewed as global risks that threaten all parts of the world. In some cases, this has the effect of making adolescents more cautious and even skeptical about the ever accelerating rate of technological innovation.

The third element of postmodernism–the adoption of a highly processive view of life–also was evident in this research. This is a sense that the markers of personal identity formation and movement through the life cycle are no longer stable. Personal identity will not be achieved merely once during late adolescence but will be reconstructed repeatedly over the course of a person's life, often in dialogue with the resources of other cultures. In many instances, this leads adolescents to engage in "cultural collaging"–the piecing together of the music, dress, customs, and values of many cultures into a meaningful sense of personal identity and the construction of a life project. This provides insight into one of the most prevalent ways religious communities accommodate postmodernism as a form of global reflexivity, at least in the United States. They, too, engage in a kind of "religious collaging," piecing together music, forms of worship, spiritual disciplines, and moral stances from many different sources in the attempt to accommodate the particular needs, interests, and tastes of their diverse membership.[13]

To summarize, globalization as a historical-interpretive framework brings into focus a range of social processes that represent a qualitatively new and different set of challenges to contemporary religious communities. Already, it has sparked new forms of global reflexivity—a heightened awareness of cultural "others" and the construction of diverse images of the global whole. Three quite different forms of global reflexivity have been identified, which have begun to effect religious communities around the world: (1) resurgent tribalism, which often takes the form of religious fundamentalism; (2) the "new cosmopolitanism," which often takes the form of a highly privatized pattern of religion and legitimates a diminished sense of responsibility for the common good; and (3) postmodernism, which often takes the form of a "religious collaging" that seeks to accommodate the various interests and tastes of a diverse religious membership. It is not difficult to identify certain problems in each of these forms of global reflexivity, especially their religious forms. Are there alternatives to a fearful fundamentalism, a morally restricted cosmopolitanism, and a relativistic postmodernism? We believe there are and find James Fowler's theory of faith development a helpful dialogue partner in rethinking the contribution of religion to our rapidly globalizing, multicultural world.

2. Global Reflexivity–A Developmental Perspective

Many of the analysts mentioned in the first section of this chapter come from the field of sociology. Authors such as Anthony Giddens or Ulrich Beck, for example, start out with a sociological approach that, in the course of their work, is broadened to a global scope.[14] This implies that they do not make individual consciousness their starting point. Rather, they first look at the more palpable social factors of the worldwide economy, international information flows, travel, and so forth in order to then ask about the implications of such factors at the individual level. In addition to sociology or to a sociological theory of globalization, practical theology and religious education also are interested in subjective factors. First of all, they must address the subjective factor in their work of teaching, preaching, program planning, and so forth. Moreover, an interest in the education or formation of persons— children, adolescents, and adults—is central to their work.

One way of looking at how globalization affects the individual person's thinking or viewing of the world is to conceive of globalization as presenting certain cognitive challenges that people inescapably encounter in a globalizing world. This view corresponds to what others have called the "mental demands of modern life."[15] In this case, the focus is on the demands that changing life situations force on us quite independently of our ability to cope with such challenges. To put it simply, from this perspective, global reflexivity is an outgrowth of the social conditions of globalization. It is what globalization does to us in terms of changing our consciousness.

It is apparent that there also is another way of looking at this situation. Global reflexivity may represent certain cognitive challenges, but not all people are able to respond to these challenges in an adequate manner. They are lacking the abilities that are required for this kind of reflexivity. This is why it makes sense to think of global reflexivity not only as a demand but also as a mental capacity. And this capacity is not an automatic given but is an achievement, at least judging from our initial observations in the interview study mentioned above. Clearly, not all the adolescents interviewed in this study have achieved this capacity. It is difficult if not impossible for them to address global issues and to interpret or to evaluate them while keeping their global implications in mind. Moreover, many of them seem to hold naïve views of globalization, welcoming the many choices that it gives to them as consumers without critically balancing the advantages and disadvantages of economic globalization.

To our knowledge, at this point, there is no systematic study available on the mental capacities required by global reflexivity. So it makes sense to explore the possibility of putting together some of our observations on the one hand and a developmental perspective–that is, Fowler's faith development theory– on the other.

A first observation concerns the clear age trend in the interviews. The younger the respondents, the harder they found it to think and to speak about globalization. They do not seem to fully grasp what globalization means. This observation can easily be connected to faith development theory. Several of the structural "aspects" that Fowler uses to trace the development of faith from stage to stage are important.

(1) An obvious category related to global reflexivity is the aspect of the "Bounds of Social Awareness."[16] Faith development theory describes these bounds as widening circles, starting with one's own family and ending with an "identification with the species." According to Fowler's data, most adolescents cannot be expected to think beyond the groups to which they are related in a direct interpersonal manner (Stage 3). Only the highest stages (Stages 4, 5, and 6) appear to be in line with the mental demands of global reflexivity, and these stages are achieved much later in life–if ever. Stage 4 affords the ability to reflect on processes of globalization in a systemic fashion. This is an important achievement. Yet globalization also includes many intersystemic processes and relationships–for example, intercultural and interreligious relationships and encounters. This creates a demand for the capacities connected to Stages 5 and 6.

(2) Another way of conceptualizing global reflexivity in terms of faith development arises from the aspect "Perspective taking." Global reflexivity

can be understood to mean global perspective taking–to consider events and processes by interpreting them in light of their global meaning, including the perspectives of cultural "others." And again, it is only at the three highest stages that, according to Fowler, taking the perspective of "groups, classes and traditions 'other' than one's own" become a possibility.

(3) Globalization also has normative implications. In this respect, it is connected to the aspect of moral development that Fowler, partly following Lawrence Kohlberg's pioneering work, sees as proceeding from a preconventional to a conventional to, finally, a postconventional level. Only the postconventional level implies a kind of moral judgment that is not limited by a given society and its social order–a capacity that probably is directly required for moral judgments about problems and challenges at a global level. In any case, the systemic thinking of Kohlberg's Stage 4 again indicates an indispensable presupposition for normative considerations at a global level.

The aspect of moral development vis-à-vis global challenges can also be considered from a somewhat different but related perspective. From the perspective of Christian theology, one central challenge has to do with the task of finding and defining ethical standards or criteria that can guide the process of globalization and that can help to shape it according to such criteria.[17] If this is not to mean that globalization is to be confronted with moral claims that exclude careful analysis of the various aspects and implications of globalization, it necessarily includes a very complex and demanding task of interrelating different disciplines and systems of thought. This would involve, for example, systemic perspectives on the various social, cultural, and economic processes of globalization, as well as on different ethical viewpoints. This requires exactly the sort of cognitive capacities that are not available to many or most in contemporary society, according to the research of Fowler and others.[18]

One of the striking observations in our interview study concerns the question of how globalization has affected the religious attitudes of young people. Many of the interviewees in our study found it difficult to respond to this question. Not only had it probably not occurred to them to think about this question but, more importantly, the question seemed to go beyond their present cognitive capacities–even more so than in the case of general questions about the effects of globalization. Obviously, it is quite demanding to think about oneself in terms of abstract categories like religion. In addition to this, it is also demanding to think about globalization as more than a global economy and to consider the effects it might have on one's own person. The task of connecting these two highly demanding perspectives and of applying them to oneself is too complex for many adolescents.

As we conclude this section, it is important to remind readers of the preliminary character of these interpretations of global reflexivity in terms of faith development theory. While they appear quite plausible, at least to us, they are not based on empirical studies beyond our preliminary interviews. In this sense, these interpretations should be considered hypotheses that are in need of further examination. The research required for this purpose might well broaden the traditional model of faith development in order to include aspects of global reflexivity more intentionally than was possible twenty or more years ago when Fowler first gave shape to his model. But even in its present form, faith development theory brings into focus certain tasks that practical theology and religious education must pursue vis-à-vis the challenges of globalization.

3. Perspectives for Practical Theology and Religious Education

Interpreting different forms of global reflexivity in the context of practical theology and religious education is not just an academic exercise. Ultimately, the purpose of this interpretation is to improve the *paideia*–the education of the public–in which the church must participate in order to contribute to more humane and responsible forms of globalization.[19] It is our understanding that faith development theory can indeed help us in designing educational and other church-related approaches to preparing people for the challenges of a globalizing world. In this last section of the present chapter, we want to point out four important considerations that faith development theory might contribute.

(1) Our first perspective concerns the importance of keeping the structural aspects of the cognitive demands of global reflexivity in mind. Since the concept of structure has a specific meaning in the context of faith development theory, it is probably helpful to remind readers of this meaning. The structuralist design is actually one of the main characteristics of faith development theory. Like other theories in the Piagetian tradition, this theory is based on a distinction between structure and content. The stages of faith are not defined by specific content–for example, by particular beliefs–but rather by the patterns of meaning making that people use to compose their centers of value and meaning, or what Fowler sometimes calls the ultimate environment of existence. This means that, for example, a child at the stage of "Mythic-Literal faith" can adhere to very different beliefs depending on what he or she has been offered by the religious environment. But as long as this stage prevails, the child's faith will always be literal in the sense of construing religious images, symbols, or metaphors literally, whether they come from the Bible, the Koran, or from poetry.

This distinction between structure and content has important implications for practical work. Many churches that have come to realize the importance of addressing issues of globalization tend to assume that this task focuses primarily on designing programs that offer information about globalization and that make people aware of what globalization means. In other words, their focus is on content, not on structure. Yet if it is true that global reflexivity does indeed require comprehension in the sense of Stages 4, 5, or 6, exposing people to information about globalization will not get them very far. Most likely, they will not be able to integrate this kind of information, let alone be able to work on related tasks such as critically evaluating what kind of globalization is taking place or relating processes of globalization to the perspectives of Christian ethics.

Clearly, it would not be helpful if faith development theory could only tell us that preparing people for the challenges of globalization is difficult, if not impossible, in most cases. But there also is no point in overlooking the developmental or educational presuppositions of grappling with globalization. To put it differently, it will not be possible to involve people in sharing the responsibility for humane forms of globalization unless there are prolonged and sustained efforts at educating the public for this task.

Prolonged and sustained efforts are needed for two reasons highlighted by research on faith development. First, stage change is difficult to achieve. It is not possible, for example, to design learning programs that guarantee stage change in a few weeks' time. This is why we need to include attention to structural developmental aspects in all of our educational efforts. Second, concerning higher stages of development (Stage 4 and beyond), the time of late adolescence and early adulthood is of special importance.[20] In this sense, global reflexivity has important implications, for example, for college ministry. But as faith development theory also makes clear, there is the need and possibility of continued growth throughout life, not only in terms of the continuing life cycle but in terms of structural change as well.

(2) Beyond this general plea for an education that supports ongoing faith development across adolescence and adulthood, the question remains if there are educational possibilities that are more accessible at earlier stages. Faith development theory also offers important insights on this matter. It refers us to the capacities that are already present with persons at all levels of development, and it invites us to work within their specific frameworks. In other words, faith development theory does not just point to the importance of supporting and stimulating structural stage change, but it also provides a perspective that allows us to better understand where people are. This allows for forms of education toward global reflexivity that are stage-appropriate— forms that are especially important in working with children and adolescents but also with adults.

In his writings on "faith nurture" and the "public church," Fowler has pointed out that it makes sense to think about possibilities for stage-appropriate approaches to cognitive challenges of pluralistic, "postmodern" societies, which require the cognitive capacities of the higher stages of his theory.[21] For example, while children will not be able to understand the complex relationships between different religions as separate bodies or as institutions, they are certainly able to meet people from different backgrounds and to build up relationships with them. Such early encounters can be a powerful way of preparing them for the achievement at later points of more open-minded and sophisticated views demanded in a multicultural and multireligious social context.

Already, some curriculums are attempting to prepare children for the development toward global reflexivity along these lines. Here again, faith development theory is helpful. In one instance, for example, the story of a child growing up in poverty in a Third-World country is introduced to children in order to give them a chance to identify with this child and to develop an empathic relationship. This way of familiarizing children with global problems such as hunger or injustice is certainly more meaningful than giving them statistical information or international comparisons based on abstract economic figures. Yet, once again, faith development theory adds an important warning not to be naïve in our use of such approaches. We have to keep in mind the specific framework from which children view the world and perceive—or construct—other people. For children, the one child whom they come to know through the teacher's presentation will never be merely "an example," as is the case for adolescents and adults. This implies a difficulty that may distort or even flaw the whole effort. The children may actually want to help the one child by doing something for him or her. And if they never hear from that child, they will probably conclude that such efforts are hopeless or that the particular person does not really matter. It is also no solution to just tell the children that the child was not real and that someone just used a picture for educational purposes. In other words, faith development theory reminds us of the need to take children very seriously and to think through what we are offering to them in our teaching very carefully from the beginning.

The example of the child also reminds us of the need to go beyond such early attempts. While beginnings are necessary, they also remain beginnings that are not the whole story. Stage-appropriate education and working toward higher stages must go hand in hand. What we need is an ongoing educational process that supports global reflexivity through the various stages and ages, and a sensitive balance between stage-appropriate approaches and new challenges that stimulate people toward higher stages. Faith development theory can be a helpful guide for this difficult balance.

(3) Working with adolescents in the context of global reflexivity, it seems especially important to support development beyond the conventional faith of Stage 3. This view not only is based on faith development theory but also came to the fore in two parallel observations of the interview study mentioned above. The first observation concerns naïve and distorted views of globalization. Especially the German sample produced responses that can most aptly be understood by applying the distinction between global reflexivity as a mental demand imposed by globalization and as a mental capacity required for global responsibility. It seems that many of the adolescents (and probably many adults as well) face cognitive demands that they cannot fully handle because they are trapped in the limitations of conventional thinking (Stage 3). The result of this mismatch between mental demands and their present capacities is *not* so much that adolescents just close their eyes and ears to globalization in order to focus on their own life worlds. Rather, there seems to be a danger that they develop what might be called *ideological* views of globalization. In our interviews, this often took the form of very positive and naïve evaluations of globalization. Globalization is considered good and helpful

because it gives people more choices and opens up more possibilities. In some cases, these views of globalization resembled a shopping-mall attitude, with no awareness of the risks of globalization.

The second observation comes from the American sample. This sample included a significant minority of adolescents who were critical of globalization and raised questions about it. They seemed to be youth in the midst of a transition between Stages 3 and 4, beginning to take a systemic perspective on globalization. In several cases, they had participated in church mission trips in the United States and abroad that had been linked to critical forms of education, helping them to reflect on their firsthand experience of the effects of globalization and to integrate such experiences. This kind of combination of firsthand encounters, of consciousness-expanding education, and of support toward stage transition seems to be an important source of growth toward global reflexivity, especially in adolescence when the transition between Stages 3 and 4 is at stake.

(4) Our final consideration has to do with the search for a normative vision that can ground a humane form of globalization. Here again, we believe faith development theory has an important contribution to make, going beyond its use of structuralist psychology to help us conceptualize global reflexivity as a subjective and psychological process. The normative vision of this theory becomes visible most clearly in the ways that Fowler describes the aim of faith development (Stage 6). When Fowler first spelled out his understanding of a final stage, he was well aware of its far-reaching normative implications. Even if globalization was not a major topic at that time, his views remain important because they anticipate many normative aspects that are now considered to be of central importance in the context of globalization.

It is easy to see that Stage 6, Universalizing faith, is based on the widest perspective that one can take. It presupposes what Fowler portrays as identifying with and taking the perspective of the "commonwealth of being."[22] The "universalizing apprehensions" of this stage can easily be connected with the sorts of global perspectives necessary for global reflexivity in its highest forms. It includes a valuing of the worth and dignity of all humans, as well as all cultures and religions around the world. It is truly an ecumenical perspective of worldwide peace and justice. Moreover, the "commonwealth of being" extends beyond humankind to include all of God's creation, animals no less than humans, but also plants and other natural forms of life. In this sense, the normative vision on which faith development theory is based clearly anticipates what more recently has been discussed under the rubrics of a "global ethic" and a "new catholicity."[23]

Fowler's vision of the aim of development has often been criticized for, on the one hand, claiming universal validity and, on the other, being clearly influenced by the Christian tradition.[24] Fowler has never accepted this criticism but has repeated his understanding that universalism and the reference to particular traditions cannot be separated unless one accepts a shallow or even empty and meaningless version of universalism. He maintains that the biblical origin of his descriptions does not speak against their (potential) universal validity—a view that Fowler supports by referring to the "absoluteness of the particular."[25] This is not the place to go into the details of the complex philosophical and theological discussions on universalism. It is enough to point out that, from our perspective, there is a clear link between faith development theory's normative vision and today's new appreciation of the importance of affirming cultural and religious "otherness."

Unlike Kantian notions of universality and the public, which strip away all cultural and religious differences as persons enter the moral domain of public life, Fowler's portrayal of Stage 6 affirms the intrinsic value of cultural and religious differences. As early as Stage 5, he begins to project an implicit model of public life in which people draw on the symbolic potentials of their own particular traditions in ways that open them to both the limitations of their own traditions and the need for dialogue with perspectives other than their own. In his descriptions of Stage 6, this notion of universality is maintained and deepened. Universality is inclusive of the pluriformity and diversity of life, not its elimination in some sort of abstract universalism. It is an appreciation of this richness and diversity and the recognition of its grounding in the commonwealth. Moreover, this sort of universalizing apprehension can only be elicited by and take the form of particular cultural, moral, and/or religious traditions. It is the apprehension of the universal in and through the particular.

Over the course of this chapter, we have pointed to a variety of ways in which faith development theory is an important dialogue partner in the emerging discussion of globalization and the struggle of religious communities to help shape the various processes associated with globalization toward more just and humane forms of life. If globalization elicits global reflexivity as a set of cognitive challenges, on the one hand, and if global reflexivity must be nurtured and educated in ways that support the emergence of higher stages of cognitive, moral, and faith development, on the other, then it is likely that Fowler's work will continue to make an important contribution in the foreseeable future.

In order to come to terms with globalization religiously, we need a vision that leads beyond tribalist fundamentalism, the new religious cosmopolitanism, and the religious collaging of postmodernism identified in our introductory section. Clearly, we need to know more about how psychological presuppositions and demands of global reflexivity work together. Enough has been said to make clear why we are convinced that faith development theory can help us to attain a nondefensive yet critical attitude toward globalization. If this is true, there can be no doubt that this theory will continue to contribute to theorizing, research, and practice seeking to understand and shape public life in a rapidly globalizing world.

Notes

[1]Richard Osmer and Friedrich Schweitzer, *Religious Education between Modernization and Globalization: New Perspectives on the United States and Germany* (Grand Rapids, Mich.: Eerdmans, 2003). The Princeton Project on Youth, Globalization, and the Church is a research project sponsored by the Princeton Theological Seminary Institute for Youth Ministry.

[2]See, for example, the widely influential book by Peter Berger and Thomas Luckmann, *The Social Construction of Reality: A Treatise in the Sociology of Knowledge* (Garden City, N.Y.: Doubleday, 1966). The adoption of this framework is widespread in practical theology. See, for instance, Johannes A. van der Ven, *Ecclesiology in Context* (Grand Rapids, Mich.: Eerdmans,1993), which draws exclusively on the framework of modernization.

[3]Writing on globalization has proliferated in recent years. See the following as helpful introductory texts: Malcolm Waters, *Globalization* (New York: Routledge, 1995); Roland Robertson, *Globalization: Social Theory and Global Culture* (Thousand Oaks, Calif.: Sage, 1992); Peter Beyer, *Religion and Globalization* (London: Sage, 1994).

[4]We take up the theme of global reflexivity in Osmer and Schweitzer, *Religious Education,* ch. 2. See also Robert Schreiter, *The New Catholicity: Theology between the Local and the Global* (Maryknoll, N.Y.: Orbis Books, 1997).

[5]Homogenization is treated along these line by Waters, *Globalization,* ch. 2, in terms of convergence theory. See also his further discussion in ch. 6.

[6]Benjamin Barber, *Jihad vs. McWorld: How Globalism and Tribalism Are Reshaping the World* (New York: Ballentine Books, 1995).

[7]Robertson provides particularly helpful insights on this issue in *Globalization,* ch. 6.

[8]For an excellent discussion of this trend on a worldwide basis, see William McNeill, "Fundamentalism and the World of the 1990s," in *Fundamentalisms and Society: Reclaiming the Sciences, the Family, and Education,* ed. M. Marty and S. Appleby (Chicago: University of Chicago Press, 1995).

[9]Barber, *Jihad vs. McWorld,* 9.

[10]Waters takes this up in *Globalization,* 133–39. See also Charles Reich, *The Work of Nations* (New York: Vintage Books, 1991).

[11]This is described with special poignancy by Reich, *Work of Nations.*

[12]The following authors are particularly helpful in describing postmodernism in relation to a set of social and institutional conditions: David Harvey, *The Condition of Postmodernity: An Enquiry into the Origins of Cultural Change* (Oxford: Blackwell, 1980); David Lyon, *Postmodernity,* 2d ed. (Minneapolis: University of Minnesota Press, 1999); Mark Poster, *The Mode of Information: Poststructuralism and Social Context* (Chicago: University of Chicago Press, 1990); Zygmunt Bauman, *Postmodenity and Its Discontents* (Washington Square, N.Y.: New York University Press, 1997); idem, *Intimations of Postmodernity* (New York: Routledge, 1992).

[13]Arguably, this sort of "religious collaging" is consistent with the type of congregation identified by Penny Becker as community congregations in *Congregations in Conflict: Cultural Models of Local Religious Life* (Cambridge: Cambridge University Press, 1999), ch. 5.

[14]Ulrich Beck, Anthony Giddens, and Scott Lash, *Reflexive Modernization: Politics, Tradition, and Aesthetics in the Modern Social Order* (Stanford, Calif.: Stanford University Press, 1994); Anthony Giddens, *Modernity and Self-Identity: Self and Society in the Late Modern Age* (Stanford, Calif.: Stanford University Press, 1991).

[15]See Robert Kegan, *In Over Our Heads: The Mental Demands of Modern Life* (Cambridge, Mass.: Harvard University Press, 1994).

[16]See the chart in James W. Fowler, *Stages of Faith: The Psychology of Human Development and the Quest for Meaning* (San Francisco: Harper & Row, 1981), 244.

[17]Schreiter, *New Catholicity.*

[18]See, for example, Kegan, *In Over Our Heads,* 335.

[19]We discuss the concept of *paideia* in Osmer and Schweitzer, *Religious Education.* Our use of this concept has been strongly influenced by the work of James Fowler.

[20]See the important study by Sharon Parks, *The Critical Years: The Young Adult Search for a Faith to Live By* (San Francisco: Harper & Row, 1986).

[21]James W. Fowler, *Weaving the New Creation: Stages of Faith and the Public Church* (San Francisco: Harper & Row, 1999), 189.

[22]Fowler, *Stages of Faith,* 245.

[23]Hans Küng, *A Global Ethic for Global Politics and Economics* (New York: Oxford University Press, 1998); Schreiter, *New Catholicity.*

[24]See, for example, the discussions in James W. Fowler, Karl Ernst Nipkow, and Friedrich Schweitzer, eds., *Stages of Faith and Religious Development: Implications for Church, Education, and Society* (New York: Crossroad, 1991).

[25]Fowler, *Stages of Faith,* 206–9.

9

Postconventional Faith for Public Life

1. Introduction

Since its inception, the whole process of modernization has influenced human life and consciousness in significant and varied ways. In the West since the nineteenth century and more recently in the East, modernization has continued in the wake of transitions from traditional to industrial to late modern societies, resulting in new types of opportunities and risks.[1] In North American society, we are experiencing a new era in which the consequences of modernity, both opportunities and risks, are radicalized more than ever before.[2] The development of modern social institutions has created significant opportunities for people to enjoy a secure existence, but it also has fostered uncertainties about life and moral and religious crises in people's minds. In other words, modernity, including its positive and negative aspects, radically alters the nature of public life and affects the most personal aspect of our religious experience, namely, Christian faith.[3]

First, in light of this problematic situation facing contemporary Christians, I will explore the consequences of modernity that radically affect Christians in ways different from traditional and earlier modern societies. I will discuss the manner in which the demands of public life challenge the faith of Christians today. Second, based on a threefold concept of the self, which provides a foundation for the achievement of an alternative Christian faith, I will deal with the necessity of postconventional faith for public life. Third, drawing upon various types of "postconventionality," I will propose my own definition of "postconventionality" and an accompanying alternative approach to faith for Christians confronted by the challenges of a rapidly changing society. My definition is based on a critical correlation of Jürgen Habermas's theory of communicative action and James Fowler's theory of faith development. Fourth, I will present suggestions for Christian education for public life. This approach to Christian education attempts to support and challenge Christians to develop this alternative Christian faith in the modern context. Again, I have termed this "postconventional faith for the public life."

2. The Challenges of Public Life in the Modern Context

Since the beginning of modernization, many scholars have criticized the Enlightenment project because of its strong trust in reason and progress. Max Weber, one of the first critics of the optimistic vision of modernization,[4] argued that the legacy of the Enlightenment did not lead to the concrete realization of "universal freedom," but rather to the creation of an "iron cage" of purposive-instrumental rationality, *Zweckrationalität,* from which there seemed to be no escape.[5] Although a significantly different tradition, the first generation of the Frankfurt school resonated with Weber's analysis. They chastised the Enlightenment project for its instrumental reason, blind domination of nature, and the abandonment of its own unrealized potential.[6] Given the present discontents of modernity—for example, an incoherent sense of community and identity, individualism, and alienation—recent neoconservative and postmodern voices also have produced, from their divergent perspectives, a critique of the Enlightenment notion of universal reason. They have demonstrated reason's inadequacy to deal with both indeterminacy and a plurality of contexts and life situations.[7]

While building on Weber's analysis of modernization, Habermas criticizes him for his narrow focus on merely one aspect of cultural rationalization, *Zweckrationalität* (purposive-instrumental rationality). Habermas argues that Weber's interpretation of the process of modernization can lead to despair and relativism and, consequently, to relinquishment of the Enlightenment project. Emphasizing the complex, multidimensionality of modernity and its potential to stimulate learning, Habermas reinterprets Weber's theory with its three levels of rationalization—religious, societal, and cultural—by focusing on the opportunities and risks created by modernization. In this regard, Habermas proposes a more precise conceptual framework for understanding the positive *and* negative aspects of modernity, and thus, he attempts to elucidate the unfinished project of modernity.[8]

2.1 Individualization and Institutionalization

The academic discussion of modernization provides a conceptual framework to understand the consequences of modernity, as it presents a description of sociological phenomena related to the constitution of a self and Christian faith. I would like to address three characteristics of public life in the modern context based on various sociological perspectives. The first characteristic that has affected Christians in the public sphere of modern society is "individualization"—that is, the ways modern society gives more freedom to, and also places more burden on, the individual.[9] With the emergence of a "post-traditional society,"[10] the influence and security of traditional communities have diminished severely.[11] Individuals increasingly are burdened by the need to arrange the competing spheres of their lives and to determine their own choices. The individual becomes the unit of reproduction for the social order in the modern context, rather than social class or family. As Ulrich Beck writes, "Individuals inside and outside the family become the agents of their livelihood mediated by the market as well as by their biographical planning and organization."[12] In other words, individualization requires modern people to reflect on their given traditions and conventions and to determine the course of their lives based on open and reflexive decision.

Ironically, this individualization process tends to be accompanied by a uniformity and standardization of lifestyle choice. These forces of uniformity and standardization structure individuals' life stories and circumstances through institutionalization.[13] This first characteristic of modernity, individualization in company with institutionalization, confronts those who have trouble establishing security in the Christian tradition. Whereas tradition formerly played a crucial role in maintaining the Christian faith, individualization requires them to arrange various life spheres without traditional support. At the same time, Christians are exposed to external control and standardization by way of institutions, which differ from those in traditional society. This situation challenges Christians to develop a capacity to achieve a sense of self, not in isolation, but in intersubjective relationship. It forces them to deal with the tension between individual freedom and choice, on the one hand, and institutional pressure for standardization, on the other. In the context of unsettled tension between individualization and institutionalization in public life, Christians are caught between extreme relativism and dogmatism, or individualism and communitarianism. As a way of bridging this tension, Christians search for a clear yet dynamic sense of self and an approach to their faith that is relevant to public life.

2.2 Structural Differentiation and Pluralism

Another characteristic of highly industrialized modern society that has affected Christians is "structural differentiation." Since the beginning of modernization, society has been characterized by a variety of institutions that structure social practices in ways relatively autonomous to one another. The differentiation in institutions, which Weber explained by way of religious-metaphysical, societal, and cultural distinctions,[14] divides society into multiple life spheres. More broadly, society is separated into the public and private spheres.[15] As a result of modernization, religious-metaphysical thinking has been confined to the private sphere, thus reducing its adequacy as a resource for critiquing societal differentiation and for reconciling the divisions among multiple spheres in the modern context. This privatization of Christianity in structurally differentiated society poses a problem for making Christian faith relevant to all spheres of life.[16] In other words, Christians are challenged to maintain their religious faith in both private and public spheres in the midst of rapid social change. Further, they must integrate multiple demands from both spheres into internalized principles.

Individualization and structural differentiation are related closely to a third characteristic of modern society, "cultural pluralism"–that is, the division of society into groups with distinct cultural traditions. In a highly differentiated society, various ethnic and racial subcultures exist in proximity to one another. Thus, pluralism is a fact of everyday life. Moreover, at the level of high culture, postmodern thinking confronts society with the realities of difference, otherness, and philosophical nonfoundationalism. This cultural and intellectual pluralism results in the relativization of all cultural traditions and the maximization of human choice in establishing moral and religious convictions.[17]

In contrast, the more recent phenomenon of globalization[18] has generated a strong fundamentalist reaction in our modern context.[19] Given the discontents of modernity–for example, alienation, homelessness, anomie and anomia, rootlessness, and so on–fundamentalism attracts people because it attempts to reorganize all spheres of life by means of a particular set of absolute values. F. L. Lechner claims, "Where the discontents of modernity are felt more keenly and defined more sharply, new and stronger fundamentalist movements are likely to emerge."[20] These phenomena resulting from cultural pluralism and globalization challenge Christians to address both the relativization of tradition and the reactionary fundamentalist movement. The question of Christian faith becomes more pertinent in this context, as Christians are challenged to engage openly in genuine dialogue with other religious and cultural perspectives in public life. In other words, Christians living in a pluralistic and global society confront situations that require reflexive thinking, open conversation with other cultures and religious traditions, and continued commitment to their own tradition.

There is no doubt that these three characteristics of the modern society are interconnected and mutually reinforcing.[21] Together, these social phenomena in modern society create conditions under which traditional integrative faith is challenged and threatened. Contemporary people often are frustrated by the cognitive demands (1) of modern life, especially public life, (2) to integrate multiple claims into internalized principles, and (3) to make their Christian faith relevant to public life.[22] Moreover, modern people, when challenged to engage in dialogue with other perspectives and worldviews, still center their identities and Christian faith on outside authorities and a homogeneous tradition. In other words, modern people live in a postconventional world, yet they do not respond to the challenges of public life in a postconventional manner.

Positively, however, these threatening consequences of modernity may provide an opportunity for a new beginning. Though Weber's critique of the optimism of the Enlightenment thinkers is helpful, to a degree, in analyzing the consequences of modernity, his conceptualization of modernity is based on the selective process of purposive rationality, which leads to pessimism and nihilism. Instead, I would propose that modernity provides us with an opportunity to learn such skills as the ability to criticize and challenge conventional tradition and religion and, consequently, to move beyond our own limits through dialogue with others. In sum, modernity can provide us with the conceptual means of constructing a reflexive or self-critical perspective, thereby facilitating a move beyond the "conventional" mode of thinking/ valuing characteristic of traditional society and toward the "postconventional" level.

3. The Necessity of Postconventional Faith for Public Life

As described above, changes arising from modernization—that is, individualization, structural differentiation, and pluralism—confront Christian churches in contemporary Western society. Individual Christians must mature in such a way that their faith is relevant to modern public life.

3.1 The Modern Religious Crisis for Christians

José Casanova has studied the phenomena arising from modernity since its inception, and, particularly, he has attempted to explain the religious crisis of relevancy, a crisis often considered to be the result of secularization. According to Casanova, many scholars who utilize secularization theories to interpret the modern context define secularization as (1) religious decline, (2) social differentiation, and (3) privatization of religion. These theorists have analyzed, in part, the decline of mainline churches and the increased relativism of moral and religious values. Thus, they tend to assume that religion will vanish with progressive modernization and that modern differentiation necessarily results in the "marginalization" and "privatization of religion."[23] Even though Casanova believes that the sudden eruption of religion into the public sphere in the 1980s indicates that differentiation and the loss of societal functions do not necessarily result in religious privatization,[24] this differentiation and the loss of societal functions still create a context that seems threatening to modern Christians.

First, religion in general and Christianity in particular no longer play the once near-universal role of providing people with systematic normative integration. The differentiation of society into public and private spheres creates a context in which Christianity tends to be confined to the private sphere. Consequently, Christianity is ill-equipped to address effectively those issues derived from living in two distinct spheres.

Second, Christianity has lost its social function as a public religion due to the process of modernization. On the one hand, social functions formerly carried out by Christianity have been usurped by other social agencies.[25] On the other hand, Christianity has failed to help modern Christians handle the social situations that they confront on an everyday basis, and it has failed to help them in reflexively reconstructing their own normative foundations.

This tension creates the possibility for the formation of an alternative Christian faith that is relevant to the modern world, especially public life. The modern context can be quite threatening or challenging for some Christians. Yet it can provide an educational context that supports and challenges Christians to develop a faith relevant to the public life, rather than an assumed faith embedded in conventional values and norms. Thus, I would argue that there are urgent demands for an alternative Christian faith relevant to public life in modern society. Given the three demands of modern public life placed on Christians, I will suggest a threefold concept of the self that is related closely to the development of postconventional faith.

3.2 The Relational, Equal, and Open Self

The first demand of public life calls for a *relational self* that is situated in an intersubjective web of relationships. This demand comes from the recognition that relationality, not separation or differentiation in isolation, plays an important role in achieving a sense of self in the modern context.[26] Several feminist scholars and other theorists argue that the concept of a "relational self" is helpful in understanding both male and female development.[27] The self achieves a sense of identity and mature Christian faith in this modern context by evolving, not through isolation, but through relationship with others.[28] In light of individualization and institutionalization, a relational self is necessary. The relational self maintains individual faith through a web of intersubjective relationships that can provide both mutual freedom and dependence, relationality and individuality.

Second, modern society requires an *equal self*, a self that regulates and authorizes the multiple roles played in both the private and public spheres. In his book *The Moral Judgment of the Child,* Jean Piaget connects logical development with moral development by the process of learning to respect others and follow rules based on mutual agreement and reciprocity rather than on tradition.[29] Piaget argues that the child develops from the world of authority to the world of bilateral cooperation, where relationships are more equal and mutual.[30] This theory implies that the self progresses from constraint to cooperation, from dependence on external authority to dependence on consensus and commitment, from conformity to family tradition to questioning tradition and to the dissociation from particular family roles and conventions. Confronted by structural differentiation in modern society, the equal self is needed for numerous reasons: (1) to regulate multiple demands from private and public spheres, (2) to integrate these demands into internalized principles, and (3) to achieve and redefine Christian faith relevant to public life. In other words, this second requirement of modern society calls for a self responsible to the church and to society as a whole.

The third and last demand of the public sphere is an *open self*, a self capable of conversation with other perspectives in a relatively egalitarian and open communicative "space." Fowler explains this openness via the concept of "second naïveté" in his theory of faith development.[31] The "second naïveté," a concept first used by Paul Ricoeur, is defined by Fowler as "a postcritical receptivity and readiness for participation in the reality brought to expression in symbol and myth."[32]

> This means a genuine openness to the truths of traditions and communities other than one's own. This openness, however, is not to be

equated with a relativistic agnosticism (literally, a "not knowing"). Rather, it is a disciplined openness to truths of those who are "other," based precisely on the experience of a deep and particular commitment to one's own tradition and the recognition that truth requires a dialectical interplay of such perspectives.[33]

This notion of "second naïveté" produces a boundary issue. Typically, closed boundaries have been considered necessary for developing a stable sense of self and for maturity in Christian faith. Yet from Fowler's perspective of Conjunctive faith, the question, "Who am I?" is not answered by isolating the self but by engaging in open conversation with others. As Fowler states, this openness indicates a combination of committed belief in and through the particularities of a tradition *and* the recognition that the "truth that any of our traditions can offer needs continual correction and challenge."[34] This openness to the voices of others and to the ongoing reformation of our religious tradition presupposes that an open self and individual faith are formed, not in isolation, but in continual conversation with others. In critically constructive appropriation of the symbolic depths of a particular religious tradition, the self discovers resources that potentially ground its participation in public life—an openness to plurality, the nurture of a utopian imagination, and the importance of affirming the fundamental dignity and equality of all persons. In a pluralistic, global society, it is not difficult to understand why an open self is required. That is, the self continually confronts situations that demand reflexive thinking and open conversation with many diverse perspectives.

In light of this definition of the threefold self (relational, equal, and open) that public life requires of Christians, I propose that an important task of Christian education is to create an educational context in which modern people are supported and challenged to redefine their conventional Christian faith and move toward "postconventional faith" for public life. By "postconventional faith," I mean an individual and collective faith that (1) allows a personality system to secure religious continuity and consistency in relationships in the midst of rapid social change, (2) enables Christians to have genuine dialogue with others and allows them to move beyond their own limits in a pluralistic and global society, and (3) redefines and activates their Christian faith in commitment to, and involvement in, religious action in the world. My description of public life in modernity as the context in which Christian faith must be achieved propels me to advocate for a "postconventional faith," a faith characterized by a reflexive attitude toward one's own context and hermeneutical foundations.

4. The Concept of Postconventionality and Christian Faith

As delineated above, postconventional faith is necessary for public life in modern society. I will now define "postconventionality" by placing different psychological theories in close proximity to the notion of postconventional faith.

4.1 Defining Postconventionality

The term *postconventional* was used originally by Lawrence Kohlberg, and more recently by scholars such as Carol Gilligan[35] and Jürgen Habermas. These scholars appropriate this term in their developmental psychology and in their discussion of culture and society as a means of describing adults who have matured beyond the conventional stages. Others, such as Fowler[36] and Robert Kegan,[37] do not use the term *postconventional* to describe their developmental psychology but display similar characteristics in their understandings of mature adult development. These similar yet dissimilar definitions of "postconventionality" illustrate postconventional faith from different angles.

The term *postconventionality* is based mainly on Habermas's theory. However, other approaches to postconventionality are beneficial as well. For example, Kegan and Gilligan have provided a helpful discussion of relationality that is grounded in a social view of the self.[38] According to Gilligan, the concept of relationality occupies an important place in the process of moving toward postconventionality. Kohlberg's theory of moral development establishes the normative context for moral regard and equality.[39] Based on John Rawls's theory of justice, Kohlberg defines the area of judgments of justice in the process of development. Fowler's theory provides the concept of principled openness in the Conjunctive stage, in which a person is grounded in a particular tradition, yet also moves beyond it through genuine conversation with others. These various theories encourage a multifaceted comprehension of postconventionality. There is a plurality of approaches to postconventionality, marked by both distinction and similarity.

In order to understand *postconventionality,* it is necessary to define *conventionality.* Conventionality, according to Kohlberg and Habermas, is morality that is based on shared norms and values, inherited tradition, and family religion. In other words, conventional morality equates the right or good with the maintenance of existing norms and values. At the conventional level, there are two important characteristics. First, the locus of value and duties is external; the person will follow either role behavior attributed by a familiar group or society or normatively governed interaction guided by an ethical system. Second, at the conventional level, the "social world is still embedded in the lifeworld and reinforced by its certainties."[40] At this point, morality and the ethics of an unquestioned, habitual, particular form of life have not yet been distinguished. In other words, religious ethics and philosophical ethics understand and justify the moral not on their own terms, but rather within the life world of a larger soteriological or cosmological whole.[41]

The transition from the conventional to the postconventional level occurs when an individual begins to reject conventional moral reasoning due to perceived relativism. In other words, he or she acknowledges that social value, both in fact and in theory, and obligations bequeathed from conventional tradition are only one among many options.[42] At the postconventional level of morality, a person first will challenge tradition, convention, and family religion, and moreover distance him/herself from particular social roles and their content. However, this does not mean that the person will reject all conventional and habitual social roles and tradition. Instead, the individual is encouraged to establish a new relationship with habitual social roles and tradition. The person participates in a particular tradition, but at the same time opens him/herself to conversation with adherents of other belief systems. The formal structure of postconventional moral reasoning provides rules or principles that test and justify traditional norms and principles of society. This testing occurs when the idealized form of reciprocity characterizes discourse.

4.2 Habermas and Kohlberg

Habermas attempts to combine philosophical argumentation with the sociomoral perspective proposed by Kohlberg. Habermas appropriates the concept of "postconventional" from Kohlberg's developmental stage at which moral judgment becomes dissociated from the local, conventional, and historical coloration of a particular form of life.[43] In Kohlberg's theory, the postconventional level has two stages. The prevailing characteristic of Stage 5 is a social contract legalistic orientation, while Stage 6 is oriented toward a universal ethical principle.

> Stage 5: *The social-contract legalistic orientation,* generally with utilitarian overtones. Right action tends to be defined in terms of general individual rights, and standards which have been critically examined and agreed upon by the whole society. There is a clear awareness of the relativism of personal values and opinions and a corresponding emphasis upon procedural rules for reaching consensus.

> Stage 6: *The universal ethical principle orientation.* Right is defined by the decision of conscience in accord with self-chosen *ethical principles* appealing to logical comprehensiveness, universality and consistency. These principles are abstract and ethical (the Golden Rule, the categorical imperative); they are not concrete moral rules like the Ten Commandments. At heart, these are universal principles of *justice,* of the *reciprocity* and *equality* of human *rights,* and of respect for the dignity of human beings as *individual persons.*[44]

At this level, moral reasoning is based on values and principles[45] that are valid and applicable apart from the "individual's identification with a particular family, group or nation."[46] It assumes an autonomous ego that develops through the integration of internal nature into the structure of language, thought, and action. When the individual reaches higher stages of development, he or she becomes autonomous, obtains personal independence, is more efficient in solving problems, can take more differentiated perspectives toward the external world, and experiences "a greater sense of personal unity and psychological consistency."[47]

Nonetheless, Habermas claims that Kohlberg's theory needs to be reconceptualized according to a "social perspective." According to Habermas, the achievement of postconventional morality enables individuals (1) to reflect on their own presuppositions, values, and norms of action, and (2) to judge existing norms and values according to a normative and critical criterion provided by discourse ethics. In Habermas's appropriation, Kohlberg's postconventional level can be defined as the ability to engage in communication in a manner that respects communicative partners as moral others. That is, postconventional communicative action is characterized by reversibility of perspective, universality, and reciprocity.[48] More specifically, Habermas defines postconventional as the level of moral and legal consciousness at which values and norms are generalized and social action is released from concrete traditional patterns of behavior. At this level, distinctions are drawn between contexts of instrumental or strategic action and those that rest on or aim at normative consensus. A person recognizes and commits to the validity of principles.[49] Habermas argues that this postconventional developmental stage can be achieved through dialogical, procedural communication, the communally followed method of redeeming normative validity claims discursively.[50] In sum, Habermas particularly emphasizes the principles of mutuality and equality in order to demonstrate both intersubjective recognition and equal accountability in open conversation in moving toward postconventionality.

4.3 Critical Appropriation of Habermas and Fowler

I am deeply indebted to Habermas's notion of postconventionality, which is based on principles of mutual respect and equal accountability.[51] His demonstration of the interactional aspect of postconventionality is most helpful. Moreover, his postconventional level has several important moral aspects, namely, reversibility, universalizability, and impartiality for the understanding of Christian faith in public life. However, his theory of postconventional ethics does not attend adequately to the role of religion, specifically Christianity, within human life and society. As several theologians argue in the book *Habermas, Modernity, and Public Theology,*[52] Habermas ignores powerful resources that might allow Christians to achieve a "postconventional faith." He neglects the positive way in which religion can be emancipatory as well as utopian.

Furthermore, Habermas's conception of postconventionality still is based on Kohlberg's postconventional level, which, in turn, is deeply rooted in the individualism and universalism of a neo-Kantian perspective on public life. I would like to move beyond Kohlberg's and Habermas's theories by pointing to an alternative account of public life that is articulated explicitly in Fowler's various writings and implicitly in his theory of faith development. Simply stated, Habermas views postconventionality in terms of what humans have in common. In order to engage in rational communication and achieve postconventionality in the modern context, he believes that people must relinquish their cultural and religious differences and move to the "common ground" of shared rationality. In contrast, Fowler points toward a postmodern notion of public life—that is, a public life in which cultural, gender, and religious differences are affirmed as necessary, constitutive dimensions of public life that cannot be surpassed by the affirmation of a universal rational core.[53] Fowler's discussion of stages of faith development beyond Synthetic-Conventional faith yields significant insights regarding (1) the nature of public life under the social conditions described at the outset of this chapter, and (2) the developmental processes contributing to a postconventional faith stance within this social context. Fowler does not utilize explicitly the language of postconventionality (à la Habermas and Kohlberg). However, his theory provides clear concepts of openness and relationality based on a critical appropriation of the symbolic depths of a religious or moral tradition, which, potentially, enable openness to others who are different across the public spectrum.

Building on H. Richard Niebuhr's portrayal of faith, Fowler describes faith along two lines: (1) faith as a human universal, and (2) Christian faith as trust in and loyalty to the God revealed in Jesus Christ. As a human universal, faith is "our way of finding coherence in and giving meaning to the multiple forces and relations that make up our lives."[54] All persons have faith in this sense. They compose centers of value and meaning or what Fowler sometimes refers to as the "ultimate context of existence." Drawing on the structural developmental tradition of psychology, Fowler embarked on empirical research that identified stages of faith development. He is best known, perhaps, for the theory emerging out of this research.

Equally important and often overlooked, however, is Fowler's second understanding of faith. Defined in explicitly Christian terms, this faith is trust in and loyalty to the God revealed in Jesus Christ. In other words, this definition of faith is rooted in a particular religious tradition—the Christian tradition. Faith, in this sense, is mediated to the members of the Christian community. As Fowler states, human faith (his first definition) is formed and transformed into Christian faith (his second definition) via the Christian community. At various points, Fowler offers theological descriptions of God's action in and through the Christian community, clarifying the relationship between God's action and human action in and through the beliefs and practices of this particular faith community. While he does not discuss extensively the ways that non-Christian religious communities transform the human faith of their members into patterns of belief and practice consistent with their respective religious visions, his theory is, in principle, open to this sort of process in a manner consistent with his description of the Christian community. Religious communities, thus, play both a shaping and transforming role in the nurture of faith. At the end of this chapter, I will point briefly to some of the related implications for Christian education.

It is especially important to note that Fowler signifies the potential, inherent in the symbolic depths of religion, to advance persons toward a postconventional faith stance. Here, we arrive at the heart of his difference with Habermas and Kohlberg. Rather than necessarily "leaving behind" the particularities of one's religious tradition in moving toward postconventionality, the members of a religious community appropriate the symbolic depths of their tradition in ways that lead them to "see through" the tradition in two ways. They not only form a critical perspective on their tradition—"seeing through" its limitations, especially in the particular form practiced by their own community—but also draw upon its various beliefs and practices as a means of acquiring new openness to the perspectives of others—"seeing through" its symbols to the value and dignity of others. In other words, they achieve a postcritical stance toward their own tradition—the second naïveté that Fowler appropriates from Ricoeur in order to describe Conjunctive faith. Abandoning the particularities of one's own cultural and religious heritage is not a prerequisite to acquiring the communicative and cognitive competencies necessary for participation in a pluralistic public domain. Religious tradition, if appropriated along the lines described above, enables openness to otherness, reflexivity, and commitment to the equality and dignity of all. As indicated above, these are precisely the sorts of cognitive and communicative competencies necessary in an institutionally differentiated and culturally pluralistic public life.

As a means of proposing my own definition of postconventional Christian faith, I have established a mutually critical dialogue between Fowler's perspective and Habermas's theory of communicative action. Postconventional faith can be understood as having a symbolic structure that permits the personality to acquire constancy of the self as a Christian despite environmental changes and individual growth. It permits a belief in God's love through experiencing what God has done for us in the midst of difficult times and thus moves us toward the realization of the realm of God. This postconventional faith cannot be achieved in isolation, but in *mutual relationship* among *equal* participants with *open* conversation. The relational, equal, and open self participates in a continual learning dialogue (openness) based on discursive procedure (relationality) and reciprocal participation of those who are different (equality).

5. Christian Education for Postconventional Faith

Most Christians live in an individualized, structurally differentiated, and pluralistic society. They are confronted with moral diversity and inconsistency. Modern people are not supported adequately with objective references that enable them to make meaning and maintain their Christian faith in a relativistic context. In the midst of diverse options, Christians are challenged to achieve and sustain a coherent but continuously revised faith. In other words, Christians are challenged to maintain a constant self and Christian identity, while simultaneously engaging in genuine dialogue with other perspectives.

As Kegan describes in his book *In Over Our Heads,* there are cultural and societal demands on modern people to move to a higher stage of development, characterized by a postconventional approach to morality and society. While only a minority of modern people actually are postconventional in orientation, many live in a postconventional culture or society. These individuals face the developmental task of shaping their morality so that it coheres with the reality of moral diversity and inconsistency in public life. This task is achieved by the development of "postconventionality," that is, the formation of principled morality as well as the construction of the self as relational, equal, and open in the process of communicative action.

This present moral and religious crisis can lead to the development of "postconventional faith" and thereby furnish Christians with the competence necessary to confront the tasks of interpreting and reconstructing their experience as Christians. Moreover, postconventional faith assists us in rethinking the role of religion, in general, and Christianity, in particular, in the private (individual) and public spheres of modern societies. (Again, this differs significantly with the role of Christianity in traditional societies.) Thus, I would argue that postconventional faith is developed in a context in which Christians are treated with mutual respect and equal accountability in open conversation, thereby enabling them to examine their faith (validity claims) and reinterpret and reconstruct their experiences (redeeming these validity claims) in light of the Christian tradition.[55]

Postconventional education for pubic life is an alternative model that helps Christians (1) reflect, understand, and critique their own culture and tradition, (2) move beyond the conventional norms and values of society, and (3) achieve postconventional faith. In other words, Christian education for postconventional faith, anchored in the principles of relationality, equality, and openness, attempts to provide an educational context (both formal and informal) in which Christians are encouraged to reflect on and criticize given assumptions and conventions. Christian education for postconventional faith encourages Christians to move toward a more mature level of moral development in hope for the realm of God. This theory of postconventional education for public life, based on the critical correlation of Habermas's theory of communicative action and Fowler's theory of faith development, accounts for the purposes, places, persons, and processes involved in teaching and learning by providing an "ideal educational context." In this context, learners receive "equal opportunities" to participate in communication without coercion, to speak and listen with "openness" to different claims, and to exercise "mutuality" and "relationality," while empathizing with others.

Certainly, this theory of Christian education for public life has limits at both the theoretical and practical levels.[56] However, it is crucial to achieve and redefine Christian faith for public life in such a way that Christians living in modern society might produce and establish, in response to genuine dialogue with others, Christian moral norms and values relevant for contemporary culture. Christian education for public life must assume the task of supporting the development of "postconventional Christian faith." This task can be accomplished by providing postconventional education in which relationality, equality, and openness are emphasized and reflected in the lives of Christians as they participate in public conversation.

Notes

[1]Ulrich Beck, "The Reinvention of Politics: Toward a Theory of Reflexive Modernization," in *Reflexive Modernization: Politics, Tradition, and Aesthetics in the Modern Social Order,* Ulrich Beck, Anthony Giddens, and Scott Lash (Stanford, Calif.: Stanford University Press, 1994), 6. See also Ulrich Beck, *Risk Society: Toward a New Modernity,* trans. Mark Ritter (London: Sage, 1992), 1–90.

[2]Giddens argues that modernity diminishes the "overall riskiness" of certain areas and modes of life, yet at the same time brings "new risk parameters" completely unfamiliar to previous eras. Anthony Giddens, *Modernity and Self-Identity: Self and Society in the Late Modern Age* (Stanford, Calif.: Stanford University Press, 1991), 4.

[3]Giddens, *Modernity and Self-Identity,* 1–9; see Beck, Giddens, and Lash, *Reflexive Modernization;* see also Anthony Giddens, *The Consequences of Modernity* (Stanford, Calif.: Stanford University Press, 1990).

[4]See Max Weber, *The Protestant Ethic and the Spirit of Capitalism,* trans. Talcott Parsons (New York: Charles Scribner & Sons, 1958); Stephen K. White, *The Recent Work of Jürgen Habermas: Reason, Justice and Modernity* (New York: Cambridge University Press, 1988), 93–94; Jürgen Habermas, *The Theory of Communicative Action,* trans. Thomas McCarthy, 2 vols. (Boston: Beacon Press, 1984), 1:157–58.

[5]Richard J. Bernstein, "Introduction," in *Habermas and Modernity,* ed. Richard J. Bernstein (Cambridge, Mass.: MIT Press, 1994), 5.

[6]See Theodor W. Adorno and Max Horkheimer, *Dialectic of Enlightenment,* trans. John Cumming (New York: Seabury Press, 1972).

[7]Calvin O. Schrag, *The Resources of Rationality: A Response to the Postmodern Challenge* (Bloomington: Indiana University Press, 1992), 13–49; Nicholas Rescher, *Pluralism: Against the Demand for Consensus* (Oxford: Clarendon Press, 1993).

[8]Jürgen Habermas, "Modernity: An Unfinished Project," in *Habermas and the Unfinished Project of Modernity: Critical Essays on the Philosophical Discourse of Modernity,* ed. Maurizio Passerin d'Entreves and Seyla Benhabib (Cambridge, Mass.: MIT Press, 1997), 38–55; Habermas, *Theory of Communicative Action,* 2:326–29.

[9]Richard R. Osmer, *Confirmation: Presbyterian Practices in Ecumenical Perspective* (Louisville, Ky.: Geneva Press, 1996), 9.

[10]Anthony Giddens, "Living in a Post-Traditional Society," in *Reflexive Modernization,* Beck, Giddens, and Lash, 56–109.

[11]Giddens argues that when tradition, which provided the stabilizing frameworks, dissolves, it becomes more problematic in respect to the construction of identity and the meaning of social norms. Ibid., 67.

[12]Beck, *Risk Society,* 130.

[13]According to Beck, this individualization takes effect precisely under general social conditions, which do not allow individuals to have autonomous private existence. In other words, individualization has come to refer to the institutional shaping of individuals' lives. Ibid., 130–34.

[14]Habermas describes Max Weber's modernization process according to the customary division into "society," "culture," and "personality." Weber conceives the modernization of society as the differentiation of the capitalist economy and the modern state, and he sees cultural modernization in modern science and technology, autonomous art, and ethics. And he apprehends the modernization of the personality system as the "methodical conduct of life." Habermas, *Theory of Communicative Action,* 1:57–68.

[15]The distinction between pubic and private spheres has been a subject of study for sociology, philosophy, and religion. This discussion leads us to explore the role of religion in the public space more seriously, since religion and the private sphere seem to be equated in the modern context.

[16]Christianity in the modern context has concentrated only on providing its members guidance with regard to personal, moral, and existential meanings, and not to questions regarding social life as a whole.

[17]Richard R. Osmer, *A Teachable Spirit: Recovering the Teaching Office in the Church* (Louisville, Ky.: Westminster John Knox Press, 1990), 27–30.

[18]As to globalization, Roland Robertson asserts that globalization primarily means the "compression of the entire world into a single place." Twentieth-century globalization is "a form of institutionalization of world order," which is controlled by "globally diffused ideas concerning societies, individuals, international relations and humankind." This "compression of the entire

world into a single place" results in relativization of religious traditions, considerable religious diversity, and religious reconstitution of locality. Roland Robertson, "The Globalization Paradigm: Thinking Globally," in *Religion and the Social Order: New Developments in Theory and Research,* vol. 1, ed. David G. Bromley (Greenwich, Conn.: JAI Press, 1991), 216. See also idem, *Globalization: Social Theory and Global Culture* (London: Sage, 1992).

[19]Robertson, *Globalization,* 169–70.

[20]F. L. Lechner, "Fundamentalism Revisited," in *In God We Trust: New Patterns of Religious Pluralism in America,* ed. T. Robbins and D. Anthony (New Brunswick, N.J.: Transaction Books, 1990), 95, quoted by Robertson, *Globalization,* 170.

[21]Peter Berger points out that there are "interconnections between secularity and pluralism." However, he also argues that secularization is neither as prevalent nor as irreversible as had been argued. The description of these different phenomena is closely interconnected and not easily analyzed separately. Peter L. Berger, "From the Crisis of Religion to the Crisis of Secularity," in *Religion and America: Spiritual Life in a Secular Age,* ed. Mary Douglas and Steven Tipton (Boston: Beacon Press, 1983), 14–15.

[22]Robert Kegan, *In Over Our Heads: The Mental Demands of Modern Life* (Cambridge, Mass.: Harvard University Press, 1994), 73–304.

[23]José Casanova, *Public Religions in the Modern World* (Chicago: University of Chicago Press, 1994), 7.

[24]Ibid., 19.

[25]Bryan Wilson illustrates the phenomena in relation to the functions that religion has carried out. First, religion has come to have less place in strengthening social control and social regulation. Second, religion does not provide interpretation of the "physical universe." Third, as to the matter of identity, most modern states become basically secular in conception. Fourth, there are active competing agencies for emotional life, such as television, films, or music. Bryan Wilson, *Religion in Sociological Perspective* (Oxford: Oxford University Press, 1982), 32–42; see also Émile Durkheim, *The Elementary Forms of the Religious Life* (New York: The Free Press, 1915); idem, *The Division of Labor in Society* (Glencoe, Ill.: The Free Press, 1947).

[26]George Herbert Mead argues that the construction of the self always includes an experience of another. This implies that the self is made through relations with others, and when others' response becomes a part of the individual, the self appears. Moreover, the individual is reacting not only to others, but also to a community, which is society. George Herbert Mead, *Mind, Self, and Society* (Chicago: University of Chicago Press, 1974), 192–200, quoted in *Know Thyself: Collected Readings on Identity,* ed. David Cernic and Linda Longmire (New York: Paulist Press, 1987), 301–7.

[27]Mead, *Mind, Self, and Society,* in *Know Thyself,* ed. Cernic and Longmire, 301–7. See Carol Gilligan, *In a Different Voice: Psychological Theory and Women's Development* (Cambridge, Mass.: Harvard University Press, 1982). See also Judith V. Jordan, Alexandra G. Kaplan, Jean Baker Miller, Irene P. Stiver, and Janet L. Surrey, *Women's Growth in Connection: Writings from the Stone Center* (New York: The Guilford Press, 1991).

[28]Martin Buber argues that humans in general exist anthropologically not in isolation, but in the completeness of the relation between humans. While criticizing the modern tendency of taking an analytical and reductive approach to humans, he emphasizes the importance of reciprocity and relationality in understanding the nature of humanity. Martin Buber, *The Knowledge of Man: Selected Essays,* ed. Maurice Friedman, trans. Maurice Friedman and Roland Gregor Smith (New York: Harper & Row, 1965), 80–84.

[29]Jean Piaget deals with the question of morality through the analysis of child psychology and shows how this is undertaken. He acknowledges that games do not seem to be moral in their contents, but this is the place where morality starts, in respect for rules. See Jean Piaget, *The Moral Judgment of the Child,* trans. Marjorie Gabain (New York: Harcourt, Brace, 1932), 1–2, 79, 90–91. See also Jean Piaget and Barbel Inhelder, *The Psychology of the Child,* trans. Helen Weaver (New York: Basic Books, 1969).

[30]When children grow, they gradually separate themselves from their family circle. Piaget argues that "the more they escape from family conformity, the greater change their consciousness of rules will undergo." Piaget, *Moral Judgment of the Child,* 98.

[31]See Paul Ricoeur, *The Symbolism of Evil,* trans. Emerson Buchanan (Boston: Beacon Press, 1967), 19, 351–53, 356. Paul Ricoeur defines the "second naïveté" as "the modern mode of belief in symbols, an expression of the distress of modernity and a remedy for that distress" (352). He goes on to argue that the second naïveté will be a second Copernican revolution: "The being which posits itself in the *Cogito* has still to discover that the very act by which it abstracts itself from the whole does not cease to share in the being that challenges it in every symbol" (356).

[32]James Fowler, *Becoming Adult, Becoming Christian* (San Francisco: Harper & Row, 1984), 65.

[33]Ibid., 65–66.

[34]Ibid., 66.

[35]Carol Gilligan contends that care and responsibility play a crucial role in achieving "postconventionality" in women's development, leading to a "postconventional contextual ethic." This is different from Kohlberg's "postconventional formal ethic," which corresponds closely to the path that men's development takes. J. M. Murphy and C. Gilligan, "Moral Development in Late Adolescence and Adulthood: A Critique and Reconstruction of Kohlberg's Theory," *Human Development* 23 (1980): 77–104; see also Carol Gilligan, *In a Different Voice.*

[36]In Fowler's faith development, the stage of postconventionality could be identified with Individuative-Reflective faith and Conjunctive faith.

[37]In Kegan's theory, the fourth and fifth orders of consciousness display the characteristics of "postconventionality." According to his theory, the fourth order of consciousness demonstrates the self's new ability to be an internal judge, in other words, a self-evaluating, self-governing system. The fifth order of consciousness demonstrates the understanding that the self is not unitary, but multiple and interrelated. This understanding of the multiself provides room for the acknowledgment of difference and the necessity of open discourse across the difference by emphasizing relationality. See Kegan, *In Over Our Heads.*

[38]Robert Kegan acutely describes the self as meaning making between self and other. The constructive-developmental tradition mainly focuses on development as a meaning-making process in which the self emerges in the increasing understanding of the relationship between subject and object. In his theory, personality development occurs through "interactions between the organism and the environment." The self is constructed through the relations between self and other throughout the developmental stages. Robert Kegan, *Evolving Self: Problem and Process in Human Development* (Cambridge, Mass.: Harvard University Press, 1982), 3–11; Kegan, *In Over Our Heads,* 21–36.

[39]Kohlberg, who coined the term *postconventional,* defined this term as a move toward autonomous moral principles that have validity and application apart from the authority of the groups or persons. Based on the Kantian idea of the autonomous self and the concept of justice, Kohlberg uses this term to describe the higher level toward which a mature person is moving. Lawrence Kohlberg and Carol Gilligan, "The Adolescent as a Philosopher: The Discovery of the Self in a Postconventional World," *Daedalus* 100 (Fall 1971): 1066–67.

[40]Jürgen Habermas, *Moral Consciousness and Communicative Action,* trans. Christian Lenhardt and Shierry Weber Nicholson (Cambridge, Mass.: MIT Press, 1995), 164.

[41]Habermas explains his argument with the distinction between questions of justice and questions of good life. He argues that, at the conventional level, duties are intertwined with habitual and unquestioned concrete life practices. Ibid., 164–65.

[42]Kohlberg and Gilligan argue that in adolescence, "the child has the cognitive capability for moving from a conventional to a postconventional, reflective, or philosophic view of values and society." Also in adolescence, the child experiences the possibility for either identity formation or identity crisis. With the emergence of the capacity for "formal operational" thinking (Piaget) as well as interpersonal perspective taking (Selman), adolescents are able to reflect on their identity, with questions such as "Where am I from?" "Who am I?" and "What will I be?" in relation to moral and religious issues. They start questioning conventional thinking and begin to formulate postconventional understanding of the self, society and culture. Kohlberg and Gilligan, "Adolescent as a Philosopher," 1072.

[43]Habermas, *Moral Consciousness and Communicative Action,* 161.

[44]Lawrence Kohlberg, "From Is to Ought," in *Cognitive Development and Epistemology,* ed. Theodor Mischel (New York: Academic Press, 1971), 165.

[45]The difference between the conventional level and postconventional level in Habermas's and Kohlberg's theories is found clearly in the absence of principles at the conventional level. At the conventional level, morality is more subject to particular content and to influence "by group definition of the situation than is principle morality." Habermas, *Moral Consciousness and Communicative Action,* 178.

[46]Ibid., 164.

[47]Robert Wuthnow, James Davison Hunter, Albert Bergesen, and Edith Kurzweil, *Cultural Analysis: The Work of Peter Berger, Mary Douglas, Michel Foucault, and Jürgen Habermas* (New York: Routledge & Kegan Paul, 1984), 201.

[48]Habermas, *Moral Consciousness and Communicative Action,* 122.

[49]Ibid., 124–25, 160–63.

[50]See Seyla Benhabib and Fred Dallmayr, eds., *The Communicative Ethics Controversy* (Cambridge, Mass.: MIT Press, 1991); Seyla Benhabib, *Situating the Self: Gender, Community, and Postmodernism in Contemporary Ethics* (New York: Routledge, 1992).

[51]For Habermas, the desirable endpoint of development is as follows: (1) the "continual revision of traditions" that have become reflexive, (2) the "dependency of legitimate orders" on formal procedures for the justification of norms, and (3) the "continually self-steered stabilization" of a highly abstract ego-identity. Jürgen Habermas, *Theorie des kommunikativen Handelns,* vol. 2, *Zur kritik der functionalistischen Vernunft* (Frankfurt: Suhrkamp, 1981), 219–20, quoted in White, *Recent Work of Jürgen Habermas,* 99.

[52]See Don S. Browning and Francis Schüssler Fiorenza, eds., *Habermas, Modernity, and Public Theology* (New York: Crossroad, 1992).

[53]James Fowler, *Faithful Change: The Personal and Public Challenges of Postmodern Life* (Nashville, Tenn.: Abingdon Press, 1996), 147–59.

[54]James Fowler, *Stages of Faith: The Psychology of Human Development and the Quest for Meaning* (San Francisco: Harper & Row, 1981), 4.

[55]Habermas argues that communicative action or interaction works as the medium for the reproduction of the life world. This reproduction of the life world can be described in three ways according to the differentiation of the life world into culture, society, and personality: "cultural reproduction," "social integration," and "socialization." These processes of reproduction involve "continuation of valid knowledge," a "stabilization of group solidarity," and a "formation of responsible actions." White, *The Recent Work of Jürgen Habermas,* 99–100.

[56]The limitations of "postconventional education" can be explained in three ways. (1) One can raise questions of openness in the construction of theory building. In other words, one needs to have a clear sense of who he or she is and understand his/her own tradition in order to engage in this open conversation with different perspectives for a common understanding. (2) Postconventional education can be criticized easily for its utopian tendency in envisioning an ideal educational context and an eschatological hope for the realm of God. (3) Postconventional education is in danger of overemphasizing the rationalistic dimension of education by advocating the concept of "postconventionality" proposed by Habermas.

10

Speak Truth to Power: Theology and Public Policy

DUNCAN B. FORRESTER

Jim Fowler has been a leading figure in the recrudescence of concern with ethics in professional life and public policy, and it is highly significant that he comes to this position unashamedly as a theologian. Karl Barth is probably correct in suggesting that one cannot separate dogmatics and belief from ethics and discipleship, and an ethics that floats free of our ultimate convictions about God, the world, and human beings is inherently volatile. In his recent major concern with ethics in public life, Fowler stands in a great tradition. And some parts of this tradition are particularly deeply rooted in Scotland and from there were implanted into the American academy.

Reformed theology in Scotland, as I hope to show, was from its beginning concerned with transforming the social order and with the responsible use of power. In the universities, this expressed itself in the long tradition, which continued at least up to John Macmurray's tenure of the chair of moral philosophy in the University of Edinburgh in the 1950s, that at the heart of the academic enterprise stood a theologically informed moral philosophy. This subject was expected to address real issues of the sort professional people met in their day-to-day practice, rather than abstract linguistic issues. It was common for doctors, lawyers, and ministers from the area to attend moral philosophy lectures alongside students from various faculties and to find them relevant and challenging to their practice. This was the heart of what a university was about: encouraging reflective excellence in practice, and challenging people—particularly powerful and influential people—to lives of altruism, service, and goodness. This tradition was adopted in many of the older collegiate foundations in the United States that had been influenced from Scotland. It was not uncommon for the president of the college to lecture on just the kind of practice-oriented moral philosophy we have been outlining to the entire student body. For the college was understood to be concerned not just with skills—important as these are—but with goodness and moral excellence in practice, the qualities Aristotle labeled practical wisdom.

This noble tradition has been deeply challenged, and in many places destroyed, by the fragmentation of university life on the one hand, and, on the other, by the long dominance of a kind of analytical philosophy that neither had time for theology nor engaged with the kind of dilemmas that people face in daily life. Instead of being the integrative core of the university, moral philosophy at the same time sat rather loosely to its own tradition and became just one speciality among many in the university. The result, where this has happened, has been a massive impoverishment of university life, which easily slides into a central concern with cleverness and enterprise rather than with practical wisdom, goodness, and the service by the powerful of the weak, the poor, and the marginalized. Centers such as the Center for Ethics in Public Policy and the Professions, headed by Jim Fowler at Emory, and the Edinburgh University Centre for Theology and Public Issues are trying to turn the tide. In this chapter, I want to reflect on some of the lessons we have learned in Edinburgh, which may, I hope, be of interest elsewhere. In this field, we all have to learn from one another.

1. A Parable

I start with a parable that seems to me to illustrate aptly the Scottish tradition that we have inherited. It explains some of the emphases that we try to express in the work of the Centre for Theology and Public Issues. It comes from the wonderful morality play by Sir David Lindsay, *Ane Satyre of the Thrie Estaites,* which was first performed at the Palace of Linlithgow before Mary Queen of Scots and her court in 1540, early in the disturbances that led to the Scottish Reformation. It was sensationally revived at the first Edinburgh International Festival and has been performed many times since then.

At the climax of the play, "Poor John the Commonweal" moves center stage for the first time. His voice has been but rarely heard until this point in the drama. Now, it comes loud and clear from the heart of the action. Poor John is supported and encouraged by two other characters. On his right is Divine Correctioun, while on his left stands Gude Counsel, grasping the book of the gospels. Poor John, the ordinary Scot, the one who is commonly forgotten in high places, whose interests and feelings are rarely taken into account, now denounces the oppression and the injustice, the self-obsession and the arrogance of each of the "thrie estaites" in turn—the burgesses (merchants), the nobility, and the church. John calls for justice and for peace, for a purification of church and state, for a society that is fair and decent and gives priority to the interests of the weak and the poor and the forgotten.

Poor John's speech to the powerful, his call to them to do justice and love mercy and walk humbly with their God, became a central concern of the Scottish Reformation. Alongside purity of doctrine and worship, the establishment of justice, the ending of oppression, and what would today be called a "preferential option for the poor" were central concerns in the early Reformation period. Church courts, according to *The First Book of Discipline,* were concerned with charges of "oppressing of the poore by exactions" and "deceiving of them in buying and selling by wrang met and measure." Knox himself taught that "the dear commonalty of Scotland" were responsible to God for the behavior of their rulers and ought to demand justice and fair dealing from them, as Poor John the Commonweal had done.

Here, surely, is a great heritage and a mandate for speaking truth to power!

2. The Relevance of the Radical Scottish Tradition

Rather to the surprise of many people in Scotland, Karl Barth chose to frame his 1938 Gifford Lectures, which in one sense were wrestling with the concrete issues of the German church struggle and the growing power of Nazism and in another way engaging with perennial issues of theology and life, around a then almost forgotten document from the Reformation period, the *Scots Confession* of 1560. The reasons for this are not hard to seek. Barth found the *Scots Confession* christological through and through. Unlike the later *Westminster Confession,* the *Scots Confession* does not speak of a natural theology complementing revealed theology. It eschews rational or scholastic theology. The times demand clear and unambiguous Christian confession and a call to active obedience. And this call to obedience is uncompromising.

The *Scots Confession* is among the most radical Reformation documents, delimiting strictly the powers of the ruler, distinguishing church and state without neglecting their responsibilities to each other, and actually affirming a right, indeed a duty, of resistance to unjust rule. The *Scots Confession* teaches that human nature since the fall is fundamentally flawed: nature is fallen and corrupt; there is no way to God other than by faith and grace; and by nature human beings are incapable of serving or knowing God. Barth saw the *Scots Confession* as anticipating his own rejection of natural theology.

From the sixteenth century, Scotland has maintained a somewhat distinctive understanding of the relationship of church and state, church and society. The ruler has not been recognized as "Supreme Governor" of the church, as in England, or as *primus episcopus,* as in many of the Lutheran lands of the continent of Europe. The ruler should be a member of the church and has responsibilities toward the church. Andrew Melville, the leader of the Second Reformation who in an encounter with James VI at Falkland in 1596 called the king "bot God's sillie vassall," typified the early relationship between church and state. Melville sees his task at a time of crisis for church and crown to speak truth to power and clarify what he sees as the true Reformed relationship of church and state. Here is a strong affirmation of the sole lordship of Christ, which relativizes all earthly sovereignties, and a powerful suggestion that this is mediated to the civil authorities by the Kirk, which in a special sense is the kingdom of Christ. This distinctively Scottish version of the two kingdoms theory may from time to time have been open to the opposite dangers to those latent in the Anglican Reformation's affirmation of the royal supremacy.[1] It certainly involved a claim on the part of the church to spiritual independence, which was seen by royalists in the sixteenth and seventeenth centuries as an unacceptable limitation on royal power, and which could easily become theocracy, or even the unqualified power of ministers.

The Scots Reformed tradition also stresses peculiarly strongly the responsibilities laid upon ordinary people. They were responsible to God for their government's actions and shared with government responsibility for establishing justice and opposing tyranny and oppression. The resistance to a tyrant that was grudgingly conceded by Luther and Calvin, under strictly defined conditions, in the *Scots Confession* became a duty.

The Scots Reformed tradition of social theology is thus, as I have tried very briefly to show, strongly confessional and biblical. It stresses that the church and the state are distinct communities that have reciprocal responsibilities. All power flows from God, and human beings are responsible to God for the way they exercise this power. The community as a whole is in a covenantal relationship with God; its whole life is to be lived toward God. But the church is not simply the one united community viewed from a different angle, with all citizens being regarded as disciples and all disciples as citizens, and usually with the monarch as the common head of church and state. Although the nations might be a covenanted community, the church was a sign and a challenge to the whole community because it was an anticipation and a kind of working model of God's coming reign.

3. A Living Tradition

The radical strand in the Scottish tradition of social theology has always emphasized the necessity for theology and the church to offer a distinctive perspective. It still shows itself today in a sometimes quite obsessive determination in the Church of Scotland to ground its public statements in the Bible. At its best, this results in the church's making a recognized and significant contribution to public debate, as did the Church and Nation Committee's 1989 report on the Constitution, which demonstrated with great clarity that there was a distinct and democratic Scottish tradition of thought on sovereignty and the constitution that was grounded in theology and widely recognized as highly relevant to the developing debate on devolution and the reform of the constitution.

There is that in the tradition of social theology that I have sketched[2] which is no longer relevant in a pluralistic, secular age. And there are distinctive dangers in the tradition that still need to be addressed. But we have also seen developments in the last fifty years or so that suggest that it may have continuing vitality and relevance in these days. For example, the Theological Declaration of Barmen of 1934 was an immensely influential confessional statement against Hitler and Nazism; and the struggle against apartheid in South Africa had close to its heart arguments about biblical interpretation, a series of confessional statements, and the ecumenical declarations that apartheid was a confessional issue of such gravity that those Christians who defended apartheid should be excluded from the fellowship of the church. The critique of natural law developed by Barth and discerned by him as already there in the early documents of the Scottish Reformation apparently retains its saliency. Nature, as we observe and experience it, is according to Reformed theology fallen, a broken remnant of God's original order and final purpose. God's purposes, being, and commands cannot now be read off nature as we find it. Natural theology easily reflects back the conventional wisdom of the age—but biblical and confessional arguments, too, may be used to buttress prejudices or conceal interests.

The Scottish Reformation had a strong conviction that reformation involved not just doctrine, worship, and the life of the church, but that the whole of society should be reformed. The *Scots Confession* itself said many things about the responsibilities of rulers and of subjects. It was complemented by *The First Book of Discipline* of 1560, which not only outlined the reconstruction of the Kirk that was required but also outlined a program by which the whole life of the community and the nation was to be shaped in accordance with God's commands and should reflect the divine purpose of justice and love.[3] This broad concern was expressed down the ages in the church's involvement in education, poor relief, and social justice, as well as individual behavior, with the commitment to what Thomas Chalmers in the nineteenth century called "the Christian good of Scotland." And the concern encompasses far more than Scotland.

Interestingly enough, Roman Catholic social teaching has in recent years moved from an almost sole dependence on natural law reasoning to a far greater reliance on scripture and serious and sustained endeavors to discern what God is doing in our times and calling us to do. This is perhaps most marked in John Paul II's encyclical *Centesimus Annus* (1991), but it is a general development in the wake of the Second Vatican Council. That encyclical not only celebrates the centenary of *Rerum Novarum*, but very seriously asks what God is doing and saying in "the New Things of Today," and especially seeks to interpret theologically the momentous events of "The Year 1989." Thus today, a shared commitment to the serious task of discerning the signs of the times together with a joint conviction of the centrality of scripture bring together Christians from various traditions in the development of a social theology responsive to the needs, problems, and opportunities of today.

The Scottish tradition of social theology is, I believe, largely confessional and evangelical. It has a gospel to share, good news to proclaim. It attends to the Bible and the tradition of faith at the same time as it attempts to discern the signs of the times and to understand what is going on in the light of the gospel. Since the seventeenth century, this has often been linked to a classical or Enlightenment form of natural theology, as in that of Samuel Rutherford or Thomas Chalmers. In the pluralist, fragmented, and secular society of today, the question of natural theology is raised with a new urgency as the only way of uniting believers and others in pursuit of a common good that is understood as unrelated to religious specifics and the understanding of which is accessible to everyone. While there is much in these efforts to forge a consensus around shared ideas of the good that is attractive and valuable, there is a danger that public debate may be impoverished by being denied the distinctive truths and insights of Christian faith. It is not only in times of crisis, such as the rise of Nazism or the struggle against apartheid, that a confessional approach has much to commend itself, even in a plural society. It is by turns a challenge, a corrective, or a complement to approaches that are in some way or another based on natural theology.

4. Speak Out for Those Who Cannot Speak

John the Commonweal was able to speak for himself, albeit encouraged by Divine Correctioun and Gude Counsel. But it is far more common for the poor and weak to be denied a voice. Liberation theologians characteristically see a central part of their role as standing with and speaking for the poor and the excluded, the ones who are commonly without a voice, fulfilling the biblical injunction:

> Speak out for those who cannot speak,
>   for the rights of all the destitute.
> Speak out, judge righteously,
>   defend the rights of the poor and needy.[4]

The liberation theologians, I believe, are right in affirming this role of the theologians, to speak for the poor and weak and voiceless. Only those who stand with those who are denied a voice can articulate their voice and contribute thus to the search for truth, not allowing the meanings of the powerful and intellectual to dominate the discussion and exclude or despise other voices. A proper objectivity is often compatible with taking sides; indeed taking sides, commitment, can be an avenue to truth. The liberation theologians' insight at this point is of broad relevance and importance.

It is, I believe, bad in principle and bad in practice to talk about people behind their backs, particularly if they are relatively powerless people who are often labeled "problems" and one is talking about their problems and how to solve them

In social theology, there is a need to put scientific study of the situation at the service of a more affective or emotional approach[5] that enables us to see things through others' eyes and leads to a more adequate and rounded understanding of the situation. I am trying to avoid using words like "sympathy" or "compassion" because they have been so devalued in common usage. But they both in origin mean feeling together, putting oneself in the other person's shoes and sharing at the level of feeling in order to deepen the understanding and strengthen the will to do something to improve the situation. And this is precisely what I am talking about.

5. An Experiment in Public Theology

The Centre for Theology and Public Issues (CTPI) in the University of Edinburgh was initially established to attempt to meet a widely expressed need for a serious Christian think tank in Scotland on social, constitutional, and political issues, which could act as a resource for the churches and others in contributing to public debate. It should be ecumenical and seek academic rigor in all its work. It was to engage with specific issues: where people are hurting; where there is much uncertainty; and often where serious communication among those of differing commitments, experiences, and views has more or less broken down. The Centre was to try to predict and engage with the issues that would be on the public agenda tomorrow, or next year, rather than with the issues that everyone was talking about and studying at the present moment. This forward look was to ensure that we did not simply repeat what everyone was saying anyway or duplicate research that was going on elsewhere. Instead, we were to try to equip the churches and theologians to prepare seriously for tomorrow's debates.

CTPI was intended to be, and from the beginning was, in fact, a thoroughly interdisciplinary operation, involving people from many different specialities and various kinds of experience in its work. It had, and has, a special care for the place of theology. This is a remarkably tricky matter, partly as a result of academic specialization, which has pushed much theology into cultivating what is considered its own cabbage patch and seldom looking over the garden fence, let alone talking with the neighbors. Occasionally, we succeeded in CTPI in offering theological insights that were regarded as strikingly relevant, but sometimes the theology didn't connect. Increasingly, we discovered that people became involved in our work because we provided a highly unusual kind of forum, and they were eager, even if they had no Christian commitment, to hear whether theology had anything relevant and interesting to say. There are many people in academic and public life who embrace Christian attitudes and values and whose lives often put us card-carrying Christians to shame, people who want to know about the roots of the values they know to be true and who want to know if Christianity makes a difference.

We also had in the work of CTPI, from very early on, a determination not to speak about people and their problems behind their backs. It was important to embrace and understand the human reality of social problems, to share feelings and emotions as well as thoughts and ideas. So when we are discussing poverty, we have poor people as full participants; when we are talking about homelessness, there are homeless people present. This often has interesting and important results. I remember occasions when, after extremely fine and humane presentations by leading scholars, a poor or homeless person has got up and shouted angrily, "You don't know what you are talking about!" In a very important sense, that cry is true. Some academics, and some theologians, turn away from such angry, inarticulate, and confusing debate to more orderly academic discourse, while others see attending to such voices as a very central part of engaging *together* with the hurt and the pain that many people are suffering. Then, and only then, there sometimes comes the time when there is a responsibility of speaking for those who have no voice.

Sometimes, the motivation for a sustained study comes from experience of a situation where communication has broken down, where people are speaking past one another rather than attending to what others have to say.

For example, some years ago we had a conference on finance and ethics. The input was of a high quality, but it quickly became clear that there was no communication between those who had great responsibilities in the Scottish financial world, and who tended to be very cautious in their public utterances, and the critics, who saw no way forward other than the dismantling of the financial system and its replacement by something that is totally different and morally entirely unobjectionable. Gathering a mixed group from all sides of the question and arranging for them to meet in private sessions under an agreement of confidentiality gradually led to a different and more productive kind of discourse. The leading financiers were able in such a context to admit that they sometimes had doubts about the moral acceptability of processes and decisions in which they were involved; the critics came to see that they needed to talk of change, reform, and improvement rather than simply challenge and confrontation. As the members of the group gained confidence in one another, they decided that they should stay together; therefore they formed a Finance and Ethics Network, which continues to meet today, and they began publishing a *Finance and Ethics Quarterly*.

I will now say a little about three projects that attempted to embody these principles.

In 1984, we were asked by the Church and Nation Committee of the Church of Scotland to undertake a study of the distribution of wealth, income, and benefits. A working group was established, composed of people with a wide range of experience and expertise. It met regularly for more than two years and received opinions, advice, and information from a wide variety of sources. A brief report was presented to the General Assembly of the Church of Scotland in 1987, and congregations and Kirk Sessions were encouraged to discuss these matters further. The fuller version of the report was published as a book, *Just Sharing: A Christian Approach to the Distribution of Wealth, Income, and Benefits.*[6] This book was presented to the then Prime Minister, Margaret Thatcher by the moderator when she visited the General Assembly to deliver her "Sermon on the Mound." It was also discussed widely in churches and community groups, and with politicians and academics.

The first task of the group was to face the facts and discover something of what these facts mean in human terms for individuals, for families, and for the nation. We then moved on to reflection and interpretation, looking to the Bible and the Christian tradition for clues, insights, signals, and challenges. Finally, we discussed how we should respond to what we had found—theologically, the question of how we should respond to Jesus Christ and the neighbors he has given us today. We felt that to be serious, we had to respond on three fronts simultaneously: looking at issues of personal lifestyle, then at the life of the church, and only then at questions of public policy.

None of the working group was themselves poor, although we attended to the voices of poor people. We all had a kind of security, which meant that we had never experienced from the inside the powerlessness and vulnerability of the poor. We had not had our children going hungry to bed, been unable to make ends meet, or felt politically impotent. But some of us had been challenged deeply by involvement in situations of great poverty and inequality. Some of us had had our understanding of ourselves, of our faith, and of how we should lead our lives fundamentally transformed by finding ourselves implicated in situations of poverty and maldistribution. We listened to poor people, and one of the things we heard from a woman in Easterhouse was this: "The church should be teaching people about God. So everything's its business."

And it wasn't only the working group that listened. As part of the "reception" of *Just Sharing,* much unusual and significant listening took place. I remember well a conference in a deprived council estate [subsidized housing], organized by local community groups, political parties, and churches, to which we were invited essentially to listen. I was asked by a group of wealthy and influential businessmen if they could attend. After consultation with the conference organizers, I said yes, on two conditions–that a small number of them came so as not to swamp the conference, and that they devoted their time to listening rather than talking. I spent much of the afternoon in a small group with one of the most powerful businessmen in the city, as local women spoke of the dampness and bad design of many of their homes, the poor medical services in the area, the problems at the schools, the inadequacy of the public transport, and how they were coping with a pervasive drug problem and insensitive policing. The businessman had never heard this kind of thing before. It was a learning experience for him.

Another area in which we have done work involves prisons and punishment.[7] It all started with a conference in the course of which it became clear that the Scottish prison system, and much of the criminal justice system, was in a state of disarray, and this confusion was deeply harmful to society. We set up an interdisciplinary working group that included prison governors, chaplains, and educational officers; a couple of bright young criminologists; theologians; and a minister of the Church of Scotland who had been in prison for murder. His case was interesting in itself, for there had been, a couple of years before the group was convened, a notable debate in the General Assembly of the Church of Scotland about whether this man and another man who had been imprisoned for embezzlement were eligible to be ordained. The debate polarized around a large minority who argued that the standing of the Christian ministry depended on ministers being above reproach, and a small majority who argued that Christian ministry was about a gospel of grace and forgiveness and that a personal experience of great forgiveness qualified a minister to speak of grace from his own experience. A friend of mine who was a prison chaplain told me that when he was on his rounds not long after this debate, he found a prisoner in tears. He told the chaplain that he had been an elder, and his wife had visited him and told him that last Sunday, for the first time since his conviction, she had felt able to go to church, as she now realized that the church really believed in the forgiveness of sins.

The turning point in the working group's deliberations was this. After a long and depressing (because it was so unrelated to what actually went on in prisons) look at the current theories of punishment–rehabilitation, retribution, deterrence, and so forth–a Christian woman prison governor said, very quietly: "There are two things that few people pay much attention to in Scottish prisons these days–guilt, as a process with which individuals have to come to terms, and forgiveness, healing, and restoration of community." This started a very exciting two hours of discussion, at the end of which we all agreed that any system of punishment that was not directed toward the goal of reconciliation, healing, and forgiveness was seriously lacking in Christian and moral acceptability. Here we were, in fact, quarrying into central aspects of the Christian tradition to find help for public policy today. In this tradition, we found a challenge to the modern assumption that the world is divided neatly and unambiguously into the guilty and the innocent. We are all offenders, standing under the judgment and the grace of God.

Out of the experience of this project we found that there was a role for Christian social theology: in supporting conscientious and caring people working within the system, often fighting against much discouragement; in influencing public opinion, beginning with the churches, because public opinion often is savage and unforgiving; in constructive suggestions to policymakers; and in demonstrating that Christian insights may be of importance and relevance in public life today.

My final case is very brief, but still, I think, important. On two occasions, in 1987 and in 1998, we have had conferences in which we have brought together a diversity of people from Northern Ireland, from Scotland, and from the Irish Republic to speak together and to listen on the basis of a shared Christian faith. I remember very vividly at the 1987 conference on "Northern Ireland–A Challenge to Theology,"[8] how Garret Fitzgerald, at that time still Taoiseach of the Republic and one who has Protestant as well as Roman Catholic roots, honestly outlined his vision for the future, in dialogue with Enda McDonagh and Terry McCaughey. And I remember Enda McDonagh's controversial suggestion that only a clear disjunction between Catholicism and nationalism and Protestantism and unionism will enable Christian faith to survive, and Frank Wright's remarkable discussion of the reconciliation of memories.

And in the 1998 conference on "A Turning Point in Scotland and Ireland? The Challenge to the Churches and Theology Today,"[9] I recall the stress on the similarities between the Scottish and the Irish situation, and the suggestion that we can learn, positively and negatively, from one another. Reconciliation may be a long drawn out process, but, for Christians, it is the recognition and expression of what God has achieved for us in Christ.

And above all, I remember that saintly Irish Presbyterian theologian Alan Lewis, who died so tragically young, telling us that we must learn in Scotland and Ireland how to speak the truth to one another in love.

And that, in a real sense, is what we are about in CTPI, learning how to speak truth to power in love and in justice.

6. Theological Fragments

Public theology needs to learn how to concern itself with the concrete and the specific, with the particular needs of neighbors, far and near. Commitment to great moral or political systems and ideals can sometimes conflict directly with an ethical attitude to the concrete *other*. In its concern with the concrete, with action and existence, and with freedom, and in its suspicion of grandiose and impersonal schemes and systems, postmodernity presents opportunities and challenges to the mission of the church. Indeed, the recognition of fragmentation opens a whole range of evangelistic opportunities.

I have suggested the deployment of "theological fragments" not because I buy into the postmodernist scenario (although I find it quite illuminating, particularly in its view of grand theories as oppressive), but because, in a situation where most people are both ignorant and suspicious of Christian doctrine and practice, there is really no other way forward than presenting or offering "fragments" that may be seen as relevant and true, illuminating and helpful for just practice.

A theologian should not, I think, be ashamed of offering initially in public debate in the conditions of postmodernity no more than "fragments" of insight. Postmodernists (and sociologists of knowledge) are, after all, right in affirming that systematic, carefully developed theories can sometimes conceal practices that are inhumane and brutalizing; ideologies can serve as the emperor's new clothes, so that the theologian's task, as a little child, is to cry out, "But the emperor's got no clothes on!" A fragment of truth reveals that to which most people have allowed themselves to be blinded. Truth telling in a fragmentary way becomes even more important when the scheme to conceal the emperor's nakedness is something that is hurting people and destroying community.[10]

Moral and theological fragments come from specific quarries—or visions, if you prefer that terminology. We know that theological fragments by which Christians live and that shape their practice have their home in a community of shared faith, the church, which, if it is true to its calling and its mission, does not wistfully look back to an unrecoverable past; instead it looks forward with expectation to God's future and meanwhile offers its fragments as a contribution to the common store and seeks to embody its insights in its life. Only at the end will the fragments, the "puzzling reflections in a mirror," give way to a face-to-face encounter with the Truth.

When a fragment is recognized as in some sense true, one should expect an interest in its provenance, in its embeddedness in a broader truth. Is a compelling task and opportunity today the bringing together of "theological fragments" that have been illuminating, instructive, or provocative in grappling with issues of practice "on the ground," reflecting on them and on their embeddedness in the structure of Christian faith, and inquiring whether this gives clues as to a constructive contribution in the public realm today? This may well be the way toward the renewal and recovery of Christian social vision in the conditions of today.

By "fragments," I mean a wide range of things–the importance of forgiveness in any decent criminal justice system, confessional statements such as the 1934 Theological Declaration of Barmen that established the German Confessing Church in opposition to Nazism, recent suggestions that a "Christian" view of human nature is necessary for a viable welfare system, and many others. Fragments may be irritants (the grit in the oyster that gathers a pearl?), stories or parables, the Socratic questioning of received assumptions, or even the "road metal" for straight paths.

Fragments, of course, come from somewhere; they have been quarried. My purpose in talking this way about real happenings and possibilities is partly evangelical: Some people who recognize a Christian fragment as true may trace it back to the quarry from which it comes. But I am also increasingly aware that fragments detached from the quarry are particularly liable to be abused or misunderstood and distorted. Thus, the theological task is, I believe, twofold: injecting or offering theological fragments in public debate and, simultaneously, laboring in the quarry or mine–work that may be largely invisible and regarded by most as irrelevant, but which is, in fact, essential. This, I believe, is precisely how Barth behaved in the 1930s: hard, unrelenting work on the Dogmatics "as if nothing had happened" (his phrase), and simultaneously bombarding the Nazis and the German Christians with a fusillade of fragments, which for many people provided a strong discernment of what was actually happening and how a Christian should respond. What I am profoundly opposed to is a facile presentation of idealistic commonplaces as if they were theological fragments!

Another parallel analogy, which in some ways is a corrective to the fragments and quarry image and is far more deeply rooted in Christian thought and liturgical practice, is that of the loaf and the crumbs or grains. The separate grains are ground and kneaded and baked into bread, the one loaf that is the sign of the body of Christ–both the body broken on the cross and the body of believers who gather and are dispersed in the world to bring forth fruit. For the work of salvation, for the work of God in the world, the body/loaf must be broken into crumbs, only to be gathered together into one at the end of time. At the heart of Christian faith and action is the breaking of the bread for the nourishment of God's people. The crumbs are food for a pilgrim people.

Some fragments are like pieces of glass or gems that catch the light and display its wonderful colors or generate a vision that many can share–glimpses into another world. It is perhaps better that visions and hopes of utopias should be generated in this way than by one of the huge ideologies that seem now to have collapsed. People and societies need to be liberated from being confined in the prison of "the real world," unable to dream the dreams that will shape the practice of tomorrow and become ultimately the practice of the reign of God.

So let's go back to the quarry, to obtain the fragments that give us road metal, that provoke the oyster to make pearls, that concentrate the light into visions, that generate utopias, that build up jigsaws puzzles of meaning, and that nourish the activity of truthfulness, love, and justice that is the practice of the reign of God!

Notes

[1]On the development of the idea of royal supremacy in the early English Reformation, see especially Diarmid MacCulloch, *Thomas Cranmer* (New Haven, Conn.: Yale University Press, 1996), esp. 278, 349, 364, 576ff., 617.

[2]I have discussed this more fully in chapter 11 of my *Truthful Action: Explorations in Practical Theology* (Edinburgh: T. & T. Clark, 2000).

[3]James K. Cameron, ed., *The First Book of Discipline* (Edinburgh: St. Andrew Press, 1972).

[4]Prov. 31:8–9.

[5]This is a process that reminds us of David Hume's famous saying, "Reason is, and ought to be, the slave of the passions." But we are suggesting particular kinds of passion that reason should serve.

[6]*Just Sharing: A Christian Approach to the Distribution of Wealth, Income and Benefits,* ed. Duncan B. Forrester and Danus Skene (London: Epworth Press, 1988).

[7]See Chris Wood, *The End of Punishment: Christian Perspectives on the Crisis in Criminal Justice* (Edinburgh: CTPI, 1991); "Law and Order–Prospects for the Future," *CTPI Occasional Paper,* no. 10 (1986); "Justice, Guilt and Forgiveness in the Penal System," *CTPI Occasional Paper,* no. 18 (1990); "Penal Policy: The Way Forward," *CTPI Occasional Paper,* no. 27 (1991).

[8]"Northern Ireland–A Challenge to Theology," *CTPI Occasional Paper,* no. 12 (1987).

[9]"A Turning Point in Scotland and Ireland? The Challenge to the Churches and Theology Today," ed. Andrew Morton, *CTPI Occasional Paper,* no. 43 (1998).

[10]Notice that Z. Bauman characterizes "the post-modern perspective" as "above all the tearing off of the mask of illusions; the recognition of certain pretences as false and certain objectives as neither attainable or, for that matter, desirable" (*Postmodern Ethics* [London: Blackwell, 1993], 3).

11

Religious Freedom and the Public Church

JOHANNES A. VAN DER VEN

The terrorist attack on the Twin Towers on September 11, 2001, has highlighted the problem of the relation between religion and society. The attack is legitimized with references to a "holy war" against decadent Western society to which Islam summons and enjoins its followers and for which they are prepared to give their all–even their lives. Despite obvious economic, political, and cultural causes behind the attack, there is an undeniable religious component in the form of the will to wage a holy war. Religion can topple a society, can undermine it, and may even destroy it totally. This happens particularly when a religion exerts a politically legitimized influence on one society, which then uses that influence to destroy another society.

Europe has a long history of bloody religious warfare, and in places such as Northern Ireland and the Balkans, it is still with us. But what we learned from the horrendous religious wars of the sixteenth and seventeenth centuries is that the risk of such wars diminishes appreciably if church and state are strictly separated and freedom of religion is entrenched in a constitution. This is not to banish religion from society but to declare it an object of personal freedom, a choice that people, in fact, make: for one religion or another, for no religion at all, or even against religion. In the same way that religious communities can use their freedom of expression and the freedom of the press within the framework of a constitutional state to expand their support through their preaching, so atheistic communities have the right to condemn the values and norms from which religious communities draw their inspiration.[1] To non-Western societies that are still based on an alliance between state and religion, this is manifestly indigestible and unacceptable. Moreover, to those non-Western societies that have felt oppressed by the West–both colonially and neocolonially–for decades and even centuries, this very alliance between throne and altar provides religious grounds to rebel, not merely against Western religious depravity but also against Western economic, social, and cultural exploitation. How does the West respond to this? Not by waging a holy war from its side, for the separation of church and state does not permit that, but by waging an allegedly just war, accompanied by a solemn declaration that the war is not directed against the religion in question (in this case, Islam) but against terrorists and countries that give them asylum and support.

Yet this solemn declaration does not solve the problem. After all, if we take the separation of church and state at all seriously, how should we deal with societies that do not recognize these fundamental human rights, including freedom of religion? How does one combine religious freedom with expressions of unfreedom that are legitimized by invoking religion? Should such expressions be respected, or at least tolerated, on grounds of religious freedom? The answer must be negative if, with a fundamentalist appeal to Islam, polygamy is permitted whilst every new marriage results in a prior family being orphaned, unmarried mothers are stoned whereas the man goes unpunished, blood feuds are enjoined as a moral duty, and decapitation is imposed as a penalty. Is the limit of religious freedom such unfreedom, the limit of religious tolerance such intolerance? Where do we draw the line between freedom and unfreedom, between tolerance and intolerance? The newly selected Nobel prize winner for literature, V. S. Naipaul, who defines himself as "a-religious," is consistently critical of religious unfreedom, specifically under fundamentalist Islam, in the four countries that he describes so vividly (Pakistan, Iran, Malaysia, and Indonesia), first in his *Among the Believers* (1981) and seventeen years later in his *Beyond Belief* (1998).[2] Especially in this second work, he suggests that religion only becomes acceptable or even meaningful if one crosses the boundary of everything pertaining to conventional, institutional religion (hence "beyond belief") and it is simply assimilated and internalized in the inner life of individuals as spirituality: beyond all enforced laws and rules, all imposed rites and myths, all dictated doctrines and dogma, without the pressure of the "total institution" (as Goffman calls an institution with an all-pervading control mechanism), which religion in its fundamentalist forms employs—not merely this particular Abrahamic religion but also the other two, Judaism and Christianity.[3]

On reading both the Islamic journeys, as Naipaul calls them, in the aftermath of September 11th, I was involuntarily reminded of James Fowler's stages of faith research. The question that came to mind was this: Under what conditions is it possible to cross the boundary beyond belief toward religious freedom? Of course, the question is far too broadly phrased, for it involves a virtually infinite number of economic, political, and cultural factors, and the field covered by these factors falls beyond my qualifications. But it also entails developmental-psychological factors, and some of these feature in the field of religion, which is the field to which James Fowler's life work pertains. Hence, the question under discussion in this article is this: In the field of religious development psychology, under what conditions is it possible to cross the boundary beyond belief toward religious freedom? And following from this, what can the public church contribute to the realization of these conditions?

This, in fact, defines the two parts of this article, which I dedicate to James Fowler with all my heart. In the first part, I dwell on the stages of faith that may be described as postconventional faith and on the conditions to actualize them in the perspective of religious freedom. In the second part, I consider how the public church can contribute to the realization of this postconventional faith in the context of religious freedom.

1. Religious Freedom and the Stages of Faith

For the sake of clarity, I should point out at once that the term "stages of faith beyond belief" does not derive from Fowler. As mentioned already, I am borrowing it from the book by V. S. Naipaul referred to above. What Naipaul calls belief, Fowler would call conventional faith, referring to the self-evident faith according to which a particular believer lives, thinks, and acts unquestioningly and without any doubts.[4] What Naipaul further stresses, far more strongly than Fowler, is the oppressive system of fixed patterns—cognitive, emotional, moral, and ritual—in this traditional faith, as well as the restrictive institutionalization of that faith. I regard this not as a contradiction, but rather as an explication and accentuation of what is implicit in Fowler's argument. After all, the distinctive feature of Fowler's conventional faith is conformism "in the sense that it is acutely tuned to the expectations and judgments of significant others and as yet does not have a sure enough grasp on its own identity and autonomous judgment to construct and maintain an independent perspective."[5] This prompts Sharon Parks to speak of "the tyranny of the they,"[6] of which the individual is not even aware. What Naipaul calls belief is what Fowler calls conventional faith; and what Naipaul calls beyond belief is what Fowler calls—I shall return to this later—beyond conventional faith.

I realize that this is to simplify Fowler's searching inquiry into faith development. Whereas my distinction makes it seem that his distinction between "belief" and "beyond belief," or between "conventional faith" and "beyond conventional faith," recognizes only two stages of faith, his interview research led him to distinguish between not just two but six stages of faith. These are: Intuitive-Projective faith, Mythic-Literal faith, Synthetic-Conventional faith, Individuative-Reflective faith, Conjunctive faith, and, finally, Universalizing faith.

Apart from the fact that the last stage (Universalizing faith) is strongly determined by the kingdom of God symbol of Judaism and Christianity and hence cannot serve as a general stage of faith, besides featuring infrequently or not at all in empirical studies, the other five stages of faith also raise some questions.[7]

The first three stages—Intuitive-Projective faith, Mythic-Literal faith, and Synthetic-Conventional faith—are clearly identifiable in the empirical findings. But are they in fact stages? According to the general theory of stages, individual psychic development consists in higher stages superseding lower ones, because the higher stage represents a more advanced level of cognitive, emotional, and/or moral functioning. Fowler, on the other hand, speaks of inclusion rather than substitution, implying that the higher stage includes the lower ones. Instead of linear development, he refers to a "spiralling movement of stages."[8] One might question whether this usage of the term *stage* is adequate and whether a term such as *soft stage* or, better still, *style* might not be more appropriate. There is certainly development, namely, development on a continuum. However, not all development is stage based. Stage-based development does not occur on a continuum but in a succession of discrete, interruptive intervals, so that individuals learn to handle their environment, so to speak, in a series of qualitatively changing spurts.

This jeopardizes the three claims postulated in general stage theory, namely, that the stages are invariable, irreversible, and universal. Invariable implies that they occur only in a given sequence: first Stage 1, next Stage 2, and then Stage 3. Irreversible means that, in normal circumstances, there is no possibility that a person can regress from a higher stage, at which he or she has actually been functioning, to a lower stage. And universal implies that this invariable, irreversible sequence is cross-cultural: Whether one does one's research in the United States or in Europe, in Africa or in Asia, the findings will be the same. The question is, Is this true?

While the first three stages, even if in no way hard stages, are certainly identifiable as distinct "styles" in empirical reality, the distinction between Stage 4 (Individuative-Reflective faith) and Stage 5 (Conjunctive faith) is difficult to discern empirically. What can be postulated is just one style, postconventional faith—a term used by Fowler himself when presenting his work synoptically and relating his faith development research to the public church. There, he makes a distinction between conventional faith and postconventional faith, defining the latter as "Individuative-Reflective or beyond."[9] The fact that Fowler himself speaks about conventional and postconventional faith in the context of the mission of the public church legitimizes my use of this distinction in my contribution to the reflection on the mission of the public church.

The questions posed thus far warrant further cross-cultural and longitudinal research. The more serious issues that an empirical theory such as Fowler's raises, and the more seriously all kinds of serious researchers probe these issues, the more it says for the empirical theory in question and the scientific reputation of its designer.

My question is, Does this apply equally to Fowler's further claim that the ontogenetic development of an individual's faith parallels the phylogenetic development of the society in which the person lives? Fowler maintains that conventional faith is associated with premodern society, Individuative-Reflective faith with modern society, and Conjunctive faith with postmodern society.[10] I thought long and hard whether I could concede this claim theoretically, in the absence of any historical and empirical research. Because of the undeniable interaction between individuals and their interpersonal, social, and societal environment, and because of the influence of this interaction on their change and even development, some relationship between the stages or styles and the society in which people live cannot be ruled out in advance. But that puts the claim to universality under pressure!

Yet another point that troubles me is the relation between modernity and postmodernity. I can form a clear picture of the distinction between modern and postmodern in the case of architecture—where the term *postmodern* was first used—and also in the case of modern and postmodern art, even in that of modern and postmodern culture. But the distinction between a modern and a postmodern society—at any rate if society is understood in Habermas's sense as the economic and political systems and the life world colonized by these systems—fails to make sense to me.[11] All I can conceive of is that the notion of a *Dialektik der Moderne* includes critical reflection on modernity. All sorts of phenomena that are currently associated with postmodernism on this basis are direct effects of modernity, such as economic, political, and information-technological globalization; I can discern nothing postmodern in them, despite Fowler's claims in this regard.[12] The various sociocultural phenomena that people relate to postmodernism—such as individualization, pluralization, fragmentation, privatization, detraditionalization, and deinstitutionalization—can be described, understood, and explained perfectly adequately in terms of modernization. They require no separate concept such as postmodernism. On the principle of conceptual parsimony, I prefer to leave it at that.

At all events, this need not be a fatal obstacle to Fowler's claim regarding the parallel between ontogenetic and phylogenetic development. In my view, we can disregard not only the distinction between modernity and postmodernity but also the distinction between Individuative-Reflective faith and Conjunctive faith, since the latter—as I have argued earlier—is dissolved in the single term "postconventional faith."[13]

This boils down to the following, more modest claim: There is a parallel between (1) the development from premodernity to modernity and (2) the development from conventional faith to postconventional faith.

Can one say, then, that religious freedom does not and cannot belong to the phylogenetic stage of premodernism but only to the stage of modernism, nor does it or can it belong to the ontogenetic stage of conventional faith but only to the stage of postconventional faith? This is an important question, because if answered affirmatively, one could, on the basis of Fowler's stages of faith research, create the conditions to achieve religious freedom. One could then infer what the public church can contribute to the realization of these conditions, which is what the second part of this article is about. And there are, in fact, arguments to answer the question, at least approximately, in the affirmative.

Premodern society is characterized, as indicated already, by an alliance between throne and altar or, put differently, between crown and temple, palace and mosque. Religion functions as the mortar of society in that it constitutes its foundation and cornerstone; it provides institutional coherence in that it holds the various institutions together and creates order among them; and it provides individual coherence in that it assigns meaning to the vicissitudes of human life, especially when it is marked by contingency and finitude–for instance, in the events of birth, suffering, and death.

In modern society, which grew via innumerable economic and political factors over many centuries, this is no longer the case. Modern society is characterized by awareness of a plurality of religions and nonreligious, secular worldviews, the dissolution of the link between state and religion, and the relegation of religion or any nonreligious worldview to the realm of free individual choice. Although the Enlightenment is regarded as the cradle of every individual's right to religious freedom and of the separation of church and state, this evolution can be traced back, via the Reformation and the Renaissance, to the Investiture Struggle (*Investiturstreit*) that culminated in the compromise of the Edict of Worms in 1122.[14]

One might well ask what holds modern society together now that God and religion no longer constitute its foundation and cornerstone. Modern political philosophy has not merely abolished God as the unifying center of democracy.[15] Every metaphysical entity whose "essence" could form the basis of democracy has vanished from it, be it the essence of human beings allegedly consisting in "reason" or authentic creativity, or the essence of the state, the nation, the market, or productive activity. Modern research into primates has eroded the division between humans and animals and between their rationality and authenticity; besides, human beings are more than just citizens, compatriots, consumers, or producers. They are all these along with countless other things, such as members of a household or a family, professionals, employers or employees, participants in all sorts of recreational contexts; they also have a hand in the communal provision of such amenities as the national education system, health care system, and traffic system, albeit in diverse ways at different times in their lives.[16] In fact, democracy is based on the insight that all of us fulfill many different functions and roles, and that both we and the various groups to which we belong pursue different short- or long-term goals and put these goals in a broader context according to diverse norms and values. What keeps us together is discussion, dialogue in which we jointly consider the legality and legitimacy of our goals and determine what goals, norms, and values should be ranked in what order. In other words, there is no metaphysical premise from which to infer the decisions to be taken: There is no core identity, no substantial core, the center is void; there is no center, as is expressed architecturally in the Dutch house of parliament. The one thing we can and must do is communicate, deliberate, argue, and negotiate about the values and interests that require or do not require positive choice, and that merit or do not merit priority over others. Conflicts of values and interests are not decided with weapons; they are clarified through argumentative communication and thus resolved. Does that not mean that human rights are the basis of Western democracy? Quite apart from the fact that their embodiment in practical measures cannot be accomplished other than through discussion and negotiation, they should, according to Habermas, be regarded as the institutional conditions under which every individual and group can take part in the aforementioned argumentative communication.[17] Furthermore, there is no definitive solution to any conflict: Argumentative communication is an endless, open process.[18]

In the religious sphere, too, such argumentative communication is vitally important. The significant point here is that, in this field, it can only take place on the basis of postconventional faith in Fowler's sense. Postconventional faith implies that one can distance oneself from the conventional faith that one has taken for granted from childhood, can confront this conventional faith and compare it with different forms of conventional faith in other traditions within one's own religion, in other religions, and in other—including secular—worldviews. It also implies that one autonomously appropriates those elements of one's own and (possibly) other traditions, religions, and worldviews that one finds meaningful for the development of one's own identity. It further implies that one accepts in one's very being that other people, when forming their own identity, make different choices and decisions; that these should be interpreted in terms of the assumptions and intentions that those people consider important; and that one understands the experiential, emotional, motivational, and cognitive reasons that they advance for their choice.

The quality entailed by postconventional faith is based on what are known (in the tradition of Jean Piaget and Lawrence Kohlberg, in which Fowler's study was conducted) as role taking and perspective exchange. Role taking means that one is capable of understanding not just the roles that one is deemed to play oneself but also those played by those with whom one interacts, and that one can tune one's conduct accordingly. Perspective exchange means that, apart from viewing the world from one's own perspective, one can also adopt the other's perspective and allow for it in one's behavior.

Role taking and perspective exchange are not confined to postconventional faith; they also occur in the earlier stages. But the principle underlying their functioning in the various stages differs, at any rate, if one can interpret Fowler's work in this regard in terms of Kohlberg's study.[19] Inasmuch as role taking and perspective exchange feature in Intuitive-Projective faith and Mythic-Literal faith, they are unilateral, implying that the other's role and perspective is considered only to the extent that it furthers one's own interest, which may be called unilateral instrumentalism. In Synthetic-Conventional faith, this unilateral instrumentality is replaced by the principle of reversibility, which means that one is able genuinely to put oneself in the other's place and view the world through that person's eyes, *in the same way* that he or she sees it and according to *that person's* assumptions, preconceptions, values, norms, and goals. In postconventional faith, the capacity for role taking and perspective exchange is based on an even higher principle, namely, that of the dignity of the human being. This principle of human dignity is part of our fundamental human rights, which include religious freedom, on which the human rights are based. The principle that human rights in their turn symbolize in practice is that of justice—at any rate, in John Rawls's school, on which Kohlberg relies.

In other words, role taking and perspective exchange occur in all stages, only the principle on which they are based or the reasons advanced for them differ, ranging from unilateral instrumentality to reversibility to justice.[20]

From Kohlberg, I take the notion—also mentioned by Fowler though not worked out in detail—that, with adequate guidance, people can be stimulated to reach the highest level of development, for instance, the supreme levels of moral and religious development. Kohlberg arrived at this by designing and investigating what are known as n+1 programs, in which "n" represents people's actual level of development and "+1" the closest higher level that one seeks to stimulate them to achieve. Kohlberg's main object with this exercise was educative programs for (albeit not exclusively) young people, but his insights appear to be applicable to adults as well, and hence to the intergenerational community of adults and youths. Here, his notions about peer-directed guidance are particularly useful, implying that adults guide adults and youths guide youths, but not to the detriment of adult-directed guidance of youths by adults.[21] Given this finding, these ideas can be transferred to the religious sphere, in this case that of interreligious dialogue. Peer-directed guidance can certainly be used in the dialogue between autochthonous and allochthonous groups of adults and youths from different religious traditions in Western societies. And finally, peer-directed guidance could definitely be applied in the dialogue between representatives of diverse religious traditions in Western and non-Western societies. In all this—to sum up what we have said here—the process of role taking and perspective exchange with a view to achieving freedom of religion at the level of postconventional faith plays a crucial role: It provides the necessary, albeit not sufficient, conditions for the full realization of religious freedom.

2. The Public Church

Honesty obliges us to admit that, viewed from this angle, societies marked by premodernity still have a long way to go, should they wish to go this way at all, particularly in regard to freedom of religion. This in no way implies that the form that Western democracies have in effect assumed should be seen as the supreme goal of development. On the contrary, they are fallible, and their failure is painfully apparent when one considers to what extent the inhuman discipline of the market and the iron cage of bureaucracy fall short of the principles that they profess to espouse: The divide between the ideal and the real is sometimes almost an abyss. This applies especially to the way in which developing countries, the majority of which are still in a state of dire poverty and oppression, are regarded by the West. Even though the United Nations Declaration of 1948 opens with the mellifluous and rhetorical phrase, "We, the peoples of the United Nations," two-thirds of these "we, the peoples" are living below the poverty threshold, whereas the remaining third, by comparison, live in the lap of luxury. But the most appalling fact is that there are no scenarios that will help to remedy these intolerable conditions. Who in the West can ignore the feeling in developing countries that they have been written off by the West as a "pathological case," as Richard Rorty puts it in his UNESCO lecture in 1996?[22] In view of this, it is perfectly reasonable to question whether, even if these countries are *able* to travel the road leading to modern Western democracy (including religious freedom), they would actually *wish* to do so.

Nonetheless, however many barriers and all but insurmountable obstacles block the way, we have no alternative but to cope adequately with the pluralism that exists, not only in modern society but in every society. And that applies also to religious pluralism, to which religious freedom pertains.

The question I want to raise here is: What could the church as a public church contribute to make the road passable? Can it, in fact, contribute anything? In the first place, is the fitting attitude not one of profound humility and a resolve not to forget its own guilt, especially when Western democracies to this day exploit religions and religious wars in so many developing countries such as Indonesia, Iran, Pakistan, and Afghanistan, directly or indirectly, for their own benefit? The churches either were or are unaware of this—implying culpable ignorance—or they cloaked or cloak themselves in silence and leave the protest to others, implying culpable negligence.

If, against the background of this call for humility and modesty, one can still speak of a contribution by the churches to the development of non-Western countries toward religious freedom, that contribution would be, in the first place, diaconal (here, meaning social ministries). The churches' diaconal work should be directed primarily to the hundreds of millions who are deprived of the fulfillment of the most fundamental needs to which they are explicitly entitled in terms of the United Nation Declaration of 1948, including religious freedom. Obviously, the innumerable homeless people and outcasts in the West should also be supported and helped, but one might suppose that Western democracies are able to look after their own societies. It is an abomination that the gap between rich and poor is still widening in these societies. But even more abominable is the growing gap between the affluent North and the impoverished South. Anyone who has seen those slums, squatter camps, or favellas with their own eyes must affirm this.

But what can the churches do? Genuine diaconal work is not outreach by the church for the poor but by the church with the poor or, better still, by the church of the poor. The church *for* the poor implies that the poor and the oppressed approach the church as supplicants, waiting for the compassion and charity of its members. That is degrading, both for the people and for the church. The church *of* the poor assumes that the church itself consists of the poor and the oppressed, which by and large is simply not true of churches in Western societies, despite the fact that this is the image that emerges from the gospel: The church was born of the poor and among the poor. But in the West, this is not the case, which presents a challenge to the church's very character: To what extent can Western churches claim to be churches? The church *with* the poor resolves the embarrassment caused by this question by identifying with the poor and the oppressed. "Identifying" means, "If you do this to the poor and the oppressed, you do it to me, the church; you do it to us, the church members." We are still miles away from such identification, considering the research finding that churches in the Western world—whether they like it or not—are steadily shifting to the political right. Nonetheless, against such a church we should continually protest on the basis of the church's own sources, the prophetic writings of the Hebrew Bible and the gospel. A church that denies the poor and the oppressed and fails to identify with them is denying the gospel itself.[23]

What does the diaconal/social task of the church with the poor entail? Diaconal work has always had two dimensions: one spiritual/material, the other individual/collective. Combined, they result in four quadrants: individual spiritual help, collective spiritual help, individual material assistance, and collective material assistance. Individual and collective spiritual help requires the churches to maintain a public presence in civil society as the advocate of the poor and the oppressed, protesting and indicting, demanding and exacting justice, planning aid strategies and scenarios and a support base for these. Of course, an ethical appeal is not sufficient. That appeal must emanate, as it were, spontaneously from critical analysis of the contrast experience of injustice in which the poor and the oppressed are situated and that makes anyone who confronts it cry out: This is wrong, this is evil, this cannot go on, it must stop![24] Individual and collective material assistance clearly does not merely or even primarily consist in ad hoc alleviation of need, however important that may be, but in changing the conditions that give rise to the structural sin that is at issue here. Of course, the church can only play a modest role in this respect, but, through pressure groups and public opinion, it can help to make governments consider structural policy changes. The Netherlands is one of the few countries that spends 1 percent of its gross national product on developmental aid, and even that 1 percent pales into insignificance compared with the global injustice in which two-thirds of the world's population find themselves. Where are the Netherlands, which so proudly boasts of its global solidarity? Where is the rest of Europe, Australia, Canada, the United States? If there has ever been a crying need for a *Bekennende Kirche* (Confessing Church), it is in this field.

Have I meanwhile lost sight of Fowler's development research? By no means. Before proceeding to the significance of his work for the development of religious freedom, however, it was necessary to create the right condition for it: abrogating the fundamental disruption of socioeconomic relations between Western and developing countries. For as we have indicated, asking the developing countries, in the framework of the required perspective exchange, to adopt the perspective of the affluent West alongside their own is nothing if not cynical. We can only ask these countries to exchange perspectives, and accompany them in so doing, if they really experience that we, too, are prepared to and capable of adopting their perspective—that of the most abject poverty—and will act accordingly.

When it comes to interreligious perspective exchange—the second contribution of the church to be explored here, after diaconal work—I want to emphasize the ability to transpose oneself to the partner's perspective and from that perspective to understand their ideas, beliefs, feelings, norms, and appraisals, then to exchange these and coordinate them with those arrived at from our own perspective.[25] Four processes enter into this, designated in terms of "inside" and "outside" perspectives.[26] The first process means that A interprets his own religion (A/A) from an inside perspective; the second that B interprets her own religion (B/B) from an inside perspective; the third that A, in terms of his own religion, interprets B's religion from an outside perspective (A/B); and the fourth that B, in terms of her own religion, interprets A's religion from an outside perspective (B/A).[27]

Interreligious dialogue in the paradigm of perspective exchange has hardly got off the ground yet. Thus, the theology of religions–at least inasmuch as it is determined by exclusivism, inclusivism, or a combination of inclusivism and pluralism–applies only to a personal inside perspective. One does observe the other religion, one listens to it, but purely from one's own perspective, be that the perspective of the biblical God, Christ, the Spirit, the kingdom of God, or the Trinity.[28] This means that no dialogue is established, nor can it be established, because the aim of perspective exchange is not strived for.

Not striving to exchange perspectives is one thing; striving to do so and failing is another. When do people fail to exchange perspectives?[29] Let me mention a few sociopsychological processes. The exchange may fail inasmuch as one's image of the partner is negative, as when the partner is seen as stupid, ambitious, aggressive, inhuman; inasmuch as information about beliefs, values, and feelings is conveyed or received selectively; inasmuch as rhetorical clichés and ploys are in evidence; inasmuch as emotional transference and counter transference processes occur, and resentment, mistrust, or jealousy cannot be overcome.[30] These sociopsychological processes may stem partly from sociocultural and sociostructural factors beyond the control of the respective dialogue partners. A major sociocultural factor, for example, is the perceived supremacy of one culture and religion over another, a phenomenon found more commonly among church members than among nonmembers.[31] In such cases, one can have all the dialogue in the world, but there will be no exchange of perspectives. An important sociostructural factor is actual and/or perceived inequality in an economic or political sense. Why should poverty-stricken Muslims in the Arab countries put themselves in the position of affluent Westerners and adopt their perspective while the only thing they desire is justice?[32] To put it paradoxically: It is proof of a lack of perspective exchange to ask these Muslims to exchange perspectives!

I'd like to link a final notion to this interreligious perspective exchange, one that–however paradoxically–should be regarded as a necessary condition for the realization of religious freedom. This relates to the locus of perspective exchange. We can distinguish between two such loci: the global locus of the official religions and the local locus of the actual religions in the city, neighborhood, school, street, or apartment block where we live. Religious leaders and scholars move in the global locus of the official religions, whereas the interaction between individuals and groups takes place in the locus of the local congregation, neighborhood, street, or apartment block.[33] In the global locus, there is a mutual exchange of hermeneutic conceptual analyses of the official religious vocabularies of the religions concerned. In the local locus, it has to do with the practical ethical and practical ritual effects of this religious vocabulary on day-to-day living. In addition, it has to do with the normative religious images that govern everyday life in the home, at work, in the sphere of recreation, and in other social contexts, and that influence, orient, and color these.[34]

3. Conclusion

Is it not part of the church's task as a public church to compile developmental programs aimed at interreligious perspective exchange in the locus of the local congregation, neighborhood, street, or apartment block? And is it not part of the church's task as a public church to implement and evaluate such programs *in situ* in its missionary activity in developing countries, the very countries where conflict specifically between Christians and Muslims, between Christians and Hindus, and between Muslims and Hindus is most virulent?

Notes

[1]This is the implication if the right to religious freedom is declared applicable also to nonreligious and explicitly antireligious people, as the European Court of Human Rights did in 1993; see M. D. Evans, "Religious Diversity and Religious Liberty as Human Right" (paper read at the UNESCO International Conference "Human Rights and Our Responsibilities Towards Future Generations: An Inter-religious Perspective," Valetta, Malta, May 6–8, 1999), 5.

[2]V. S. Naipaul, *Among the Believers: An Islamic Journey* (New York: Vintage Books, 1981); *Beyond Belief: Islamic Excursions Among the Converted Peoples* (London: Little, Brown, 1998; 2d ed. London: Abacus, 1999).

[3]E. Goffmann, *Totale Instituties* (Rotterdam 1975).

[4]James W. Fowler, *Stages of Faith: The Psychology of Human Development and the Quest for Meaning* (San Francisco: Harper & Row, 1981), 151ff.

[5]Ibid., 172–73.

[6]Sharon Parks, "Faith Development and Imagination in the Context of Higher Education" (Th.D. diss., Harvard Divinity School, 1980).

[7]Here, I rely on the review of stages of faith research in various countries compiled by C. G. Vergouwen, "Een hemelsbrede gelijkenis. Geloofsopvoeding in godsdienstpsychologisch perspectief" (diss., CU Nijmegen Kok Kampen, 2001). See C. A. M. Hermans, *Participerend leren. Grondslagen van religieuze vorming in een globaliserende samenleving* (Budel: Damon, 2001), 263–71.

[8]Fowler, *Stages of Faith*, 287.

[9]James W. Fowler, *Weaving the New Creation: Stages of Faith and the Public Church* (San Francisco: Harper & Row, 1991), 169.

[10]James W. Fowler, *Faithful Change: The Personal and Public Challenge of Postmodern Life* (Nashville, Tenn.: Abingdon Press, 1996), 160–78.

[11]Jürgen Habermas, *Theorie des kommunikativen Handelns,* 2 vols. (Frankfurt: Suhrkamp, 1982).

[12]See Fowler, *Faithful Change,* 173.

[13]Besides, a definition such as "convention-critical reflective faith" would be more appropriate than the term "postconventional faith," because the latter suggests that one has abandoned the religious tradition in which one was socialized, whereas critical reflection on that tradition as suggested by the first term may result in a purged, critical reappropriation of that tradition, as I

argued in regard to moral development in my *Formation of the Moral Self* (Grand Rapids, Mich.: Eerdmans, 1998), 227ff.

[14]Franz Xaver Kaufmann, *Religion und Modernität* (Tübingen: Mohr, 1989); idem, *Wie überlebt das Christentum?* (Freiburg: Herder, 2000).

[15]References to God do not occur in the constitutions of Western democracies, although they do sometimes appear in the preambles, such as the preamble to the French Declaration on the Rights of Man and the Citizen (1789). Here, there is a reference to "droits naturels, inaliénables et sacrés," whose natural, inalienable, and sacrosanct character derives from "l'Être suprême," the supreme Being. The preambles to the constitutions of other countries likewise contain references to God—for instance those of the United States, Germany, the Netherlands, South Africa, and Ireland (see J. M. Piret, "Burgerreligie. De religieuze 'fundering' van de liberale rechtsstaat," *Nexus* (1992): 2, 3–36). Here, it is important to distinguish between the various linguistic nuances. Thus, the Swiss constitution has an *invocatio Dei* ("In the name of God the Almighty"), Germany has a *nominatio Dei* ("While conscious of its responsibility to God and the human being"), and the South African constitution refers to God in what may be described as the style of a *rhetorical petition prayer* ("God bless South Africa"). It is significant that in the United Nations Declaration of 1948, human rights are no longer described as "sacrosanct" but simply as "inalienable," and that God has disappeared from the preamble (see E. Fuchs, P.-A. Stucki, *Au nomme de l'autre: essay sur le fondement des droits de l'homme* [Geneva: Labor et Fides, 1985]). What God could it refer to, since the United Nations in principle embraces all peoples with their diverse religions, including such ones as official Buddhism that recognize no God? Or should God be seen as the consummation rather than the basis of the project of democracy, which preserves even the memory of those who have suffered innocently or died as victims, and who are taken up in God who is all in all (see G. Essen, "Der 'Präambelgott.' Verfassungsanker oder Verfassungsstörer? Theologische Anmerkungen zur verfassungsrechtlichen und rechtsphilosophischen Bedeutung der nominatio dei im Grundgesetz für die Bundesrepublik Deutschland," *Kirche und Recht* [2001]: 143–56). Paul Ricoeur also believes that the foundation of the constitution is not God but rather the symbol "people of God" in terms of anteriority (see Paul Ricoeur, *La critique et la conviction* [Paris: Calman-Lévy, 1995], 100ff.).

[16]M. Walzer, "The Civil Society Argument," in *Dimensions of Radical Democracy, Pluralism, Citizenship, Community,* ed. Chantal Mouffe (New York: Verso, Phronesis, 1992), 89–107.

[17]Jürgen Habermas, *Faktizität und Geltung. Beiträge zur Diskurstheorie des Rechts und des demokratischen Rechtsstaats* (Frankfurt: Suhrkamp, 1992).

[18]Richard Herzinger, *Republik ohne Mitte* (Berlin: Siedler-Verlag, 2001).

[19]Fowler himself admits to having been influenced to a considerable extent by the work of Piaget, Kohlberg, and Selman, even though he is explicitly conscious of its limitations (Fowler, *Stages of Faith,* 98–105).

[20]Lawrence Kohlberg, *Essays on Moral Development,* vol. 2 of *The Psychology of Moral Development* (San Francisco: Harper & Row, 1984), 624–39; see van der Ven, *Formation of the Moral Self,* 202–5.

[21]M. Blatt, and L. Kohlberg, "The Effects of Classroom Moral Discussion upon Children's Level of Moral Judgment," *Journal of Moral Education* 4, no. 2 (1975): 129–61; Lawrence Kohlberg, *Essays on Moral Development,* vol. 1 of *The Philosophy of Moral Development* (San Francisco: Harper & Row, 1981).

[22]Richard Rorty, *Moral Universalism and Economic Triage,* http://www.unesco.org/phiweb/uk/2rpu/rort/rort.html.

[23]Johannes A. van der Ven, *Ecclesiology in Context* (Grand Rapids, Mich.: Eerdmans, 1996), 508–23.

[24]For contrast experience, see Edward Schillebeeckx, *Mensen als verhaal van God* (Baarn: Nelissen, 1989), 24–26.

[25]Robert L. Selman, *The Growth of Interpersonal Understanding: Developmental and Clinical Analyses* (New York: Academic Press, 1980); R. L. Selman and D.F. Byrne, "A Structural-developmental Analysis of Levels of Role-taking in Middle Childhood," *Child Development* 45 (1974–1975): 83–86.

[26]When applying the paired concepts of inside and outside perspective to religions, one should allow for the fact that religions are not constant entities but living, dynamic processes that influence one another syncretistically, with polycentric structures containing synchronically and diachronically polyvalent meanings. This applies not just to religions but also to cultures; see W. Welsch, "Transkulturaliät. Die Veränderte Verfassung heutiger Kulturen," in *Die Vielheit in der Einheit,* F. Due et al. (Frankfurt. 1994), 83–122; idem, *Unsere postmoderne Moderne* (Berlin, 1997).

202 Developing a Public Faith

[27]Perspective exchange is even more complex than I have indicated here; see van der Ven, *Formation of the Moral Self,* 272, where I add a further two processes to the four mentioned here: interpretation of A's inside perspective interpretation by B, and interpretation of B's inside perspective interpretation by A. Failure to exchange perspectives, which can cause the dialogue itself to break down, threatens if B gives an outside perspective interpretation of A's inside perspective interpretation (B/B[A/A]]) and if A gives an outside perspective interpretation of B's inside perspective interpretation (A/A[B/B]).

[28]See K. Rahner, "Einzigkeit und Dreifältigkeit Gottes," in *Der Gott des Christentums und des Islams,* ed. Andreas Bsteh (Mödling: Verl. St. Gabriel, 1978), 119–36; Jacques Dupuis, *Toward a Christian Theology of Religious Pluralism* (Maryknoll, N.Y.: Orbis Books, 1997); Gisbert Greshake, *Der dreieine Gott, Eine trinitarische Theologie* (Freiburg: Herder, 1997), 499–522. For a lucid survey, see W. Valkenberg, "Christ and the Spirit: Towards a Bifocal Christian Theology of Religions," in *The Myriad Christ: Plurality and the Quest for Unity in Contemporary Christology,* ed. T. Merrigan and J. Haers (Louvain: University Press, 2000), 121–29; P. Valkenberg, "Christelijke identiteit en religieuze verscheidenheid," *Wereld en Zending* 30, no. 3 (2001): 20–27. Ultimately, this is a Christian interpretation of "non-Christian religions" that makes use of the conceptual structure of "anonymous Christianity." In the absence of perspective exchange, which easily rouses suspicions of a mixing of dialogue with mission, adherents of other religions understandably react with mistrust and rejection; see C. Hasselmann, "De wereldethiek-verklaring van Chicago 1993," *Concilium* 37, no. 4 (2001): 24–37, esp. 31.

[29]Johannes A. van der Ven, *Practical Theology: An Empirical Approach* (Louvain: Peeters, 1996), 53–59.

[30]Julie Feldbrugge, *Commitment to the Committed: Treatment as Interaction in a Forensic Mental Hospital* (diss., CU Nijmegen, Lisse, 1986); Sheldon Cashdan, *Object Relations Therapy* (New York: Norton, 1988).

[31]Religious supremacy should be understood as a focus on the religious sphere of the cultural complex of chauvinism, as distinct from patriotism. The former consists in an unconditionally uncritical positive attitude toward one's own group, accompanied by ethnic exclusivism. The latter refers to pride in and love for one's own group, based on a conditional and critical positive attitude, usually without any exclusivism toward immigrants and political refugees; see M. Coenders, *Nationalistic Attitudes and Ethnic Exclusionism in a Comparative Perspective: An Empirical Study of Attitudes Toward the Country and Ethnic Immigrants in 22 Countries* (diss., CU Nijmegen, 2001); M. Lubbers, *Exclusionistic Electorates, Extreme Right-Wing Voting in Western Europe* (diss., CU Nijmegen, 2001).

[32]P. Valkenberg, "The Myth of a Dialogue between Equals: Who Needs Interreligious Dialogue in Western Europe?" in *The Polemical Dialogue,* ed. W. Valkenberg and F. Wijsen (Saarbrücken, 1997), 85–104.

[33]I use the term "locus of perspective exchange" by analogy with "locus of policy"; see van der Ven, *Wetenschappelijke Raad voor het Regeringsbeleid, Nederland als immigratieland* (Den Haag, 2001), 29–30.

[34]Normative images–that is ones that contain a normative orientation based on an image, can be divided into somatic and cultural images. Somatic images play a role, for example, in the choice of a partner (hair style, physique, height, skin color). Cultural normative images affect forms of interpersonal dealings, work ethic, solidarity, and so forth; see van der Ven, *Wetenschappelijke Raad voor het Regeringsbeleid,* 197–99. Religious normative images may be seen as a category of cultural normative images. They also influence day-to-day living, as Max Weber demonstrated–by way of analogy–in the case of the Calvinist work ethic (*Die protestantische Ethik und der Geist des Kapitalismus* [Hamburg, 1969]), and as M. ter Voert did in regard to the Christian work ethic generally ("Religie en het burgerlijk-kapitalistisch ethos" [diss., CU Nijmegen, 1994]).

12

Children and Parents

Two-way Partners in Faith Development

THOMAS GROOME

Our paths first crossed when we were "young"–Jim Fowler's and mine. This I count a particular blessing to my life. Even back then, before it was well tested, I recognized the great value of Jim's work. He was illuminating how the faith journey unfolds, enabling us to see further and clearer than ever before. For my interest as a religious educator, his schema of stages became suggestive for how to mentor people along the way.

After meeting Jim, I never though of faith the same again and, at least on good days, performed religious education a little more adequately. Whether crafting a first-grade curriculum, or teaching faith-bewildered undergraduates, or accompanying a struggling adult as spiritual companion, my vision was a little clearer because of the Fowler lens. For this I'm truly grateful, and, if I may be so bold, I express the gratitude of countless colleagues in religious education. I feel honored to contribute an essay to honor Jim here.

The theme I've chosen–parenting–is one dear to Jim's heart. I remember chatting with him many times about his own parenting with Luerline of their two lovely daughters. Now, after a bit of a late start, I find myself "young" again, this time at being a dad. As our little son Theodore Thomas Griffith-Groome–mercifully shortened to Ted–celebrates his first birthday, I'm recognizing a new "stage" in my own faith development. I'm not sure where it fits on Jim's schema, but it feels a bit miscellaneous to my mid-fifties. However, I can say for sure that Ted's coming home has been a profound experience of faith development–for him and for us. I've long been convinced that parents are the primary faith educators of their children. Now, I'm realizing that children can be powerful educators in the faith of their parents. I will write from both perspectives here–as teacher and learner–for parenting is truly a two-way partnership.

Upon hearing of Ted's arrival in our lives, an old friend commented, "Ah, this will be the real test of Groome's approach to religious education." I might have done so anyhow, but that remark occasioned so much anxiety that I determined to begin immediately with Ted's education in faith. So, I found myself in the early hours of the morning, besides singing old lullabies from my childhood, mumbling the Lord's Prayer in his ear, and to good effect– he'd fall back to sleep. Ted's religious education began the first week of his life.

Then I noticed that this little boy often touches into my own heart's core– my soul. His blind trust evokes how I should live my life; his total dependence reminds me of my constant need for God's grace; the great love I feel for him bespeaks the love in God's heart–and a thousand times more–for each of us. So yes, Colleen and I will be his primary religious educators, but if we are open to it, Ted will nurture us in faith as well. Let's reflect on both sides of this coin.

1. Parents as Primary Religious Educators of Children

To take seriously our responsibility to educate our children in faith, parents need to (1) debunk the schooling paradigm and (2) imagine the family as "domestic church."

1.1 Needed: To Deschool and Expand Our Educational Consciousness

Long before the social sciences verified it, parents had known that *they* have the most influence on who their children become. Nothing teaches with greater effect than the ethos and example of the home. Indeed, "the apples don't fall far from the trees." So why do we find that parents now need to be so reminded? I propose that our sense of ourselves as primary educators has been overwhelmed–even nullified–by "the school."

The notion of universal education emerged slowly in the Western world and represented a major breakthrough in social consciousness. Plato first made the philosophical argument that all citizens should be educated (though remember that "citizen" included less than 10 percent of the population). The first real attempt at universal education came when the emperor Charlemagne decreed (circa 800 C.E.) that the monastic schools must be open to all boys of the empire, not only to those interested in becoming monks. Note, the idea that girls should have equal access to education would take another thousand years.

The watershed came with the great Reformation catch-cry of "*scriptura sola*," calling all Christians to read the Bible for themselves, thereby encouraging universal literacy. And the specific catalyst toward "public education" was Martin Luther's letter of 1524 to the German nobles urging them to establish and fund schools that would educate every child–boys and girls. They did! Note well, however, that Luther never intended schooling to replace family education. In fact, he advised that boys attend school for no more than two hours each day and girls for only one, lest their schooling diminish their education at home and in the world around them.[1]

Alas, Martin's caution fell on deaf ears. Before long, the whole Western world had bought hook, line, and sinker into the "schooling paradigm," equating universal education—a fine ideal—with universal schooling. The latter became a totalizing affair in that it subsumed everything that could pass for education, with the parental role reduced to seeing to it that children "attend" a didactic process by professional teachers in an institution designed to "school" them. And though the professionalizing of teaching was a breakthrough, its unfortunate underside was the impression that amateurs—such as parents—have nothing to contribute to the education of children.

In sum, the triumph of schooling caused parents to pull back from their own educational role, to assume (1) that education equals didaction, and (2) that this is done solely by experts—teachers—in schools. Though Huckelberry Finn said that he tried not to let his schooling interfere with his education, the rest of the world wasn't nearly so wise.

Religious educators embraced the schooling model with equal gusto. This is not to dismiss the great work of the Sunday school movement, of the Confraternity for Christian Doctrine (CCD), or of parochial schools. However, the schooling paradigm also colonized parental consciousness regarding education in faith. Again, the notion came to prevail that the parental role in religious education is to see to it that children attend some kind of school or formal program of catechesis. Ridiculous as it may sound, the church encouraged parents to think that if they "dropped off" their kids for a one-hour, once-a-week program, they could later "pick up" Christians.

There were a few dissenting voices to totalizing the school. Regarding religious education, and writing first circa 1845, Horace Bushnell proposed that family nurture must be the primary mode of faith formation. "That the child is to grow up a Christian, and never know himself as being otherwise" depends upon parental example and the ethos of the home.[2] In the early 1970s, Ivan Illich proposed "deschooling society" as a strategy for educational reform. Though sounding too radical to get a hearing, Illich was only trying to shift consciousness beyond the idea that "education equals schooling" and was proposing to engage all social agencies to educate intentionally. In particular, he wanted parents to reclaim their role as primary educators.[3] Alas, his prophetic call was heard as utopian—impossible.

More recently, the greatest challenge to the schooling paradigm has been mounted by the "home-school" movement. Over two million U.S. children are being educated in their own homes—without ever "going to school"—most often by their parents, many of whom have had minimal schooling themselves. Yet with the help of appropriate curriculum, coupled with local resources and the limitless possibilities to be found on the Internet, these parents seem to be very effective in educating their children. During my years at Boston College, some of the best students I've taught were previously home-schooled.

Now, I'm not favoring or recommending the home-school movement. I call attention to it only because it can help to debunk our total dependence on schools for education. Nor am I opposed to schools as such—I work in one. I'm simply proposing that we reconfigure our consciousness to see all of life as educational, and that schools, though highly significant, should be only one aspect of education, including education in faith. We must disabuse ourselves of the myth that education is synonymous with formal schooling. In particular, our whole Western culture needs to reclaim the function of parents as primary educators and encourage them to intentionally fulfill their crucial role.

Our churches, of course, regularly proclaim that parents are the primary religious educators of their children. The Second Vatican Council, for example, declared that "parents must be acknowledged as the first and foremost educators of their children." Then, to drive home the point but also laying a potential guilt trip on parents, it added, "Their role as educators is so decisive that scarcely anything can compensate for their failure in it."[4] Alas, such rhetoric has not been matched by action on the church's part; in fact, it can be counterproductive. For "education" is still heard as "schooling," so parents hear that they should be more didactic with their children, sitting them down regularly for periods of instruction. Overwhelmed by this prospect–especially in our "too busy" families–and terrified that nothing can make up for their failure, they redouble their efforts to find professionals to do it for them, using teachers in schools or congregational programs. Whereas to really appreciate parents as educators–in faith or otherwise–we must think outside the box of schooling. Here, a truism from the social sciences might be helpful.

All the social sciences agree that we become who we become–in large part–through the influence of our sociocultural contexts. We interiorize the worldview, value system, and self-image mediated to us from our surrounding communities, and nothing is more influential than the primary socialization of family. So to raise a person with a Polish identity requires a Polish family, and to raise a Spanish person takes a Spanish family. Likewise, to raise a Christian person takes a Christian family.

Now when we broaden education beyond schooling to include socialization and inculturation, the fundamental role of parents comes vividly into view. For it is the ethos of the home, the shared life as a family that is most educational. Parents don't need to become didactic teachers–any more than usual–but they must more consciously attend to the value system, worldview, and self-understanding mediated through the whole family milieu. For religious education in particular, a family's faith is more caught than taught; its communal life *is* its catechetical curriculum. Parents must intentionally structure the lifestyle and ethos of the home to educate in faith.

For its part, the church should abandon its exclusive investment in the schooling paradigm to fulfill its faith education ministry. Local parishes and congregations must make a concerted effort to "nurture the nurturers"–commissioning, training, resourcing, and encouraging parents as the primary religious educators of their children. After family catechesis has due priority, including real financial support, then "schools" can be a helpful supplement.

Years ago, in his description of "undifferentiated" faith, Fowler recognized the make-or-break influence of family nurture on the subsequent faith journey. He wrote, "The quality of mutuality and the strength of trust, autonomy, hope and courage (or their opposites) developed in this phase underlie (or threaten to undermine) all that comes later in faith development."[5] Jim was making a powerful point. But sadly and despite a lot of lip service, as church we don't really take it seriously. We say "rah, rah" for family, but we invest exclusively in schools and congregational programs. I'm certainly not opposed to the latter or suggesting that we abandon them. But first and foremost, we must attend to the primary locus of faith education. My proposal is that we imagine the family as "the domestic church" and proceed accordingly.

1.2 Family as Domestic Church

By "family," I intend any and every community of domestic life. In other words, we must shift our imaginations beyond the nuclear family of a mom, dad, and two kids living in suburbia, to include extended and blended families; single-, double-, and triple-parent families; straight, gay, and bent families. Family is *any bonded network of domestic life and nurture.* And here, let me make an important parenthetical point.

I love to ask gatherings of religious educators, "How many of you grew up in a perfect family?" Invariably, no matter how big the crowd, no one ever puts up a hand. The truth is that likely 95 percent of our families are "dysfunctional"—to use the fashionable term. But since when has God been choosy about instruments? If God were, I'd certainly be out of work. My friend Trish is likely one of the best parents I know, with irrefutable evidence in the two wonderful children she has raised. Yet Trish has faced more social problems than most people even imagine. From an immigrant family, with little formal education and low earning power, as a single parent living in poor housing, Trish had an extraordinary capacity to love her kids, and she raised them with the best of Christian values. Come to think of it, the "holy family" of Nazareth began with a teenage pregnancy out of wedlock, yet look at the wonderful child they raised.

My point is that every family should be able to mount the intentional catechesis I outline below. At least, this is my hope, as I recognize the shortcomings of my own family and yet pray that we will be able to fulfill our responsibilities as Ted's primary religious educators.

The Second Vatican Council described the family as "the domestic church."[6] Though an ancient notion from the first Christian communities, it may come to be ranked with the more revolutionary developments heralded by Vatican II. Let us unpack what this image might suggest by way of family as religious educator.

Now, if the family is the "domestic church," then it should carry on or have represented within its life all the functions of ministry. And because the whole ethos of the home educates—or miseducates—in faith, all its efforts at ministry, and not only that of "the Word," should be suffused with an intentional catechetical consciousness. So every aspect of family life should be likely to educate in faith.

We can outline the church's ministries in many ways. Since the earliest days, however, six Greek terms have had pride of place in naming the constitutive functions of Christian ministry:

Koinonia—to be a life-giving community;

Marturia—to bear witness to Christian faith;

Kerygma—to evangelize and share the good news;

Didache—to teach scripture and tradition;

Leitourgia—to worship as a community; and

Diakonia—to care for human needs.

For convenience, I will summarize them in a fourfold schema (pairing *marturia* with *koinonia,* and *didache* with *kerygma*) as the functions of *Witness, Worship, Welfare,* and *Word.* I place *Word* last because it is the obvious mode of faith education, whereas we need to raise catechetical consciousness around the other three. So let us imagine a family realizing each function of ministry within its common life, all geared to educate in faith.

Family as witness means that the whole life of the home should be suffused with the values and perspectives of Christian faith. This requires that the members constantly review the family's environment and ethos, lifestyle and priorities, relationships and gender roles, language patterns and conversations, work and recreation—every aspect—to monitor how well it reflects the convictions and commitments of Christian faith. In sum, everything about the Christian family should bear *witness* to its faith; this is how it educates.

Family as a worshipping community calls it to integrate shared prayer and sacred ritual into its patterns of daily life. To be effective as religious educator, every Christian family needs its own "liturgy" to symbolize and celebrate its faith. I once asked a devout Jewish friend how she came by her strong Jewish identity; she immediately responded, "Oh, from the rituals in my home." Surely, every Christian family can create or rediscover—old Christian cultures had plenty of them—sacred rituals for the home that will nurture the Christian identity of its members. Without family prayer and sacred symbols, the home is less likely to educate in faith.

Family as agent of welfare requires care for the spiritual, physical, and emotional well-being of its own members, rippling outward to responsibility for others and society. Family life must reflect love and compassion toward all, promoting justice within itself and the social values of God's reign in the world. If children grow up and adults dwell within a family that lives the values of mercy and compassion, of justice and peace, they are more likely to embrace the social responsibilities of Christian faith to the world.

Family as community of Word calls it to share its faith around scripture and tradition, within itself and in the broader community. While participating in the formal programs of congregations and schools, every Christian should be "home-schooled" in scripture and tradition. Parishes must empower parents—with resources, training, suggestions, support, encouragement, expectation—for encountering God's word within the conversations of family life. I know a family who every week gathers together for "a family scripture moment." They reread a passage from the Sunday lectionary and then share what each one heard from the text for their lives. Imagine the long-term faith education effect on both parents and children.

Let me reiterate that all of the above requires intentionality, especially on the part of the adults in a family. Little of faith education "just happens" by accident. Parents must craft the whole environment of the home and engage all the functions of Christian ministry to educate in Christian faith.

2. Children as Faith Educators of Their Parents

If we're open to it, our children can educate us in faith (1) by what we share with them and (2) by what they share with us.

2.1 Sharing Faith and Educating Ourselves

According to gospel math, what we give away in faith returns a hundredfold. So every effort to share our faith greatly enriches our own. Ask Sunday school teachers if their faith has grown and deepened through their efforts to teach it, and they will immediately say yes, even thinking of the question as rhetorical. Simply put, the faith of parents will deepen if they genuinely try to share it with their children. Parents who make a deliberate effort at Christian nurture will find their own faith constantly drawn upon, exercised, and renewed.

I have an old friend who likes to say, "Ah, 'twas my grandkids that brought my kids back to their faith." What a common pastoral experience this is. A young couple is indifferent to or alienated from their religious roots, but then along come children; now their sense of parental responsibility brings a new opportunity in their own faith journey. Before long, they find themselves in a baptism preparation program; if done well, it may rekindle their own faith. Personally, I believe that the most effective effort at adult faith education in the Catholic church of recent times has been the sacramental preparation programs that require parental participation. As parents are tutored and then help prepare their children to welcome First Eucharist or celebrate Confirmation, these efforts often rekindle their own faith.

But even more compelling than formal programs is what children invite us to craft within the home itself. On an election morning, I asked a colleague if he had voted yet, and he replied, "Ah, I always vote now; the boys would notice if I didn't." Here was a father trying to give a good example of responsible citizenship to his twin eight-year-old sons. And doesn't every conscientious parent try to do as much—across the board. Even already, I can see how Ted is helping to reform some of my own "vocabulary," eliminating words that I wouldn't want him to learn, at least not from his father. And I can only imagine as yet what other reforms he will bring to my life.

When Colleen and I were discussing how to decorate Ted's nursery, we looked at wall prints and hangings that had the Disney characters, and Harry Potter, and themes from nursery rhymes. But then we wondered, why not a biblical story or image. So now, Ted's room has a large hanging of the story of Noah's ark and a reproduction of Jesus the Good Shepherd cuddling a lamb—

and fairly good art. Ted is totally taken with the animals and seems to hold his favorite teddy a little tighter when he looks up at the Good Shepherd. The day will soon come when he will ask and we will tell the great stories behind those pictures. Meanwhile, every time I enter his room, that rainbow and shepherd remind *me* of God's unrelenting love and the kind of loving life to which I'm called.

We have also begun to develop family rituals—domestic liturgy—that may nurture Ted in Christian faith. For example, since a few days after he came home to us, I've found myself taking a deliberate moment every morning when I get his attention to look him in the eye and say with a big smile, "Ted, God loves you, we love you, and Jesus is your best friend." And I intend to do this most days until he leaves for college. Now, I don't know for sure what it will do to Ted's faith identity, but with the help of God's grace, he's likely to grow up confident of God's love, of our love, and that he has a friend in Jesus. With that, won't we have ingrained the foundations of his faith—for life? And whatever that simple ritual does for Ted, I know what it does to my own faith. I find myself wondering if I really believe in God's love and how well I'm living as a friend of Jesus.

There is also our reading. Indeed, we love *Good Night Moon* and *Where's Spot?* and so does Ted. But we were amazed at the number of children's Bibles available—yes, even for a one-year old. Friends gave them to us, presuming that we would like to read them to Ted. And indeed we do, though Ted seems oblivious to anything other than the colorful pictures. It's amazing what a baby version of a great Bible story can say to one's own heart—like a second naïveté. And we've found a whole line of delightful "holy" books to share with Ted—ones that reflect our curriculum choices for him. A particular favorite is *What Is God's Name?* with text by Sandy Eisenberg Sasso and illustrations by Phoebe Stone.[7] It beautifully teaches that God has many names; we and Ted all need to learn this, over and over, and more than ever in these times. And only God knows what else our sharing of "the Word" with Ted will bring to our own lives over the years.

I could go on, but the point is made. Our efforts to nurture Ted in faith are nurturing our own as well. I'm confident that all our efforts, even the poor ones, will "return" a hundredfold.

2.2 Children as Sacramental to Parents' Lives

The old Christian principle of sacramentality reflects the conviction that God outreaches to us with saving intent through the ordinary and everyday of life and that we respond likewise. God's presence with us and the Spirit's grace most typically "work" in very ordinary ways. Likewise, our own efforts, made by God's grace, to live as disciples of Jesus are through everyday life and are usually quite ordinary. Now, if parents have this sense of the sacramentality of life—not just about church on Sunday—then they will often encounter God's presence and outreach through their children, as sacramental to their lives.

Though my experience is very limited as yet, already and many times I've encountered the presence of God through Ted. I will never forget his first smile; even if it was wind, I experienced the presence of God in that little grin. It was as if God had smiled just at me and was right there with us. What a special moment!

Ted's trust and simplicity ever evoke a renewed sense of how my own life should be lived. So many times, too, I've looked down at him with a great feeling of unconditional love welling up in my heart. Then, I often reflect that God's love for me is like that—unconditional, really unconditional. And I've often experienced the feeling that no matter what Ted ever does in life, I will always love him. What a feeble effort is my love compared to God's; how much more God continues to love us, no matter what we ever do.

Ted is giving me a whole new way of looking at life, of noticing things that I had taken for granted, of stopping to "smell the roses." One morning, we were out for a walk, and the wind rose and blew through the autumn leaves, bringing a shower of them to the ground. Suddenly, I became aware that Ted was mesmerized by this; I could literally "see" him listening to the wind as it rustled through the trees and being amazed at the showers of falling leaves. Then I, too, stopped and marveled at the wind—that I had not noticed before—and found myself enveloped in an autumnal meditation on my own mortality.

Or take how Ted greets the new day—especially after a good night's sleep. Maybe all little people do as much, but Ted has a way of embracing the day with the greatest delight. We walk in when he wakes, and, upon seeing us, he simply bursts with glee, so excited, gurgling and banging his two little fists on the mattress. It's as if he is thrilled to be alive, to see us, to have a whole new day to enjoy. Every morning he reminds me of a favorite saying of my grandmother, "Whenever we wake up, throw out our arms, and don't feel the sides of a coffin—that's a great day." Ted is helping us to welcome the gift of each day and to live it as a gift.

Ted has certainly brought us "back to basics," reminding us forcefully of our own bodiliness. One is delighted to get a good burp at the end of a feeding, and his morning bowel movement is cause for rejoicing—especially if he hasn't had one for a few days. And watching those teeth ever so slowly peeping through—his pain and discomfort remind us of the travails of life and that little of real value comes easily. But then, if we are open to it, this vivid and daily encounter with his bodiliness could return us to a healthy spirituality of our own bodies. Christians ought to have as much: We believe that God made us to reflect the divine image as a unity of body and soul; that "the Word became flesh and lived among us" in Jesus (Jn. 1:14). Why, we even claim to expect "the resurrection of the body" (Apostles' Creed). Ted may help us to really believe such confessions as we see the glory of God in his little body.

Having written for years about parents as the religious educators of their children, I'm beginning to really know what I was talking about. And beyond that, I'm recognizing the truth of the converse: that children can be primary religious educators of their parents, if we have the imagination and openness to accept. Who knows, should I ever reach Stage 6 of faith development, it will be thanks in no small measure to Ted.

Notes

[1]See Martin Luther, "To the Councilmen of All Cities in Germany that They Establish and Maintain Christian Schools," in *Basic Writings in Christian Education,* ed. Kendig Cully (Philadelphia: Westminster Press, 1960), 137–49.

[2]Horace Bushnell, *Christian Nurture* (New Haven, Conn.: Yale University Press, 1947), 4.

[3]See Ivan Illich, *Deschooling Society* (New York: Harper & Row, 1971).

[4]"Decree on Education," no. 3 in *The Documents of Vatican II,* ed. Walter Abbott (New York: America Press, 1966), 641.

[5]James W. Fowler, *The Stages of Faith* (San Francisco: Harper & Row, 1981), 121.

[6]"Constitution on the Church," no. 11, in *Documents,* ed. Abbott, 29.

[7]This is one of a whole series in early childhood spirituality from SkyLight Paths Publishing, Woodstock, Vermont.

13

Family and Moral and Spiritual Development

DON BROWNING

This chapter investigates the role of parental investment in moral and faith development. The word *investment* is chosen intentionally. It points to the factors of emotional energy and identification that help fuel, but do not totally account for, parental commitment and care. Of course, parents with high degrees of emotional investment and identification with their children do not always make the best parents; furthermore, these qualities do not always translate into moral and spiritual growth for children. It is unlikely, however, that low or nonexistent emotional investment by parents will correlate with high levels of moral and faith development.

This chapter addresses the so-called structuralist dimension of moral and faith development–the idea that, in both lines of development, there is a strong formal cognitive component that goes through a series of crises, transformations, and reorganizations at successively more encompassing levels.[1] Both the faith development theory of James Fowler and the moral development theory of Lawrence Kohlberg use structuralism to conceptualize the cognitive dimensions of these two lines of development.[2] I affirm this aspect of their thought.

But I agree with Fowler that structuralism is not sufficient to account fully for either moral or faith development. In the case of faith development, Fowler has brought Piagetian and Kohlbergian structuralism together with Erik Erikson's psychoanalytic theory of emotional development and the narrative theory found in Stanley Hauerwas and Alasdair MacIntyre. To understand faith development, he shows how cognitive and emotional lines of development also interact with the religious narratives of specific communities of faith.[3] Fowler's synthesis of structuralism, psychoanalysis, and narrative theory for understanding faith as a universal mode of being is a major contribution.

But there is room in his theory, I believe, for one more addition. As it stands, it is susceptible–as are all theories highly dependent on structuralism–to an element of abstractness. For instance, there is little concrete discussion of the role of intact families in moral and faith development. Fowler certainly has addressed the general question of the role of families in faith development, especially in his important essay titled "Faith Development through the Family Life Cycle," where he correlates faith development, family life-cycle theory, and styles of family systems.[4] But I am asking in this chapter the question of the importance of the natural conjugal couple to moral and faith development.

Even this formulation of the issue is too abstract. A fuller question would go like this: What is the role of intact families in raising children to be moral and faithful persons in the context of a culture and social system dominated by both individualism and market rationality? Posing the question like this suggests that raising children with morality and faith may be more daunting today than it was in times when individualism and market rationality were less central to our lives.

1. Morality and Faith in an Individualistic and Market-driven Society

Certainly we live in an individualistic culture, and it has become increasingly so at least since the Enlightenment. But some people argue that the seeds of Western individualism have multiple sources, many of which precede the Enlightenment. Some list as a source the belief in the dignity of each person implied by the Jewish and Christian doctrine of the *imago Dei,* others the value accorded to both theoretical and practical reason in Greek philosophy, and still others the centrality of the individual conscience in the Protestant Reformation.

And there are those who make the discussion more complex by showing how the cultural sources of modern individualism interact with and are embellished by technical and market rationality.[5] Technical rationality, as identified by the great German sociologist Max Weber, is the application of powerful means-ends thinking to the enhancement of life satisfactions.[6] Market rationality, on the other hand, is the application of technical rationality to the maximization of efficiency and profit in production and distribution.[7] Scholars as diverse as Jürgen Habermas, Robert Bellah, and Alan Wolfe believe that when cultural individualism interacts with market rationality in a capitalist society, they together unleash a calculative and ethical-egoist mentality into the entire social fabric—even into the most intimate aspects of interpersonal life such as love, family, and marriage. People in such societies become more self-centered, more interested in immediate gratification, and more calculating. We become, as Bellah and his associates have said, simultaneously expressive and utilitarian individualists.[8]

One might hope that the moral socializing capacities of families would counterbalance these cultural and social-systemic trends. But the same forces making citizens more individualistic in their moral thinking also increase family instability, rendering them less able to socialize the young to resist these pressures. Although the United States leads the world in statistics on family disruption, most Western democracies nearly match us and in some categories exceed us. To remind the reader of what is widely available in the newspapers, here is a brief summary of the pertinent facts about family disruption. The divorce rate in the United States is slightly below 50 percent; one-third of all babies are born out of wedlock (an overall increase of six times since 1960 and an increase of ten times in the white community); the rate of cohabitation has increased eight times since 1970, with two-thirds of couples now cohabiting before marriage;[9] and around 45 percent of all children live at least three years prior to age sixteen in a single-parent home.[10]

What are the implications of these trends for the moral and spiritual socialization of children? The answers seem somewhat sobering. Cohabitation is far more fragile than legal marriage, and increasingly children are born into these arrangements.[11] Detailed longitudinal research by Sara McLanahan and Gary Sandefur show that children raised apart from both biological parents are two to three times more likely to drop out of school, have difficulty getting jobs, or become single parents themselves; and they are one-and-one-half times more likely to be idle in adulthood.[12] Income makes a difference, but it only cuts these statistics in half. Men in jails are disproportionately more likely to have been raised in a disrupted home, generally without the presence of a father.[13] Family disruption has, on average, negative consequences for children, some of which seem to be moral and spiritual in nature.

2. Two Views of the Role of Families

So our basic question has become clearer. It reads like this: In a time when individualism and market rationality are stronger and the family is weaker, how will we raise our children to have moral competence and faith? There have been a variety of answers given to this question, but two I characterize as basically minimalist in nature. One response goes back to Plato's *Republic.* It has to do with how the capacities for universalistic thinking and identifications arise. His theories are pertinent to the question of universalism in both morality and faith, although he is addressing primarily the moral line of development. Plato believed that the main cause of conflict in the city (the *polis*) was too much, not too little, family strength. He held that strong and cohesive families led to nepotism—the preferred treatment of blood kin at the expense of the just treatment of all people no matter what their family connection. So Plato proposed taking children away from their biological mothers and fathers, raising them in state-supervised nurseries, and making certain that parents and children could not develop special attachments between each other. Destroying family ties, he thought, would lead to a society of universal justice devoid of the biases of kin preference.[14] A modern-day variation of Plato's view was put forth by Mark Poster in his *Critical Theory of the Family,* where he argues that families must lose their "possessiveness" if a more universal ethic is to arise. He believed that multiple family forms must exist and that family ties must become weaker "so that feelings of affection can expand throughout the community." He advocated the extension of the kibbutz to the entire society so that children raised together and dwelling separately from their parents "can select figures for identification from a wider group of adults."[15]

In short, Plato and his modern day followers believed that the weakening of families would lead to more universalistic attitudes and sensibilities, especially if they are measured by the category of universal justice of the kind we today associate with the moral philosophy of Immanuel Kant or the highest stage of moral development as conceived by Kohlberg.[16] All of these positions relate the higher levels of moral thinking with the transcendence, if not the suppression, of kin attachments and kin altruism. I do not believe, however, that the modern followers of Plato understand the dynamics of individualism and market rationality and how they function to exacerbate detachment, if not alienation, from family connections. Nor do they comprehend what contemporary German social theorist Jürgen Habermas has characterized as the "colonization" of everyday life by the technical rationality of both market and government bureaucracy.[17] He means by this the spread of both the cost-benefit logics of the market and the dependency-producing logics of government bureaucracy into the rhythms of daily life, even the lives of families. With these dynamics in mind, loosening ties between parents and children might just as easily lead to the abandonment of children to the individualistic logics of the market rather than liberating them for some grand new capacity for universal justice.

Aristotle, on the other hand, had a different point of view. He thought, as do some of his modern-day followers, that strong families were essential for raising moral children. Aristotle believed that humans share with animals the desire to give birth to children, that is, "to leave behind them an image of themselves."[18] In holding this view, his thought was consistent with modern-day evolutionary psychologists who believe that kin altruism and inclusive fitness (the inborn tendency to produce and care for individuals carrying one's own genes) are major forces motivating all living beings, even humans, whether they know it or not. Recognizing the reality of this pervasive desire led Aristotle to argue in his *Politics* that Plato's thought experiment about the state raising children and suppressing kin affections was doomed to failure. Biological parents, he wrote, are motivated to invest and care for their offspring with an intensity that no general substitutes can match. Furthermore, he wrote, "that which is common to the greatest number has the least care bestowed upon it."[19] According to Aristotle, Plato's ideal city where parents relinquish their children to state nurseries would contain within it far more violence; the natural inhibitions created by kin relatedness and investment would deteriorate; and anger and murder would become rampant.[20] Love would become "watery," diluted, and without substance; it would apply to people in general and to no one in particular. The moral fabric of the community would decline.

This insight into human nature became firmly wedded within Christian thought at various points, especially in the Christian Aristotelianism of Thomas Aquinas. Christian love was seen by him as building on and extending, without dismantling or rejecting, Aristotle's basic insights into what we today would call kin altruism.[21] Kin altruism was, for Aquinas, part of the structure of God's good creation, a gift of God that inclined us to care for those we bring into the world. Although God was the ultimate Creator and was to be honored as such, natural fathers and mothers were also principles of creation; they passed their life on to their children and should care for them first and foremost as gifts of God then, second, as continuations of themselves.[22] Both sets of reasons counted as a ground for parental love in the Thomistic view.

This strand of thinking has continued in Roman Catholic thought, providing the intellectual core of its pro-family social teachings. It is particularly visible in the social thought of Pope Leo XIII, Pius XI, the Roman Catholic doctrine of subsidiarity, and many of the documents of the Second Vatican Council.[23] It has influenced legal thought wherever Thomism has extended its influence, which certainly includes all primarily Roman Catholic countries and many Protestant countries and colonies that absorbed into their legal theory elements of Catholic canon law, with its Aristotelian assumptions. Aristotle's theory of the centrality of natural families for the moral development of children has been basic to much of Western family and moral theory.

3. Evolutionary Psychology and Christian Thomism

Christian Thomism has clear analogies to certain tenets of contemporary evolutionary psychology. Both hold that the deeper investment of natural parents in their children can contribute to the moral and spiritual development of their offspring. Both hold that this investment meets certain needs in the parents, just as it contributes to the well-being of infants and children. However, Thomism carries with it many additional insights into human development, several of which come from its wider theology and ecclesiology. My argument will be that evolutionary psychology contains important insights into the grounds of human development but requires supplementation from Aristotle, Thomas, and new perspectives on Kant, Kohlberg, and Fowler gained from the moral philosophy of Paul Ricoeur.

3.1 Peter Singer, Kin Altruism, and Moral Reason

The evolutionary psychological views of moral theorist Peter Singer are useful for my argument. He addresses the moral line of development, but what he says has implications, as we will later see, for faith as well. Singer, the controversial Australian moralist now at Princeton University, uses evolutionary psychology in his *The Expanding Circle: Ethics and Sociobiology*.[24] I will use Singer to show the relevance of evolutionary psychology to the issue I am pursuing. I just as usefully could have discussed the writings of James Q. Wilson, Robert Wright, Frans de Waal, or Richard Alexander.[25] Each of them believes that evolutionary psychology uncovers a substratum of natural sociality that constitutes the core of our moral inclinations. I use Singer because he is more explicit about the philosophical assumptions of his argument.

Singer argues that human ethical systems are grounded in two forms of altruism. The first, and most basic, is kin altruism—the tendency of parents and children to become attached, identify with one another, and give preferential treatment to one another because they share 50 percent of the same genes. The second is reciprocal altruism, the tendency of the members of many species, especially humans, to help others as a way of assuring that they in turn will be assisted when they are in need.[26] The inclination toward reciprocal altruism in part stems from the generosity of a prior kin altruism; because invested parents first give to their infants and children, these young ones are inclined to return the favor to both parents and others, thereby keeping the mutually beneficial process of giving and receiving alive for everyone's advantage.

Singer contrasts his theory of ethical development with the antisocial and egoistic view of humans in the state of nature found in Rousseau and Hobbes.[27] Their views that humans were originally isolated and in a state of constant warfare are inconsistent with what we know from both archaeology and biology about the innate sociality of humans. Singer believes that morality grows out of this sociality—this natural tendency to care for our young and be reciprocally altruistic with our neighbors in order to enhance mutual advantage. According to Singer, Rousseau and Hobbes, who both believe that morality stems from a contract between otherwise hostile individuals, fail to take account of these premoral inclinations toward care of kin and reciprocity with neighbor. Singer applies his criticism of the classic contractualism of these two Enlightenment thinkers to the contemporary contractualism of John Rawls.[28] All are unrealistic about the substratum of human sociality on which morality builds.

But Singer admits that this substratum of sociality does not itself fully account for either ethical theory or moral development. Fully moral capacities, he argues, require the universalizing logic of the kind of moral reason that Kohlberg associates with the highest levels of moral thinking.[29] Reason, in effect, extends the prosocial impulses of kin altruism beyond the natural boundaries of kinship and neighbor reciprocity. Singer here is bridging the gap between Aristotle and Kant by connecting Kohlberg's Kantian-oriented theory of moral thinking to its elementary energizing roots in kin altruism. Without the extensions of reason, kin altruism and reciprocal altruism can end in the kin and tribal preferentiality that Plato of the *Republic* so desperately feared or that Kohlberg somewhat disparaging calls the "conventional."[30] But without the elementary attachments, investments, and associated empathy of kin altruism, moral reason is without energy and emotional content. Singer acknowledges that fully mature morality is defined by universality. A judgment to be fully moral must apply in principle to all human beings; in fact, for Singer, it must apply to all creatures with conscious sentience and the capacity to experience pain and suffering.[31] So Singer sees morality as an "expanding circle," which was, you will recall, the title of his 1981 book. It begins with the sociality of kin and reciprocal altruism, but these impulses are dragged by the analogical extension of reason to apply to all creatures who show any flicker of self-consciousness similar to that of the humans we first come to love and appreciate—our family and friends.

Singer borrows from the structuralist moral psychology of Kohlberg to explain how reason is analogically expanded to include but also go beyond kin and helping neighbor. Singer appears to agree with Kohlberg: Moral reason is expanded by disequilibria or conflict between conflicting interests in the context of free interaction. When my interests conflict with those of another, I am forced to move to a higher and more inclusive level of moral reason in order to recognize and accommodate the interests of us both. In this way, I gradually move through a series of stages toward a more universal and reversible point of view. Although Singer associates higher levels of morality with reason's capacity to expand analogically our animal sociality to identify with the interests of others beyond kin and immediate reciprocators, he finally is skeptical of a disembodied universalism. He rejects Kant's specific articulation of universalism because of its abstractness, its narrow emphasis on respect for the rational self of the other, and its disconnection from the motivations of affectional human interests. But he is also skeptical of an ethic that restricts itself to an abstract utilitarianism based only on interests and universal reason. Singer ends by emphasizing the importance of inherited rules and customs as carriers of moral wisdom and supplements to more abstract principles of moral reason. The rules of custom, he believes, systematize the past results of the universalizing tendencies of reason, thereby saving us from always needing to do our reasoning afresh.[32] Rules also tie prescriptions to concrete situations, individuals, and groups, hence building on our biological tendencies to help specific people such as kin and neighbor. Nonetheless, a society's customary rules generally prescribe actions that tilt behavior toward the common good—that is, toward an equal consideration of all interests, a goal that it is difficult for reason alone to motivate us actually to accomplish. Settled rules help us to turn toward a universality that reason requires but cannot itself easily bring us to attain.

In summary, what then is Singer telling us about how to raise humans with universalistic inclinations? He is saying that we should build on natural family inclinations toward kin altruism. We should also build on natural inclinations toward reciprocal altruism. To this extent, he is siding with Aristotle, Thomism, and modern Roman Catholic social teachings, although he extends them with references to Kant and Kohlberg on moral reason. He stands against Plato and modern critical theorists such as Poster. If the family is falling apart, this, for Singer, would logically be a matter of grave concern. Although Singer says little about such issues, he doubtless would favor cultural and social measures that might help resist the disruptive influence to families of individualism and its exacerbation by market rationality. Because of his affirmative stance on other issues such as animal rights and the killing of deformed fetuses, it is strange to think of Singer as an ally of the Vatican on anything at all. But, on the issue of the moral relevance of intact families and the conditions for the development of a moral self, he would in many respects be on the side of the pope.

Although Singer agrees with the Thomists and Catholic social teachings that kin and reciprocal altruism contribute to the development of more universalistic sensibilities, he would also agree that they do not alone assure it. More is needed. For Singer, the more is reason and rules, with reason providing the measure but rules giving the concrete instantiation. More is needed as well for the Thomists and modern Catholic thought. Although reason and rules are affirmed by the Thomists, even more than these are necessary to educate humans for universalistic capacities.

3.2 Affect, Reason, and Narrative in Ricoeur

Rather than turning to the Thomists, I want to pursue the question of "what more is needed" by turning to the thought of the French hermeneutic philosopher Paul Ricoeur. Ricoeur is one of the major philosophers of the twentieth century, increasingly placed in the company of such giants as William James, John Dewey, Martin Heidegger, and Ludwig Wittgenstein. In recent years, he has turned to the field of moral philosophy, especially in his Gifford Lectures published in 1992 under the title of *Oneself as Another*.[33] The relation of morality to faith has been a growing theme in his huge corpus.

Singer and Ricoeur might seem to be strange thinkers to bring into dialogue. But I believe that a fruitful conversation is possible. For instance, although the psychology of Sigmund Freud has influenced Ricoeur's philosophy and moral theory, only recently has he begun to consider the moral claims of evolutionary psychology and, even then, not extensively.[34] Nonetheless, Ricoeur has appreciation for the Aristotelian tradition of moral philosophy, as does Singer. He believes that ethics is primarily teleological in nature—that is, it is about the realization of the good and the actualizing for self and others. This would be formally consistent with Singer's belief that morality builds on and extends the basic affections of natural human sociality. But there are at least four important differences between Singer and Ricoeur, and these differences illuminate the "more" that is needed to expand kin and reciprocal altruism in the direction of wider universal sensibilities, whether seen from the perspective of morality or faith.

These four elements are Ricoeur's emphasis on practices, his appreciation for the role of narrative in the moral life, his respect for the role of the Kantian categorical imperative (hence, the kind of structuralist moral thinking associated with Kohlberg and Fowler), and his understanding of the role of wisdom or *phronêsis* in the full rhythm of the moral action. I will summarize his position on each of these four concepts and use them to recontextualize Singer's contributions.

First, practices: Ricoeur and Singer agree, as I have indicated above, that the moral life evolves out of our teleological inclinations. Before the moral life becomes a matter of duty, it is first of all a drive to realize the goods of life. For Singer, as we have seen, the goods of life are illuminated by kin and reciprocal altruism. In speaking about these goods, Singer generally talks more about interests than desires, but the teleological point of his argument is still there. The moral life for him has to do with giving equal consideration to all interests, both our own and others. These include interests such as "avoiding pain, developing abilities, having adequate food and shelter, enjoying good personal relationships."[35] Ricoeur speaks more of desire than interests and interprets desire as plastic, more in the fashion of Freud's concept of *eros* than the thicker idea of kin and reciprocal altruism found in evolutionary psychology.[36]

Ricoeur's main point, however, is that we only know our desires and the goods they aim at through practices that have been linguistically interpreted by community traditions. We do not know our desires and interests directly through unmediated bodily states, as Singer appears to hold. These bodily urges exist, but they become desires through interpretation and amplification by the language games of surrounding communities. "Why am I eating? It is because I am hungry." Hunger may be a vague bodily state, but our social practices link this diffuse physical condition to the specifics of sitting down, using a fork and knife, and saying, "I believe it is time for dinner." Whereas Singer, and almost all the evolutionary psychologists, would lead us to concentrate directly on our desires, interests, and the rules that organize them, Ricoeur would have us discover the goods of life through the interpreted practices into which we are born and socialized.[37] It is true: Singer speaks of rules and Ricoeur writes about practices, and there are similarities between the two ideas. But Ricoeur's concept of practices is a much thicker idea. For Ricoeur, our desires are known through practices that connect them to realizable social patterns; these practices in turn are given significance by wider narratives or stories that tell us about the meaning and direction of our practices.

This leads to the second point about the "more" that is needed to account for universalism in morality and faith. The moral life is, for Ricoeur, a storied life; it is a story that reveals some overarching meaning to our practices.[38] It is a story that is mediated to us by a more-or-less cohesive community of tradition. The overarching narratives that define our lives are never a product of science in the narrow sense of that word. In fact, the classic religious narratives of the West that give meaning to our practices include symbolic ways of stating and affirming the moral worth of human beings. *In Judaism and Christianity, the picture of humans made in the image of God has constituted the symbolic grounds on which Christians have come to believe that before the eyes of God, nonkin members— even strangers and enemies—have value equal to their kin and other reciprocating partners.* This belief, generally first mediated by parents and their community of faith, functions as a leverage calling us to balance preference for kin and friend with awareness of the needs of those beyond these intimate circles. Stated in the terms of Kohlberg and Fowler, this is a narratively grounded belief on which higher-level formal intellectual operations function to generate our capacity for universal respect for others. But in contrast to Kohlberg, formal intellectual operations and their universalizing functions do not create the belief in the status of others; rather, they are called out by and function on a prior storied belief about the ontological status of all other persons. But to make this point clear, I need to say something in addition about the other two points that distinguish Singer and Ricoeur on the "more" needed to explain and anchor universals in morality, and also in faith.

I must say more on the third point—the role of reason. Singer, as we have seen, does contain a place for reason in its universalizing mode, although he also believes it becomes morally misleading and impotent in its abstract and disembodied forms. Ricoeur believes that universalizing reason also has a place, but not at the beginning of moral thinking, as was the case for Kant, but toward the end of the process. Kant held that moral thinking must be ruled from beginning to end by the categorical imperative that, in its second form, read, "Act so that you treat humanity, whether in your own person or in that of another, always as an end and never as a means only."[39] This abstract principle, for Kant, was the essence of morality. This was the universal law that Kant taught should be applied to all humans who, as rational creatures, deserved to be treated as ends in themselves and never as mere means to ends beyond themselves.

Rather than using the categorical imperative as the sole principle ruling moral thought, Ricoeur uses it as a test of the narratively interpreted practices that embody the goods and rules entailed in the pursuit of the ethical life, that is, the good life.[40] When our ethical practices confront obstacles, when the goods we pursue fall into conflict with one another and create potential violence, when we meet resistance from the other, then our practices must pass, according to Ricoeur, the *test* of universalization. In Ricoeur's formulation, universalizing reason becomes a test for our tradition-laden ethical practices. As Aristotle would say it, we must first learn and consistently reenact ethical practices—ethical habits—in pursuit of life's goods. But then, in the midst of conflicts and crises, we must learn to apply the universalizing tests of reason. To say it more simply, to be a moral person, we must first be socialized into a tradition of moral practices and only then, on occasion, learn to test these practices with reason. But even then, as we have seen, reason cannot do its work of generalization unless its inherited practices and narratives inform it with the belief, or faith, that others—all others—deserve to be equally considered. Moral development requires faith in the ontological status of self and other—an insight that Ricoeur and Fowler would share.

This leads me to the fourth difference between Ricoeur and Singer. Ricoeur teaches that the last stage of moral thought and action is what he calls *phronêsis.*[41] This is the task of accumulating the best of our narratively interpreted moral practices, testing them with universalizing reason, and *then* returning to the original concrete situation to either confirm or amend our customary practices. In returning to the concrete situation, we have to exercise wisdom; neither customary habit nor universalizing reason are sufficient alone. We have to make judgments about what concrete steps toward the universal are indeed possible without, in the end, disrupting enhancing practices beyond repair.

3.3 Conclusion

These are the criticisms that Ricoeur rightly can make of Singer: He does not take with sufficient seriousness narratively interpreted traditional practices as the beginning point of ethics. Singer jumps from kin and reciprocal altruism to rules and bypasses both practices and their interpretation in light of wider inherited narratives about the meaning of life. This has practical ramifications for how Singer conceives the first states of moral formation. Singer would use kin-based parent-child attachments to teach the young rules and hope that these rules build on our natural sociality; however, he does not conceive of this as a process of socializing the young into communities of narratively informed shared practices. Ricoeur would see socializing the young into communities of shared practice as the central step of moral formation; we should help the young learn the shared moral practices of a well-formed religio-moral community, and we should help the young learn the narratives that define and generate our faith in these practices.

After this initial process of formation has occurred, we should then help the young to be *reflective* about what they have learned. We would help them acknowledge and confront the tensions and conflicts within these practices—conflicts that inevitably emerge, especially as circumstances change and new challenges evolve. Ricoeur would agree that Singer in one respect is right; the essence of morality is found in the universalizing impulse of moral reason. It is here that ethics moves beyond provinciality—whether based in kin or reciprocal altruism or something else—to equal concern for the respect and well-being of all others. Singer and Ricoeur would also agree that the premature drive into universalization can be destructive for everyone, especially the young. But rather than backing away from universalization, as Singer did, we should follow Ricoeur in locating its use as respecting, but then testing, the deeply learned conventional wisdom of tradition-laden practices.

Finally, Singer does not understand the importance of the last stage of *phronêsis,* or moral wisdom. Singer is right to fear the abstractions of universalizing reason, but he is wrong to retreat to a morality of rules. He needs to move through the critique of universalization but then return to the initial concrete situation to determine what steps can be taken to move toward the ideal. Good moral education entails socializing the young into narratively informed communities of moral practice, learning how to test these practices by universalizing reason, but then learning as well how to make realistic moral reconstructions back in the original situation.

4. Family and Universality in Morality and Faith

So far, it would seem that Ricoeur is getting the upper hand in this dialogue and that Singer and the evolutionary psychology that he espouses have little to offer to an adequate understanding of morality and the juncture between morality and faith. This conclusion, however, would be premature. Singer does have big contributions to make. He and the entire field of evolutionary psychology point to a significant truth that Ricoeur and others like him should take to heart—that is, the importance of kin altruism in initiating the young into the moral practices of a tradition. The investments, family affections, and identifications that the theory of kin altruism helps us to understand are crucial for socializing children into the moral and faith demands of narratively grounded traditional practices. They may be equally important for modeling critical reflection that goes beyond conventionality and moves toward universality. As family strength declines, church and society should do what it can to reverse these trends, not only in the name of the family, but in the name of the moral and faith formation of our children. This, in part, entails learning how to curtail the forces of individualism and market rationality that undercut all communities of the life world, including families. It is difficult to imagine any other agency of socialization that will have the on-average leverage needed to induct children into the practices of a religious and moral tradition and then model what it means to apply our structural cognitive capacities to these traditional practices.

Rather than the movement toward universalization in morality and faith occurring in opposition to the family, as Plato and Poster imagined, it is far more likely that it will happen with the aid of families–families who are themselves grounded in narratively based practices on which reason and *phronêsis* can do their work. To make this statement is not to attack the institution of adoption or the skills and commitments of many single parents. It is to say that their unusual gifts should not blind us to the likely impossibility of finding a more general institution outside of intact families that will, on the whole, do the task as well. My point is to reject the proposals of Plato and his modern offshoots.

I make no argument for an idolatry of the family–a charge often made, with some justification, against the Christian Right. Families, within Christian practice, are relative goods, always to be seen as in service to and subordinate to the kingdom of God. My argument, rather, is that the intact conjugal couple, when properly informed by narratively enriched practices, can contribute a limited but essential element to the task of a more universal morality and faith.

But, how to rebuild and reformulate families in face of the growing power of individualism and market rationality is another discussion, one that the Religion, Culture, and Family Project has addressed at length.[42]

Notes

[1]For the importance of the structural point of view in moral development, see Lawrence Kohlberg, *The Philosophy of Moral Development,* vol. 1 (San Francisco: Harper & Row, 1981), 15–16.

[2]James W. Fowler, *Stages of Faith* (San Francisco: Harper & Row, 1981), 269–76.

[3]For a discussion of faith and emotional development from the perspective of Erik Erikson, see ibid., 107–10; a full investigation of Fowler's view of the relation of the cognitive-structuralist perspective on development and narrative theory is found in *Becoming Adult, Becoming Christian* (San Francisco: Harper & Row, 1984), 82–84.

[4]James W. Fowler, "Faith Development through the Family Life Cycle," *Growing in Faith: A Catholic Family Sourcebook* (New Rochelle, N.Y.: Salesian Society, 1990), 99–126.

[5]Ron Lesthaege, "A Century of Demographic Change in Western Europe: An Exploration of Underlying Dimensions," *Population and Development Review* 9, no. 33 (September 1983): 411–32.

[6]Max Weber, *The Protestant Ethic and the Spirit of Capitalism* (New York: Charles Scribner's Sons, 1958), 180–82.

[7]For a discussion of market rationality that builds on Jürgen Habermas's theory of purposive rationality, see Alan Wolfe, *Whose Keeper? Social Science and Moral Obligation* (Berkeley and Los Angeles: University of California Press, 1989), 27–31.

[8]Robert Bellah, Richard Madsen, William Sullivan, Ann Swidler, and Steven Tipton, *Habits of the Heart: Individualism and Commitment in American Life* (New York: Harper & Row, 1985), 27, 32–35.

[9]Tom Smith, "The Emerging 21st Century American Family" (Chicago: National Opinion Research Center, 1999), 1.

[10]Larry Bumpass and James Sweet, "Children's Experience in Single-Parent Homes: Implications of Cohabitation and Marital Transitions," *Family Planning Perspectives* 21 (Nov/Dec 1989): 256–60.

[11]For information on the instability of cohabitation, see Linda Waite and Maggie Gallagher, *The Case for Marriage: Why Married People Are Happier, Healthier, and Better Off Financially* (New York: Doubleday, 2000), 36–46; Linda Waite, "The Negative Effects of Cohabitation," *The Responsive Community* (Winter 2000): 31; David Popenoe and Barbara Dafoe Whitehead, "Should We Live Together? What Young Adults Need to Know about Cohabitation before Marriage" (New Brunswick, N.J.: Rutgers University, The National Marriage Project, 1999), 1, 4–5.

[12]Sara McLanahan and Gary Sandefur, *Growing Up with a Single Mother* (Cambridge, Mass.: Harvard University Press, 1994), 1, 37–63.

[13]David Popenoe, *Life Without Father* (New York: The Free Press, 1996), 9.

[14]Plato, *The Republic* (New York: Basic Books, 1968), Bk. V.

[15]Mark Poster, *Critical Theory of the Family* (New York: Seabury Press, 1978), 204.

[16]Immanuel Kant, *Foundations of the Metaphysics of Morals* (New York: Bobbs-Merrill, 1959), 39; Kohlberg, *Philosophy of Moral Development,* vol. 1, 135.

[17]Jürgen Habermas, *Theory of Communicative Action,* vol. 2 (Boston: Beacon Press, 1987), 182–96.

[18]Aristotle, "Politics," in *The Basic Works of Aristotle* (New York: Random House, 1941), Bk. 1, 1.

[19]Ibid., Bk. 1, 3.

[20]Ibid., Bk. 2, 4.

[21]Thomas Aquinas, "The Order of Charity," in *Summa Theologica* (London: R. & T. Washbourne, 1917), II, ii, q. 26.

[22]Ibid., II, ii, q. 26, a.3, a. 7.

[23]Pope Leo XIII, "Rerum Novarum," in *Proclaiming Justice and Peace: Papal Documents* (Mystic, Conn.: Twenty-Third Publications, 1991); Pius XI, "Casti Connubi," in *The Papal Encyclical* (Wilmington, N.C.: McGrath, 1981).

[24]Peter Singer, *The Expanding Circle: Ethics and Sociobiology* (New York: Farrar, Straus & Giroux, 1981).

[25]James Q. Wilson, *The Moral Sense* (New York: The Free Press, 1993); Robert Wright, *The Moral Animal* (New York: Pantheon Books, 1994); Frans de Waal, *Good Natured* (Cambridge, Mass.: Harvard University Press, 1996); Richard Alexander, *The Biology of Moral Systems* (New York: Aldine, 1987).

[26]Singer, *Expanding Circle,* 11–18.

[27]Ibid., 1, 23–24.

[28]Ibid., 55–56.

[29]For a discussion of Kohlberg's highest Stage 6, see his *The Philosophy of Moral Development,* vol. 1, 157–68.

[30]Ibid., 410

[31]Peter Singer, *Practical Ethics* (Cambridge: Cambridge University Press, 1993), 93–108.

[32]Singer, *Expanding Circle,* 156–67.

[33]Paul Ricoeur, *Oneself as Another* (Chicago: University of Chicago Press, 1992).

[34]Jean-Pierre Changeux and Paul Ricoeur, *What Makes Us Think?* (Princeton, N.J.: Princeton University Press, 2000).

[35]Singer, *Practical Ethics,* 37.

[36]Paul Ricoeur, *Freud and Philosophy* (New Haven, Conn.: Yale University Press, 1970).

[37]Paul Ricoeur, "The Teleological and Deontological Structures of Action: Aristotle and/or Kant," in *Contemporary French Philosophy,* ed. A. Griffith Phillips (Cambridge: Cambridge University Press, 1987), 99–112.

[38]Ricoeur, *Oneself as Another,* 140–68.

[39]Kant, *Foundations of the Metaphysics of Morals,* 47.

[40]Ricoeur, *Oneself as Another,* 203–39.

[41]Ibid., 240–96.

[42]See the summary book of the Religion, Culture, and Family Project, located at the Divinity School of the University of Chicago and funded by the Division of Religion of the Lilly Endowment, Inc.: Don Browning, Bonnie Miller-McLemore, Pam Couture, Bernie Lyon, and Robert Franklin, *From Culture Wars to Common Ground: Religion and the American Family Debate* (Louisville, Ky.: Westminster John Knox Press, 1997, 2000). For more information, see the Web site of the project at www.uchicago.edu/divinity/family.

PART FOUR

A Response

Faith Development Theory
and the Challenges of
Practical Theology

14

Faith Development Theory and the Challenges of Practical Theology

JAMES W. FOWLER

Faith development theory stands at the convergence of developmental psychologies and a tradition of liberal theology deriving from Christian origins. It took form through empirical research based on in-depth interviews with children and adults, conducted initially primarily in North America. In the author's perspective, the research and theory of faith development is a principal part of a larger practical theological project. This chapter undertakes to do the following: *first,* review the elements that have converged to shape faith development theory; *second,* clarify the ways in which the theory is an account of the development of the self, in relation to others and to an ultimate environment; *third,* sketch and respond to the urgings to relinquish some features and claims of the theory in the light of postmodern critiques; and *fourth,* attempt to place the author's work on faith development in the larger framework of his efforts toward a systematic practical theology.

A final section of this chapter expresses the author's response to the articles that constitute this volume. Brief though they be, these commentaries carry deep and particular gratitude to the colleagues and friends whose contributions elegantly and rigorously enter into dialogue with many of the concerns that have animated our common work.

1. Elements That Converged to Shape Faith Development Theory[1]

It is important to recognize that faith development theory had its origins in a context of *praxis.* While writing my dissertation on the theological ethics of H. Richard Niebuhr, I accepted the role of associate director of Interpreters' House, a center for personal and vocational self-examination and growth for clergy and laity, founded by my mentor and friend, Carlyle Marney. In that role, I had the opportunity to spend a year listening to and interacting with several hundred persons in a context where they shared in-depth narratives of their lives and work and were provided with support (and challenge) for developmental and spiritual growth. During that year, I devoured the work of Erik Erikson and lectured regularly to Interpreters' House groups on his eight ages of the life cycle. I also deepened my reading of Niebuhr, with special attention to his several discussions of faith. In this context of practical involvement and reflective reading, linkages between Niebuhr's dynamic conception of faith, understood as a universal feature of humans, and the psychosocial conception of the self offered in Erikson's ego psychology began to come clearly into fruitful relationship. Part of the linkage that made this pairing seem natural results from Niebuhr's having been deeply influenced by his early study with philosopher-sociologist George Herbert Mead. It is important to indicate at this juncture how central in Niebuhr's account of human faith and selfhood the social and relational understanding of the self, which he found in the work of Mead, became.

After the year at Interpreters' House (1968–1969), I returned to Harvard Divinity School to teach and administer a program in continuing education for clergy and laity. In my teaching, I built upon the Interpreters' House experience, offering a course I titled "Theology as the Symbolization of Experience." In that context, I lectured twice a week and invited students to participate in small encounter groups of about ten each. My lectures drew theologically from Niebuhr and Paul Tillich; psychologically, they drew from Erikson, Freud, Jung, and others. In a first approach to developing a concept of postcritical faith, I began to draw on the hermeneutical work of Paul Ricoeur, Michael Polanyi, and on Owen Barfield's book *Saving the Appearances*.[2] In the weekly small group meetings, participants were encouraged, as at Interpreters' House, to bring the lectures and readings together in the context of autobiographical reflection and sharing. These late-sixties and early-seventies gatherings of students exhibited a lot of diversity. In my courses, there were Catholics, Unitarians, Sikhs, Jews, Muslims, and Protestants ranging from the Church of Christ to Lutherans, Presbyterians, Episcopalians, the United Church of Christ, and Methodists.

In the first year that I taught that course, some of my students began to mention the then new research and psychology of moral development being pursued and taught by Lawrence Kohlberg at the Harvard Graduate School of Education. Interested, I soon gathered the available Kohlberg papers and began to study his work on the emerging theory of the development of moral reasoning. Soon, I came to know Kohlberg, who graciously invited me to join the intellectual circle forming around his work. Through studying Kohlberg's work, I became a student of Jean Piaget, with his constructive developmental approach to the study of stages of cognitive development. From Kohlberg and Piaget, I gradually adopted—and adapted—the constructive developmental account of stage-like transformations in the forms of cognition and of moral reasoning. I did not, however, relinquish my dependence on Erikson and my involvement with Niebuhr's multidimensional theology. My initial excitement about Kohlberg's work provided an impetus to try to operationalize a rich concept of faith and to begin to look more systematically at faith in a constructive developmental perspective.

After some years, I would come to find myself restive with Kohlberg's lack of attention to the emotions and his turning away from study of the broader development of the self. Kohlberg made a fateful decision, which one can find described in an article titled "Stage and Sequence: The Cognitive-Developmental Approach to Socialization."[3] There, he opted for the cognitive structural-development approach of Piaget and turned away from the possibility of developing a theory of the moral self in dialogue with Mead and his social interactionist account of the self. Kohlberg seems to have felt that this step was necessary for two reasons. First, he believed that focusing on the structures of moral reasoning made his constructs more susceptible to empirical assessment. Second, the formal quality of his accounts of structural stages of moral reasoning made his work more acceptable in face of the judicial strictures on the separation of church and state operative in public schools, because it allowed the teaching of normative approaches to the teaching of moral reasoning, without having to address its religious or philosophical "contents."

In my fourth year of teaching at Harvard Divinity School (1972), I developed a new course that grew out of my postdissertation work with Erikson, Piaget, and Kohlberg. Of course, Niebuhr continued to be a central source for me, as did Erikson, and now, Piaget and Kohlberg. I called the course "Dynamics of Identity and Faith." It was built around the challenge of introducing students to the theological and developmental psychological background for faith development theory, and then involving them in the constructive work of interviewing and analyzing persons' journeys in faith through semiclinical interviews.

From the first year of teaching this course, I involved students in conducting and analyzing in-depth interviews designed to open access to their respondents' processes of developing identity and faith. This required that we work out a framework for the analysis of the recorded and transcribed interviews they conducted. During the summer of 1972, I shaped a preliminary matrix of structural aspects with which to differentiate and trace developmental patterns among the dynamic elements involved in making and holding together the patterns and processes of faith. Taken together, they give an operational depiction of faith as a complex, central—and centering—constituent of selfhood.[4] These became:

Form of Logic (derived from Piaget)
Social Perspective Taking (derived from Selman)
Form of Moral Judgment (derived from Kohlberg)
Bounds of Social Awareness
Locus of Authority
Form of World Coherence
Symbolic Function

From the mid-seventies, with this chart we developed an elaborate set of structural descriptions of stages that became the basis for research and scoring.

This has evolved to become a handbook that provides the framework for the conduct of Faith Development Interviews and for their interpretation and analysis.[5]

In 1974, a substantial grant from the Kennedy Foundation enabled me to form a research team at Harvard and to work more rigorously on approaches in empirical research and theory building in faith development studies. This led to the three major waves of data collection and analysis from 1975 to 1979. These culminated in *Stages of Faith: The Psychology of Human Development and the Quest for Meaning.* This book, published in 1981, brought faith development theory to a comprehensive first statement.

I think it is significant that, between the ending of my time in Boston (1977) and the writing of *Stages of Faith* (1979–1981), I moved to Atlanta to take up a teaching post at Emory University. There, I found able students in both the Masters of Divinity courses I taught (primarily students preparing for the ministry) and in the doctoral program I helped to form in 1980 (then, Theology and Personality; since 1997, Person, Community and Religious Practices). The Masters of Divinity students often were older than those I had taught at Harvard. By and large, they were more interested in the church and the practices of ministry than many at Harvard had been. This altered setting, and my returning to the South, which has strong storytelling traditions, both permitted and demanded an increased attention to narrative. Hence, the use of examples from film and novels in *Stages of Faith* and in my 1984 book *Becoming Adult, Becoming Christian.*

There were also life experiences and challenges that affected my work. In 1980, at age forty, I had to decide whether to accept the invitation to become dean of the divinity school of a major university. When I accepted nomination for the job, I thought surely I would take it, if offered. When the offer came, however, I found myself more divided than I had expected. *Stages of Faith* was half written. My first two graduate students in the new program had just begun their work, and my own institution made a very attractive counteroffer to underwrite the creation of a funded center to institutionalize and support research in faith and moral development. The struggle over that decision—both in turning down the job and in living with the choice—opened questions of selfhood, of vocation (in a deeper sense than profession or job), and of my primary life relationships. One result of the work I undertook with myself was the writing of *Becoming Adult, Becoming Christian,* a book that placed faith development theory in the context of studies of the self in Erikson, Daniel Levinson, and Carol Gilligan. Clearly, the motions and emotions of living found deepened engagement in that book, as did the question of what it meant to hold personal theological and faith commitments and at the same time to try to study faith as a universal feature of human beings, whether in specifically religious terms or not.

As a result of such experiences and personal learning in my forties, I began to study early child development, giving fresh attention to the primary emotions of trust, shame, guilt, and the child's earliest constructions of God.

This opened the way for expanded attention to the emotions, their forms and meanings, in relation to specific stages of faith. It also led to substantial work on shame and selfhood, in which I drew on the work of Silvan Tomkins and a number of other shame theorists who begin the study of this powerful emotion by grounding it in the neurophysiological affect system of our bodies.

These foci of work in the fifth decade of my life have found expression and place in my most recent book, *Faithful Change: The Personal and Public Challenges of Postmodern Life.*[6] In the third section of this book, I gathered and extended work in which I have used the faith development paradigm as a framework for exploring the emergence of what I have call "practical postmodern consciousness." I argue that whether contemporary persons in postindustrial, high technology, and culturally plural societies know it or acknowledge it or not, we participate in practical postmodern consciousness. In this connection, I present faith development theory as an account of the person's move from a first naïveté to critical consciousness and then to a postcritical second naïveté as offering parallels to premodern, modern, and postmodern forms of social consciousness and their techno-institutional forms. I will return to this theme later in this writing.

2. The Self in Faith Development Theory

John McDargh, in a thoughtful and constructive article, asserts that despite the usefulness and influence of faith development theory, it lacks an adequate account of the development of the self.[7] He acknowledges that the theory brings together two important strands of psychological study and theory, the "Cambridge developmentalists" (Kohlberg, Selman, Kegan, and others) on the one hand, with the ego psychology of Erikson, on the other. But he, and others whose critiques he cites, lament the lack of an explicit theory of the development of the self in faith development theory.

McDargh does point out that the first published account of faith development theory included a study of the journey in faith of Malcolm X. He applauds the interpreting of Malcolm's life story, with its developmental crises and transitions, through the structural stages of faith. And McDargh wrote appreciatively about the inclusion of "Mary's Story" in *Stages of Faith,* a case study based on a relationship that grew more out of pastoral counseling than from the conduct of a faith development research interview. There have been other psychobiographical faith development studies across the years—John Wesley, the founding spirit of Methodism,[8] and an early book of such studies done by my students at Harvard, which I edited with Robin Lovin, that included analyses of the development in faith of Anne Hutchinson, Ludwig Wittgenstein, Dietrich Bonhoeffer, and Blaise Pascal—in addition to the aforementioned study of Malcolm X.[9]

I would like to point out that faith, and the development of faith, has a triadic structure. There is the self; there are the primal and significant others in the self's relational matrix; and there is the third center of relational engagement—the ultimate Other, or the center(s) of value and power in one's life structure. The study of the self, in faith development perspective, therefore, must attend to the process of the increasingly self-aware construction of that relational matrix and of its change over time. This includes both the self's choices and affinities with others and with the holy, and the transformations and changes these relationships undergo, due both to ongoing development and to changes in the content and shape of one's life experiences. Thus, I will claim that the structural "Aspects" that constitute the matrix of faith do embrace—or constitute—a theory of the self, as well as a *story* of the self. *But it is a theory (story) of the self through time, as constructing meanings and being constructed, in the matrix of relationships and meanings that faith involves.*

Heinz Streib, drawing on hermeneutics and literary theory from Ricoeur and others,[10] has proposed that faith development theory has focused more on the formal (content empty) account of the development of cognitive and emotional operations underlying lived faith than on the "story" of the life or lives in faith. He makes an important point. One reason for the substantial readership and use of *Stages of Faith* in classroom and clinical settings is the illustrative use of narratives from interviews, biographies, and fiction that are sprinkled throughout that and other of my works. These narratives have surely been features that have accounted for readers' being drawn to the theory and for their "catching" what it is about. Critics might rightly say, however, that I have not let the idiosyncratic features of extreme cases challenge the structural theory as fully as I might. This is what I understand Professor Streib to be proposing. My hope for his work is that he will not exchange the stage theory for a theory of types, but rather will expand the theory by cross-cutting it with an empirically tested typology. It is important to remember that the structuring operations underlying faith are, at best, only half of the story of a person's development in faith. The other half has to do with the "contents" of faith, the symbols, narratives, practices, and communities—and the emotional and imaginal responses to life conditions and experiences—that exert powerful existential shaping influences on persons' patterns of interpretation, habit, mind, and action. Any adequate faith biography has to embrace both of these important halves of the story.

Robert Kegan, who was a member of the original Project in Faith Development Research in the mid- to late-seventies, has elegantly shaped his own extension of Piagetian theory to provide a developmental account of the self-in-motion and its meaning making.[11] Kegan was a member of my research team on faith development during his graduate studies. He also worked closely with Kohlberg, with Gilligan, and with William Perry. Kegan's stage theory, hammered out in the same forge as faith development theory, developed stages that have extensive parallels with those that I developed. Kegan's genius lies, I believe, in his moving beyond older dichotomies of cognition and emotion, and of structure and content, to disclose the developmentally emergent patterns of the self's constitutive meaning making. While by no means tone-deaf to faith and matters of ultimate concern, he has chosen to focus on the *self-in-motion* as "the dance" that constitutes development. I, on the other hand, have chosen to focus on the *self-other-ultimate environment trialectic* as "the dance." In holding on to the latter, my work is subject to understandings of it that look more at the aspects of the construal and construction of meanings than at the story of the self and its relations with others and with the transcendent in faith. I contend, nonetheless, that the sequence of faith stages is, itself, a formal narrative of the self in the process of constructing and reconstructing its centering and life-interpreting meanings toward a telos of mindful participation in Being-Itself. It is a theory of the journey of the faithful or religious self, with its companions and life challenges, toward increasingly reflective and responsible relation to and grounding in the holy. "You have made us for yourself and our heart is restless until it rests in you."[12]

3. Faith Development: Responses to Postmodern Critiques

Now, we turn to some reflections on the claims of faith development theory from the standpoint of postmodern theorists and critics. Jane Flax is an author who writes from a threefold grounding in psychoanalytic theory and practice, critical feminism, and philosophy. In her book *Thinking Fragments,* she points to a consensus among Jacques Derrida, Richard Rorty, Jean-Francois Lyotard, and Michel Foucault regarding six subjects of conversation necessary and appropriate for "our time":[13]

1. Contemporary Western culture—its nature and the best ways to understand it;
2. Knowledge—what it is, who or what constructs and generates it, and its relations to power;
3. Philosophy—its crisis and history, how both are to be understood, and how (if at all) it is to be practiced;
4. Power—if, where, and how domination exists and is maintained, and how and if it can be overcome;
5. Subjectivity and the self—how our concepts and experiences of them have come to be, and what, if anything, these do or can mean;
6. Difference—how to conceptualize, preserve, or rescue it.

Flax continues:

> Post modernists are also unified in their rejections of certain positions. They all reject representational and objective or rational concepts of knowledge and truth; grand, synthetic theorizing meant to comprehend Reality as and in a unified whole; and any concept of self or subjectivity in which it is not understood as produced as an effect of discursive practices.[14]

In my graduate seminar on "Faith and Selfhood," a bright and vocal minority of graduate students consistently engaged the figures we studied through the strictures imposed by this postmodern agenda. Our examination of the works of Kenneth Gergen, William James, George Herbert Mead, Erik Erikson, James Fowler, Ana-Maria Rizzuto, Katherine Keller, Robert Kegan, Charles Taylor, and Jane Flax in that seminar proved to be a bracing, if sometimes frustrating, experience.[15] Having sharpened their swords in seminars in contemporary theology and hermeneutics—which draw heavily on philosophy—the postmodernists brought their critical tools to the engagement with psychologists who, in varying ways and degrees, have formulated their theories out of contexts of practice and disciplined empirical inquiry.

For the postmodernists among my students, the most challenging book proved to be this one by Flax, from which I have quoted. She effectively criticized the postmodern theorists for their lack of specific and nuanced attention to *difference,* as in attending to minority persons' and women's *actual* experiences. For example, the "partners" in Rorty's "conversations," says Flax, "have a strangely abstract and harmonious quality. They are pieces of a 'self' that in its parts and thus as a whole arises out of nowhere and exists in no relation(s) to others, to desire, or to the body. These partners were evidently never children who had parents toward whom they felt complex feelings of love and hate."[16]

Flax writes, "Postmodernists have made important contributions to deconstructing the (apparently) universalizing forms of conceptions of the self. Postmodernists join feminist theorists in viewing these concepts as artifacts of (white, male) Western culture." She points out, however, that the postmodernist critique of subjectivity differs from both psychoanalytic and feminist views:

> Postmodernists seem to confuse two different and logically distinct concepts of the self: a "unitary" and a "core" one. All possible forms of self are confounded with the unitary, mentalist, deeroticized, masterful, and oppositional selves they rightfully criticize...I work with people suffering from "borderline syndrome." In this illness the self is in painful and disabling fragments. Borderline patients lack a core self without which the registering of and pleasure in a variety of experiencing of ourselves, others, and the outer world are simply not possible. Those who celebrate or call for a "decentered" self seem self-deceptively naïve and unaware of the basic cohesion within themselves that makes the fragmentation of experiences something other than a terrifying slide into psychosis. These writers seem to confirm the very claims of those they have contempt for, that a sense of continuity or "going on being" is so much a part of the core self that it becomes a taken-for-granted background. Persons who have a core self find the experiences of those who lack or have lacked it almost unimaginable.[17]

Flax's writings offered a powerful challenge to the book with which we began the seminar, Kenneth Gergen's *The Saturated Self: Dilemmas of Identity in Contemporary Life.* Gergen celebrated the freedom and widened interactions made possible by air travel, phone, e-mail, and the Internet to "populate" our lives with an ever-widening and enriching array of relationships, experiences, and collaborations. Only at the end of his book does he raise a few sobering questions about matters such as integrity and the shallowing that comes with spreading finite energy and consciousness in unlimited ways.

In a search in *PsychInfo* for articles relating "human development" and "postmodern" in all their variants, I located some 247 articles. Most of these did not go very far in deepening my effort to think through how those of us interested in faith development theory and research should engage and respond to postmodern critiques. The most helpful single article I found was Peter H. Kahn's article "Reinstating Modernity in Social Science Research–Or–The Status of Bullwinkle in a Post-Postmodern Era." Kahn writes with two goals:

> First, we speak to problems within postmodern theory itself. We argue that, when taken seriously, the theory leads to contradictions in epistemology, to fragmentation in knowledge, to opportunism in interpersonal relationships, and to nihilism in moral action and commitment. Second, we demonstrate how many of the legitimate concerns of postmodernists can (be) and are addressed in current "modern" research programs.[18]

Now, how do faith development research and theory relate to the postmodern challenge? At the outset, I pointed out that the origins of faith development theory lie in praxis. In a Jamesian sense of pragmatism, faith development theory took form in order to illumine a path persons follow from the origins and awakenings of faith through the interactive process of forming and reforming frames of meaning in and between communities of shared traditions and practices. However, the constituent elements and the grounding convictions underlying this work are affirmed and claimed as contestable articles of reflective, existential choice. In the way, I believe, all postmodern scholarship and intellectual production must proceed, the theory of faith development established an acknowledgedly convictional set of starting points. It conducted several waves of a qualitative research with increasingly diverse populations. On the basis of those data, it refined and reworked a developmental framework whose initial formulations selectively drew on a combination of stage theories shaped by other acute observers and the interpretative efforts of the theory-laden practitioner. Within those limits, and with those strengths, faith development theory has maintained the claim that the formally describable stages it identifies are sequential, invariant, and hierarchical. Both Piaget and Kohlberg claimed not only that their stages were sequential, invariant, and hierarchical, but that they were also universal. In that sense, both these thinkers continued the unreconstructed Enlightenment claim, rooted in Kant, that the fundamental forms of the categories underlying human thought (though in Piaget and Kohlberg, developmentally realized in some segments of populations) are established a priori (prior to experience) and are, therefore, universal.

For holding the more modest claims that faith stages are sequential, invariant, and hierarchical, I think we can make a strong case. Why have I maintained the confidence represented in these limited claims against the postmodern mood of flattening all hierarchies in obeisance to a pervasive (and allegedly indisputable) relativism?

Faith development theory selectively builds on the psychosocial framework of Erikson's theory.[19] Erikson has woven together attention to biological development, ego development, and correlated social-cultural supporting matrices for development. The bases of Erikson's work provide many reasons for confidence. In formulating his theory of the life cycle, he drew on his multicultural, multinational experiences as European and American, as Jew and Gentile. In this country, he conducted anthropological studies of the Yurok and the Sioux, as well as drawing on his work with sons and daughters of sharecroppers, steelworkers, and children and youth from privileged classes, east and west. His investigations of identity included careful work with African American and other minority populations dealing with the issue of *pseudospeciation*. He learned from his struggles with "Womanhood and Inner Space" and the early feminist critique of his work. His historical studies of European figures and the Holocaust, as well as those in Gandhi's India, provided an unusual breadth of observation and testing for his theory of psychosocial development. While our faith stages differ from Erikson's, his account of the timing and focus of the psychosocial crises of each stage and transition are part of faith development's foundational frame. Moreover, his accounts of what he calls the "virtues"—the strengths of developing personhood associated with each stage's crises—have been both useful and vindicated in our research. In the order of the stages, these include Hope (infancy), Will (early childhood), Purpose (kindergarten age), Competence (elementary years), Faith (adolescence), Love (young adulthood), Generativity (middle adulthood), and Integrity (older adulthood). Erikson helps us keep body, psyche, ideology, developmental challenges, and society in faith development studies.

The second and defining psychological source for faith development theory clearly is in the Piagetian constructivist developmental tradition, in conjunction with the work of Kohlberg, Selman, and Kegan. Piaget's pioneering theory of infancy, preoperational, concrete operational, and formal operational stages has not only contributed to framing faith development constructivist stages and criteria, it has been confirmed and expanded by our research.[20] We have augmented the Piagetian tradition's treatment of infancy and early childhood with careful attention to the work of object relations theorists inspired especially by Donald Winnicott.[21] These include the studies of infancy by Daniel Stern, studies of early childhood by Jerome Kagan, and psychoanalytic work on the development of God representations by Ana-Maria Rizzuto.[22] The work of these figures and their students has given me confidence, both in interpreting the data from the young children (age four and up) we have interviewed and in constructing a theory of the origins and dynamics of faith in early childhood.

The third, and in many ways centering and mediating, conceptual frame for faith development theory comes with the theological work of H. Richard Niebuhr. Niebuhr created an original synthesis of historical-critical, sociological, and psychosocial perspectives on the phenomenon of faith. Faith, for Niebuhr, was not limited to religious faith. He saw and illumined the relational structure of the kind of faith (or "good faith") that makes the flourishing of stable communities of strangers and neighbors possible. Faith involves ties of mutual trust and loyalty between persons and groups who commit themselves, explicitly and tacitly, to loyalty to and trust in shared centers of value and power. Shared commitments to the values of truth telling, fairness, noninjury, and the practice of procedures that guard and fulfill the common good help to constitute a viable social faith. Religious traditions help to evoke and form commitments of this sort, but they also call their members to more specific commitments and visions, including those that can provide critical and transformative perspectives in relation to routinized or corrupted forms of societal faith.

4. Toward Systematic Practical Theology

Despite the fact that I am better known for my work in faith development research, I have consistently thought of that work as an aspect of a broader calling, which I take to be that of practical theology. In concluding these remarks, I want to sketch the direction I find myself taking as a practical theologian who teaches in my discipline, but who also has the responsibility of leading the Center for Ethics in Public Policy and the Professions at Emory University. Here, I will sketch the direction of a practical theological approach to the reclaiming of the doctrine of providence. The doctrine of providence—which I will refer to here as the theology of the praxis of God—came to be among the most neglected themes of theological focus in the second half of the twentieth century. There are good reasons for that eclipse, and they are not, and will not be, easy to overcome. Nonetheless, I feel called to contribute to the recovery of that doctrine and to work at forceful and faithful depictions of the ways the Spirit of God interacts with human beings, recruits them into God's work, and, through them, can influence the systems of human interaction and the affairs of nations.

Correlated with the attempt to help reclaim a doctrine of God's providential praxis, I have pointed to the necessity and significance of reclaiming a rich and risky doctrine of human *vocation*. I want to attend to how the Spirit of God, in partnership with human agents, works to shape new patterns and systems of human interaction. There have been anticipatory expressions of this concern in my earlier work, starting with *To See the Kingdom,* my book on the theology of H. Richard Niebuhr. The themes of vocation and God's praxis play a key role in *Becoming Adult, Becoming Christian* (1984), in *Faith Development and Pastoral Care* (1987), and in both *Weaving the New Creation* (1991) and *Faithful Change* (1996). We really cannot develop a significant sense of vocation without a convictional sense and trust that God can and does call us to partnership in the divine praxis.

Preliminary Reflections on Divine Praxis and the Calling to Human Partnership

I would like to offer a few principles that guide my interest in trying to develop a systematic practical theology of the divine praxis and the human calling to partnership.

First, I and we must be clear that the praxis of God is not limited to the action or leadership of religious organizations and leaders. The Spirit of God can and does address peoples and movements involved in other faith traditions than our own. And the Spirit does, I believe, influence and call persons in secular positions of leadership toward acts of courage and self-giving in the service of justice and peace.

Second, studies of leadership in relation to the praxis of God underscore the presence and importance of respect for the humanity and the potential for moral responsiveness of those who are our "enemies." Where those on one side have deep concern about the dangers and consequences of continued estrangement, noncommunication, and violence, it is likely that there are those on the other side(s) who share similar perplexities. We must not let propaganda and negative characterizations of our "enemies" or those who are different blind us to their humanity and their capacities for at least self-interested response and perspective taking in situations of grave conflict or danger.

Third, one high-level diplomat, involved in several years of effective mediation with one of our nation's most intransigent and dangerous enemies, recently told me: "When you look back at where we have come in our relations with them, and how we have gotten to this place, you can't escape seeing in this process the work of God's providence. But," he continued, "you can't know that at the time. All you have to go on is faith."

Fourth, it is not just in the high-level affairs of relations between nation-states that this kind of role of God's praxis can be discerned. Conflicts and struggles in politics, in business, in families, and in the shaping of the priorities and distribution of "goods" in universities and seminaries also represent contexts where one may pursue, observe, and participate in the praxis of God.

Fifth, for those who want to test and grow in trying to be available to the praxis of God, there is a call to the ascesis of prayer and to growth in Spirit-sustained nonattachment to ego striving. It is humbling, but ultimately deeply reassuring, to recognize retrospectively that the Spirit of God weaves, and often has woven, our input in a given situation into a much larger gestalt of vectors involved in resolving the conflict or addressing the need at hand.

Sixth, the mention of the Spirit of God, and of the Spirit's work in awakening, in guiding, in animating moral imagination, and in giving hope and courage, reminds us that robust trust in providence is grounding for living out of the conviction of the presence and efficacy of God the Spirit in life, in systems, in human affairs.

Finally, in a dangerous, heavily armed world, we cannot ignore the fact that the capacity, courage, and will to use force to protect the innocent or to prevent abuses offers a necessary deterrent to the capricious use of violence. However, faith in the praxis of God, and the willingness to honor the human and spiritual capacities of those with whom we are in conflict, may mean that the genuine threat of force can serve the appropriate role of creating space for conversation and for the exploration of moral and humane ways to move forward.

The danger is that we, and leaders at every level and in every sector of our societies, often functionally forget or give in to doubt that the praxis of God is active and powerful. We forget that we are called to be partners who trust, in faith, that God is at work. To that degree, we may disqualify ourselves from taking on tasks that seem too big, too daunting, and too improbable of success. Or we may be resistant to the nudges of conscience and calling that touch our hearts. A practical theology of the praxis of God and a recovered doctrine of vocation, marked by a strong doctrine of the Holy Spirit, therefore, strike this practical theologian as an essential responsibility of our discipline, and of our lives and leadership.

5. Responses to Colleagues Who Have Created This Book

Reading the thoughtful and often forceful presentations of friends who have produced this volume brings a rare opportunity to see oneself, and one's work, through the eyes and judgment of respected others. The perspectives of both appreciation and challenge convey significance. They also reveal ways in which others have accepted some of what you have written and taught, while critically rejecting or objecting to other of its aspects. Both by what is said and by what is unsaid, this collection of essays that touch on dimensions of what I have written and cared about provides gifts of great worth. I hope they prove of interest to others who engage in thinking and writing in the areas on which my work touches. For me, they provide a rare opportunity for a kind of self-reflection and reckoning as to what the public side of one's life and thought looks like in the eyes of thoughtful and fair-minded peers. I am deeply grateful to them and for them. Let me share the following brief reflections in response to my colleagues.

PART ONE–FOWLER'S CONTRIBUTION: CHARACTERIZATION AND CONTRAST

Heinz Streib– I and all persons who are interested in faith development research are deeply indebted to Professor Heinz Streib of the University of Bielefeld. Professor Streib has emerged as the most comprehensive compiler and analyst of the research literature in psychology and the social sciences on faith development theory. His magisterial account of the numbers and foci of dissertations on faith development theory and research give us some sense of the impact of this work. His analytic attention to the strengths and limits of this research and its spin-offs is objective, balanced, and constructively critical. His documentation of the influence and reach of faith development theory and research is a singular and most appreciated contribution.

His own proposals for strengthening and altering research in this area grow out of his long-standing interest in narrative and his sensitivity to the stimulating yet fragmented cultural contexts in which youth and young adults today are "making meaning." His theory of types, which in some ways parallels the typology that I offered earlier in this chapter, will either cross-cut faith with faith stages or replace them in his work as a useful nondevelopmental typology. Inveterate developmentalist that I am, I would challenge him, if he fragments them into a typology, to keep an eye on longitudinal changes in his subjects that may, in fact, reveal developmental change.

Gabriele Klappenecker–An educator and researcher, Dr. Klappenecker's research for her doctoral dissertation on faith development uniquely qualifies her as an interpreter and critic of this body of research and its uses. She has paid careful attention to the influences and elements that make up the theory's development and research. She has offered her own account of the faith stages that is both accurate and insightful while showing her particular interpretative nuances. Unlike some American and English readers, she is not put off by the intermingling of psychological and theological categories in the stage descriptions. She is also attuned to the centrality of vocation as a prime category in the faith development corpus. That she can hold psychological and theological terms together in her discussion of faith development theory and research reminds us Americans that, in Germany, and in Europe, public education does not need to exclude religious particularity from school instruction.

I especially appreciate her distinctive attention to my use of Martin Marty's theme of the "public church" with its calling to help create an "ecology of care and vocation" in a culture of acknowledged pluralism. She offers a valuable recognition that, seen through faith development lenses, the challenges of secularization in our contexts of religious pluralism may be addressed aggressively, but in nondefensive ways.

Sharon Daloz Parks–Poetic and richly blessed with gifts to the imagination, Sharon Parks's chapter in this volume provides the inestimable value of both pointing to and elaborating the relationships between the metaphors of development and growth, on the one hand, and of settling and making/finding home, on the other. She points to the mobility of our lives, and those of our contemporaries, and to the capacities we have to choose and engage multiple environments. She addresses a deeper hunger, the hunger for *home,* the yearning for a sense of rootedness–in community, in a physical landscape, in a place of the heart.

She writes from Whidbey Island, located among the San Juan Islands, off the coast of northern Washington. There at the Whidbey Institute, she and the community to which she and her husband, Larry Parks Daloz, belong, teach and write and commune with the beauty of sea and trees, of wind and storms. Balancing this book's attention to development, her contribution speaks of "another powerful sensibility that pulls as deeply at the human soul–the call to dwell, to stay, to abide, to return home."

With a goodly company of witnesses, she calls us to see the earth, and our sense of "place," as also constituting "significant others" in our faith and identity formation. Her original creation of a developmental account of our relatedness to places and communities both uses and expands the purview of faith development theory. Faith development, she sees, cannot be separated from community. She calls for "public homeplaces" that beckon us out of our private lives and into communities of service, care, and celebration. "The story of the development of faith," she writes, "can be told as the account of an ongoing Journey—the pull of the tide into the sea; it can also be told as the call to return Home to the shore of the authentic self, to the Center—to the Spirit that dwells within as well as beyond."

PART TWO—PHILOSOPHICAL AND THEOLOGICAL ISSUES RAISED BY FOWLER'S WORK

Maureen Junker-Kenny—To respond fully to the informative and philosophically sophisticated critique offered by Dr. Junker-Kenny would take an entire paper. Her commentary is informed by the philosophical perspectives of Paul Ricoeur and Charles Taylor and the critique of Piaget by Ursula Peukert. On the whole, her reading of my work is generous. But by relying so heavily on Taylor's critique of Piaget, and implicitly of Kohlberg, I believe she misses some of the ways faith development theory differs from them.

In my view, Junker-Kenny fails to take fully into account the way faith development, by attending to imagination, emotion (valuing), and selfhood, enriches the strictly cognitive foci of Piaget and Kohlberg. In the main, she has not attended to the ways the Conjunctive and Universalizing stages depend on the reconstitution of meanings, as in Ricoeur's "second naïveté." Nor, I believe, has she come to terms with faith development theory's taking into account the role of the unconscious in faith. Most of all, I believe, she has failed to take note of my affirmation that the structuring of faith—the operations of knowing and valuing—constitute at most half the picture. The narratives, images, symbols, and practices that shape faith—the *contents* of faith—are of equal or greater importance. Finally, her criticism that faith development theory relies too heavily on Old Testament notions of covenant and vocation, and seeing these themes as Protestant, seems to discount another of the decisive ways this work differs from the Kantian epistemology and ethics of Piaget and Kohlberg.

I do grant her point that the Universalizing stage is difficult to characterize. However, I have come to believe that the qualitative process of transformation that leads to this stage's emergence is no less discontinuous with the stages that have gone before than those that lead from Synthetic-Conventional to Individuative-Reflective, or from Individuative-Reflective to Conjunctive. Because it does involve a culminating shift away from ego-defensiveness and striving, and because it is relatively rare, I find it understandable that it seems less developmentally continuous than previous transitions. Literary critic Northrup Frye once gave me a helpful symbolic representation of what he thought he heard me trying to describe in this transition. I share it as a symbolic gift of gratitude to Dr. Junker-Kenny. Frye drew on a chalkboard one graceful cone that sat on its base and rose evenly to a point. Then he overlaid that cone with one like it, differing only in that the latter stood on its point and gradually widened as it rose to the height of the first cone's tip. Frye then explained, "The cone rising from base to point symbolizes the gradual development of an increasingly clear and self responsible sense of identity and faith, with consequent reductions in self-concern, anxiety, and aggressive defensiveness. Concurrent with that process, and correlated with it," he suggested, "the inverted cone widens from an initial centration in self-experience and attachment to an increasingly widening gain in perspective-taking and decentration from self. This involves a powerful attribution of worth and care for other persons and groups at the Universalizing stage." In the Universalizing stage, perspective taking is least distorted by self-striving and defensiveness, and not being anxious, one is optimally freed for love and respect. Such persons bring compassion, love, and justice to the contexts of their "spending and being spent" in service to members of what they regard as a universal community bound together in God's love.

Gordon Mikoski–Presbyterian minister, second career doctoral candidate, and teaching associate in practical theology at Emory University, Gordon Mikoski has studied H. Richard Niebuhr with me and assisted me in teaching a graduate seminar in systematic practical theology. With deep roots in the Cappadocian fathers and in Calvin, Mikoski has also built strong competence in the interplay of European theology with Enlightenment philosophy and has developed special strength in the theologies of Jürgen Moltmann, Wolfhart Pannenberg, and Michael Welker.

Mikoski's essay is less focused on faith development theory than on my turn toward the above-mentioned engagement with systematic practical theology. I describe this venture as trying to work on the themes of God's praxis and humans' call to partnership in vocation in ways that, starting with the Spirit, move toward a more full-orbed trinitarian theology, but one that does its work in close proximity to reflective human experience.

In his chapter, Gordon traces the formative influences of Niebuhr on my thought, with special attention to the way the conviction of the sovereignty of God provides a core theme in Niebuhr's theological ethics, and in mine. In his careful, critical analysis he notes a growing attention to the role of God's Spirit in my work. He sees the challenge of bringing Niebuhr's use of the metaphors of God creating, God governing, and God liberating and redeeming, which have been central in my efforts, into a genuine trinitarian framework.

Michael Welker–The theme of Spirit in Christian theology provides a helpful turn to the contribution to this volume of Michael Welker. If I may be so bold, I would propose that Welker's distinctions between THEOLOGY, theology, and Theology confirm his confidence that the Spirit of God acts or impinges in history and in the present in myriad ways. His readings of scripture and his appreciation of canon show an impressive refusal to systematize or homogenize accounts and witnesses to the work of Spirit. THEOLOGY, I take it, characterizes those moments in Christian tradition where a great interpreter, or community of interpreters, has formulated a body of theological reflection and formative teachings that, by its weight and comprehensiveness, as well as its canonical social standing, has become a normative "milieu" of interpretation of scripture, teaching, and practice. "Small t" theology, if I read Welker rightly, refers to the kind of "meaning making" that persons and small groups engage in as they seek to understand their lives and participation in the theater of the present in relation to their sense or interpretations of God. Faith development interviews, in many respects, turn out to be "theologies."

In the third sense–Theology–Welker seems to point to serious efforts, in communities of interpretation, to draw on canon to shape lines of interpretation that inform and animate persons and groups in the praxis of inquiry, reflection, and spirit-responsive patterns of service and leadership in social, political, and economic life. Theology, in this sense, goes with *vocatio* and with the horizontal witness of faith that is contextual, convictional, and yet subject to dialogue and nondefensive explication.

If my surmises are correct, Welker offers a very valuable framework for the praxis of what I am, somewhat provocatively, calling "systematic practical theology." I am grateful.

Part Three–Faith Development and Public Life as Practical Theological Matters

Karl Ernst Nipkow–This contribution by one of Europe's strongest voices on religious education wrestles with how officially Christian nations (especially Great Britain and Germany) can carry out effective religious education in state-supported schools in contexts of growing religious pluralism, on the one hand, and growing public indifference, on the other. With nuanced comparisons of the differences between England, Scotland, and Germany, Nipkow counsels against a too-easy avoidance of the challenge of pluralism. He warns against embracing, by default, the replacement of religion and faith (which denote specific traditions) with "spirituality," which is at best vague, and at worst, solipsistic and vacuous.

As a Lutheran, Nipkow has maintained a certain skepticism about linking faith and development. As Luther liked to say, we human beings–Christians as well as others–are *simul justus et peccator,* simultaneously justified and yet still marked by the contradictions of sin. In this view, "progress" in faith development is suspect. At the same time, however, Nipkow has made constructive use of faith development theory in his writing and curricular designs.

Nipkow reminds us that in Protestant traditions in Germany, the idea of a public church that honors particular traditions, coupled with informed interaction and tolerance of differences, claims both precedent and promise. His account of the University of Tübingen's efforts to address the loss of students' (and teachers') groundings in faith traditions through their program of "elementarization" is an important initiative and demonstration.

Nipkow sees that the serious study of religions in schools is essential for creating public conversations that draw on the rich particularity of religious traditions, and for the modeling of valuable practices of ethical and spiritual leadership. One could wish for more address to the growing issue of interreligious pluralism and the presence of guest workers (*Gaestarbiters*) in Germany and other countries, whose children and youth populate our contextual challenges of pluralization, secularization, globalization, and religious conflict.

Richard R. Osmer and Friedrich L. Schweitzer–The chapter by the editors of this volume, Richard Osmer and Friedrich Schweitzer, examines the usefulness of faith development theory and research in the light of the ethical, religious, and educational challenges of globalization. The authors identify three pervasive patterns of response to the worldwide growing sense of globalization: (1) fundamentalism, in its many forms; (2) cosmopolitanism, with its retraction from local commitments and responsibilities; and (3) postmodernism, with it tendency to affirm pluralism, to raise awareness of the risks attending scientific research and technological developments, and to offer its "highly processive view of life."

In nuanced ways, the authors draw out the religious and secular educational implications of faith development theory for addressing the opportunities and challenges of globalization. I have genuinely learned from Osmer and Schweitzer's lucid analysis of globalization and from their use of faith development theory to clarify aspects of it. I am especially informed by their suggestions of four areas in which faith development research and theory may help form and guide, across the different religious traditions, our address to preparing people for postconventional faith and for discerning participation in shaping the religious, political, social, and ethical responses to globalization.

I am braced and encouraged by the authors' unapologetic urging that religious and secular educators pay special attention to nurturing the structural developments that underpin the formation of the Individuative, Conjunctive, and Universalizing stages of faith. In my judgment, this article is a groundbreaking contribution, growing out of research with mid-teen adolescents on each of our continents.

Hyun-Sook Kim–In ways that both parallel and complement the preceding work, Professor Hyun-Sook Kim offers a very suggestive consideration of the necessity of *postconventional faith* for addressing the challenges of modernity. Kim calls for Christians to move toward postconventional faith, which she defines as an individual and collective stance with three qualities: (1) It shapes a "personality system to secure religious continuity...in relationships in the midst of rapid social change; (2) it enables Christians to have genuine dialogue with others...and move beyond their own limits in a pluralistic and global society; and (3) it redefines and activates one's Christian faith in commitment to and involvement in religious action in the world."

Dr. Kim works with Kohlberg and Habermas in exploring the meanings of "postconventional moral reasoning," which she sees as being based on principles of mutual respect and equal accountability. She then turns to my account of a postmodern view of public life in which "cultural, gender, and religious differences are affirmed as necessary and constitutive dimensions of public life and cannot be surpassed by the affirmation of a universal rational core."

In my limited experience of Korea, I believe Dr. Kim would be well advised to include in her analysis the strong religious and cultural pressures that militate *against* the emergence of Individuative-Reflective faith and the later stages. The strong Korean cultural strain emphasizing the maintenance of group solidarity and conformity, encouraged by populist fundamentalist and conservative megachurches, make individuation in her land a strong uphill struggle, but one well worth engaging.

Duncan B. Forrester—Ethicist and theologian Duncan Forrester's contribution to this book rings with a spirit that bespeaks H. Richard Niebuhr's "Christ transforming culture" model of ethical engagement and leadership. I was captured by his reference to the 1540 play *Ane Satyre of the Thrie Estaites* by Sir David Lindsay, which was first performed at the Palace of Linlithgow before Mary Queen of Scots and her court. He describes the play's climax where Sir John Commonweal, flanked on his right by Divine Correctioun and on his left by Gude Counsel, "denounces the oppression and the injustice… of the 'thrie estaites' in turn—merchants, nobility, and church" and calls for justice, peace, a purification of church and state, and for a fair and decent society.

Under Forrester's leadership, The Centre for Theology and Public Issues at the University of Edinburgh provides a compelling model of the public church. Creating a context of interdisciplinary inquiry with broad lay participation, the research and symposia the Centre promotes engage knotty issues of public policy and practice. Drawing on scripture and Christian tradition unapologetically, the Centre demonstrates the informing power of the churches' intellectual and moral traditions in conversation with secular inquiry and resources.

In a rapidly secularizing society, Forrester's vision and commitment, and that of the Centre for Theology and Public Issues, represents an uphill battle. Yet in strange ways, in both Scotland and the United States, the shrinking support from conventional Christianity and the erasure of Christian memory from a majority offer new opportunities to start "from the ground up." The tradition in which Forrester stands, and of which he is so exemplary a representative, provides a telling instance of public church mission and ministry.

Johannes A. van der Ven—Hans van der Ven's work in practical theology builds on his strengths in the social sciences and in post–Vatican II Catholic theology and ethics. His work manifests his keen sense of ethics and social responsibility. Underlying his methodology is a strong empirical bent: He uses sociological research to test hypotheses and claims; he consistently looks for empirical ways to ground observations and explanations. Throughout his work, one senses his passion for social equity and justice and his determination to unmask the social self-deception of privileged societies and groups, including our churches.

Van der Ven's chapter helpfully keeps in focus my efforts to characterize *postconventional* faith and the ecclesial ideal of the *public church*. September 11, 2001, provides an urgent focus for looking at questions of interreligious and intercultural conflict as primary sources leading to the sneak attacks of terrorists and to the massively destructive use of technological warfare in retaliation. Van der Ven helpfully underscores how religious freedom and the separation of church and state in Europe and the United States arose out of the seventeenth-century wars of religion in Europe.

In the aftermath of September 11th, can leaders in the global community begin to sort out ways to keep retaliation and mutual suspicion attuned to the fragility of the increasingly vulnerable systems that make communication, finance, travel, education, and international cooperation possible? Can churches that embrace a "public church" stance make effective witness to justice and civil peace by modeling, in their service and witness, a firm, compassionate integrity? These are the vital questions and challenges that van der Ven's contribution presses.

Thomas Groome–Tom Groome's depth and breadth as a Christian religious educator and his and Colleen's deep joy at the arrival in their lives of Theodore (meaning "gift of God") Thomas Griffith-Groome blend together in his fine chapter. With affection and respect, I honor Tom's great happiness and his fresh restatement of his sterling contributions to the field of Christian religious education as focused in this personal way by his becoming a father.

Groome's wide ranging historical survey of ways the biblical and Christian communities have formed new generations in faith, coupled with his special attention to families as *ecclesiola* in the great *ecclesia* of Christian faith, resonates strongly with Don Browning's essay. It is instructive, however, that Groome's definition of "intact families" would be more comprehensive of different types of parental leadership than that which Browning proposes in the chapter that follows Groome's. For Groome, the definition includes "any bonded network of domestic life and nurture." Between Browning's and Groome's formulations of possible family structures in the nurture of wholeness and faith, a powerful conference and an ongoing discussion on these important issues could be nurtured.

While the *ecclesiola* (little church of the family) is primary in the intimate witness and "demonstration project" that is faith nurture, it needs the vital support and accountability of a larger intergenerational community of faith. In this regard, Groome's proposal of a shared-praxis approach to Christian and religious formation both complements and challenges Browning's stress on the intact family as the nucleus from which vital citizens and leaders in the common faith of our cities, nation, and world–and the particular faiths of our churches, synagogues, and mosques–will come.

Don Browning–Don Browning provides a key model and standard for systematic practical theology. His learned, constructive discussion of the role of families–with special focus on the responsibilities and potential strengths of "intact" families–in moral and faith development, is most informative.

Browning rightly criticizes the formal "principle-ism" of Plato and Kant and their modern follower Lawrence Kohlberg. He favors the communal nurture of habits and virtues set forth by Aristotle and his Christian interpreter, Thomas Aquinas, and their followers. And yet, in a richly developmental move, he restores the role of principled moral reasoning at precisely the point where it is needed. Mores based on familial loyalty, clan cohesion, and mutuality reach their limits when tribes have to settle disputes between them. Nation-states, grounded in notions of national self-interest, can only transcend their limits by working out notions of justice and fairness as central in international law. In a real sense, Browning is offering us the overview of a rich, substantive, pluralistic theory of moral development, which—as he recognizes—fits very well with faith development theory.

While Browning cites one of my articles on faith and the family, he has missed the one that he might most appreciate and find supportive of his strong argument for the "intact" two-parent family as being best equipped to nurture growing persons' moral and faith growth.[23] My discussion of "ontic needs" may help offset what could be taken in Browning's work as a kind of idolatry of the intact family. It is my observation and conviction that covenanted partners, in families where one or both partners have experienced divorce or where persons of the same sex with maturity and covenant commitment, can—in acknowledgedly more complex ways—create the kind of stable, loving, accountable family milieu that meets this cluster of "ontic needs" that my article sets forth.

6. A Final Expression of Thanks

To Professors Richard Osmer and Friedrich Schweitzer, who initiated this project and have edited the articles that make up this volume, I am filled with gratitude. That colleagues from several continents, whom I respect, have joined together to explore and comment on the various efforts in practical theology to which I have been party is a gift of great significance. I give thanks for the friendship and reflective gifts of so goodly a company.

Notes

[1]This section of my chapter includes material, with modifications, from my article entitled, "Faith Development Theory and the Postmodern Challenges," printed in a special issue of the *International Journal for the Psychology of Religion* 11, no. 3 (2001): 158–72. Edited by Professor Heinz Streib of the University of Bielefeld, and by editors of the *Journal*, Raymond Paloutzian, and Jozef Corveleyn, this edition of the *Journal* includes challenging articles on faith development theory by Heinz Streib, James M. Day, John McDargh, and Ana-Maria Rizzuto.

[2]Owen Barfield, *Saving The Appearances: A Study in Idolatry,* 2d ed. (Middletown, Conn.: Wesleyan University Press, 1988).

[3]See Lawrence Kohlberg, "Stage and Sequence: The Cognitive-Developmental Approach to Socialization," in *Essays on Moral Development,* vol. 2, *The Psychology of Moral Development,* ed. L. Kohlberg (San Francisco: Harper & Row, 1969).

[4]For explications of these headings, see James W. Fowler, *Stages of Faith: The Psychology of Human Development and the Quest for Meaning* (San Francisco: Harper & Row, 1981), 243–57.

[5]R. M. Moseley, D. Jarvis, and J. W. Fowler, *Manual for Faith Development Research,* 2d ed. (Atlanta: Center for Research in Faith and Moral Development, Candler School of Theology, Emory University, 1993).

[6]James W. Fowler, *Faithful Change. The Personal and Public Challenges of Postmodern Life* (Nashville, Tenn.: Abingdon Press, 1996).

[7]See John McDargh, "Faith Development Theory and the Postmodern Problem of Foundations," *International Journal for the Psychology of Religion* 11, no. 3 (2001): 185ff.

[8]See James W. Fowler, "John Wesley's Development in Faith" in *The Future of the Methodist Theological Traditions,* ed. M. Douglas Meeks (Nashville, Tenn.: Abingdon Press, 1985).

[9]See James W. Fowler and Robin Lovin, *Trajectories in Faith: Five Life Studies* (Nashville, Tenn.: Abingdon Press, 1979).

[10]See Heinz Streib, *Hermeneutics of Metaphor, Symbol, and Narrative in Faith Development Theory* (Frankfurt: Peter Lang, 1991); idem, "Off-Road Religion? A Narrative Approach to Fundamentalist and Occult Orientations of Adolescents," *Journal of Adolescence* 22 (1999): 255–67.

[11]See Robert Kegan, *The Evolving Self: Problem and Process in Human Development* (Cambridge, Mass.: Harvard University Press, 1982); idem, *In Over Our Heads: The Mental Demands of Modern Life* (Cambridge, Mass.: Harvard University Press, 1994).

[12]Saint Augustine, *Confessions: Book 1.1,* trans. H. Chadwick (London: Oxford University Press, 1991), 3.

[13]Jane Flax, *Thinking Fragments: Psychoanalysis, Feminism, and Postmodernism in the Contemporary West* (Berkeley and Los Angeles: University of California Press, 1990).

[14]Ibid., 188.

[15]See Erik H. Erikson, *Childhood and Society,* 2d ed. (New York/London: W. W. Norton, 1963); idem, *Identity, Youth and Crisis* (New York/London: W. W. Norton, 1968); idem, *Toys and Reasons: Stages in the Ritualization of Experience* (New York/London: W. W. Norton, 1977); Fowler, *Stages of Faith:* idem, *Becoming Adult, Becoming Christian* (San Francisco: Harper & Row, 1984); idem, *Faith Development and Pastoral Care* (Philadelphia: Fortress Press, 1987); idem, *Faithful Change;* Kenneth J. Gergen, *The Saturated Self: Dilemmas of Identity in Contemporary Life* (New York: Basic Books, 1991); Wiliam James, *The Varieties of Religious Experience: A Study in Human Nature* (New York: Longmans, Green, 1902); Kegan, *Evolving Self;* idem, *In Over Our Heads;* Catherine Keller, *From a Broken Web: Separation, Sexism, and Self* (Boston: Beacon Press, 1986); George Herbert Mead, *Mind, Self, and Society* (Chicago, London: University of Chicago Press, 1962); Ana-Maria Rizzuto, *The Birth of the Living God: A Psychoanalytic Study* (Chicago, London: University of Chicago Press, 1979); Charles Taylor, *Sources of Self: The Making of the Self* (Cambridge: Cambridge University Press, 1989).

[16]Flax, *Thinking Fragments,* 218.

[17]Ibid., 218–19.

[18]Peter H. Kahn, "Reinstating Modernity in Social Science Research–Or–The Status of Bullwinkle in a Post-Postmodern Era," *Human Development* 42 (1999): 92–108, quotation from 92.

[19]See Erikson, *Childhood and Society;* idem, *Identity, Youth, and Crisis;* idem, *Toys and Reason.*

[20]We have named and described the variant of formal operations characteristic of the Individuative-Reflective stage as "Dichotomizing," a logic of unitary category systems based on clear conceptual distinctions and boundaries. The variant of formal operations characteristic of the Conjunctive stage we call "Dialectical," a logic of polarities and embraced paradoxes and of multiple systems. The variant of formal operations characteristic of the Universalizing stage we call "Synthetic," a logic of wholeness that embraces, without paradox, the domains of the physical, the psychological, the scientific, and the spiritual, and their appropriate modes of study, in nonreductionistic ways. An example would be physicist David Bohm's description of the explicate and the implicate orders of being. See David Bohm, *Wholeness and the Implicate Order* (London: Routledge Kegan Paul, 1980). Another would be Gandhi's synthesis of Hindu and Christian thought and disciplines in the service of India's liberation and the formation of Indian democracy.

[21]See Donald W. Winnicott, *Playing and Reality* (London: Tavistock, 1971).

[22]See Daniel N. Stern, *The Interpersonal World of the Infant* (New York: Basic Books, 1985); Jerome Kagan, *The Nature of the Child* (New York: Basic Books, 1984); Rizzuto, *The Birth of the Living God.*

[23]See James W. Fowler, "Perspectives on the Family from the Standpoint of Faith Development Theory," *The Perkins Journal* (Perkins School of Theology, Southern Methodist University) 33, no. 1 (Fall 1979): 1–19.

Bibliography of James W. Fowler's Work

Books

To See the Kingdom: The Theological Vision of H. Richard Niebuhr. Nashville, Tenn.: Abingdon Press, 1974. Reissued by University Press of America, 1985.

(with Sam Keen) *Life Maps: Conversations on the Journey of Faith.* Edited by Jerome Berryman. Waco, Tex.: Word Books, 1978. 2d, expanded ed., Word Books, 1985.

(with Robin Lovin et al.) *Trajectories in Faith: Five Life Stories.* Nashville, Tenn.: Abingdon Press, 1980.

(with Antoine Vergote et al.) *Toward Moral and Religious Maturity.* First International Conference on Moral and Religious Development. Morristown, N.J.: Silver Burdett, 1980.

Stages of Faith: The Psychology of Human Development and the Quest for Meaning. San Francisco: Harper & Row, 1981. Also published in German, Portuguese, and in two Korean editions. Paperback ed., San Francisco: HarperSanFrancisco, 1995.

Becoming Adult, Becoming Christian: Adult Development and Christian Faith. San Francisco: Harper & Row, 1984: Rev. ed., San Francisco: Jossey-Bass, 2000.

(with Romney Moseley and David Jarvis) *Manual for Faith Development Research.* Atlanta: Center for Research in Faith and Moral Development, Emory University, 1986. Rev. ed., 1993.

Faith Development and Pastoral Care. Philadelphia: Fortress Press, 1987. Also published as *Glaubensentwicklung: Perspektiven für Seelsorge und kirchliche Bildungsarbeit.* Gütterloh: Kaiser, 1989.

Responsible Selfhood: An Interdisciplinary Approach to Ethics Education. Edited by John Shippee and Linda Johnson. (James Fowler supervised writing and editing.) Orange County (Calif.) Public Schools, 1988.

Remembrances of Lawrence Kohlberg. Edited by James W. Fowler, John Snarey, and Karen DeNicola. Atlanta: Center for Research in Faith and Moral Development, Emory University, 1988.

Caring for the Commonweal: Education for Religious and Public Life. Festschrift for Robert Lynn. Edited by Parker Palmer, Barbara Wheeler, and James W. Fowler. Macon, Ga.: Mercer University Press, 1990.

Weaving the New Creation: Stages of Faith and the Public Church. San Francisco: HarperSanFrancisco, 1991. Korean Translation, 1997.

Stages of Faith and Religious Development: Implications for Church, Education, and Society. Edited by James W. Fowler, Karl Ernst Nipkow, and Friedrich Schweitzer. New York: Crossroad Press, 1991.

Faithful Change: The Personal and Public Challenges of Postmodern Life. Nashville, Tenn.: Abingdon Press, 1996. Paperback ed., 2000.

Published Lectures, Articles, and Chapters

"Faith, Liberation, and Human Development." The Thirkield Jones Lectures, Gammon Theological Seminary. *Foundations* 39 (Spring 1971).

"Agenda Toward a New Coalition." *Engage/Social Action* 1, no. 5 (June 1973): 45–63.

"Agenda Toward a Developmental Perspective on Faith." *Religious Education* 69 (March–April 1974): 209–19.

"Stages in Faith: The Structural Developmental Approach." In *Values and Moral Education,* edited by Thomas Hennessey, 187–211. New York: Paulist Press, 1976.

"Faith Development Theory and the Aims of Religious Socialization." In *Emerging Issues in Religious Education,* edited by Gloria Durka and Joanmarie Smith, 187–211. New York: Paulist Press, 1976.

"Alienation as a Human Experience." In *From Alienation to At-oneness,* edited by Francis Eigo, O.S.A., 1–18. Proceedings of the Theological Institute, Villanova University, 1975. Villanova, Pa.: Villanova University Press, 1977.

"H. Richard Niebuhr as Philosopher." *The Journal of Religion* 57, no. 3 (July 1977): 307–13.

"Psychological Perspectives on the Faith Development of Children." In *Catechesis: Realities and Visions,* edited by M. Sawicki and B. Marthaler, 72–82. Washington, D.C.: United States Catholic Conference, 1977.

"Future Christians and Church Education." In Jürgen Moltmann with M. Douglas Meeks et al., *Hope for the Church: Moltmann in Dialogue with Practical Theology,* edited and translated by Theodore Runyon, 93–111. Nashville, Tenn.: Abingdon Press, 1979.

Foreword to *The Recovery of the Person* by Carlyle Marney. 2d ed. Nashville, Tenn.: Abingdon Press, 1979.

"Perspectives on the Family from the Standpoint of Faith Development Theory." *The Perkins Journal* (Perkins School of Theology, Southern Methodist University) 33, no. 1 (Fall 1979): 1–19.

"Faith and the Structuring of Meaning." In James Fowler, Antoine Vergote, et al. *Toward Moral and Religious Maturity.* First International Conference on Moral and Religious Development. Morristown, N.J.: Silver Burdett, 1980.

"Moral Stages and the Development of Faith." In *Moral Development, Moral Education, and Kohlberg: Basic Issues in Philosophy, Psychology, Religion, and Education,* edited by Brenda M. Munsey. Birmingham, Ala.: Religious Education Press, 1980.

"Stage 6 and the Kingdom of God." *Religious Education* 75 (May–June 1980).

(with Knud Monksgaard). "Udvikling of tro." *Religions-Laereren* (Copenhagen), January 1980, 10–14, 15–16.

"Black Theories of Liberation: A Structural-Developmental Analysis." In *The Challenge of Liberation Theology: A First-world Response*, edited by Brian Mahan and L. Dale Richesin, 69–90. Maryknoll, N.Y.: Orbis Press, 1981.

"Reflection on Loder's 'The Transforming Moment.'" *Religious Education* 77 (March–April 1982): 140–48.

"Author's Response to a Review Symposium" (responding to four reviews of *Stages of Faith*). *Horizons: The Journal of the College Theology Society* 9, no. 1 (Spring 1982): 123–26.

"Theology and Psychology in the Study of Faith Development." In *Concilium: Project X*. Nijmegen, The Netherlands, 1982.

"Stages of Faith and Adults' Life Cycles." In *Faith and the Adult Life Cycle*, edited by Kenneth Stokes. New York: W. H. Sadlier, 1982.

"The RCIA and Christian Education." *Worship* 4 (1 July 1982): 336–43.

"Practical Theology and the Shaping of Christian Lives." In *Practical Theology: The Emerging Field in Theology, Church, and World*, edited by Don S. Browning, 148–66. San Francisco: Harper & Row, 1983.

"Gifting the Imagination: Awakening and Informing Children's Faith." *Review and Expositor* (Journal of the Southern Baptist Theological Seminary, Louisville, Ky.) 80, no. 2 (Spring 1983): 189–200.

"A Gradual Introduction into the Faith." In *Concilium: Project on Practical Theology*. Nijemegan, The Netherlands, summer 1984.

"John Wesley's Development in Faith" and "Wesleyan Spirituality and Faith Development." In *The Future of the Methodist Theological Traditions*, edited by M. Douglas Meeks, 172–208. Nashville, Tenn.: Abingdon Press, 1985.

"Practical Theology and Theological Education: Some Models and Questions." *Theology Today* 41 (April 1985).

"Pluralism, Particularity, and Paideia." *Journal of Law and Religion* (Special Volume on Religion and Public Life, April 1985): 263–307.

(with Richard Osmer) "Childhood and Adolescence–A Faith Development Perspective." In *Clinical Handbook of Pastoral Counseling*, edited by Robert J. Wicks, Richard D. Parsons, and Donald E. Capps, 171–212. New York: Paulist Press, 1985.

Foreword to *To See the Promised Land: The Faith Pilgrimage of Martin Luther King, Jr.*, by Fred L. Downing, i–iii. Macon, Ga.: Mercer University Press, 1986.

"Faith and the Structuring of Meaning" and "Dialogue Toward the Future in Faith Development Studies." In *Faith Development and Fowler*, edited by Craig Dykstra and Sharon Parks, 5–42 and 275–301. Birmingham, Ala.: Religious Education Press, 1986.

"Stages of Faith." In *Women's Spirituality: Resources for Christian Development*, edited by Joan Wolski Conn, 15–42 and 226–32. New York: Paulist Press, 1986.

"Religious Congregations: Varieties of Presence in Stages of Faith." *Moral Education Forum* 12, no. 1 (Spring 1987): 4–14.

"Stages of Faith and Human Becoming." In *In the World: Reading and Writing as a Christian*, edited by John H. Timmerman and Donald R. Hettinga, 96–108. Grand Rapids, Mich.: Baker Book House, 1987.

"H. Richard Niebuhr." In *Thinkers of the Twentieth Century*, 2d ed, edited by Roland Turner, 570–72. Chicago and London: St. James Press, 1987.

"The Vocation of Faith Development Theory and Research, 1981–87." In *Glaubensentwicklung und Erziehung*, edited by Karl E. Nipkow, Friedrich Schweitzer, and James W. Fowler, 29–47. Gütesloher: Gütesloher, Gerd Mohn, 1988. Also in *Stages of Faith and Religious Development*, edited by Karl E. Nipkow, Friedrich Schweitzer, and James W. Fowler, 19–36. New York: Crossroad, 1987, 1991.

"The Enlightenment and Faith Development Theory." *Journal for Empirical Theology* (Nijmegan, The Netherlands) 1, no. 1 (1988): 29–42.

"Prophetic Vocations: Parables of the Kingdom." *Spirituality Today* 40 suppl. (Winter 1988): 96–104.

"Faith Development and Spirituality." In *Maturity and the Quest for Spiritual Meaning*, edited by Charles L. C. Kao, 19–40. Lanham, Md.: University Press of America, 1988.

"Strength for the Journey: Early Childhood Development in Selfhood and Faith" and "The Public Church: Ecology for Faith Education and Advocate for Children." In *Faith Development in Early Childhood*, edited by Doris Blazer, 1–36 and 131–54. Kansas City: Sheed & Ward, 1989.

"Öffentliche Kirche und christliche Erziehung." In *Bildung–Glaube–Aufklärung: Zur Weidergewinnung des Bildungsbegriffs in Pädagogik und Theologie*, edited by Reiner Preul, Friedrich Schweitzer, Christoph Scheilke, and Alfred Treml, 253–69. Gütersloh: Gerd Mohn, 1989.

"Reconstituting Paideia in American Public Education." In *Caring for the Commonweal: Education for Religious and Public Life*. Festschrift for Robert Lynn, edited by Parker J. Palmer, Barbara G. Wheeler, and James W. Fowler, 63–89. Macon, Ga: Mercer University Press, 1990.

Articles in *Dictionary of Pastoral Care and Counseling*. Edited by Rodney J. Hunter: "Erik H. Erikson" (360); "Faith and Belief" (394–97); "Faith Development Research" (399–401); "Identity" (565–67); "H. Richard Niebuhr" (793); and "Structuralism" (1229–30). Nashville, Tenn.: Abingdon Press, 1990.

"Faith Development through the Family Life Cycle." In *Catholic Families: Growing and Sharing Faith*, 99–126. New Rochelle, N.Y.: Don Bosco Multi Media, 1990.

Foreword to *Despair: Sin or Sickness? Hopelessness and Healing in the Christian Life* by Mary Louise Bringle. Nashville, Tenn.: Abingdon Press, 1990.

"Stages of Faith Consciousness." In *Religious Development in Developmental Psychology,* edited by George Scarlett and Fritz Oser, 27–45. San Francisco: Jossey-Bass, 1991.

"Praktische Theologie und gegenwärtige Kultur–Auf der Suche nach einem neuen Paradigma." In *Praktische Theologie und Kultur der Gegenwärt,* edited by Karl Ernst Nipkow, Dietrich Rossler, and Friedrich Schweitzer, 155–69. Gütersloh: Gerd Mohn, 1991.

"Character, Conscience, and the Education of the Public." In *The Challenge of Pluralism: Education, Politics, and Values,* edited by F. Clark Power and Daniel K. Lapsley, 225–250. Notre Dame, Ind.: University of Notre Dame Press, 1992.

Foreword to *Sponsoring Faith in Adolescence: Perspectives on Young Catholic Women,* edited by Carmel Leavey, O.P., Margaret Hetherton, Mary Brett, O.P., and Rosalie O'Neill. Newtown, Australia: E. J. Dwyer, 1992.

"Stages of Faith: Reflections on a Decade of Dialogue" *Christian Education Journal* 13, no. 1 (Autumn 1992): 13–23.

The following articles are published in *Christian Perspectives on Faith Development: A Reader,* edited by Jeff Astley and Leslie Francis. Grand Rapids, Mich.: Eerdmans, 1992. "Foreword" (ix–xv); "Faith, Liberation and Human Development" (3–14); "The Enlightenment and Faith Development Theory" (15–28); with Romney M. Moseley and David Jarvis, "Stages of Faith" (29–58); "Perspectives on the Family from the Standpoint of Faith Development Theory" (320–44); "Religious Congregations: Varieties of Presence" (370–83).

"Alcoholics Anonymous and Faith Development." In *Research on Alcoholics Anonymous: Opportunities and Alternatives,* edited by B. S. McCready and W. R. Miller, 113–35. New Brunswick, N.J.: Rutgers University, Rutgers Center of Alcohol Studies, 1993.

"Response to Helmut Reich: Overview or Apologetic?" *The International Journal for the Psychology of Religion* 3, no. 3 (Summer 1993): 173–79.

"Bio-Cultural Roots of Shame, Conscience, and Sin." *Bulletin of the Center for Theology and the Natural Sciences* 13, no. 1 (Winter 1993): 1–11.

"Shame: Toward a Practical Theological Understanding." *The Christian Century,* 25 August–1 September 1993, 816–19.

"Culture Wars and the Paradigms of Adult Faith: Some Implications for Religion, Politics, and Organizational Life." In *Omwegen door de Woestijn. Reflecties over de theologie van Prof. Dr. Gijs Dinemans bij zijn afscheid als Kerkelijk hoogleraar,* edited by Riet Bon-Storm and Libertus A. Hoedemaker, 157–74. Kampen: Utigeverij Kok, 1993.

"Keeping Faith with God and Our Children." *Religious Education* 89, no. 4 (Fall 1994): 543–60.

"Moral Education in Global Context: The Moral Sense, Conscience, and Justice." Translated into Japanese and published in Japanese and English in *Conference Papers: In Search of Moral Education in the 21st*

Century, edited by Nobumichi Iwas. Kashiwa-shi, Chiba, Japan: The
Institute of Morality, 1995.

"Perspectives on Adolescents, Personhood and Faith"; "Adolescence in the
Trinitarian *Praxis* of God"; and "Grace, Repentance, and Commitment:
Youth Initiation in Care and Formation." In *Christ and the Adolescent:
The 1996 Princeton Lectures on Youth, Church and Culture,* 1–34. Princeton,
N.J.: Institute for Youth Ministry, Princeton Theological Seminary,
1996.

"Pluralism and Oneness in Religious Experience: William James, Faith
Development Theory, and Clinical Practice." In *Religion and the Clinical
Practice of Psychology,* edited by Edward Schafranscke. Washington, D.C.:
American Psychological Association, 1996.

"The Emerging New Shape of Practical Theology." In *Pastoral Theologische
Informationen.* Fachgruppe Practische Theologie der Wissenshaftlichen
Gesellschaft für Theologie. Frankfurt: Postbank.

"Entwicklung: III. Psychologisch und religionspsychologisch." In *Religion in
Geschichte und Gegenwärt,* 4th ed., Tübingen: Mohr Siebeck, 1999.

Foreword to *The Banality of Good and Evil: Moral Lessons from the Shoah and
Jewish Tradition* by David R. Blumenthal. Washington, D.C.:
Georgetown University Press, 1999.

"Foreword." *The Journal of Adolescence.* Special issue on "Psychology of
Religion and Adolescence" (1999): 22 and 181–83.

Foreword to *Getting Ahead Without Losing Heart* by Andrew T. Fleming.
Savannah, Ga.: Frederick Biel, 1999.

"The Humanities and Humanization." In *Leadership in the Humanities.*
Atlanta: Georgia State University Press, 2000.

"Faith Development and the Postmodern Challenges." *International Journal
for the Psychology of Religion* 11 (2001): 159–72.

Feature Interviews

Interview by Linda Lawrence. *Psychology Today* (November 1983): 56–62.
Interview by Lynn Donham. *SBC Today* (January 1984): 6–7.
Interview by Susan McDonald. *Emory Magazine* (November 1985): 18–23.
"Fowler on Faith." *Christianity Today* 30, no. 9 (13 June 1986): 7–8.
"Religion and Clinical Issues: An Interview with Theologian James
Fowler." By Edward Shafranske. *Psychologists Interested in Religious Issues,*
Division 36, American Psychological Association, Newsletter 11, no. 2,
(Summer 1986): 1–4.
"Public Church: Radical Interdependence." By Dick Westley. *In the
Meantime* (Chicago) no. 5 (Fall 1993): 1–10.

Reviews Written by Fowler

Joint review of *Openings for Marxist-Christian Dialogue,* edited by T. W.
Ogletree, and *The Faith of the Atheist* by Arthur Gibson. *Religion in Life*
33 (Autumn 1969): 444–46.

Review of *Methodism's Destiny in an Ecumenical Age,* edited by Paul H. Minus. *Methodist History* 8 (April 1970).

Review of *The Nixon Theology* by Charles Henderson. *Catalyst* 4, no. 11 (November 1972).

Review of *Talking, Thinking, Growing: Language with the Young Child* by Joan Tough. *Religious Education* 70, no. 1 (January–February 1975): 95–96.

Review of *Vision and Virtue* by Stanley Hauerwas, and *Biography as Theology* by James Wm. McClendon, Jr. *Christian Century* 92, no. 13 (9 April 1975): 360–61.

Review of *The Modernist Impulse* by William R. Hutchison. *American Protestantism in Religious Media Today* (Fall 1976): 24–25.

Review of *Evil: The Shadow Side of Reality* by John Sanford. *Theology Today* 39 (1982).

Review of *Sexism and God-Talk: Toward a Feminist Theology* by Rosemary Radford Ruether. *Christian Century* 100, no. 30 (19 October 1983): 940.

Review of *The Critical Years: The Young Adult Search for a Faith to Live By* by Sharon L. Parks. *Horizons* 14, no. 2 (Fall 1987): 347–49.

Review *Conversion and Discipleship: A Christian Foundation for Ethics and Doctrine* by Stephen Happel and James J. Walter. *Journal of Religion* 67 (Fall 1987).

"The Psychology of Altruism." Article review of *The Altruistic Personality* by Samuel and Pearl Oliner. *First Things* 1, no. 4 (June/July, 1990): 43–49.